Islam, Society, and Politics in Central Asia

ISLAM

SOCIETY AND POLITICS IN CENTRAL ASIA

EDITED BY
PAULINE JONES

University of Pittsburgh Press

Published by the University of Pittsburgh Press, Pittsburgh, Pa., 15260

Manufactured in the United States of America
Printed on acid-free paper
10 9 8 7 6 5 4 3 2 1

Cataloging-in-Publication data is available from the Library of Congress

ISBN 13: 978-0-8229-6427-8
ISBN 10: 0-8229-6427-9

*In memory of my sister
Carleene Annette Jones,
whose spirit lives on.*

CONTENTS

Conclusion

INTRODUCTION

Reassessing the "Islamic Revival" in Central Asia

Pauline Jones

For most of the 1990s, there was a broad consensus that Central Asia was experiencing an "Islamic revival" analogous to what occurred throughout the Islamic world in the 1970s and 1980s,[1] and that this would have similarly negative effects on the social and political development of the five sovereign states that compose the region: Kazakhstan, Kyrgyzstan, Tajikistan, Turkmenistan, and Uzbekistan.[2] And yet, despite over two decades of research, at the end of the 2000s we still lacked a thorough understanding of: (1) the extent, nature, and meaning of Central Asia's Islamic revival, and (2) its social and political impact over time. The purpose of this edited volume is to shed light on both of these major questions by bringing together an international group of scholars from a variety of disciplines who offer a fresh perspective based on recent empirical work in one or more of the Central Asian states.

Admittedly, the chapters contained in this edited volume do not represent the first attempt to address these critical gaps in our knowledge. Most of what we know about the Islamic revival in post-Soviet Central Asia to date, however, is based on the thick description and cogent analysis of individual cases that have not been sufficiently stitched together to identify commonalities both within and across Central Asian states and societies.[3] Research to date has also largely focused on documenting the Islamic revival itself by demonstrating the increased role of Islam in citizens' daily lives and government policies designed to mitigate its social and political influence. We thus possess a rich array of detailed scholarly accounts, and yet lack a comprehensive picture that could form the basis of a cumulative body of knowledge.

This edited volume goes beyond earlier efforts by providing a more complete and aggregate portrayal of Central Asia's Islamic revival. First, it is divided into four parts, each of which examines the role that Islam has played in Central Asia since independence from a different perspective: part I, "A View from Below: Islam and Society in Central Asia," focuses on the everyday practice of Islam—its various manifestations and interpretations within and across local communities—and the role that both individuals and organized groups play in fostering these manifestations and interpretations in order to illuminate the form, content, and scope of Central Asia's Islamic revival; part II "A View from Above: Islam and the State in Central Asia," examines the evolution of state policies toward Islam, focusing on official attempts to regulate both the public and private practice of Islam through cultural, legal, and political institutions and the important ways in which these policies are distinct from Soviet religious policy; part III, "A View from Within: Sources of Religious Authority in Central Asia," describes the multitude of religious actors and specialists that compose the religious field (Bourdieu 1971) at both the local and national levels and the ways in which they are attempting to influence how communities understand and practice Islam, state policies toward Islam, and communal responses to state regulations; and finally, part IV, "A View from Outside: International Islam and Central Asia," reconsiders the extent to which increased interaction with and knowledge of the larger Islamic world is shaping both the form and content of Central Asia's Islamic revival and state responses. Second, the volume uses these perspectives to develop a set of collective insights, detailed below, that both corroborate and contradict the findings from previous research.

A Transformation, Not a Revival

Consistent with previous research (e.g., Louw 2007; Sahadeo and Zanca 2007), the chapters herein (particularly in part I) portray Islam in Central Asia as extremely diverse when it comes to both individual beliefs and daily practices across communities. Their point of departure is to suggest that this diversity warrants rethinking the common characterization of increasing public and private manifestations of Islam in Central Asia since independence as merely a *revival* but rather as a *transformation*. The former term implies that Islam has "reappear[ed] in a cyclical or more or less unchanged form" (Davis 1987, 37). This volume clearly demonstrates, however, that what we have witnessed is not simply the reemergence of beliefs and practices that were suppressed under Soviet rule, but rather, their alteration in form, nature, and appearance, as individuals and communities gain direct access to ideas and information concerning both Islam and other religions via a variety of new sources (e.g., social media, Christian missionaries, and activists as well as opportunities to travel and study abroad), encounter an evolving range of state policies toward religion, and come into contact with multiple and sometimes competing sources of religious authority.

Recharacterizing Central Asia's Islamic revival as a transformation is not only more accurate but also more consistent with the notion that Islamic beliefs and practices throughout the region should be viewed on a continuum from scriptural/textual to mystical/traditional with most people not located firmly at either end (Tucker 2013). Although these "competing discourses" have existed in Central Asia for centuries, they manifest themselves in different ways at both the individual and community levels and reflect what appears to be a "pluralization of Islam" since independence (Khalid 2007, 123). Based on an original mass survey conducted in Kyrgyzstan in 2011–12, for example, Rouslan Jalil (chapter 1) concludes that society has generally become more attached to "certain aspects of Islamic tradition" and more committed to "observ[ing] . . . Islamic rituals" but that this varies significantly across regions and ethnic groups. Moreover, he finds that "despite the low level of religious participation [measured as adherence to the five pillars of Islam], the majority of the society considers itself to be religious." His findings are consistent with two other chapters in part I that provide a more intimate examination of the multiple beliefs and practices associated with individual piety among local populations in Central Asia. As Svetlana Peshkova (chapter 2) argues, there is no singular meaning when it comes to being a pious Muslim, and thus, no one practice or behavior that constitutes piety. Rather, Muslims in Central Asia engage in a creative synthesis of multiple existing conceptions of piety to "create unique understandings of 'correct' Islam." Finally, whereas both these chapters demonstrate the salience of the mystical/traditional end of the continuum, the final chapter in this section discusses the local communities in which scriptural/textual interpretations have gained the greatest resonance. Similar to some previous studies (e.g., Babadzhanov 1999; Olcott 2007a), Vera Exnerova (chapter 3) emphasizes the domestic origins of fundamentalist beliefs and practices associated with radical political Islam in post-Soviet Central Asia. In contrast to these earlier studies, however, she argues that the Islamist groups that promote such beliefs and practices—namely, Mujaddidiya and Hizb-ut-Tahrir—are not interested in politics at all, but rather, in spiritual change within their communities. Exnerova's research also demonstrates that the desire to "purify" Islam in Central Asia has local origins rooted in a highly localized Islamic education that proliferated under Soviet rule.

Distinct State Policies

The plurality of beliefs and practices that characterize Islam in Central Asia, of course, do not exist in a political vacuum. Accordingly, the chapters in part II offer another set of collective insights regarding the evolution of state policies toward religion. In sum, they demonstrate that the avowedly secular governments of Central Asia have pursued approaches to regulating Islam that are distinct—not only from one another but also from their Soviet predecessors. David Abramson and Noah Tucker (chapter 4), for example, adeptly describe the state's response to the Islamic transformation in Uzbekistan as "inconsistent, confusing, and brutal." They argue that since independence the incumbent regime has adopted and implemented rules and procedures that are in many ways more restrictive, expansive, and invasive than under Soviet rule in an effort "to monitor, limit, and ultimately engineer Muslim religiosity" that is motivated by self-preservation. Similarly, Emily O'Dell (chapter 5) contends that the official rehabilitation of Sufism in Uzbekistan, Tajikistan, and Turkmenistan from a source of Islamic extremism under tsarist and Soviet rule to a source of moderation was spurred by the regime's need in each country for allies to support their increasingly authoritarian rule. Both chapters thus illuminate how declining legitimacy in the wake of increasing religious expression compelled Central Asian regimes governing predominantly Muslim populations to reject the Soviet brand of secularism they inherited and manufacture their own.

These insights counter the common view that the state approach toward Islam in Central Asia is essentially a continuation of Soviet religious policy. Perhaps even more important, they suggest the need to reconsider both the substance of Soviet policy and its impact. In the concluding chapter in this section, therefore, Eren Murat Tasar (chapter 6) calls into question the degree to which the Soviet state successfully controlled Islamic belief and practice by examining the persistence of "unregistered" Muslim religious leaders despite the strict registration requirements that Stalin imposed in the early 1940s. He argues convincingly that, although this outcome was "ideologically unacceptable" and "a source of consternation and worry for the leadership," like other "gray spaces" such as the underground economy, it was unavoidable given the Soviet state's emphasis on the rule of law over repression after the Second World War.

Multiple and Competing Sources of Religious Authority

Among the most important factors influencing the design and implementation of state policies toward Islam in Central Asia are the role of religious leaders and their relationship with state officials at both the local and national levels. And yet, this aspect has been relatively understudied. Part III of this edited volume is thus devoted to identifying the multiple claimants to religious authority, and how they interact with local communities, state officials, and one another.

Noor O'Neill Borbieva (chapter 7) highlights how the sources of religious authority in Central Asia—and hence, the basis for legitimately claiming such authority—have changed over time and the way in which competing sources of authority have contributed to the construction of local variants of Islam in the region. Whereas in the pre-Soviet period authority was derived from "the community and particularly the elders" who were entrusted with determining proper behavior for Muslims within their jurisdiction, both the Soviet and post-Soviet states attempted to centralize authority based on a singular interpretation of sacred texts. Focusing on the case of Kyrgyzstan, she argues that consolidation at the national level has unwittingly elevated a fundamentalist discourse over more traditional ones that have stronger resonance with the local population. In contrast, Tim Epkenhans (chapter 8) emphasizes the failure of Tajikistan's government to limit the role and influence of a variety of nonstate religious specialists, who rely on a combination of historic genealogical lineage—in particular, descent from a Sufi order—and modern economic success as their source of authority. Such figures use this authority not only to cultivate a national following, bolstered by the growing need for spiritual advice that can be easily transmitted via the Internet and other media, but also to routinely ignore the directives of state-trained and -appointed religious specialists.

While the two aforementioned chapters underscore the fact that religious authority in Central Asia is diffuse, they also suggest that it is localized. Alisher Khamidov (chapter 9) demonstrates how local informal ties and dispute resolution mechanisms developed under Soviet rule can both preserve the authority of local religious leaders vis-à-vis government officials and prevent violent confrontation between pious communities and the secular state. He argues that the Kyrgyzstan government's efforts "to tighten controls over religion" since the late 2000s have increased the likelihood for clashes between the local population and officials charged with implementing these unpopular regulations. Where local "power brokers" could work together amicably, however, they could find a peaceful resolution.

Exaggerated Influence of Transnational Islam

Finally, the chapters that compose part IV suggests that the influence of transnational Islam on Central Asia's "Islamic revival" is grossly overstated and offer a more nuanced portrayal of the way in which "foreign Islam" has affected Central Asia's Islamic transformation. Mukaram Toktogulova (chapter 10) introduces a common theme across these chapters by examining the efforts of global Tablighi Jama'at activists in Kyrgyzstan to adapt their message and approach to the local context. This process of "localization," she argues, has enabled the global Tablighi Jama'at network to promote beliefs and practices that are associated with scripture-based understandings of Islam, which have heretofore been considered "foreign" or "alien." In her account of the establishment of Islamic banking in Kazakhstan and Kyrgyzstan, Aisalkyn Botoeva (chapter 11) also emphasizes the crucial role of domestic actors in "fram[ing], translat[ing], and implement[ing]" transnational Islamic institutions for the local context. She argues that the motivations behind support for Islamic banking and other sharia-compliant businesses, moreover, vary across these actors: whereas state regulators are driven primarily by the political and economic benefits, entrepreneurs are driven by the desire to align their business practices with their religious identity as pious Muslims. Similarly, Manja Stephan-Emmrich (chapter 12) highlights the diversity of motivations in her analysis of the growing trend among young Tajiks to study abroad despite the threat of state persecution upon return. She finds that young Tajiks seek foreign religious training in order to better secure their livelihoods, for example, by improving their marriage prospects and elevating their social status in the community, rather than as an expression of individual piety.

The Pluralism of Piety

While all these collective insights improve our understanding of the extent, nature, and meaning of Central Asia's Islamic revival and its impact over time, perhaps the most important message that this edited volume conveys is the need to reconsider the presumed linkage between this revival, rising levels of religiosity, and particular social or political attitudes and behaviors. Following the collapse of the Soviet Union, the number of mosques multiplied, religious artifacts became more visible, and conservative dress proliferated among Muslims in Central Asia. Many predicted that this revival would lead to higher levels of religiosity among Central Asian Muslims, and in turn, that higher levels of religiosity would foster support for radical Islamist movements.[4]

Recasting what has occurred in Central Asia as not merely a revival but rather a transformation, however, makes drawing such links not only difficult but also counterproductive. Rising levels of religiosity in Central Asia have manifested in a diversity of beliefs and practices that cannot be measured simply in terms of Islamic orthopraxy. Thus, we also need to develop more appropriate measures of religiosity that capture this diversity and, in turn, use this diversity to rethink existing theories of how religiosity affects attitudes and behaviors (Jones Luong 2014). The variation in government policy toward Islam across the Central Asian states, moreover, further complicates these presumed linkages because we should expect these policies to have different effects—both on levels of religiosity and on the propensity for higher levels of religiosity to foster support for radical solutions. At the same time, the finding that there are multiple and competing sources of religious authority—even where government policies are the most repressive—suggests that we can expect higher levels of religiosity across these states to continue to be expressed via multiple beliefs and practices that often combine scriptural/textual and mystical/traditional interpretations of Islam. Finally, the revelation that the threat of so-called foreign Islam has been exaggerated should provide some solace to those who are concerned about the unfiltered influence of transnational groups. In order to mobilize the Central Asian population, these groups will need to build domestic constituencies, which requires a message that resonates locally. The pluralism of piety in Central Asia, however, makes it difficult for any single group or ideology to dominate.

PART I

A VIEW FROM BELOW

ISLAM AND SOCIETY
IN CENTRAL ASIA

CHAPTER ONE

The Social Significance of Islam in Post-Soviet Central Asia

The Case of Kyrgyzstan

Rouslan Jalil

The aim of this chapter is to analyze whether the process of religious revival in Kyrgyzstan has translated into increased religiosity in Kyrgyz society. The study is based on a nationwide mass survey conducted in 2011–12, which examines various dimensions of religiosity to ascertain the degree of Islamic practice, beliefs, values, and religious knowledge. (See the appendix to this chapter for details.) The findings demonstrate that the apparent outcome of religious resurgence in Kyrgyzstan is a profound growth of religious institutions and formal attachment to religion. However, this has not led to the dramatic growth of religiosity in terms of participation in religious rituals and mosque attendance. The findings also reveal significant regional and ethnic differences in religious observance and attachment to certain aspects of Islamic tradition. Overall, the outcomes of the study substantiate the view that although Islam in Kyrgyzstan serves as a means of traditional self-identification, Kyrgyz society prefers to believe but not belong to the Islamic faith.

Islam: A Significant Social Constant or Superficial Cultural Element?

The disintegration of the Soviet Union in 1991 gave new momentum to the resurgence of Islam across the Central Asian societies. This process has been marked by the dramatic growth of Islamic institutions, increased religious observance, and the institutionalization of religious categories in society. It is evident that the role and meaning of Islam have changed in both the private and public domains. One question that needs to be asked, however, is whether the society has become more religious and more attached to religion as a result of this change.

After the collapse of the Soviet Union, two main views on the future of Islam in Central Asia prevailed among the scientific community. One view held that Islam would go through revitalization and gain considerable influence in the region. A number of scholars (Rashid 2002; Roy 2000) have projected the dynamic growth of religion and eventual transformation of Islam into a separate social constant, which would play, if not the main role, a significant one in sociopolitical developments in the region. Others (Seifert 2008) have reinforced the idea that Islam had the full potential to become a religious, cultural, and to some extent, a socionormative element of Central Asian societies due to the disappearance of Communist ideology and liberalization of religion. Shireen Akiner (2003b) has stressed that the so-called Islamic factor would become a key aspect in determining political processes in the region.

The thesis of the growing influence of Islam is primarily based on the existence of Muslim populations in all five Central Asian states. Islam is the dominant religion in the region and the majority of the population in each country traditionally consider themselves Muslim. Islamic traditions have always been an integral part of the cultural identity of indigenous people. Though heavily suppressed during the Soviet era, this self-identification existed unofficially and was sustained by means of cultural norms, traditions, and sacralized rituals. Soviet atheism was not able to totally uproot Islam and its elements from the lifestyles or traditions of Muslim people. Therefore, embracing Islam and religious traditions after independence "meant a rediscovery of a cultural heritage that was much restrained during the Soviet era" (Khalid 2007, 120). The overall society, at least the greatest majority, viewed Islam as its own religious, cultural, and socionormative determinant or weltanschauung that fit, if not perfectly but legitimately, the local social and cultural structures. This does not imply, however, that the role of Islam in social structures has not been challenged, criticized, or even opposed. Islam, as a sociopolitical constant, has been under scrupulous scrutiny in diverse contexts and has often created contention in societies. Nevertheless, the revival of Islam in Muslim Central Asia may be regarded as a natural phenomenon. It is not a revolutionary process that has resulted in an absolute shift of cultural, traditional, or social values. To be more accurate, this process may be characterized as evolutionary insofar as existing cultural structures and values are going through a gradual transformation.

If a Muslim population can be regarded as an *internal* factor determining the development of Islam in Central Asia, the influence of foreign players such as Islamic movements and parties or Islamic countries may be seen as an *external* aspect of this thesis. A number of analysts (Khalid 2007; Rashid 2002) agree that foreign players have influenced the Islamic revival in one form or another. Shortly after the collapse of the Soviet Union, an array of Islamic groups from Iran, Saudi Arabia, Turkey, and elsewhere rushed into Central Asia to support Islamic institutions by distributing generous financial contributions, as well as to establish their presence and political influence. As Adeeb Khalid (2007, 123) points out, these groups "came bearing different messages and with different agendas, which all added to the pluralization of Islam in the region."

On the other hand, some scholars (Khalid 2007; Malashenko 1999; Privratsky 2001) have been skeptical about Islam's prospects of gaining a significant position in the region. They argue that Islam may gain some momentum as a traditional cultural element of people; however, it is hardly possible for Islam to grow into one of the key factors in transforming Central Asian societies. For them, religion is likely to remain an insignificant factor because it has gone through considerable erosion during the Soviet period. Moreover, given the firm commitment of regional leaders to rely on secular categories in the nation-building process and to encourage ethnocentric nationalism, the attachment to Islam may barely go beyond self-identification in Central Asia. In addition, Islam in the eyes of the current generation of ruling elite is seen as a counterweight and a direct competitor in the struggle for power and control over the state structures. For political elites, Islam continues to be regarded as an obsolete dogmatic system—"an opium for the masses"—unable to accept modernity let alone provide any viable alternative vision for society. Therefore, the regional governments are extremely cautious about the idea of integrating Islam into sociopolitical structures. Given all these factors, Islam, according to this thesis, is not capable of transforming from a traditional-cultural identification into a sociopolitical institution of socialization of Central Asian people.

This study contributes to the current debate on the role and meaning of Islam in post-Soviet Central Asia by examining the social attitudes toward religion in present-day Kyrgyzstan. The research is guided by the question of whether society has become more religious as an aftermath of Islamic revival. The study examines various dimensions of religiosity to learn the degree of Islamic practice, beliefs, values, and religious knowledge. Then, by analyzing the data using statistical methods, the study makes inferences about general society to illuminate in what ways religion is socially significant.

Religiosity or Secularism

So what is the picture of Islam after twenty years of religious change? Is religiosity increasing in postcommunist Central Asia? Have the societies of the region become more religious in the past twenty years? What are the social attitudes toward Islam and to what extent is Islam significant in Central Asia? These questions are vital in assessing the impact of the religious resurgence taking place in the region. The existing literature provides rather ambiguous analyses of this subject that either support or reject the claim of increasing religiosity. For example, a recent report on the religious situation in Muslim countries (Ladbury and Khan 2008) affirms a growing inclination toward religion in Muslim societies over the past two decades. The report suggests that growing incidents of religious practice such as fasting, mosque attendance, and women's wearing of veils are evidence of increased religiosity. In his study of Muslim communities, Mehran Kamrava (2006) claims that religiosity and self-identification with Islam has grown dramatically in Muslim countries compared to the past few decades. Ernest Gellner (1993, 36) points out that contrary to the secularization theory, Islam has not lost its authority over Muslims but rather strengthened its influence and presence in recent decades. Furthermore, another recent study that examines religiosity across Muslim countries reveals an increasing trend of religiosity among Muslims, which is marked by high frequency of mosque attendance and participation in religious services (Fish 2011, 46). Other observers (Khalid 2007; Roy 2000) emphasize the growing number of religious institutions such as mosques, madrasas, Islamic movements, and so on, in supporting the thesis of growing religiosity in Central Asia.

On the other hand, some studies report low or superficial levels of religiosity in Central Asia. Khalid (2007) argues that Islam in Central Asian societies exists more as an element of cultural identity than as a faith that serves as spiritual guidance for individuals. Islam is embedded in traditions of the people and serves as a structural component of existing social norms. Bruce Privratsky (2001, 56) uses the term "religious minimalism" to describe the loose and superficial attachment to Islam among the societies of Central Asia. He notes that although people might identify strongly with Islam, participation in public and personal ritual practice is often a low priority. A compelling explanation for the low level of religiosity is usually ascribed to the legacy of Soviet atheism. According to this view, during Soviet times any signs of religiosity in both public and private domains were discouraged, which led to the massive secularization of society and a weakened role of Islam as an element of social mobilization. What currently seems a religious revival, according to Pippa Norris and Ronald Ingelhart (2011, 115), is merely "a short-term reaction to the disappearance of state atheism."

Central Asian Islam

Given the vast interest in Central Asian Islam, a great volume of research on this subject is done by both local and foreign scholars. Many of these studies are ethnographic or anthropological observations that examine local religious practices or "everyday" Islam, which, according to Tim Epkenhans (2011, 82) suggests the existence of a "dichotomy between local religious practices and . . . normative doctrines and principles." These studies accentuate the need for essentializing the local forms of Islam in understanding the role of religion in the region. In effect, socially reconstructed forms of Islam or folk Islam, which gets its legitimacy from various sources including traditions, popular beliefs, legends, veneration of saints, and so forth, is regarded as a "true Islam" even if it bears only a vague resemblance to the normative, scriptural Islam. In the Central Asian context, Islam is understood differently and is manifested in different ethnological behaviors and actors (see, for example, Abashin 2006; Khalid 2007; Louw 2007; Privratsky 2001).

Along with importing local customs, traditions, and even some elements of primordial beliefs such as Tengrianism or Shamanism, Islam has ceased to carry much spiritual significance and is reduced to being part of the cultural sphere that is seen more as a conduct of morality. For example, the lack of knowledge or observance of the main Islamic pillars does not contradict the common understanding of a "good Muslim," which is defined by the notion of having a "pure heart" (Khalid 2007). As Svetlana Peshkova argues in chapter 2 of this volume, Islamic piety is a fluid concept that can change its form according to one's understanding. Thus, Islam, especially prior to the disintegration of the Soviet Union, existed not so much as a separate, independent constant but more as a social construct in different forms and facets. Similarly, there was no single definition of what Islam constituted or meant in the region. Therefore, the religious change in post-Soviet Central Asia should not be understood as a process of the "simple" revival of one essential form of Islam that had been lost during Soviet times. Rather, as Pauline Jones argues in the Introduction to this volume, this process can be better termed as the *transformation of Islam* due to the multifaceted development of religion after independence.

Islamic Revival and Its Implications in Kyrgyzstan

The population of Kyrgyzstan is approximately 5.5 million and the majority consider themselves Muslims (CIA Factbook 2013). Islamic traditions had been largely weakened in the country during Soviet times. Because the Soviet *nomenklatura* saw religion as a challenge to both political authority and state ideology, religion was heavily suppressed under the Communist regime. As a result, all religious denominations, including Islam, became the targets of the state and were to a great extent diminished from the public sphere.

The disintegration of the Soviet Union in 1991 brought religious freedom, which gave rise to the resurgence of Islam. This process has been marked by a dramatic growth of Islamic institutions, the institutionalization of religious categories in society, and increased religious observance. As Khalid (2007, 138) notes, the most visible aspect of the Islamic change was the rush to open mosques and to revive shrines. The number of mosques has risen dramatically during the past two decades. According to the Muftiyat (2013),[1] a semiofficial body that regulates religious affairs in the country, the number of officially registered mosques rose from 39 in 1991 to 2,362 in 2013 (see figure 1.1). The population, especially the younger generation, initially got free access to learning more about religion through media, publications, and educational institutions. There has been a gradual rise in the number of madrasas or Islamic schools: from four in 1998 to fifty-one in 2013 (Muftiyat 2013). By 2013 seven Islamic institutions of higher education had been opened that prepare students for a career in religious institutions. Moreover, a growing number of Kyrgyz students are receiving Islamic education abroad (Abramson 2010).

Apart from the growth of Islamic institutions, new religious categories such as halal food industry (religious diet), hijab (religious attire for wom-

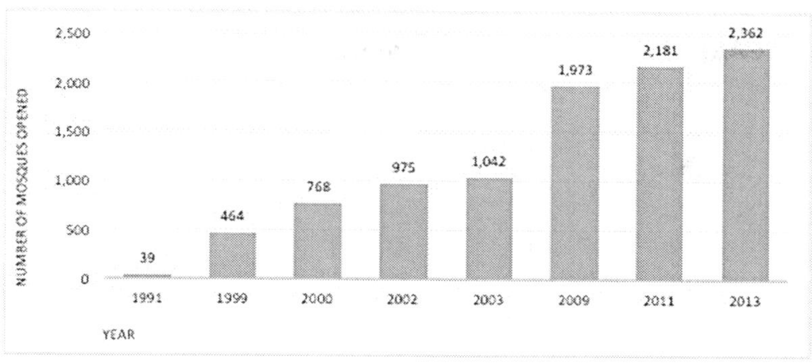

FIGURE 1.1. Officially Registered Mosques in Kyrgyzstan, 1991–2013.
Sources: Muftiyat (2013); State Agency for Religious Affairs.

en), and others have gradually been institutionalized in the society. The halal industry has started to boom in recent years and is gaining significant market value. According to a Muftiyat official,[2] approximately 10 percent of all dietary products sold in Kyrgyzstan carry the halal label. Aiming to regulate this growing market, the Muftiyat has also launched a major project to introduce common standards for the halal industry. There are no official numbers on how many women are wearing the hijab, but it has become a common custom not only in traditionally conservative areas but also in the more secularized capital of Bishkek. The Muslims of Kyrgyzstan are among the most populous group in Central Asia who perform the Islamic pilgrimage hajj. The Muftiyat reports that approximately five thousand Kyrgyz citizens visit Mecca for hajj every year. Furthermore, a great number of different Islamic groups and organizations operate in Kyrgyzstan that contribute to the pluralization of Islam. These groups include Sufi lodges, *dawah* movements (which aim at proselytizing), modernist movements (e.g., the Gulen community), Wahhabi or Salafi groups, Islamist parties such as the Islamic Movement of Uzbekistan (IMU) or Hizb-ut-Tahrir. Among these groups, the Tablighi Jama'at is considered one of the more numerous and influential movements. In this volume, Mukaram Toktogulova (chapter 10) argues that the Tablighis managed to penetrate Kyrgyz society on a massive scale by means of "localizing" the Islamic teachings. The Muslims of Central Asia have traditionally been followers of Hanafi school of law, but this started to change with the influence of various Islamic groups and the return of Kyrgyz students from their studies in different Islamic countries (Abramson 2010).

The changes experienced during the process of Islamic resurgence over the past two decades remain unprecedented. There is an obvious tendency toward an increase of religious institutional structures, ritual observance, and public discourse on issues related to Islam. One question that needs to be addressed, however, is what the religious revival means for the society. In other words, to what extent and in what ways is Islam significant in the society? Finding an answer to this question is equally important for both scholars and policymakers. The Kyrgyz state, which is formally secular by constitution, seems to have limited control over the process of religious transformation. Nonetheless, the government has to find a way to accommodate the growing Islamic presence or at least reach a modus vivendi. It cannot ignore the Islamic factor and needs to make important projections for the future: how will the society be shaped several decades from now if religiosity continues to grow according to the current dynamic? What should policymakers do to prevent possible conflicts of interests between secularism (state) and religion (society)?

The existing literature may suggest some provisional answers to the question of whether religion plays a significant role in the lives of people in Kyrgyzstan. The anthropological or ethnographic approach used in most studies on Central Asian Islam is good for examining personal attachments to religion in particular local communities. These studies are helpful for explaining the underlying reasons and motivations or causal relations with regard to the manifestation of religion in specific contexts. However, they are unable to capture the social attitudes toward religion in society as a whole and the findings cannot be sufficiently used to make projections. Moreover, such studies cannot properly reveal whether meaningful correlations exist across different variables such as age, ethnicity, level of education, region, and so forth. For this reason, a quantitative approach based on a nationwide mass survey can be extremely useful for identifying statistical relations as well as making inferences about society in general. Empirical data from a quantitative study can also be useful for analyzing findings or testing hypotheses drawn from qualitative studies done by scholars of Islam in Central Asia.

Measuring Religiosity

Can a concept like religiosity be quantified to produce a sophisticated analysis? This might be a tricky task, for the reason that religion is a highly complex phenomenon that involves "attitudes, behaviour, values, commitment, social psychology, belief, self identification" and many other categories (McAndrew and Voas 2011, 1). Similarly, formulating a precise definition of religiosity can also be difficult. Religiosity can be described as a " self-expression of personal faith" (Ladbury and Khan 2008, 26) in regard to "belief, practice, formal membership, informal affiliation, ritual initiation, doctrinal knowledge, moral values [and] core values" (Siobhan and Voas 2011, 2). In the conventional literature, social scientists operationalize religiosity using three dimensions: "belief, practice, and affiliation" (McAndrew and Voas 2011, 3). *Belief* in God and other core elements of faith constitute the central aspect of a religion. *Practice* is measured by participation in religious rituals and attendance at services. *Affiliation* is measured by formal or informal identification with a religious denomination (McAndrew and Voas 2011, 3). Norris and Ingelhart (2011, 45) suggest another dimension of religiosity: *Religious values*, which are measured by the degree of importance that religion carries for the individual.

Some observers (e.g., Froese 2008; Krauss, Hamzah, and Idris, 2007; Moaddel 2007) argue that Islamic religiosity cannot be adequately measured using only habitual dimensions such as belief, belonging, and behavior because they are "insufficient to capture the fluidity of religious life in the public and private spheres" (González 2011, 340). The existing models of religiosity were elaborated mainly in Western scholarship, and therefore might be more applicable to the context of Judeo-Christian environments. The literature (Froese 2008; Krauss, Hamzah, and Idris, 2007) suggests using additional variables that may enable capturing specifics of Islamic religiosity such as personal piety, the particulars of Islamic practices, the significance of physical appearance such as dress code or beard, and so forth. The Pew Research Center (2013), in its worldwide survey of Muslim communities, employs questions that address specific elements of Islamic beliefs and practices in an explicit way. For example, it asks about observance of the five pillars of Islam, belief in articles of Islamic faith, and religious identity. These variables may provide a good baseline for measuring Islamic religiosity. The World Values Survey (WVS) is another study that is carried out across a large number of countries to explore people's values and beliefs. The questions it uses are helpful for measuring religious values and particularly for understanding how people relate religion to politics. The present study employs some of the questions used in these surveys, but also uses additional questions that allow a more nuanced analysis of personal religiosity. These include questions about the sources of religious knowledge, attention to Islamic diet or halal food, and attitudes toward religious institutions. In this

Table 1.1. Distribution of Survey Participants by Age (*N* = 2,483; the data for 82 respondents are missing)

Age	Number of respondents	Percentage of total
17–25	912	37.2
26–40	871	35.5
41–55	499	20.4
56+	169	6.9
Total	2,451	100

regard, the findings of this study might be more accurate in exploring religious attitudes than are the findings of the WVS or Pew Research Center.

Research Design

The research is based on a nationwide mass survey carried out in Kyrgyzstan during 2011–12. With the participation of about 2,900 people, the response rate was about 80 percent, or 2,483 people. The survey was carried out in four districts (oblasts) of the country that cover both the southern and northern parts. In addition, government officials, community leaders, religious activists, and members of the clergy were interviewed as a part of a qualitative examination.

Procedure

The survey implements a multidimensional approach in exploring religiosity and consists of forty-three questions grouped into six blocks: (1) demographic information, (2) religious belief, (3) religious participation, (4) religious values, (5) religious knowledge, and (6) religion and politics. The survey questions are designed to examine various aspects of religiosity such as participation in rituals, commitment to faith, degree of belief, religious education, place of religion in politics, and others. The results allow the testing of hypotheses on how ethnicity, age, education, place of residence, income, and so forth relate to certain aspects of religiosity. The survey was prepared in three languages Kyrgyz, Russian, and Uzbek. A group of research assistants, mainly undergraduate students from the American University in Central Asia and International Atatürk-Alatoo University, conducted the interviews.

Table 1.2. Distribution of Survey Participants by Birthplace and Place of Residence (*N* = 2,483)

Region	Residence (%)	Birthplace (%)
Bishkek	36.6	11.1
Chuy	5.4	4.8
Issyk-Kul	0.3	5.1
Naryn	0	5.4
Talas	0	4.3
North subtotal	**42.3**	**30.7**
Batken	0	2.0
Jalal-Abad	1.1	7.4
Osh city	27.6	35.5
Osh oblast	29.0	24.4
South subtotal	**57.7**	**69.3**
Total	**100**	**100**

Participants

The focus group consisted of local people who identifed themselves as Muslims. The respondents were selected on a random basis with special attention to include all age and different social groups (young and old, rural population, students, etc.). Out of 2,483 people 52 percent were female and 48 percent male. The majority of respondents were Kyrgyz 63.4 percent, Uzbeks 30.5 percent, Uyghurs 2.7 percent, and 3.4 percent other ethnicities including unspecified. About one-fourth (22.7 percent) earned 5,000–10,000 som and the other one-fourth (27 percent) 10,000–30,000 som.[3] Approximately 53 percent of respondents were surveyed in Osh oblast including the city of Osh, 43.4 percent in Bishkek and Chuy oblast, and the remainder in other regions. Table 1.1 shows the age distribution of the survey participants.

The data on birthplace of respondents indicate that almost one-fifth (18.9 percent) of all respondents who reside in the northern part of the country, including Bishkek, initially come from the southern region (see table 1.2). Regional differences are important in the country. There are certain cultural deviations between the residents of the northern and southern regions who are thought to have varying degrees of inclination toward religion. The North includes the capital city Bishkek, Chuy, Talas, Naryn, and Issyk-Kul, whereas Osh, Jalal-Abad, and Batken belong to the South. It is a common perception that the residents of the South tend to be more religious than their northern compatriots. In this study, belonging to a particular region was determined by birthplace and self-ascription of the respondents during the interviews.

Findings and Discussion

The study presents the data in the form of descriptive statistics as well as in the form of statistical analysis. Some of the findings are run through regression analysis to identify whether certain variables have a statistical effect on religiosity. In survey research, gender, age, educational attainment, and income are often regarded as determinants of personal religiosity (Fish 2011, 26); therefore, these indicators serve as independent variables. Because the study also aims at determining how ethnicity and region are related to religiosity, these are used as additional independent variables in the regression analysis.

Religious Belief and Identity

The religion of Islam prescribes that Muslims believe in certain articles of faith, which include belief in God, belief in the Prophet Muhammad, belief in the Koran, and belief in afterlife. The overwhelming majority of the survey participants say that they believe in articles of Islamic faith. Belief in the existence of God is nearly universal (95 percent), while 88.3 percent believe that Muhammad is a Prophet sent by God. Almost 85 percent of people believe in resurrection and the judgment day, while 12 percent are unsure about this. Of the respondents, 91.3 percent believe that the Koran is revealed by God and only 7.3 percent have doubts about the divine origin of the holy book of Islam.

About 96 percent of those who participated in this survey identified themselves as Muslims. The study aimed at finding out why people consider themselves Muslims and what other identities they affiliate with. Over half of the respondents (58.8 percent) say they consider themselves Muslim because their social environment or parents happen to be Muslims, while one-third (31.6 percent) say that Islam is their conscious choice. When the respondents were asked how they describe themselves best, they replied as

Muslims (less than half, 45.6 percent), human beings (29.8 percent), and Kyrgyzstani citizens (9.2 percent).

Overall, the majority of people can be characterized as "traditional Muslims" because their self-identification with Islam is based on fact that their families or social surroundings are Muslim. The Muslim identity strongly correlates with ethnicity as 98 percent of Kyrgyz, 96 percent of Uzbeks, and 100 percent of Uyghurs in the survey belong to the Islamic denomination. In this sample, none of the Russians identified themselves as Muslim. It is interesting to note that the larger part of Muslims in Kyrgyzstan, regardless of their ethnic and regional origin or socioeconomic status, accept and believe in the tenets of faith. This finding seems to be consistent with the study done by the Pew Research Center (2013), which reports that 94 percent of Kyrgyz Muslims believe in God and the Prophet Muhammad and 89 percent believe in the afterlife.

Religious Participation

Participation in religious practices is an essential element of personal religiosity. The observance of religious rituals and attendance at services reveal the extent to which an individual is committed to his or her faith. The survey uses four of the five pillars of Islam as core measures of religious participation:[4] *salat* (*namaz*), the five daily prayers; fasting during the month of Ramadan; hajj, pilgrimage to Mecca; and *zakat*, religious almsgiving. The question on namaz asked people whether and how often they perform daily prayers. One-third (32.7 percent) perform prayers on a daily basis, almost half of the respondents (47.9 percent) say that they do not perform daily prayers at all, while the rest (19.5 percent) perform prayers a few times a month, usually attending the Friday prayers. When asked whether they fast during Ramadan, half of those interviewed (49.4 percent) replied that they observe fasting, while one-third (29.9 percent) do not fast. The number of those who performed Islamic pilgrimage or hajj is relatively low (4.3 percent), however, an impressive 76.8 percent of respondents wish to go to hajj in the future. Furthermore, the data indicate that almost two-thirds of respondents (64.3 percent) observe zakat regularly, while 15 percent do not give zakat.

Table 1.3 presents the result of an ordinal probit regression of four indicators of religious participation. In addition, an aggregate value of these indicators is presented as a separate variable. This analysis demonstrates

Table 1.3. Ordinal Probit Regression for "Religious Participation"

Independent variables	Prayer (*namaz*)	Fasting	*Zakat*	Hajj	Aggregated
		Dependent variables			
Gender	.345 * (.133)	.406*** (.134)	.226 (.145)	.257* (.149)	.323*** (.124)
Age	.005 (.005)	.013** (.005)	−.006 (.006)	.014 (.006)	.003 (.005)
Ethnicity	.403*** (.119)	.390*** (.126)	−.056 (.127)	.132 (.132)	.466*** (.111)
Region	.569*** (.163)	.549*** (.157)	.305 * (.177)	.846*** (.181)	.718*** (.153)
Education	−.173** (.071)	.025 (.072)	−.004 (.076)	−.016 (.078)	−.055 (.065)
Income	.005 (.035)	−.017 (.035)	.053 (.040)	.034 (.038)	.006 (.034)

*p < .10; **p < .05; ***p < .01.
Note: Standard errors are given in parentheses.

that region has a statistically significant and positive effect on observance of the main religious practices. In other words, people in the South are more likely to perform daily prayers, fast during Ramadan, and go to hajj. The effect of ethnicity on daily prayers and fasting is statistically significant and positive as well. Being an Uzbek increases the likelihood of performance of namaz and fasting. In this sample, 45.9 percent of Uzbeks perform prayers on a daily basis compared to 24.3 percent of Kyrgyz. Income and age have no statistically significant effect on any of the parameters of religious participation, with the slight exception of fasting. Younger people are more likely to observe fasting during the month of Ramadan. Education correlates only with prayers, although the effect is negative and slight. Advanced educational attainment decreases the likelihood that a person will perform namaz prayers. Furthermore, gender is positively associated with religious participation. Men are more likely to observe Islamic practices (fasting, prayers, and hajj) than women are.

In addition, the survey explored other forms of religious participation, including mosque attendance, contemplation of God outside of religious services, observance of Islamic dietary prescriptions, and participation in religious activities such as attending sermons, religious lectures, and the like. Less than one-third of respondents (28.4 percent) say that they attend mosque once a week or more. Half of respondents (54.4 percent) report that they never attend other religious services, while 23.3 percent say they attend other services on special occasions, usually during Islamic holidays.

Slightly over 50 percent of survey participants say they always pay attention to ensure that what they consume is in accordance with religious dietary prescriptions or halal food, and only 12 percent hardly ever pay attention to this. The rate of halal food consumption varies considerably in both regions of the country with 64 percent and 24 percent in the South and North, respectively. Two-thirds of respondents (63.2 percent in total, 70 percent and 50 percent in the South and North, respectively) report that they consume no alcohol.

Overall, the survey finds that religious participation is relatively low in the country. The Pew Research Center (2013) arrives at the same conclusion in its study, which indicates that only 18 percent of people in Kyrgyzstan pray several times a day, 23 percent attend mosque at least once a week, and 53 percent fast during Ramadan. The high rate of positive response to the observance of zakat in the present study (64.3 percent) may be explained by the lack of adequate understanding of the notion of zakat and its difference from ordinary charity among Muslims in Kyrgyzstan. Another important observation based on the data is the emergence of a distinct pattern: region and ethnicity have a strong effect on religious participation. Being from the South and being an Uzbek increase the chances that a person will be committed to the observance of Islamic rituals. On the other hand, income and age have no statistical significance on religious participation, although 35 percent of those under forty years old perform prayers on a daily basis.

Religious Values

The other indicator of personal religiosity is the degree of importance that religion carries for individuals. The survey reveals that religion and its aspects are not equally important in the lives of all people in Kyrgyzstan. About half (54.6 percent) of the respondents say that religion is very important in their lives and another 69 percent say that God is very important to them as well. Two-thirds (69.7 percent) report that they support the increase of Islamic institutions in the country. With no substantial regional or ethnic differences, less than half of the survey participants (45.8 percent) describe their reaction to women who wear the hijab as affirmative or very affirmative, while 22.6 percent view the hijab negatively. Less than two-thirds of the respondents (58.3 percent) consider themselves religious, whereas half (54.4 percent) state that they have become more interested in Islam in the past five years.

The results of a statistical model demonstrate that region has a statistically significant effect on changes in personal religiosity and on how

Table 1.4. Ordinal Probit Regression for "Religious Values"

Independent variables	Dependent variables		
	Importance of religion	Reaction to rise of Islam	Personal religiosity change
Gender	.165 (.130)	.141 (.122)	.189 (.134)
Age	−.002 (.005)	−.002 (.005)	−.011* (.005)
Ethnicity	.127 (.118)	−. 089 (.108)	.147 (.120)
Region	.578 *** (.155)	.248* (.146)	.520*** (.165)
Education	−.004 (.070)	.091 (.065)	.068 (.074)
Income	.017 (.034)	−.058* (.032)	−.053 (.037)

*p < .10; **p < .05; ***p < .01.
Note: Standard errors are given in parentheses.

people personally regard religion (see table 1.4 for details). Being from the South increases the likelihood that a person will view religion as very important in his or her life. Moreover, being from the South also increases the likelihood that a person will become more interested in Islam as time passes. Age correlates with personal religiosity change, although the effect is negative and slight. As age increases, the likelihood of a person's interest in Islam decreases. Income has a slight negative effect on people's attitudes toward the rise of Islamic institutions. As income rises, the reaction to the increase of religious institutions becomes more negative. From the data in table, it is apparent that neither gender nor ethnicity has a statistically significant effect on a person's religious values.

In general, Muslims in Kyrgyzstan have positive attitudes toward the manifestation of religion in public sphere. There is substantial support for the increase of religious institutions such as mosques and madrasas. However, people show only moderate approval for women who wear the hijab. Interestingly, despite the low level of religious participation, the majority of society considers itself religious. This is more evident in the South than in the North.

Religious Knowledge

During Soviet rule, the means of obtaining a religious education were very limited throughout Central Asia, which many presume to have led to wide-

Table 1.5. Breakdown of Religious Literacy by Age Group (based on response to the question "Do you know the main principles of Islam?")

Response	Age group				
	17–25	26–40	41–55	56+	Total
No	21.4	18.3	11.8	43.5	19.9
Not completely	41.2	20.0	35.3	30.4	32.0
Yes	37.4	61.7	52.9	26.1	48.1
Total	100	100	100	100	100

spread religious illiteracy. The present study examined how this situation has changed at present and how believers attain knowledge about their religion. The survey revealed that despite their faith, many Kyrgyz Muslims are ignorant of the main facts concerning their own religion. Only 46.6 percent of respondents acknowledge that they know the core principles of Islam, while 33.2 percent have incomplete knowledge. The majority (72.4 percent) note, however, that they plan to obtain more knowledge about Islam in the future. The main sources of religious knowledge for believers are friends and peers (30.5 percent), members of the family (25.2 percent), mosque sermons (13.9 percent), and publications (12.7 percent). Only 3 percent attend religious schools to learn about their own faith. Furthermore, the survey asked respondents whether they read a translation of the Koran as a source of religious knowledge and divine guidance. About 27 percent hardly ever read the Koran and less than 25 percent read it on a regular basis. The great majority of respondents (80 percent) admit, however, that they would encourage their children to get a basic Islamic education in the future. An impressive 73 percent (80 percent in the South and 57 percent in the North) support the idea that Islamic education should be a part of the official curriculum at schools in Kyrgyzstan.

The results of this survey show a strong correlation between religious literacy and religious participation. Having a fair amount of knowledge about one's faith is necessary for exercising one's own religion. For example, about 75 percent of those who have knowledge about the main principles of Islam perform prayers (namaz) on a daily basis, and 75 percent of those who have incomplete or no knowledge about Islam do not perform prayers at all. Contrary to expectations, the age factor does not seem to be a significant determinant of religious literacy. Younger respondents do not necessarily have more knowledge about Islam than older respondents (see table 1.5). On the other hand, the study finds a positive correlation between region and religious literacy. People from the South appear to have a greater degree of religious knowledge and are more likely to support Islamic education at schools.

Religion and Politics

Islam is considered an all-encompassing religion that regulates all aspects of individual and social life. Islamic theology holds distinct views on how the societal or political order should be constructed and what characteristics a Muslim leader should possess. Some argue that the idea that "only a religious leader can provide a good government for the Muslim community" (Al-Suwaidi 1995, 87) is deeply rooted in the consciousness of Muslim *ummah*. As a part of this ummah, do Muslims of Kyrgyzstan share aspirations for political authority influenced by religion? The last section of the survey was structured to find an answer to this question and to examine general views on religion and politics.

Five items in the questionnaire are used to measure political attitudes. One-third of respondents (36.7 percent) agree or strongly agree with the statement that "politicians who do not believe in God are unfit for public office," while 28.8 percent disagree or strongly disagree. On the other hand, the majority (56.8 percent) agree that more people with strong religious beliefs should hold public office in Kyrgyzstan, whereas only 18.2 percent disagree with this. In response to the question of whether they would vote for an Islamic political party if it participated in elections, 36.4 percent of the survey participants give an affirmative answer and 28.4 percent a negative answer. Another question on the separation of religion and state in Kyrgyzstan yielded moderately proportionate responses with 36 percent in favor and 32.4 percent against. In addition, over half of those surveyed (57 percent) agree with the statement that Kyrgyzstan should cooperate more with Islamic countries, and only 15.5 percent disagree.

The results obtained from the regression analysis shown in table 1.6 demonstrate the persistence of a pattern observed in earlier statistical models. Region again has a positive and significant effect on the likelihood that a person supports the fusion of religious and political authority. People from the South are prone to favor religious politicians in the government and to support an Islamic political party. Gender and education are negatively associated with the belief that politicians who do not believe in God

Table 1.6. Ordinal Probit Regression for "Religion and Politics"

Independent variables	Dependent variables				
	Politicians who do not believe in God are unfit for public office	People with strong religious beliefs should hold public office	Vote for Islamic political party	Religion and state should be separated	Kyrgyzstan should cooperate more with Islamic countries
Gender	$-.250^{**}$ (.123)	.010 (.123)	$-.306^{**}$ (.123)	$.426^{***}$ (.123)	.160 (.124)
Age	.005 (.005)	.007 (.005)	.006 (.005)	$-.005$ (.005)	$-.003$ (.005)
Ethnicity	.016 (.108)	$-.249^{**}$ (.109)	$-.136$ (.109)	$.227^{*}$ (.108)	.122 (.110)
Region	$.361^{**}$ (.147)	$.552^{***}$ (.148)	$.375^{**}$ (.149)	.053 (.147)	$.351^{**}$ (.149)
Education	$-.171^{**}$ (.066)	.047 (.066)	.004 (.066)	.045 (.066)	149^{**} (.067)
Income	.025 (.032)	$-.053$ (.033)	$-.039$ (.032)	$-.130^{***}$ (.033)	$-.111^{***}$ (.033)

$^{*}p < .10; {}^{**}p < .05; {}^{***}p < .01.$
Note: Standard errors are given in parentheses.

are unfit for public office. Men with advanced educational attainment are more likely to tolerate secular politicians in the government. Moreover, men are more likely to support the separation of religion and state and would be less likely to vote for an Islamic political party if it participated in the elections. Interestingly, income has a statistically negative effect on the separation of religion and state in Kyrgyzstan. People with higher incomes are less likely to support secular government. Furthermore, income has a statistically significant and negative impact on the statement that Kyrgyzstan should cooperate more with Islamic countries. As personal income increases, agreement with this statement decreases. On the other hand, those with higher levels of education are more likely to agree that Kyrgyzstan should enhance cooperation with Islamic countries. In this model, age is the only variable that does not have any statistical significance.

Popular attitudes toward the role of religion in politics fluctuate unevenly across the different strata of Kyrgyz society. Men generally tolerate nonbelieving politicians and strongly support a secular government. Individuals with higher levels of education are also tolerant of atheists in high office. A more surprising correlation is found between income and secularism: those with higher economic status are against the separation of religion and state in Kyrgyzstan. The analysis of previous models did not show any significant correlations between income and self-reported or actual personal religiosity. Therefore, it is difficult to explain this result, but it might be related to the fact that the economically less-advantaged population is uncomfortable with any possible clerical influence of the government. Nonetheless, another interesting observation to emerge from the data comparison is the persistence of the regional pattern. Muslims from the South are more inclined to favor a fusion of religion and politics. Support for religious politicians, an Islamic political party, or cooperation with Islamic countries is especially strong in the southern region.

Belief without Belonging

The present study was designed to examine whether Kyrgyz society has become more religious as an aftermath of Islamic resurgence since independence from Soviet rule. The data collected during the research provide multiple ways of assessing various dimensions of religiosity. The statistical models presented in the chapter offer an analysis of how certain socio-economic variables influence specific aspects of religiosity. The data show social attitudes toward religion, and explain how religious the society is at present and how this religiosity is manifested across different segments of society. The lack of comparable data for earlier years, however, limits the evaluation of the findings. The data do not reveal whether the society has become more or less religious since independence. Despite this limitation, the empirical findings in this study make several contributions to understanding the outcomes of religious change in Central Asia.

First, this study has shown that the evident outcome of religious resurgence in Kyrgyzstan is the dramatic growth of religious institutions. The number of mosques and religious educational institutions has substantially increased in recent decades. Moreover, new religious categories such as halal food or hijab attire have gained considerable significance among Kyrgyz Muslims. Furthermore, an array of different Islamic groups and organizations has emerged in the country, which will eventually contribute to the pluralization of Islam in Kyrgyzstan.

Second, the findings indicate a great disparity in *belonging* and *attending* in Islamic praxis. Though the majority of the society belongs to the Islamic denomination, participation in religious rituals is a low priority. The evidence suggests that Kyrgyz society has not become religious in terms of participation and attendance of religious practices. Only a small fraction of respondents actively participates in religious rituals, which include regular mosque attendance (28.4 percent), performing a daily prayer (32.7 percent), reading the Koran (25 percent), and fasting during the month of Ramadan (49.4 percent). Another important outcome of the study is the persistence of region as a powerful factor influencing religiosity. People in the South are more likely to be religious in terms of Islamic practice, attitudes toward religion and politics, religious education, and commitment to religious values.

The disparity between religious practice and adherence to religion is not surprising if we compare the findings of similar studies conducted elsewhere in post-Soviet space. For example, the Pew Research Center's (2014) study on Russia states that "Russians return to religion, but not to church." In the past twenty years, identification with the Orthodox Church and other religious groups has risen significantly in Russia; however, religious observation and attendance at religious services remains at a disproportionately low level.

Third, the survey reveals that Kyrgyz society has relatively poor levels of religious literacy. Despite their faith, many people in Kyrgyzstan are ignorant of the main facts about their own religion. Less than half of the population knows the core principles of Islam. The people obtain religious knowledge mainly through their friends and peers or family members. Contrary to expectations, younger people do not necessarily have more religious knowledge than the older generation. In fact, no statistically substantial evidence is found to claim that younger people are at the forefront of religious change. Only one-third of those younger than forty regularly perform daily prayers and another 40 percent attend mosque at least a few times a week.

Finally, the research suggests that the majority of people can be characterized as "traditional Muslims," whose self-identification with Islam is drawn from the collective Muslim identity of society. Kyrgyz Muslims adhere to the local form of Islam or "traditional Islam" that is manifested in various cultural forms. Therefore, an understanding of what religiosity means can vary enormously for different Muslims in different contexts. One example of this can be found in the survey outcome. Despite the low level of religious participation, the majority of the society regards itself as religious. It shows that Muslims have differentiated perceptions of what Islam is and what it means for them in their lives. Overall, the outcome of this study supports the results of existing anthropological observations on Central Asian Islam that report apparent disparities between local religious practices and normative doctrines of Islam. This conclusion accentuates the fact that survey research in combination with anthropological studies may generate a more comprehensive understanding of Islam in Central Asia.

Appendix: Survey Questionnaire

Part I. Demographic Information

V1. Gender:
    1. Female   2. Male

V2. Marital Status:
    0. Single   1. Married   2. Divorced
    3. Widowed   4. Cohabitating

V3. Age: ___________

V4. Education:
    0. No formal education   1. High school graduate
    2. University student   3. University graduate
    4. Master or PhD

V5. Ethnicity:
    0. Kyrgyz   1. Uzbek   2. Russian
    3. Uyghur   4. Other: ___________

V6. Birthplace: In what part of the country were you born?
    1. Bishkek   2. Chui   3. Osh oblast
    4. Osh city   5. Talas   6. Jalalabad
    7. Naryn   8. Issyk-Kul   9. Batken
    10. Other: _____________

V7. Where do you currently live?
    1. Bishkek   2. Chui   3. Osh oblast
    4. Osh city   5. Talas   6. Jalalabad
    7. Naryn   8. Issyk-Kul   9. Batken
    10. Other: _____________

V8. Where were you brought up?
    1. City (Indicate where: ___________)
    2. Rural (Indicate where: ___________)
    3. Both

V.9 Do you belong to any religious denomination? If yes, which one?
    1. Yes. I am a Muslim
    2. Orthodox Christian
    3. Other: _____________
    4. No. I do not belong to any religious denomination

V10. What is the average monthly income of your household counting all wages, salaries, pensions, and other incomes that come in?

    0. No income   1. Less than 1,000 som

    2. 1,000–3,000 som   3. 3,000–5,000 som

    4. 5,000–10,000 som   5. 10,000–20,000 som

    6. 20,000–30,000 som   7. 30,000–50,000 som

    8. More than 50,000 som

Part II. Religious Belief

V11. Do you believe in the existence of God?

    0. No   1. I don't know   2. Yes

V12. Do you believe in life after death and that you will be judged according to your deeds?

    0. No   1. I don't know   2. Yes

V13. Do you believe that Muhammad was the prophet guided by God?

    0. No   1. I don't know   2. Yes

V14. Do you believe that the Koran—the holy book of Islam—is revealed by God (God's word)?

    0. No   1. I don't know   2. Yes

Part III. Religious Participation

V15. Do you perform the five prescribed prayers—namaz? If yes, how frequently?

    0. No, I don't pray

    1. One or two times a month

    2. One or two times a week

    3. Every day

V16. How often do you attend a mosque?

    0. Never

    1. Only on special occasions (e.g., Feast of sacrifice, Ramadan feast)

    2. Only on Friday prayers

    3. Few times a week

    4. At least once a day

    5. Five times a day

V17. How often do you attend other religious services (davat, etc.)?

    0. Never   1. Once a year

    2. Only on special occasions   3. Once a month

    4. Once a week

V18. How often do you pray to God (contemplate) outside of religious services, would you say?
    0. Never   1. Only in times of crisis
    2. Hardly ever   3. Sometimes   4. Often

V19. Do you fast during the month of Ramadan?
    0. No   1. Sometimes   2. Yes

V20. Do you give zakat (to give out 2.5 percent of wealth to needy people on an annual basis)?
    0. No   1. Sometimes   2. Yes

V21. Have you performed hajj (pilgrimage to Mecca)?
    0. No. I don't plan it   1. No. But I plan it in the future   2. Yes

Part IV. Religious Values

V22. The reason I consider myself Muslim is:
(Choose only one answer)
    1. Because my parents are Muslims
    2. Because I am a Kyrgyz/Uzbek/Uyghur, etc.
    3. Because I chose Islam as my religion
    4. Because everyone around me is Muslim
    5. Because _______________________________

V23. How important is God in your life?
    0. Not at all important   1. A little important
    2. Somewhat important   3. Important
    4. Very important

V24. How important is religion in your life?
    0. Not at all important   1. A little important
    2. Somewhat important   3. Important
    4. Very important

V25 How often do you follow religious prescriptions in your life?
    0. Never   1. Hardly ever   2. Sometimes
    3. Often   4. Always

V26. Do you pay attention that what you consume is in accordance with Islamic dietary prescriptions or halal food?
    0. Never   1. Hardly ever   2. Sometimes
    3. Often   4. Always

V27. Do you consume alcohol?
    0. No   1. Sometimes   2. Yes

V28. What is your reaction to the increase of Islamic institutions (mosques, madrasas, etc.) in Kyrgyzstan?
    0. Very negative   1. Negative   2. Neutral
    3. Affirmative   4. Very affirmative

V29. What is your reaction to the women who wear a hijab?
    0. Very negative   1. Negative   2. Neutral
    3. Affirmative   4. Very affirmative

V30. How would you identify yourself? Give a value from 1 to 5, where 1 is the main ID and 5 is the least important ID.
    0. Not applicable.
    1. I a am Bishkek/Osh citizen (geographical affiliation)
    2. I am a Muslim (Religion)
    3. I am a Kyrgyz/Uzbek/Russian, etc. (Ethnicity)
    4. I am a Kyrgyzstan citizen
    5. I am a World citizen

V31. Independently of whether you pray, attend a mosque or not, would you say you are
    0. A convinced atheist
    1. Not a religious person
    2. Not religious but a spiritual person
    3. A religious person
    4. I don't know
    5. Other: _______________________

V32. Have your religious beliefs changed in the past three to five years compared to today?

0. Yes, I lost my interest in Islam/I am not religious at all now
1. Yes, I became less interested in Islam/I became less religious
2. No, there are no changes
3. Yes, I became somewhat interested in Islam/I became religious
4. Yes, I became more interested in Islam/I became more religious

Part V. Religious knowledge

V33. Do you know the pillars/principles of Islam?
    0. No   1. Not completely   2. Yes

V34. How often do you read a translation of the Koran as a divine guidance?
    0. Never   1. Hardly ever   2. Sometimes
    3. Often   4. Always

V35. Please indicate the main source(s) of your religious knowledge:
1. Friends, peers
2. Members of the family
3. Mosque (sermons)
4. Religious school/madrasa
5. Publications: books, newspapers
6. Media: TV, radio, Internet
7. University
8. Other: _______________
9. I don't know
10. I don't have any religious knowledge

V36. Do you plan to get more knowledge about Islam in the future?

    0. No   1. I don't know   2. Yes

V37. If you have children, would you encourage them to get a basic Islamic education?

    0. No   1. I don't know   2. Yes

V38. The majority of the population in Kyrgyzstan is Muslim. So, Islam should be a part of official curriculum at schools.

    0. Strongly disagree   1. Disagree
    2. Neither agree nor disagree   3. Agree
    4. Strongly agree

Part VI. Religion and Politics

To what extent do you agree with the following statements? 0—Strongly disagree, 1—Disagree, 2—Neither agree nor disagree, 3—Agree, 4—Strongly agree

V39. Politicians who do not believe in God are unfit for public office

    0   1   2   3   4

V40. It would be better for Kyrgyzstan if more people with strong religious beliefs held public office

    0   1   2   3   4

V41. If an Islamic political party participated in the next elections, I would vote for it

    0   1   2   3   4

V42. Religion and state should be separated in Kyrgyzstan

    0   1   2   3   4

V43. Kyrgyzstan should cooperate more with Islamic countries

    0   1   2   3   4

CHAPTER TWO

Beyond Piety

Self-Related Muslims in Uzbekistan

Svetlana Peshkova

In this chapter I focus on the individual uniqueness of Central Asian Muslims and challenge prevalent analytical assumptions about Muslim piety that obscure religious diversity in the region and the rich religious history informing it. These assumptions limit individual piety to a set of cultural symbolic behaviors, including a regular ritual practice (Ar. *salat,* Uz. *namoz*), dietary restrictions, religious education, modest covered dress, and sometimes increased political activism. In order to gain deeper insights into the role of religion in the daily lives of local populations, I propose to refocus the analysis from external manifestations of piety to its internal constitution and experience. This analytical focus can lead scholarly and policymaking communities away from overarching politicized generalizations about the region and Islam, and beyond the recognition and assertion of religious diversity, toward an understanding of the implications and causes of such diversity.

Central Asian Diversity

There is a plethora of scholarly works about Central Asia's internal cultural diversity and complex social history. Some discuss the region's incorporation into the Soviet Union through an intense secularization campaign during the first part of the twentieth century, and others focus on the role of a "safe"

Islam in the reformulation of national identities by regional postindependence elites and governments and local social movements' resistance to this effort (Adams 2010; Kamp 2006; McGlinchey 2011; Nazarov and Sinor 1993; Northrop 2004). Scholars aiming to understand transformations of religious observance of local populations during the past two decades (1990s–2010s) often disagree on the criterion used to assess the quality of these changes—whether it should be the number of religious institutions, the frequency of mosque attendance, or an interest in religious education and sociopolitical activism, or all of the above (e.g., Jalil, chapter 1, this volume). Despite this variance, all of them conclude that in the post-Soviet era religious observance among Central Asian Muslims has increased (e.g., Khalid 2007; McGlinchey 2007; Peshkova 2009; Rasanayagam 2010). Yet, as Rouslan Jalil (chapter 1, this volume) points out, these transformations are not a "'simple' revival of one essential form of Islam that had been lost during Soviet times . . . [but] the pluralization of Islam." The increased importance of religious knowledge, sensibilities, and behaviors in the daily lives of self-identifying Muslims in the Fergana Valley exemplifies such qualitative shifts.

The Fergana Valley is a mainly agricultural area shared among the post-Soviet independent countries of Uzbekistan, Kyrgyzstan, and Tajikistan. Different peoples inhabit the Valley, including Uzbeks, Tajiks, Kyrgyz, Koreans, Russians, Roma, and Jews, who variously profess Islam, Christianity, Judaism, Buddhism, and atheism. Similar to Christians, Jews, and others, being Muslim is expressed in a variety of ways. The majority of existing political, journalistic, and scholarly discussions of the Valley, however, tend to focus on Muslims only.[1] Moreover, while applying a preconceived understanding of Muslim piety, these analyses by and large tend to center on those Muslims who consistently perform ritual prayers, participate in communal religious rituals, observe dietary restrictions, adopt particular forms of covered dress, cultivate piety through spiritual exercises (e.g., *zikr*) and religious education, and/or can advocate for an Islamic state and exhibit political ethics potentially leading to violence (e.g., Bat, Kochan, and Littman 2002; Lubin and Rubin 1999; Mayer 2006; Najibullah 2003; Omelicheva 2007; Rashid 1994). As a result, despite the internal diversity, existing analyses often reduce inhabitants of the Valley to their religious and political identities (e.g., Chaudet 2008; Hunter, Thomas, and Melikishvili 2004; Naumkin 2005; Roy 2000; Yemelianova 2010).[2]

Julie McBrien and Mathijs Pelkmans (2008, 89) argue that a focus on such Muslims (only) leaves out the regional "secular" majority, which includes individuals who self-identify as Muslim but either do not believe in God or understand their "atheism" as being "good" and "moderate" Muslims, different from other "bad" Muslims zealously expressing and propagating their "correct" understandings of Islam. This also applies to Muslims who recently converted to Christianity. McBrien and Pelkmans (2008) and other scholars (e.g., Kamp 2001) explain such identities as a result of the Soviet fusion of religion and nationality (see also Borbieva, chapter 7, this volume), whereby many local individuals feel and claim to be Muslim and secular at the same time.[3]

Preoccupation with questions of religious authenticity is not unique to Muslims in the region either. Sebastien Peyrouse (2007) and Johan Rasanayagam (2010) argue that regional believers representing different denominations of Christianity also engage these questions. Through proselytizing and the establishment of prayer houses and churches, they challenge each other and Muslims' claims to the one true faith and right beliefs. Following Rasanayagam (2010) and McBrien and Pelkmans (2008), in this chapter I focus on individuals whose understandings of and feelings about being Muslim are *beyond* existing understandings of individual piety limited to a set of cultural symbolic behaviors that are often assumed to capture the essence of being or becoming a pious Muslim. These measurements of one's active religious consciousness and participation reflect particular discourses on how to be and act Muslim that some scholars in this volume refer to as "scriptural," "orthodox," or "text-based scholarly" (e.g., Jalil, chapter 1 and Borbieva, chapter 9, this volume). As a result, they obscure the variety of ways that religious consciousness and participation thrive in Central Asia and elsewhere (e.g., Grant 2011). Following Bruce Grant (2011) and Gabriele Marranci (2008, 98), I understand piety as active religious consciousness that is experienced and expressed through "acts of identity" that are symbolic and not limited to ritual performance and verbal statements. By refocusing away from piety's external manifestation to its internal constitution and experience, I aim to challenge normative discourses about Islam and piety and to contribute to the body of literature (e.g., Heathershaw and Megoran 2011) interrogating existing claims that Islam is the cause of political ethics and violence in the region. Below I limit my discussion to the part of the Fergana Valley that belongs to Uzbekistan.

"Real" Muslims

Since Uzbekistan's independence from the Soviet Union in 1991, an "enlightened and tolerant" Islam became the primary element in the discourse on national identity (Asad 1999, 186; see also, e.g., Rasanayagam 2010). This discourse, articulated by intellectual elites and promoted by Uzbekistan's government, has materialized in a variety of ways including mosque building, the (re)opening of religious schools (madrasas), the training of some (overwhelmingly male) clergy overseas, and numerous artistic productions celebrating the unique cultural history of the country (e.g., Abramson 2010; Adams 2010; see also Jalil, chapter 1, this volume). At the same time, discourses and behaviors challenging the existing state's leadership and structure in terms of Islam were penalized; according to the government's representatives, they promoted politically charged religious ethics leading to only one outcome—violence (McGlinchey 2007, 2011; see also Vera Exnerova's discussion of the Adolat Islami [Islamic Justice Movement], chapter 3, this volume).

Against this backdrop, I conducted ethnographic research about gender, Islam, and religious leadership. During repeat visits to the Valley in 2001, 2002, 2003, and 2011, I spent time interviewing, observing, sharing stories with, and learning about "correct" Islam and how to be a better human from local women and men. Over the years I met many individuals who self-identified as "real" Muslims in the Valley. They often differed in their understandings of and feelings about how to lead a "truly" Islamic life. Some, disappointed with the existing state structure, advocated theocracy, since democracy was discredited by the Uzbek government's corruption, violence, and failed promises of financial stability and political freedom. Among these individuals, I met those who wanted to have "a just *khalifa* [ruler], like the Prophet Muhammad" (author's personal communication, 2003).[4] Others, consistent with the state's discourse on "enlightened and tolerant" national Islam, understood Islam as a "tradition" that had nothing to do with politics (Fathi 2006; Louw 2007; Rasanayagam 2010; also see Exnerova's discussion of the conflict between the Mujaddidiya [reformers] and traditional Hanafi *ulema* [religious authorities], chapter 3, this volume).

My research centered on individuals who took Islam to be an ethical message guiding personal moral transformation from ignorance to knowledge; they claimed that through ritual prayers, dietary restrictions, religious education, modest covered dress, and various spiritual exercises, local individuals could become better Muslims and would eventually create a different moral society (e.g., Peshkova 2006, 2009, 2014). Yet this (my) analytical radar, propelled by the assumption that an individual's commitment to Islam and active religious consciousness and participation have to be manifested in one particular way, left some Muslims undetected and/or sidelined (e.g., Deeb 2006; Hafez 2011; Henkel 2007; Mahmood 2005). In the post-Soviet space these Muslims also reoriented their lives toward what they considered to be "correct" Islam. Their commitment to Islam, however, was animated by *other* acts of identity, not limited to ritual prayers, religious education, and particular forms of modest dress, and purified (*halal*) food. These acts of identity included drawing on divinely enhanced bioenergy to promote physical healing, using professed psychic and spiritual abilities to predict the future and communicate with the dead, and talking to extra-terrestrial beings. One of these individuals was Nafisahon Ulchieva and another was Hayethon Kurbanova. At the time Hayethon self-identified as a "Ruhshonoz"—a term she translated as "one who heals souls."[5]

Several academic works detail diversity and the contextual nature of religious beliefs and practices in Uzbekistan and elsewhere. They argue that even though practitioners may claim that their understanding of Islam is the "correct" one, from an anthropological standpoint there is no one "correct" way of being Muslim (Bowen 1993; el-Zein 1977; Khalid 2007; Makris 2007; Marranci 2008; McBrien and Pelkmans 2008; Varisco 2005). Since there is no one correct way of being Muslim, there should be no one correct definition of piety—piety is contextual. Although piety is often enacted in a social context, drawing on Nigel Rapport (2010), I argue that piety is essentially personal. In the following paragraphs, I examine piety through an empirical and analytical investigation of individual moral projects, by discussing how these two individuals felt Muslim and rationalized and acted on these feelings.

Called to Heal

Nafisahon was born in Namangan, a city in the Fergana Valley (Uzbekistan). Her parents and neighbors, she claimed, noticed her special powers early on; as a child she could predict the future. Later in life, Nafisahon worked for twenty-three years as a nurse at a local hospital in the then Soviet Socialist Republic of Uzbekistan. After work—in the privacy of her home— Nafisahon performed healing rituals by using her bioenergy, a kind of energy produced by a living organism, although in Nafisahon's case it was transcendental in nature. After Uzbekistan's independence from the Soviet Union in the early 1990s, she became a popular healer, performing these rituals not only in her home but also at large public venues such as cinema halls.[6]

In a short pamphlet about her life and healing abilities, Nafisahon's biographer, Nabi Rahimov (2002, 2), writes that in 1997, Nafisahon completed the hajj (pilgrimage to Mecca); as a result, she "became *hoji-ay*, thus accomplishing one of the five demands of Islam by visiting Kaaba in holy Mecca, and also Medina, the city of the Prophet Muhammad."[7] Performing the hajj was a deeply emotional experience for Nafisahon. At one point during the hajj, Rahimov (2002, 2–3) continues, "with tears in her eyes and a deep faith in her soul, [she] pleaded to Allah for mercy not for herself but for those who were sick, [she asked Allah] to give peace to the seekers and happiness to the sad." In return Allah granted her unusual powers to heal others.

In the context of "growing religious freedom" in post-Soviet Uzbekistan, Nafisahon was finally able to fully realize her potential as "a national healer" (author's personal communication, 2003). She claimed to have healed hundreds, even thousands of patients suffering from various maladies and to have made occasional appearances on national radio and television, as if saturating the social fabric of the whole of Uzbekistan with her healing powers. One example of Nafisahon's extraordinary ability to heal others, showcased by her biographer, was her patient's regenerated iris. In a letter addressed to Nafisahon, this patient, Gulnara, recounted how after thirteen séances, her surgically removed iris grew back:

> I consider Nafisahon [to be] my savior. I am a medical doctor—a family doctor. I know a great deal about medicine. I was blind in my left eye for six years. I had a surgery. They removed [my left] iris. The iris was gone. After the thirteenth séance the iris completely reappeared. I felt the light and my pain disappeared. After the third séance I started seeing light from the lightbulb. I saw sacred fathers [*sviatie otsy*] and they healed me, and all these days my iris grew bigger and bigger, until it became a normal size. I can see. Although I am a doctor, I believe in miracles. I believe in healing. (Gulnara, Shilva village, Dangarinski county, Fergana Valley, quoted in Rahimov 2002, 6)

Rahimov (2002) also notes that Nafisahon's patients took her ability to heal others as a manifestation of her deep faith in God; her work contributed to a circulation of Islamic knowledge among the locals. In a letter, an elderly man, another one of her former patients, thanked Nafisahon for "propagating the true Islam [and] calling people to believe in God the Almighty" in Uzbekistan and neighboring countries, such as Kyrgyzstan and Kazakhstan (Rahimov 2002, 10).

Like many other men and women I have talked to, Nafisahon insisted during our meetings in 2003 that she was "truly" Muslim. Unlike the

Muslims my research centered on, she did not exhibit the acts of identity that scholars often associate with "Islamic revival/renewal/resurgence" and use as measurements of being or becoming (more or less) Muslim (e.g., Hafez 2011; Mahmood 2005; Rashid 1994). She mentioned very little about Islamic education, did not advocate any particular form of covered modest dress, or preach ethical self-formation. She exhibited no desire for political engagement with the state and did not promote ritual prayers and dietary restrictions. Even though Nafisahon's thinking, feeling, and acting "truly" Muslim could not be measured by these cultural symbolic behaviors, she claimed to rediscover Islam and God in her own "special" way and to experience great changes in her life. Regardless of how others evaluated or perceived Nafisahon, these changes helped her, she said, to accomplish her mission—her moral project of changing others by healing their physical maladies with her divinely enhanced bioenergy.

Called to Resurrect Souls

In the summer of 2001, I met Alima, who told me about her "spiritual resurrection." Alima felt that her soul had been resurrected and she felt like "a new [and] different person." One night, "*bobolar* [ancestral spirits]" spoke to her, telling her to lead a "correct" life, to "purify" and "resurrect" her soul, and love and accept others. Since that time, Alima's life had changed. She said she had "reevaluated what was important in life" and now felt more focused on God and her soul. Alima found support and guidance from a local healer and prophetess. The seer "predicted floods in Russia, Europe, and South Korea," added Alima. Later that day I met Alima's spiritual guide, another self-identified "good and true" Muslim, Ruhshonoz.

Ruhshonoz claimed that she could heal souls and physical bodies, predict the future, and speak to the dead and interpret dreams. During our meetings in 2001, she said that we were living in an environment of "great transformations," including natural disasters and infectious diseases (author's personal communication, 2001). After 1999, these transformations, according to Ruhshonoz, became particularly intense and led to global catastrophes, which, in turn, would transform human souls—"the souls will be resurrected." The Fergana Valley had a very special role to play in this process. Ruhshonoz reminded me that chapter 12 of the Bible, known as "Revelations," talks about a woman who will give birth to a child. According to Ruhshonoz, this woman was a symbolic reference to the city of Fergana and to the Valley; the Valley will give birth to "a child"—a new spiritual movement—and will become "a center of peace and truth" (author's personal communication, 2001).

During our consecutive meetings in 2002 and 2003, Ruhshonoz, like the Uzbek government, condemned "zealous" Muslims advocating an Islamic state. She neither insisted on five-times-a-day prayers nor limited the knowledge of God's plan for humanity to the Koran. According to Ruhshonoz, ritual prayers and Kaaba were not very important, because holiness did not reside in physical structures, but internally, inside human beings.[8] She believed that a truly pious person could pray "in her heart" without performing corporal movements or verbal prayers (or directing them toward Kaaba); the whole mark of piety consisted of not the words of the prayer or its execution, but the individual's unconditional "acceptance of God's creation." "One should accept the world, accept the people, prepare oneself for a meeting with God, and be Godlike not in the body, but in the soul; the soul is priceless." Ruhshonoz said she lived what she preached.

While promoting a vision of the Fergana Valley's future as a pluralistic spiritualist society, an example of religious tolerance and coexistence for the rest of the world, Ruhshonoz's moral project was to (re)orient other Muslims' and non-Muslims' understandings of God's plan for their lives toward what she called "spiritual all-inclusive religiosity." This religiosity would begin locally and spread globally. Ruhshonoz was meant to facilitate this process, through her special powers, which, she claimed, were tested in one of Moscow's universities where she was found to be a "clear-seer" and a "clear-thinker" (*iasno vidiashchaia i iasno misliashchaia*).

Postrelational Turn

If we take seriously the claims of Nafisahon and Ruhshonoz to have reoriented their lives toward what they consider to be "correct" Islam and toward God, and to possess special powers and access to the divine, then from a traditional anthropological standpoint there are no *real* relations between these (and other) individuals and God. Therefore, a simple relational analysis cannot explain their active religious consciousness and participation. In order to engage Nafisahon's and Ruhshonoz's individual moral projects (following Pedersen 2012), I explore these *unreal* links by "inventing" them.

Morten A. Pedersen (2012) suggests that contemporary anthropology is (or should be) more relational than ever before, or "post-relational," and argues that "the task of anthropologists" is to invent relations and themselves become "the potentiality of relations" (Pedersen 2012, 60–61). In the case of Nafisahon and Ruhshonoz, we can (re)invent these relations by shifting the analytical focus from relations with others (or from how one's reorientation toward God affects others) to relations with(in) the self (or to how this reorientation affects the self): from intersubjective to intrasubjective experiences. This postrelational turn helps to capture the unexpected and unique inner world of "the self-relational person" and, as a result, challenges existing generalizations about piety as limited to a set of cultural symbolic behaviors (Pedersen 2012, 63). A focus on individual self-relatedness and the concomitant shift of focus from piety's external manifestations to its internal constitution and experience allows us to move the analysis beyond just the recognition and assertion of religious diversity toward an understanding of its implications and causes. In the following paragraphs, I use the postrelational turn to analyze Nafisahon's and Ruhshonoz's experiences of being and becoming truly Muslim, and their concomitant moral projects.

A Return to Nafisahon

Nafisahon's renewed commitment to Islam in post-Soviet Uzbekistan was fundamental to her moral project of healing others. As a "national healer," by using her extrasensory powers and *biotoki* (bioenergy), she claimed to have healed multitudes of people simultaneously. For instance, a day after our first meeting in 2003, Nafisahon went to Kyrgyzstan to conduct a healing session at a local cinema hall for "hundreds" of individuals. Both Rahimov (2002) and Nafisahon claimed that is was not unusual; while she had already healed "countless numbers" of people, many more were waiting to receive physical healing through Nafisahon's extrasensory powers and bioenergy (author's personal communication, 2003).

To me Nafisahon sounded similar to the alternative practitioners/healers claiming unique powers and abilities that I have encountered personally and read about while studying and working in the United States (see also Tucker 2002). Yet, she was also different from them. During our first meeting, Nafisahon established the cultural uniqueness and continuity of her moral project. She stated that her "strong extrasensory power and bioenergy" were very special and that they helped her to heal patients' bodies and souls. Then Nafisahon reminded me that she was not exceptional. Her power and abilities were like those of other historical and contemporary local healers (*tabibs*) and famous Central Asian individuals such as Rumi,

Alisher Navoi, and Ahmed Yassavi. She claimed to be following in their footsteps.

Although Nafisahon's power was transcendental in origin (God provided this power), it was as if fused with her physical body (as bioenergy) and manifested in material changes. According to her, one could not scientifically understand and explain her methods of healing and her psychological and extrasensory abilities. She too could not comment on or explain the "sacred power" of her magic words, her touch, or her energy, which became exponentially stronger after her experience in Mecca. But, she said, "It worked." Rahimov (2002, 5–6) too insists that there is no need to explain her abilities: "when you personally see positive changes in the condition of the sick ones during her séance . . . when you see signs and symbols appearing, then you will be convinced that Nafisahon turns her spiritual energy into material power." To her patients, their personal experiences and empirical evidence, such as qualitative shifts in their physical condition or the appearance of Arabic letters on various objects during a healing ceremony, were more important than epistemological explanations of her ability to heal.

Nafisahon said her patients' faith in her ability to heal mattered a great deal in order for her bioenergy to work; they had to believe in her God-given bioenergetic power and extrasensory abilities. She and her patients experienced her power as warmth or an invisible force, which allowed Nafisahon to "read" people during séances; she was able to detect those who did not believe in her ability and would ask them to leave. Those in an adulterated state of intoxication, Nafisahon said, "felt" her power in a sudden chest pain that they could not withstand; they too would leave her healing séances.

Not only a healer but also an activist, Nafisahon demonstrated her active engagement in the social life of Uzbek society by exploring and promoting "natural energy and information exchange" (Rahimov 2002, 34). She was a member of the International Association of Natural Healers founded in Uzbekistan in January 1995 (renamed the Avicenna Association of Traditional Medicine in the late 2000s). Both Nafisahon and Rahimov (2002) praised Uzbekistan's Ministry of Justice for registering this association after Uzbekistan's independence from the Soviet Union. According to Nafisahon, this gave local healers access to global audiences. As a result, she claimed to be known not only in the countries of the former Soviet Union but also overseas.

Nafisahon called herself an "ekstrasens," a Russian term describing a person claiming to have and exercise extrasensory abilities. She said she was the first woman in Uzbekistan to perform healing séances for over a thousand people at the same time. In addition she communicated with and received help from *bobolar* (ancestral spirits) who appeared to her in the form of long-winged birds and helped her to predict the future. Nafisahon added that she could communicate with extraterrestrials, but did not elaborate on this because she was rushing to yet another healing engagement (author's personal communication, 2003).

Her new career as a national healer offered Nafisahon new economic opportunities: "People give me gifts, although I do not ask them to, if and when I can, I support widows, orphans, the elderly, and the sick." As a "true" Muslim she performed charitable acts and reported giving money to local schools and orphanages. She also sponsored restoration efforts at some sacred sites in the Valley (Rahimov 2002, 38). Aside from economic motivations, Nafisahon continued to claim that God was fundamental to her life, self, and ability to heal. If this claim was not purely theological (ideological) or an example of a continuity of indigenous healing practices but a sign of Nafisahon's moral project, then we need to explore the *unreal* links between Nafisahon and God.

As a nurse and healer who was able to predict the future from an early age, the most significant stage of her development into a "truly" Muslim human began when she was forty, after both of her parents died (Rahimov 2002, 14). This tragic event propelled her interest in God and ancestral spirits, and eventually led her to experiential knowledge of the divine energy. At a minimum three kinds of new mutually informative relations were created and solidified through Nafisahon's renewed commitment to God and Islam. These were relations with (1) God, (2) other spiritual beings, and (3) her body's bioenergy. God, the initial source of Nafisahon's bioenergy, granted her the ability to retain this energy and give it out through healing and predicting the future in Soviet Uzbekistan. After the Soviet Union's disintegration, starting with her trip to Mecca in 1997, Nafisahon's energy was greatly enhanced by God, which made her acutely aware of having special relations with her body, its energy, and this energy's historical continuity, as her connection to other historical figures and sacred places in the region. Hence, God was the source of all other relations that Nafisahon engaged in as a self-related individual.

Relations with Other Spiritual Beings

Although Nafisahon's bioenergy was divine in nature, she was not the only receptacle for it. This energy also extended into and emanated from sacred places in Uzbekistan. Nafisahon reported that upon visiting these places, she was able to replenish her bioenergy that had been depleted through healing others. Wherever Nafisahon would travel to heal others, she said she visited local sacred places, often burial places of well-known spiritual masters (*awalyo*) such as Ahmed Yassavi (see Rasanayagam 2006b, 2010). There she would perform commemoration rituals, sacrifices, and special prayers. As part of the circuit of divine energy, the power of these sacred places and spiritual masters would become a part of *her* self, as a part of her body's bioenergy that she gave out to others.

Relations with Her Body

On the one hand, this divine energy was not limited to Nafisahon and was transcendental in nature. On the other hand, through her relations with her body, this energy was fully hers. The divine, reinvented as *relations*, unfolded into Nafisahon's life not only as her links to other, often spiritual, beings; as a self-relational person, this energy became a part of her individual self. She reported connecting to and feeling this energy through her hands when she detected cold and hot spots on human bodies during healing ceremonies. These spots gave out "signals." In response to these signals, Nafisahon's "heart" informed her "about the condition of the sick person . . . how many séances she or he has to attend" (author's personal communication, 2003). Through her self-relatedness powered by the divine in nature and now her own bioenergy, while completing the circuit from the patient's body to her hands to her heart to her hands to the patient's body, Nafisahon was able to connect to others by refilling their depleted physical energy and strength.

Relations with God

Nafisahon's relations with God were unique. These relations reflected her desire and ability to heal others with powerful bioenergy, which could have been epistemologically unfathomable but experientially effective and therefore real to her and those she had healed. According to Nafisahon, this energy was proof of her special connection to God *within* and *from outside* her body. She felt her divinely enhanced bioenergy; she had relation(ship)s with it, which she protected and reinvigorated by visiting sacred places that were potent sources of such energy. These experiences, feelings, and acts of identity—and not any one set of cultural symbolic behaviors assumed to capture the essence of being or becoming a pious Muslim—characterized Nafisahon's piety, her active religious consciousness, and her religious participation.

Exit Strategy

In the summer of 2011, I found out that Nafisahon was no longer performing healing séances in public places in Uzbekistan. In response to my question about Nafisahon, one of my local friends, who personally did not know Nafisahon but had heard about her, stated that "the Uzbeks did not accept her; she was not traditional. She was a fake. She was not a true Muslim. Kazakhs love her. They do not care about Islam. She works there now." Although this statement was one individual's opinion about Nafisahon's healing practice, it pointed to contextual discourses—different, contested, and dynamic—on what it means to be truly Muslim. In summer 2011, perhaps Nafisahon did not fit the acceptable category of "traditional" in the national discourse on "enlightened and tolerant" Islam, and her "acts of identity" were no longer accepted by Muslims who wanted to cleanse local Islam of *bid'ah* (innovation) and *shirk* (polytheism) (see Exnerova, chapter 3 and Borbieva, chapter 7, this volume).

During our meetings in 2002–3, Nafisahon defined her relationship with Islam as nonpolitical. She praised Uzbekistan's government and the Ministry of Justice for registering the International Association of National Healers, and connected herself to historical figures, such as Ahmed Yassavi and Rumi, glorified by the Uzbek nationalist discourse at the time (Rasanayagam 2010). During those years she could be "a national healer" and hold healing séances in cinema halls. I was told that in 2011, unless sanctioned and organized by the state, en masse public gatherings were prohibited and could be construed as political. Furthermore, Nafisahon's mission to bring "true" Islam to the masses, as one of her grateful patients observed, was no longer acceptable to the Uzbek state. To define and promote what *was* and *was not* "true" Islam were political matters now limited only to the state and its agents and not to individuals. It is also possible that Nafisahon's healing techniques, which employed the language of extrasensory bioenergy, did not fit into the practices advocated by the Avicenna Association of Traditional Medicine in Tashkent, which was organized in order "to revive, preserve, and promote the foundations of eastern medicine and develop international cooperation in this area," and is now headed by the president's eldest daughter Gulnara Karimova.[9] Whatever went wrong, Nafisahon had a good exit strategy. She moved her renewed commitment to Islam and concomitant identity acts to Kazakhstan where, regardless of how others evaluated her piety, she continued to identify as a "true" Muslim and carry out her moral project to the best of her abilities. Essentially personal, her piety, whether witnessed, accepted, or criticized by others, continued to be her own.

Ruhshonoz's "God" and/or "Humanity"

During our first meeting in 2001, Ruhshonoz predicted "great transformations" both in the Fergana Valley and globally (author's personal communication, 2001). She believed that these changes would be particularly difficult for those Muslims who did not believe in God at all and for zealous Muslims, whom she particularly resented. Inspired by knowledge imported from "the Arabston" (a term she used to refer to Saudi Arabia), the latter were calling for the purification of local religious practices and the creation of an Islamic state. She referred to these claims as "absurd," and added that these zealous Muslims would understand that such calls were utter fallacies after their souls experienced resurrection, just as she and her disciples had.

Illness, doubt, personal catastrophes, natural disasters, and self-education led Ruhshonoz to rediscover Islam. When she was young she did not believe in God; she was "in the darkness." Her first child was born with serious health problems. This was the first time she asked God for help. The child lived and after that, to her, "God [had become] light." From then onward, just as in Nafisahon's case, God became the source of all other relations that Ruhshonoz engaged in as a self-related individual. This initial connection to God, established on the evening of her firstborn's health crisis, led Ruhshonoz to rediscover her relations with others, including her self, angels, ancestral spirits, and other humans. These were not social relations, but spiritual ones.

One day in the 1990s, Ruhshonoz heard a voice saying, "I am in you!" Feeling confused, she wondered, "Could it be Allah?" She knew she was not crazy and decided to consult with some local Muslims who were famous for their religious knowledge. They told Ruhshonoz, "Allah talks only to the prophets." Later, while reading the Koran, she "found a *surat* [chapter] that [said] that Allah, if He wants, can talk to anyone." While following Allah's command to "Look at your life and analyze it," and evaluating her self, Ruhshonoz realized that her mission—her moral project—was to heal human souls (hers included) with the help of the spirits of "sacred ancestors" and angels; she had to establish spiritual relations with her self, these beings, and then with others, between her and their souls. According to Ruhshonoz, this mission was a "real miracle. . . . It took me twelve years to analyze and understand much of my life and to realize that one needs to live not in the body, but in the soul; there is death for the body, but not for the soul. The soul is resurrected not the body. Thus, there is no death." She continued receiving messages from God through angels. In 1993, Ruhshonoz said, she received a message from God mediated by angels, and addressed to President Karimov. The same year, she met with Karimov to deliver this message.[10]

Ruhshonoz called herself a "real" Muslim. According to her, "the healing energy" she shared with others "was God's love," which brought about knowledge of "the truth" that "we are all creatures of God; everyone has a particle of God." In Ruhshonoz's understanding, "the true message of Islam" was not just a belief in the "Oneness of God" (*tawhid*, an Islamic doctrine)— in the "Oneness of Humanity." These two were mutually informative; there could not be one without the other. In time, she said, she came to understand the Koran, some parts better than others, and sometimes better than other Muslims, and her home became a popular destination. Some came to Ruhshonoz for spiritual awakening while others wanted to understand their dreams, learn about their futures, and find lost parts of their personal histories by communicating with the spirits of their ancestors.

Despite her claims to be a "real" Muslim, some local women and men, devout and not devout, found Ruhshonoz's stories blasphemous, radical, wrong, or plainly crazy, while some local religious leaders criticized her understanding of resurrection. According to them, both the body and the soul would be resurrected, not just the soul. She responded to these criticisms by denouncing her critics' understandings of what it means to be "truly" Muslim. Ruhshonoz insisted that her rational decisions, beliefs, and actions were expressions of her free will to follow God's commands, as she understood them: "Before they judge me they should live righteous lives themselves. They should live according to the Koran . . . They need to learn humility. I am a free woman! I am not a slave! God gave me freedom of choice and I choose to follow God's calling." Despite others' criticisms, Ruhshonoz continued to predict the future, interpret dreams, and write leaflets about the Oneness of Humanity and not the Oneness of God.

Expanding Spiritual Network

During one of our meetings in 2002, I too received a message from God addressed to me and transmitted through the angels to Ruhshonoz.

She recited this message as her hand was writing it down on a piece of paper:

Like morning dew you cover [others] with the beauty of your thoughts. Mother. Woman. She carries the secret of creation. Let it be so! We Are [angels] proud that a Mother, an earthly woman, becomes a Savior of the matrix of "Earth." Dear creature carrying light . . . We Are happy that you accept Our voice. Love unites us. We Are light and love. If you will allow Us in[side], We will help you. You will feel Us healing you for ten days. We can help you to develop your "clear hearing." [At this point Ruhshonoz asks, if I want to "let them in"; in response I nod.] Thank you. We Are waiting for you. You are an educator of consciousness. You are hope. You give a gift of knowledge to the world! Everything will happen [that is supposed to happen]. Love and give warmth to others. The Heaven loves the woman, as she gave birth to great people. And her sacrifices, not recognized by others, kept her in a shadow. Now, it is an hour of a great transition. A woman as a Mother, as a Creator of a new life, should be put on the throne of the Governance, for she, as a creator, has a right to judge and make decisions. We are here to help an earthly woman to become a matrix of a new beginning. [Signed] Angels.

The poetics of the message are rather fascinating, but so is its substance. As "the one who brings light" (this is my name, Svetlana, understood literally), the message stated that my mission—my moral project—was to bring both scientific and religious knowledge to the world. It could be that by being included in a spiritual network Ruhshonoz was engaged in expending, and I was meant to facilitate her project, to make her ideas known to the world outside the Valley. If this is true, then Ruhshonoz possessed a truly extraordinary ability to create relations among people. Although not real at the time but extended into the future, these relations materialized, among other things, by my writing this chapter.

In order to facilitate the kind of moral transformation she was advocating, Ruhshonz was planning to use (or was already using) various techniques including publishing a newsletter—*A Second Way to Allah*. In 2002, she gave me two leaflets, which she said were to be included in the first issue of the newsletter. One leaflet featured a verse, both in Russian and Uzbek:

My friend, you are considered to be a representative of the most perfect religion. Why are you still not perfect? Why are you not an example for others? Before you offend anyone, remember your own pain when you were offended. Before you take something that does not belong to you, remember how someone took something from you [without asking]. Before you judge someone, remember when you were judged [unjustly by others]. Before you hurt someone [emotionally], remember how hard it is to ask for forgiveness. Do not wish death to anyone. You have not created this life [unlike God]. Do not judge others' actions before you judge yours. Before you humiliate someone, remember how you were humiliated. If this will not stop you from acting wrong, then know that you are truly lost. Do not forget that you are not the judge and not the executioner. You are simply a human covered from head to toe with your own mistakes.

Another leaflet described the human soul, love, everlasting life, and the oneness of humanity:

Human, you woke up! Your spirit woke up, and you understood that you are a particle [part] of the Oneness [of Humanity]; and you understood the meaning of your life on earth. You're an image of God! A child of God, create as your Father creates! Love as he taught you to love! Love is a fire uniting your soul and your mind. Let your generosity quench the thirst [of others]. Carry inside your soul service to humanity. Remember, God is known through its little particles [parts]. Be kind! Be able to accept the kindness of others; do not judge the size, for even a little kindness is a kindness. Do not preoccupy your mind with unnecessary preexisting thoughts, but learn how to think differently, create new [thoughts] in your mind. Let your feelings decorate and give shape to your thoughts; the actions based on these thoughts will be written in the book of your destiny. Be able to forgive others' imperfections, as your [way to] perfection should teach you to be merciful and caring. Rain on everything and everyone around you with a clear water of Aquarius and faith in God. Be able to be a human. You have been given a great guidance: now it is your turn to live out this guidance in the Book of Life! Love for the sake of love! Live for the sake of life everlasting! Accept your eternal life; remove the heavy seal of time and bitter tear of death! Remember, you are a particle of Oneness! Amen.

In Central Asia, poetry is a very popular genre of self- and artistic expression employed by famous personalities, such as Rumi. In addition to their rich substance, which deserves a separate analysis, I see these verses—which articulate poetically both the message of the oneness of humanity and a moral criticism of certain feelings and behaviors—as Ruhshonoz's pragmatic technique aimed at facilitating her mission. Not only her lectures, seminars, mediations with ancestral spirits, and teachings while healing, but also this pragmatic technique make her message easier to comprehend and remember—a message that delivers moral criticism to accept and reflect on. Publishing this information in printed and online media sources would make Ruhshonoz's moral message more accessible to a much wider general public, whether digitally literate or not. Therefore, the newsletter as a method of communication was also a pragmatic technique that reflected the substance and goal of Ruhshonoz's (truly) moral project of social transformation that begins with an individual.

Relations with the Self and Others

Similar to Nafisahon, Ruhshonoz's life and feeling of being truly Muslim was "a unique relational transformation" (Pedersen 2012, 63). This transformation started sometime during the late 1980s and early 1990s, after God saved Ruhshonoz's child. It then took her twelve years to reorient her self toward Islam, toward God. During this process, as an intratensional (or in Pedersen's [2012] terms "intensional") self-related individual she felt doubt, pain, fear, and confusion over God's attempts to speak to her and to reinvigorate relations with her. Finally heeding the call, as a way of solidifying the relations between her self and God, she developed relations with ancestral spirits and angels, since, according to Ruhshonoz, a human being could not speak to God directly. This was a process of realizing the importance of love and coming to terms with her personal "clear thinking" and "clear visions." During this process, Ruhshonoz came to experience, understand, and insist on individual holiness as humanity's wholeness, a potentiality that resided internally in her (and every) self. Her relations with her own soul were an example of and proof that the same (or some) kind of relations can be established intrasubjectively *within*, and then intersubjectively *with* others.

Like Nafisahon, Ruhshonoz's becoming and being "truly" Muslim was not animated by a set of cultural symbolic behaviors that are often used to manifest one's piety. She neither insisted on five-times-a-day prayer nor limited knowledge of God to the Koran. Unlike Nafisahon, she did not visit or perform rituals, sacrifices, and occasional prayers at the sacred places in the Valley. Rather, Ruhshonz's piety was manifested in her ability to feel, envision, experience, and invent relations within herself and then among others all around her in her own unique ways. She first formed these relations inside her existential expansive universe, intrasubjectively. Although not fully accessible to anyone, these intrasubjective relations helped Ruhshonoz to realize that she had the potential to unite (*with*) everyone, precisely because, according to Ruhshonoz, her self and everyone had a "particle of God" in them. These particles were meant to come together through one God who is love resulting in the "Oneness of Humanity." This was the "true" message of Islam. In spite of others' criticism of her ways of becoming and being Muslim, Ruhshonoz, like Nafisahon, continued to pursue her moral project to the best of her abilities. Whether or not others witnessed or doubted her piety, it continued to be essentially her own.

Exit Strategy

In August 2011, during a visit to a beauty parlor in Tashkent, I overheard three women talking about Ruhshonoz. They discussed the recent death (in April 2011) of an Indian holy man—Satya Sai Baba—lamenting that only two hundred people from Uzbekistan had a chance to visit him. Ruhshonoz, however, was among these few. One of the women insisted that Ruhshonoz had a special connection to Satya Sai Baba, who gave *her* "a special assignment." This assignment had something to do with collecting water from "seven rivers." I was unable to find out the details of this assignment, but on my arrival back to the Valley, I inquired about Ruhshonoz's whereabouts. Indeed, I was told that she traveled widely in India and Africa, where she met and became a disciple of "some holy man" (author's personal communication, 2011). Since then, she no longer resided in Fergana Valley but only visited there.

I wondered whether a "special assignment" was the reason Ruhshonoz visited the Valley only occasionally. During our meetings in 2002 and 2003, she, like the Uzbek government officials, spoke against "zealous" Muslims who advocated for an Islamic state. Her preaching of spiritual resurrection was similar to the government's emphasis on the historical coexistence of Christianity, Islam, and Judaism in Central Asia, while her understanding of spiritual resurrection was *beyond* Islam, in the sense that it was not limited to Muslims. But then again, she talked about change. She called for a spiritualist society that was pluralist, and some people listened to her. Like the state representatives, she talked about tolerance (Rasanayagam 2010, 106). Unlike them, Ruhshonoz stated that this tolerance could be achieved only as a result of freedom of expression and choice, which the government of Uzbekistan promoted discursively, but curtailed habitually. She called on people to think differently, to think for themselves and on their own terms, not on terms provided (and enforced) by others such as the government's representatives and the state's religious leadership.

Finally, during 2002–3, Ruhshonoz publicly proclaimed her views (e.g., by distributing leaflets). She had students, disciples, and followers. Yet, she was among the "unregistered" with state religious leaders and teachers.[11] Eight years later, in 2011, the Uzbek government's persecution of "unregistered" and unsanctioned religious instruction and practice increased; leaflets containing esoteric poetry could be construed as antigovernment messages inciting the local population to protest. This persecution did not affect Ruhshonoz spiritually and could not affect her territorially. In 2013 a colleague from a Russian university, a follower of Ruhshonoz's teachings, told me that Ruhshonoz was no longer traveling between countries and continents—now she resided mainly in Moscow, where she continued her spiritual mission as a founder and director of the School of the Spirit.

Genealogy of Extrasensory Healing and Vision

In the previous paragraphs, I have argued that Nafisahon's and Ruhshonoz's manifestations of piety were unique and not limited to a particular set of cultural symbolic behaviors. It is therefore tempting to see their experiences—feelings about and understandings of human relations with God, and their identity acts, such as healing with bioenergy and claiming to have extrasensory abilities—as exceptional. However, even though these women certainly do not represent every Muslim in the Fergana Valley, their abilities to heal and see the future are not unprecedented (see, e.g., Abramson and Karimov 2007; Rasanayagam 2006b, 2010). A brief detour into a rich religious history during the Soviet period helps in giving an understanding of these existing manifestations of individual piety (Asad 2003; Bringa 2002).

In the Soviet Union of the late 1980s to early 1990s, individual claims of extrasensory and telepathic abilities and UFO sightings were common occurrences. "Town halls that had once hosted Communist Party meetings now saw sorcerers armed with ouija boards attempting to conjure up Lenin. Old women openly sold magical charms against AIDS in city markets. State journalists transformed overnight into wild-eyed psychic healers. Pravda [the main Soviet newspaper] ran horoscopes" (Bennetts 2010). Particularly popular were televised healing shows, where physical transformations were expected to occur through biotoki possessed by individuals such as Anatoli Kashpirovsky and Alan Chumak. According to

Bennetts (2010), these men's healing shows attracted about three hundred million viewers throughout Eastern Europe.[12]

Tele-healers were not the only ones claiming the ability to influence events and mold physical bodies. Local healers were always popular in the Soviet Union de facto, even if discouraged de jure. Unlike these local healers using herbs and prayers to treat various diseases, tele-healers used their personal bioenergy fields. Anatoli Kashpirovsky and Alan Chumak, not God or some other natural or supernatural agent, promised to relieve the masses of all strain, stress, and pain, to heal them and change their behavior. They claimed to be able to perform miraculous surgeries without anesthetic, to help people lose weight (about thirty-eight kilos a week), gain sight, or become pregnant. They charged objects such as water with their healing bioenergy, and led various scholars to conduct scientific experiments that were meant to ascertain the validity of their bioenergetic healing through an increased electrophotonic glow—a combination of electric and radiant energy (light) glow (Bennetts 2010; Chalko 2001; Falkowski 1989).

Female healers like Baba Vanga and Djuna were legendary as well.[13] Djuna acted as healer for the Soviet Union's leaders such as Leonid Brezhnev.[14] (Nafisahon's biographer, Rahimov [2002, 11], also mentions Djuna's "special connection" to Uzbekistan.) Baba Vanga, famous throughout Eastern Europe and the Soviet Union, was a healer and prophetess, who predicted "the end of days" (Naumescu 2007). During the 1980s–1990s, prognosticators abounded in every corner of the former Soviet Union.

Scholars and journalists propose different explanations for the popularity of what they refer to as "occult" practices of that time. Some argue that this popularity reflected personal psychological anxieties about sociopolitical changes during the disintegration of the Soviet Union. Bennetts (2010) states that "perestroika and glasnost had driven the entire nation out of its collective mind. The country was gripped by a frenzy of visions and hallucinations, alien sightings and mystic revelations." Belousova (2002) suggests that in the late 1980s the general public expected the collapse of everything—the end of days. Therefore, eschatological expectations led to an increased mass interest in supernatural help. Belousova (2002, 53) writes, "Healers, sorcerers, astrologists and hypnotists became extremely popular. . . . Private business became legal, and numerous small publishers and newspapers began specializing in books on dreams, the interpretation of omens, folk healing and the supernatural."

Other scholars suggest that the public's interest in occult practices in the disintegrating Soviet Union was not a novel phenomenon. While referring to an array of religious phenomena, including the aforementioned activities, Demyan Belyaev, for example, notes:

> [Such] heterodox religious worldviews . . . are rooted quite deeply in Russian culture. They were common in many forms and in different parts of society long before the demise of the Soviet Union and were preserved not only among Russian émigrés but even within the Soviet leadership . . . although the intensity of interest in heterodox religiosity and the scale of its proliferation among the population constitute a phenomenon which has occurred mainly since the end of communism, an interest in this kind of religiosity was present in society long before that time. (Belyaev 2010, 141, 143)

Therefore, occult practices during the 1980s–1990s exemplify historical continuity rather than a unique manifestation of religious consciousness and participation in the Soviet Union.

What Belyaev (2010) calls "heterodox religious worldviews" were not unique to Russia, but popular throughout the former Soviet space.[15] Tasawwuf (Sufism) is a set of spiritual exercises, ideas, ideals, and knowledge passed from masters to disciples by following sacred spiritual lineages, represented by prominent members of Muslim communities. As such, it also provided resources for "heterodox religiosities" in various parts of the former Soviet Union, including the territory of the Central Asian Soviet Socialist Republics, which in the 1990s became independent countries (on Sufism, see Ernst [2011]). In Muslim communities of the former Soviet Union, Islam (and other religious traditions) "transformed by socialist rubrics" has already been "pluralized" (see Jalil, chapter 1, this volume) and manifested as combinations, partial accommodations, "evasions, and unexpected incorporations" (Grant 2011, 659, 656). This has resulted in "'a very inclusive' Islamic ethos" that, in some cases, incorporates practices such as healing with bioenergy, communicating with ancestors' spirits, and predicting the future (Seteney Shami 1999, 190, quoted in Grant 2011, 670).

In the context of spiritual kinship, Rahimov (2002, 11–13) places Nafisahon among other historical occult leaders and healers such as Nostradamus, W. Messing, Djuna, and G. Gurdjieff. These individuals also claimed to have special gifts and special spiritual energies truly known only to their selves. There was an important difference between Nafisahon and Ruhshonoz and famous healers like Anatoli Kashpirovsky or Djuna. While the latter claimed to be *the source* of their bioenergy or ability to predict the future, Nafisahon's bioenergy came from Allah and local (and global, such as the Kaaba) sacred places. She was a vessel, albeit an important one: she did not self-generate, but recharged this energy by visiting local sacred places that housed the spirits of sacred ancestors. Ruhshonoz's knowledge and ability to resurrect souls also had a transcendental ontology; she was not a vessel but a particle of God.

Both Nafisahon and Ruhshonoz were self-relational individuals who had relations with God as a "network" of other relations (to paraphrase Holdraad [2004] quoted in Pedersen [2012, 62]). Their moral projects were aimed at healing and resurrecting, not teaching about Islam's history or theology. In Uzbekistan, their patients and disciples included Russians, Koreans, and others; they did not need to be Muslims. Nafisahon's patients did not even have to *really* believe in God, but to believe in *her* ability to materialize spiritual energy and bring about physical change in their condition. Ruhshonoz's followers, as particles of God, rather than focusing on One God—the Creator *apart from* humanity, a fact that some consider central to Islamic theology—had to focus on being *a part of* "One Humanity" and accept Ruhshonoz's ability to communicate with angels and the spirits of their ancestors.

Susan Ackerman (2005, 509) argues that "the growth of the middle classes in modernizing societies with vibrant popular spiritual traditions is a fertile ground for the creation of globalized spiritual products that can appeal to New Age lifestyle consumers anywhere in the world." Although it is possible that the abilities of Nafisahon and Ruhshonoz were business-like responses to the demands of post-Soviet middle class "consumers" in Uzbekistan, I contend that economic incentives do not explain their moral projects. If, indeed, these women were entrepreneurs, and their moral projects were just products meant to be sold, then why not find less contested merchandise to trade in Uzbekistan's cultural supermarket (for a discussion of contested discourses on Islam in Central Asia, see Exnerova, chapter 3 and Borbieva, chapter 7, this volume)? Or in the spirit of good entrepreneurship, rather than moving their businesses elsewhere, why not abandon this product and find another one in demand by local consumers?

I do not possess the final word on the motivations behind these women's goals. Yet instead of adopting a framework of religious economy, I argue that these women's moral projects were particular individual verbalizations of piety and acts of identity that were produced in response to and became formative of their social context at the time. The statements and identity acts of Nafisahon and Ruhshonoz were informed by the stories about religion (including occult practices and foretelling the future) familiar to them, and by the women's unique individual experiences, which were in many ways reflective of their active pursuit of moral projects. They blended virtues of and discourses on healing, bioenergy, beauty, spirituality, prognostication, the occult, love, and devotion to God and society. In other words, Ruhshonoz and Nafisahon ideologically rethought, authored, and authorized in new and different ways "certain sensibilities, knowledge and behaviors" formative of various historic and contextual discourses about relationships between human and divine worlds not limited to sacred books, particular modes of dress, ritual prayers, and political ethics articulated in Islamic terms (Asad 2003, 25).

We could interpret the message from God that Ruhshonoz transmitted for me as an advertisement for her entrepreneurial skills and her moral project as a product, or as the Sufi or spiritualist, or New Age-like ideas popular among the middle classes in the global cultural supermarket at the time. However, by exploring the contextual genealogy of healing and extrasensory abilities in the post-Soviet space, I take this to be a moral message promoting virtues of love, care, sacrifice, kindness, and hope; these virtues are not limited to any one spiritualist, Sufi, or New Age discourse. Shared by many these virtues were not unfamiliar to Ruhshonoz and are fitting to describe her experiences of and feelings about God's plan for humanity.[16]

"Useful" Religion beyond Piety

My research and that of other scholars focuses on those Muslims who claim to have reoriented their lives toward "correct" Islam. Their spiritual transformation was animated by the consistent performance of ritual prayers, participation in communal religious rituals, observance of dietary restrictions, the adoption of particular forms of covered modest dress, and the cultivation of piety through spiritual exercises and religious education. The more I think about the aforementioned cultural symbolic traits and behaviors as measurements of one's piety, the more unsettling this understanding of piety becomes in terms of what it excludes. It leaves out Muslims such as Nafisahon and Ruhshonoz, who also, yet in different ways, reoriented their lives toward what *they* considered to be correct Islam. As my analysis demonstrates, their finding of God was animated by different acts of identity.

There are many ways one can be Muslim in Central Asia: from wanting an Islamic state, or retreating from the communities one considers to be morally corrupt, to teaching "correct" Islam, to resurrecting souls, or using bioenergy to heal physical illnesses and perform miracles, and even possibly to talking to ETs (e.g., Ilkhamov 2006; Louw 2007; McBrien 2009; Rasanayagam 2010). The chapters in this edited volume showcase this diversity. If we closely analyze the relations of Nafisahon and Ruhshonoz with their own bodies, their (bio)energy, the sources of this energy (such as God and sacred sites), and their intratensional and intentional moral projects to change others, then this diversity is no longer the end of the social analysis of religious dynamics in Central Asia. All local Muslims and non-Muslims, just as these two women, are self-related individuals with unexpected and unique relations springing forth in their inner worlds toward their selves, the divine, and toward others (cf. Pedersen 2012). And each and every case of such *being* can challenge generalizations about piety and individual experiences of reorienting lives toward God in Uzbekistan and elsewhere. In other words, there will always be contradictory behaviors and situational human choices that continue to destabilize our generalizations about humans, challenging us to empathize with, rather than be afraid of their *other* ways.

In this chapter I have discussed how and in what ways Nafisahon's and Ruhshonoz's moral projects take us *beyond* dominant understandings of piety. These examples confirm that different ways of being Muslim coexist in the Valley, and this diversity and coexistence are not limited to the region. As Paul Rabinow (2003, 23) argues, "claims to hegemony are typical of [a] moral landscape, but the practices of coexistence are equally representative." In some places and times these different ways of being Muslim might compete with one another, as Exnerova (chapter 3, this volume) and Borbieva (chapter 7, this volume) demonstrate, while in other places and times and in regard to particular issues, they might complement each other or be "simply copresent" (Rabinow 2003, 23).

I have also argued and demonstrated that our understanding of what it means to be Muslim in the post-Soviet space can directly benefit from attending not only to the social context but also to the concept of the self-related individual. The insights into individual moral projects themselves become potentialities for challenging a normalized perception of Central Asian Islam that is often reduced to violence and the Islamic ethic that is oppositional to the state. These insights are helpful for finding similarities with those inhabiting the region because they help us to recognize our human capability for "introverted acts of self-evaluation" and the sheer vastness of our "inner existential expanse," whether we are born-again or not, whether we are Muslims, Christians, or atheists (Pedersen 2012, 63). Finally, these insights can help us to remain attentive to state discourses about what is and is not Islam and what is and is not political. The Roman Stoic philosopher of the first century, Seneca the Younger, is believed to have said, "Religion is regarded by the common people as true, by the wise as false, and by the rulers as useful." In the case of Uzbekistan, we often look for danger in the wrong places. Perhaps our analytical lens needs to be shifted away from those labeled as dangerous, and refocused on those who find religion useful and claim to *define* danger, piety, and tradition. It is not Islam that drives individuals to violence. Rather, some individuals, as Mahmood (2006) rightly points out, may express their contention vis-à-vis the state in terms of religious ethics, among other possible terms, particularly if the state's self-proclaimed secularism and democracy are systematically expressed through violence. Uzbekistan's post-Soviet history exemplifies this dynamic.

CHAPTER THREE

Radical Islam from Below

The Mujaddidiya and Hizb-ut-Tahrir in the Ferghana Valley

Vera Exnerova

For many in Central Asia the Mujaddidiya and Hizb–ut–Tahrir (HBT) movements represent the most active and prominent radical Islamist groups to have emerged over the past four decades.[1] The Mujaddidiya is known for its role in the appearance of radical political Islam in Uzbekistan both prior to and after the collapse of the Soviet Union and its culmination in the violent jihad of the Islamic Movement of Uzbekistan (IMU) against governments in Central Asia in the 1990s. The HBT has been scrutinized for its role as the most attractive radical Islamic group in the region since the 2000s as well as for its ultimate aim to regulate everyday life according to sharia law under a caliphate.[2]

In the scholarly literature, authors have explored the discourse of the Mujaddidiya and its critics with the aim of explaining the roots of radical Islam in the Soviet period and have sought to identify individual devout Muslims who should be considered as posing a threat to the secular post-Soviet regimes (Babadzhanov, Muminov, and von Kügelgen 2007; Frank and Mamatov 2006; Olcott 2007a). Others have analyzed the relative success of HBT in mobilizing its social base, or have considered the role HBT ideology plays in attracting support for this group in the Central Asian region (Collins 2007; Karagiannis 2009). In reaction to it, some scholars have argued that Islamic revivalism, including support for movements such as HBT, has been a strategy for coping with an increasingly ineffective central state (ICG 2009b; McGlinchey 2009), and have warned against the discourse of danger in relation to Central Asia (Heathershaw and Megoran 2011).

This chapter takes us beyond such a debate and instead aims to assess the practice and discourse of the two Islamic movements from below, in the local context of the Ferghana Valley, which is characterized by multiple and competing sources of religious and social authority.[3] Specifically, it explores the Mujaddidiya group in the context of the Uzbek Ferghana Valley, where it originated and was most active, during the late Soviet period and around the time of its dissolution. The chapter also explores HBT's practice in the context of the Kyrgyz Ferghana Valley since the late 1990s.[4] Placing the two groups in their local contexts allows us to avoid the traditional focus on the implications of "radical Islam" for the current state. It describes how the proponents of the Mujaddidiya and HBT have pursued authority when compared with other diverse local actors and provides a more nuanced understanding of the role of radical Islam in the region.

This analysis contributes to the recent scholarship on Central Asia, which has argued that Islamic congregations have performed pragmatic functions in the context of social and economic change in the region during both the Soviet and post-Soviet eras,[5] and has emphasized the importance of a local perspective when seeking to understand the various manifestations of Islam and "Islamic politics" (Heathershaw and Roche 2011; Khamidov, chapter 9, this volume).

This chapter builds on the existing scholarly resources in relation to both the practice and discourse of the two movements as well as on multisite ethnographic research. The approach traces multiple sites of power *and* counterpower exercise, and it subordinates the questions of resistance to other questions "about the shape of systemic processes themselves and complicities within these processes among variously positioned subjects" (Kubik 2009, 47–48; Marcus 1995, 85).[6] In the first phase of the research, about sixty semistructured interviews and informal discussions were conducted regarding the practice of Islamic authorities in the Soviet period, primarily in the Uzbek Ferghana Valley (September 2007 and May–June 2008), and in Tajikistan (October 2008 and June 2009) and Kyrgyz Ferghana Valley (June 2009). Those interviewed included representatives of the Islamic authorities, rural and urban civilians, state officials from both the Soviet regime and the current regimes, politicians, and local civil society activists.[7] In the second phase of the research, the discourse and counterar-

guments relating to radical Islamic groups in Central Asia were analyzed
(as articulated in leaflets, Web sites, or texts published in secondary historical and political sources, and the public discourse) and about twenty additional interviews and informal conversations on the theme were collected
in Kyrgyzstan and Tajikistan (June–July 2011).[8]

The Mujaddidiya in the Uzbek Ferghana Valley

"Those who undertake renewal," in Arabic the "Mujaddidiya," was the
self-styled name of a group that gained ground in the Ferghana Valley of
Soviet Uzbekistan in the late 1970s, and later in other neighboring regions
(Babadzhanov and Kamilov 2001a). This was not a particularly coherent
group. The Mujaddidiya, representing a movement of individuals who were
locally referred to as the "young mullahs" (in Uzbek, *mulla bachas*),[9] were
united in their desire to reform Islam in their local communities.

At the time of their expansion in the Ferghana Valley in the 1970s, the
Soviet apparatus periodically harassed and persecuted public manifestations of Islam in relation to most of the population of the region.[10] Despite
the constitutional right to religious freedom, people were taught that pioneers, komsomols, and Communists were not allowed to have religious
convictions, thus preventing religious observance for the vast majority of
the population. Students and workers were officially monitored and discouraged from observing periods of fasting, sometimes being forcefully
compelled by the authorities and teachers to drink water or eat when in
school or at work.[11] At times, the Soviet apparatus used a comprehensive
surveillance and persecution system to prevent the manifestation of informal religious practices among the population. Those who were reported
for transmitting religious knowledge were imprisoned or fined, as well as
publicly denounced and ridiculed at meetings and in the newspapers. Their
"crimes" were reported in the official documentation sent to republic-level
and Union-level bodies.[12] The Soviet authorities did not formally persecute
people who were retired and nonactive members of Soviet economic and
public life, thus allowing the elders, including those who worked within
the Soviet ideological apparatus during their careers, to travel for Friday
prayers to one of the few registered mosques.[13]

However, in certain cases the Soviet authorities relied on the authority
of official Islamic actors when seeking to promote their goals and boost
their legitimacy. Most notably, the Central Asian Spiritual Board of Muslims (SADUM), which had been established in 1943 by the Communist

regime, partly in an attempt to generate support among the Central Asian Muslims for the war effort during the First World War, represented religious life in the Soviet Union and had the task of spreading a positive image among potential comrade states within the Muslim family of nations.[14] Individual workers within the Soviet apparatus had also supported the practice of Islam. For instance, the first secretary of the Communist Party in Yozyovon raion in the Ferghana Valley, Rakhmon Safarov, after his appointment in 1981, allowed the reconstruction of the Qarasakal *mazar* (saintly place), which was visited by people on pilgrimage, especially during Nauruz and at the beginning of the autumn, concealing this activity as a vacation prior to the beginning of the cotton-picking season.[15] There were also instances at a local level when, for example, the kolkhoz administration asked local Islamic authorities to act as site supervisors at cotton storage centers in order to prevent the regular theft of cotton.[16]

In such an environment only a minimal number of people had access to religious education within the state, and it was available mostly to people from ordinary family backgrounds (the authorities made sure that the person was not a descendant of a respected religious family), the sons of religious figures who were cooperating with the government, or members of the Spiritual Administration, such as the mufti Ishon Babakhan from the Musakhon-tura family.[17] The ulema who matriculated through the official system of religious education sometimes acknowledged that the quality of the provided education could not compete with the religious instruction provided via informal networks.[18]

In towns and *qishloqs* (villages), those individuals who were interested in Islam were able to study the basics in the evening under the guidance of religiously literate people in their neighborhoods, or receive their knowledge through other members of the family. In some cases, families secured religious education for one of their children by sending the child to live in the households of religious scholars, or by supporting their studies over many years.[19] In Qoqand, for example, students lodged with their host families for free, with children often helping the teacher in his or her workshop and adults coming in the early morning or late in the evening. Individuals established guilds where students officially worked as guards, while in practice dedicating their time to religious studies, such as in the case of Abdul Kunduz Khoja (died in 1960) in Marghelan.[20]

The content of lessons depended on the teacher's educational background, level of knowledge, and the books he or she possessed. For instance, Toj Mohammad received his initial education in the 1960s in

Qoqand. First he studied with his sisters under Hamro otin-bibi (died 1982 when she was approximately ninety years old), who used, among other resources, the primer *Ustád-i-awwal* by Said Rasul Khoja, and also the Koran. His next teacher, Mohammad Ali Qori, besides teaching him the Koran, also taught him literature and grammar. In addition, every day he was required to rewrite one page from the textbook of the jadidist reformer, Abdullah Awlani.[21] In the same town Hakimjon qori, a supporter of the Ahl-i-Qur'an movement, advocated the interpretation of Islam only on the basis of the Qur'an and taught his pupils about the unacceptable nature of certain rites and rituals practiced in the region and sanctioned by other local ulema.[22] According to some sources, Hakimjon qori slowly established a substantial library, including multivolume works by Ibn Taymmiya and the fundamentalist commentary of the Koran written by Ibn al-Kathir during this period, from those who were allowed to perform the hajj and travel outside the Soviet Union (Olcott 2007a, 13).

It was also possible to buy a variety of books at the informal book markets that operated close to Friday mosques or former madrasas, such as Medrese Mir in Qoqand, which was held each Friday during the 1970s. From the classical portfolio there were Arabic-language grammars, *tafsir* (exegesis), hadith, *mawlid* (texts recited to celebrate the Prophet Muhammed's birth), various Sufi poetry collections, jadidist textbooks, *Haftiyak, Chor Kitob*. Of the new publications, there were *Janokh at-Talib* (Student's wings, Arabic-language textbooks) produced by the proponent of the Mujaddidiya, Rahmatulla Alloma, Oltinkhon-tura's books (Said Mahmud Tarzi, the author from Turkestan who in the 1970s published commentaries on the Koran and printed them in Saudi Arabia), and, from the end of 1970s, cassettes with commentaries from proponents of the Mujaddidiya, Abduvali Qori and Rahmatulla Alloma, as well as their former teacher, Mohammad Hindustani.[23] Other books published in the 1970s were also available (such as Sverkhontura's *Ilkhomir Rahmon*—the basics of religion and *namaz* [prayer]—and *Hadith Qudsiy*), which were backdated by fifty to sixty years in order to trick the Soviet authorities and reduce the risk of danger to the author.[24]

During the Soviet invasion of Afghanistan in the 1980s other versions of the Koran, brought by Central Asian soldiers fighting across the Amu Darya River, began to appear on the market.[25] The leaders of the Mujaddidiya group at that time also established contact with students from Arabic countries in Tashkent, who provided lessons on Islam and distributed literature by Islamist thinkers such as Sayyid Qutb and al-Mawdudi.

This continued until their contact with locals was restricted by the Uzbek authorities in the late 1970s.[26] In addition, some of the young people also studied Arabic within the official Soviet education system. According to official figures, in Marghelan alone during the five-year period 1975–80, 850 people passed through two special schools established by the Ministry of Higher Education of the Soviet Union for Arabic language and literature studies, thus gaining the opportunity to directly access primary sources relating to Islam.[27]

Nonetheless, the majority of people in the Ferghana Valley at that time learned about and experienced Islam primarily through their participation in different informal family and community events and life-cycle rituals, where prayers were read and rites were carried out under the leadership of locally respected personalities, elders, irrespective of whether or not they were self-educated, sons of mullahs, *ishans* (Sufi spiritual leaders), sheikhs, or *hojis* (those who have performed the hajj), that is, the source of their religious authority.

In such an environment of diversity and the continuous transformation of Islamic practices (Dudoignon and Noack 2014; Jones, Introduction, this volume), it was also the case that the religious authorities and descendants of Islamic scholars in the Ferghana Valley pursued a variety of approaches. Initially, some of those who survived the Soviet purges of the 1920s and 1930s and did not flee to Afghanistan or Saudi Arabia went into hiding or chose a life of total separation from the reality that was the Soviet Union. For example, Okhunjon Qori (1872–1958), a pupil of Mohammad Yusuf Marghiloni (referred to as Hazrat Domla, 1836–1917), did not leave his house from 1928 until his death. During the thirty years of his voluntary confinement at home he wrote twenty books and provided lessons to those interested in studying Islam.[28] Later, most Islamic scholars entered public life as ordinary Soviet citizens and worked to preserve the knowledge of Islam in a variety of ways that were complementary with the system.[29] Sverkhontura (Sheikh Abu Mohammad Makhbubi al Margilani, 1928–2007) worked during the day in the field in Yozyovon, for example, and in the evenings drove to different locations—toward the Leninabad (Khojent) region, the Jalalabad oblast, and Osh, teaching people sometimes in four or five places in one night, lecturing until two o'clock in the morning.[30]

A specific but very small group of Islamic scholars from the region, most famously the family of Ishan Babakhan, maintained their religious authority by working for the Soviet system and the institution of SADUM. This group publicly strove to motivate Muslims to adapt to the realities of Soviet authority, while claiming to uphold the Islamic community by discouraging activities that violated Islamic law. Their arguments were inspired, for example, by the local "reformist" scholar Shamli Domullah, and they later relied on Salafi theologians, including Taqiuddin Ahmad ibn Taymiya (1263–1368) and Ahmad ibn Hanbal (780–855), at the time when Ishan Babakhan's son, Ziyautdin Babakhan, served as mufti of SADUM (Babadzhanov 2003, 12).[31] Despite the common tendency in the literature to divide Islam during the Soviet period into its "official" and "unofficial" parts,[32] some Islamic scholars operated in proximity to each other and there was always some kind of a contact between them on individual or scholarly levels.[33]

The Mujaddidiya's Practice and Discourse

In comparison with other local actors, who either accepted the status quo, challenged the official Muslim establishment, or worked for the Soviet regime, those who associated themselves with the Mujaddidiya group did not aim to subjugate themselves to other existing sources of authority in their individual contexts.[34]

Initially, the mulla bachas mainly questioned the legality of practices among local Muslims in informal circles. The group denounced the recitation of certain *ayats* (prayers) from the Koran at funerals and the worshipping of saints or the treating of their gravesites as shrines or holy places. They opposed the acceptance of payment for the recitation of the Koran and healing ceremonies. The Mujaddidiya also called for a change in the rituals associated with the offering of namaz (Babadzhanov and Kamilov 2001a). According to the group, these customs and most of the local Islamic way of life were in direct violation of the true way that these rituals should be performed, as described in the early Arabic texts. In other words, from the perspective of the Mujaddidiya proponents, these practices were drawing Muslims in the Ferghana Valley away from true Islam.[35] "He, the Prophet, Muhammad said, May God's curse be on whomever slaughters for other than God" or "May God's curse be on the Jews and the Christians, for they have taken their prophets' graves as places of worship," were some of the hadiths that one of its main proponents Abduvali Qori from Andijan quoted in support of his authority.[36]

During the late 1970s and 1980s, the group's proponents sought to spread their ideas to other places in the Ferghana Valley where informal religious education was taking place. A mullah from Toshloq raion in the Ferghana oblast remembered how he had been studying with the scholar

Ahmadjon-aka when, during the preparation of their lessons in 1978, the "Wahhabis" had for the first time appeared and entered into discussions with others.[37] The Mujaddidiya leaders also expressed their opinions when participating in different local Islamic feasts. In 1979, one of its leaders, Rahmatulla Alloma, for example, related to participants at a feast of *sunnat-toi* (circumcision) the scenario in which if someone had a slight ache, they asked the imams or a religiously literate person to read out an ayat or a short sura from the Koran, and the mullahs then got paid for reciting the prayers.[38] "Well, it's better to simply go to the pharmacy and buy aspirin or some other medicine to be cured. Is it really worth asking God's help for such insignificant matters when more significant issues are facing the Muslim community, and about which we give no thought?" he argued (Babadzhanov, Muminov, and von Gügelgen 2007, 26). Later, the Mujaddidiya started to offer their own courses in Islamic education with the aim of generating new nontraditional interpretations of Islam and freeing Islam from Soviet influences (Babadzhanov 2014, 219).

During informal discussions with religious scholars at that time, the Mujaddidiya leaders persuaded other local scholars to actively change sides and join their group.[39] Initially, the Mujaddidiya proponents did not wish to offend the elder religious scholars and their peers. Later, the conflict was to grow and Rahmatulla Alloma and others accused the older ulema of fanaticism, criticizing, for example, their former teacher Mohammad Hindustani by claiming that although he had learned the "Qur'an from the beginning to end, he has not really believed," and comparing the scholar to a blind man with a torch and a donkey bedecked with books.[40]

Over time, the Mujaddidiya proponents also began to question the unwillingness of other local actors and religious scholars, including their own teachers such as Hakimjon qori who advocated a fundamentalist interpretation of Islam, to move toward public demonstrations of the Islamic faith. The mulla bachas contrasted this position with the courage of the jihad of Dukchi Ishan in 1898 or Afghan *mujahids* fighting against the Soviets in Afghanistan (al-Hindustani 1988, 117, 123). According to them, Islam would not be revived unless the proponents of the faith were more aggressive. What they had in mind was that people would print and distribute religious literature more actively and move toward more public demonstrations of the Islamic faith. Specifically, they argued that people should act as true Muslims, by wearing the hijab, long hair, beards and no ties for men, even if this made them stand out in the Soviet schools (Babadzhanov and Kamilov 2001, 218–19).[41]

Other informal Islamic scholars actively opposed the views of the Mujaddidiya. Sverkhontura warned his students that to offend the saintly places (mazars) was to offend God, citing ayat 2:154 from Bakara: "Do not say: 'They are dead!' about anyone who is killed for God's sake. Rather they are living, even though you do not notice it." He also referred to the wisdom transferred to him by his teachers through the system that had been operating in Islam for centuries, citing the example of his teacher, Musharofkhon (a respected *alim* from Marghelan), and his warnings from seventy years earlier when he said: "Islam has existed for 1,400 years and probably people will come who want to make the path too narrow or too wide, but you should firmly follow the path, be firm and stand in your path, do not agree with anyone."[42] Additionally, Sverkhontura tried to teach his students and his family members to always avoid any conflict with the authorities. Mohammad Hindustani, who was personally offended by the claims of Abduvali Qori and other young mullahs, took the lead in disputations with them, which he recorded and distributed among the people in the Valley. Hindustani criticized the fact that the Mujaddidiya had strayed from the Hanafi dogma in the case of ritual worship and pilgrimages to shrines and the tombs of saints. With regard to the Soviet invasion of Afghanistan and the jihad, Hindustani claimed that Muslims should not support jihad if there was no reasonable hope of success. According to him, the sufferings inflicted on Muslims during the Soviet era was a test of faith, and the amelioration of the religious situation, particularly during the Perestroika era,[43] was a sign of God's favor (Babadzhanov and Kamilov 2001a, 117; see also al-Hindustani 1988).

However, formally no one addressed the group. SADUM's mufti Ziyautddin Babakhan promoted similar ideas and was inspired by similar literature when he claimed to be carrying out the fight against "all negative occurrences which happen in the everyday lives of Muslims and draw them away from all kinds of superstitions and *bidayat*," explaining it by appeals to sharia (Saroyan 1997, 51). The actions of young mullahs also coincided with one of the last Soviet campaigns against the pilgrimage to the saintly places that Abdullaeva initiated in 1984 in the Uzbek SSR (Krivosheev, Rustamov, and Hasanov 1987, 69–71). As a result, according to some sources, from 1983 onward those religious actors opposing the veneration of saints and pilgrimage as well as other common Islamic rituals were even able to access Soviet television and the press (Frank and Mamatov 2006, xii; Babadzhanov 1999).[44] Often, on a local level, the authorities did not pay attention to the phenomenon whereby Islamic education in the villages became more popular than the secular variety.[45]

The situation in the Ferghana Valley became polarized in the latter 1980s with the gradual collapse of the Soviet institutions and the overall atmosphere of glasnost. In some of the villages and rural areas at that time, those who sympathized with the Mujaddidiya began to openly denounce the older generations, along with the morals and ruling order that they guaranteed at both community and family levels. "You are no longer my father or mother if you do not read namaz five times per day or wear the hijab," were the arguments that some of the youth began to use, for example.[46] The young mullahs ignored not only the local elders (*oqsoqols*) and the informal mullahs, but also the official Islamic representation and the state.

During this period, various individual actors in the villages and parts of the old towns of the Ferghana Valley began to demand the registration of their local mosques by the Soviet authorities or the construction of new mosques at the places where the Soviet regime had destroyed them during the purges of the 1920s and 1930s.[47] Some imams registered with SADUM, who during Soviet times had been sent to different locations, also gained permission to establish mosques in their home communities.[48] From 1989 onward the newly appointed mufti, originally from Andijan, Mohammad Sodiq, abolished the official practice of nominating imams of the Friday mosques from above and allowed individual communities to elect the imams themselves.[49] The individual Mujaddidiya proponents, however, often through self-nomination and without the confirmation of SADUM, took over the positions of imams and khatibs in some of the major mosques of the Ferghana as well as in the villages. They ostentatiously refused to take a salary from the funds allocated to mosques and instead claimed to be purifying local Islam and protecting the *ummah* (community) from those religious scholars who had been conserving it. Abduvali Qori set up his own trading company under the Friday mosque in Andijan, whose income he publicly used to meet religious needs (Mirsaitov and Saipov 2006). He accused SADUM's mufti (as did part of the disaffected religious elite in Tashkent) of corruption in the case of the sale of Korans donated by Saudi Arabia (Olcott 2007a, 19). In his lectures he criticized the individuality of "local Islam" as the main obstruction to the real integration of "one Islamic *Umma*" in the Ferghana Valley at that time (Babadzhanov and Kamilov 2001a).

A similar situation occurred in other cities in the Valley, such as Qoqand, Marghelan, and Namangan. In Qoqand, Mohammad Radjab-qori, for example, invited other followers of the young mullahs from Namangan, Andijan, and Marghelan to the opening of the Qoqand Friday mosque and the election of the imam, hoping to gain control of the mosque. He also threatened other local respected scholars, such as Munavvar Qori, so as to prevent them from raising their voices against his candidature (see, e.g., Toychiyev 2007).[50] In Namangan, reportedly, groups of young mullahs attacked weddings, entered private homes and workplaces without permission and confiscated alcohol, smashing the bottles. They used sticks to beat women who were not covered by the hijab, and so forth.[51] Young people trained in karate assisted private entrepreneurs and Islamic leaders in protecting their property and upholding public order. One such group, called Justice (Adolat), came under the influence of young mullahs and it was renamed as Islamic Justice (Adolat Islami). From 1990, this group, which had access to the centrally located Gumbaz mosque, used this as a base from which to control parts of Namangan, to punish criminals in accordance with sharia law, and to pin the verdicts to the bodies of those who had received punishment and display them for a period of time in public places (Olcott 2007a, 20).[52] In 1991 in Namangan a group of young people, shouting Alahu Akbar, even seized several governmental buildings in the city and placed green flags on the *hokimiyat* (city hall) under the pretext that the time of Islam had returned.[53] For several months they monitored the application of sharia in the city before they agreed to leave the building.[54]

Other Islamic scholars opposed the activities of the young mullahs at that time. Initially, some sought to facilitate a discussion. In May 1990 SADUM's mufti organized a disputation between "Wahhabis" and Hanafites in Tashkent (Babadzhanov and Kamilov 2001, 68). In addition, in Namangan, Umar-khon Domulla initially organized regular Saturday debates on Islamic issues (Olcott 2007a, 20). The local elders warned their youth that the Wahhabis were not the real authority in relation to Islam.[55] People typically complained in the following way: "I am also Muslim, and I know the sharia; even in the Soviet times I read namaz but I never ordered others around. I did it for myself but I could not say to my neighbor that they were wrong because they did not read namaz."[56] After the forceful demonstrations of power that the young mullahs applied, many people became scared of the unknown phenomenon and the apparent strength of this version of Islam in the new context (Hilgers 2009). In some cases, the elders and families expelled the Mujaddidiya youth from the villages in an attempt to maintain Hannafi integrity or to protect the families and communities from government repression.[57] Across the region in the early 1990s skirmishes between the "Wahhabi" and Hanafi proponents often ended in violent fights, and Hanafi proponents were also engaged in expelling "Wahhabis" from their mosques (Babadzhanov and Kamilov 2001, 68). As Babadzhanov mentions in the case of Khojawot village in Namangan region, the "elders were not united and there were individual groups and family clans with their own interests and local leaders. However, on the question of the candidature of the imam they were united. To be more precise, this unity was directed against the radical 'young people'" (Babadzhanov 2014, 243–44).

The conflict that took place outside of the framework created by the government was eventually handled, at least partially, at the oblast level and by the security authorities. Especially after the 1991 events in Namangan, when the youth seized the government buildings, the state moved to eliminate or persecute most imams of large Friday mosques in the Ferghana Valley, including those from the Kyrgyz part. The government gradually reinstituted their control over Islam, similar to that exercised during the Soviet period (Mirsaitov and Saipov 2006; see also Hilgers 2009). Many of the Islamic youth fled to Tajikistan and joined the civil war there, some later moving to Afghanistan. One of the main proponents of the Mujaddidiya at that time, Abduvali Qori, was, however, allowed to remain as imam khatib in "his" mosque in Andijan (Jome Mosque) for some time after these events.[58]

In his sermons he reassured his listeners that "the enemies of Islam will always be confounded by someone who understands true Islam, brothers. They'll always be confounded by someone who knows the Qur'an and hadith perfectly. This is because there's no doubt in Islam's purity" (Frank and Mamatov 2006, 92), thus suggesting ignorance on the part of the existing sources of authority, including state power. He also advocated a need for the purification of Islam, including the "health" of the Islamic creed following a century of oppression:

> The Islamic creed is considered the foundation upon which the edifice of the Muslim communities is built. Every community's potential and well-being—that community's progress—is tied to the health of its creed. And that community's worldview is connected to its health. . . . The communities that maintained that creed found progress and were happy. All of the communities that did not maintain that creed encountered decadence and were unhappy. Know that every licit and correct thing you see that exists in irreligious nations came into being as a result of the Prophets' summons. Atheists who have acted justly recognize this too, brothers. (Frank and Mamatov 2006, 33–34)

During these years, Abduvali Qori continued to operate a trading company in his mosque and did not accept any payment from believers,[59] although he was under the constant surveillance and harassment of the secret service.[60] In 1995 he disappeared under unknown circumstances. By 1999 the Uzbek government had eliminated or silenced the activities of scholars and groups associated with the Mujaddidiya or young mullahs in the Ferghana Valley. Some returned to their home villages after the end of the Tajik civil war but did not involve themselves in the active promotion of their previously held views. Abduvali Qori's interpretations continued to spread in the form of literature and on the Internet. His sermons from the period between 1990 and 1994 were placed on different Web sites and his interpretation of the Koran was published in Saudi Arabia. Despite his disappearance, Abduvali Qori has been conceptualized locally by his supporters as someone who "interpreted the Qur'an not according to what the government, or any other political forces wanted," thus representing the only real authority in Islam. As his relative, who was living in Kara-Suu in the Kyrgyz Ferghana Valley, explained in a rare interview:

> Abduvali Qori unconditionally, and implicitly, fulfilled the legacy of the Prophet. . . . Until now the authorities fear these people, because Abduvali Qori . . . did not go against Allah, did not want to comment on the Qur'an and the legacy of the Prophet in accordance with the politics of the Uzbek authorities, who asked from him particularly to do so. [He] did not turn the mosque into an agitation-propaganda organization of the Uzbek regime in the same way that other *imams* did. (Firdavsii 2006)

Hizb-ut-Tahrir in the Kyrgyz Ferghana Valley

The party of Islamic Liberation (in Arabic *Hizb-ut-Tahrir al-Islami*, hereafter HBT) is the name of the transnational group that was founded in 1952 in Palestine. Its ideas spread in the Ferghana Valley in the late 1990s. It has functioned as a semisecret nonviolent group, united in the desire to reestablish an Islamic culture that is "vital to every Muslim . . . a means of strengthening the *'Aqeedah* [Islamic belief] and of understanding the Message of Islam, and thereby guaranteeing the consistent application of Islam" (An-Nabhani 1998, 29). Ultimately, HBT members have aimed to bring Muslims back to a position where they are living an Islamic way of life in Dar al-Islam, in an Islamic society where all life's affairs are administered according to sharia, and the viewpoint was the halal (what is permissible to use or engage in, according to Islamic law) and the *haram* (what is sinful—in Islam, any act that angers or displeases God)—under the shade of the caliphate (HBT official Web site).

At the time of HBT's expansion in the Kyrgyz Ferghana Valley, the official policy on Islam can be characterized by a commitment to religious tolerance, but also by reference to the rising authoritarianism in the country and the influence of the antiterrorism agenda. At times, considerable attempts have been made by state bodies to control Islam. As an official admitted in 2003: "In Kyrgyzstan, we say that the state does not interfere in the affairs of religion, but if there is an instruction from above, *imams* have to carry it out completely" (ICG 2003b, 25). The repression increased during Bakiyev's era in 2005–10, when the situation in the view of some people in the Kyrgyzstan part of the Ferghana Valley resembled the harassment that had been prevalent in the Soviet Union or in post-Soviet Uzbekistan. Girls wearing the hijab were sometimes not allowed to enter school compounds or to attend lessons, an act that was intended to maintain Kyrgyzstani national security and achieve the goal of eliminating terrorism.[61] Public manifestations of Islam were in some cases equated to terrorism, and some government officials argued that only people over sixty years old should be allowed to visit mosques, with a demand that imams should list the names of believers on the doors of their mosques. The religious scholars who argued, among other things, that drinking vodka or eating horse meat was forbidden in Islam, were accused of crossing over the forbidden line separating politics and religion.[62] Primarily in the Uzbek *mahallas* (neighborhoods) in the Kyrgyz Ferghana Valley, special forces sometimes carried out forced raids and tortured and persecuted those who were found to be studying or allegedly possessing extremist religious literature.[63]

At the same time, the Kyrgyz authorities continued to rely on different Islamic authorities to promote their goals or boost their legitimacy. The formally independent institution of muftiate, inherited from Soviet times, issued fatwas and instructed on different questions, including the permissibility of borrowing money from a bank, and imams discussed plans to forbid children under eighteen years old from visiting mosques.[64] President Bakiyev described the muftiate as representing the "true essence of Islam, its tolerance and peacefulness" and saw the muftiate's role as critical in informing Muslims in Kyrgyzstan that "true Islam has nothing to do with religious extremism" (McGlinchey 2009, 18). Since the ousting of Bakiyev and the 2010 ethnic riots in southern Kyrgyzstan during Roza Otunbayeva's presidency (2010–11), the issue of regulating Islam has not been so prominent.[65] Nonetheless, attempts to control Islam in the country in the name of preserving the Kyrgyz nation and its security have gradually reappeared.[66] "Now, they already want to give licenses to imams for the reading of the *nikokh* and *janoza* (religious marriage and funeral prayers). This is after all impossible; I myself can read *nikokh, janoza*. If they are my relatives, I am supposed to read it. This is still in the phase of discussion, the government wants to get everything under its control as in Uzbekistan and the muftiate really fulfills a formal role in it," complained a businessman in Jalalabad in 2011.[67] Government officials have also at times visited local mosques, even promising and providing funds for the construction of new ones, thus reacting to the changing electorate and its relationship to Islam, especially in rural areas where lots of people have not had access to state education and have not read newspapers.[68]

Most people in the Kyrgyz Ferghana Valley have learned the basics of Islam from their parents and also from the imam in their local mosque. The possibility of studying Islam at state-run religious institutions has been open to everyone; however, its graduates have often found it difficult to secure a job in a mosque and have often remained unemployed, working at the bazaar, or teaching in madrasas. As one informant of the ICG survey explained: "People don't accept graduates from theological colleges, even if they are well-educated. They don't dress correctly, they don't have authority. Even if they go around in a cap, like other young people, this is not liked."[69]

In towns and raion centers, youth have sometimes studied in religious schools funded or financially supported by foreign Muslim countries. On the one hand, the younger generation has considered them to be more religious and knowledgeable in relation to Islam than older generations and representatives of official Islam, and these schools have supported this idea: "In mosques *imams* do not know Islam very well and do not have any information about the outside world. We want them to know both the outside world and Islam," explained one of the teachers of the Batyrov Friendship of Peoples University in Jalalabad.[70] On the other hand, the semiprivate religious schools have attracted students by providing social services and support. For instance, for students at the Osh Theological College the provision of three daily meals and, if needed, a dorm room, has reportedly figured prominently in their decisions regarding higher education choices (McGlinchey 2009, 26). Similarly, the Imam Bakyt School in Osh has educated women who could not afford to pay tuition fees at Osh State University.[71]

Individual people in the Kyrgyz Ferghana Valley have learned about Islam through the clandestine provision of lessons and informal circles focusing on readings from the Koran organized by Wahhabi groups, HBT or other organizations. A variety of people were attracted to them when they saw that the religious actors had built a nice center, provided help and a warm room in which to read namaz,[72] or when they experienced or were subjected to violence or injustice at the hands of government officials.[73] Furthermore, these Islamic institutions did not demand that students should understand Arabic or know the Koran. In particular, young males from Kyrgyz Ferghana Valley also studied Islam abroad in other Islamic countries.[74]

Most religious leaders exercised authority in their mosques at a very local level in mahallas and qishloqs and they did not seek to cross the boundaries between their local community and politics.[75] Particular groups of Islamic scholars have worked for the state and pursued their authority through this relationship. Specifically, they have worked in the local branches of the muftiate, administering permissions to embark on hajj and the registration of religious associations.[76] Their role has been to provide expertise on judicial verdicts in relation to suspects accused of religious extremism and the possession of religious literature. Their authority in religious affairs has often been openly challenged, both by other religious scholars and by lawyers: "In general, they do not know Arabic, in madrasas there are two or three directors who know Arabic but it does not mean that they know the principles of Islam fully. Therefore, in the majority of cases these expert agreements have been neither precise nor objective. They are always one-sided; they fulfill the policy of the government, and, in reality, the government has full control over the process," explained a lawyer in Osh.[77]

There have also been Islamic scholars in the Kyrgyz Ferghana Valley who have derived their authority from belonging to famous local religious families and from their knowledge of Arabic, the Koran, and Sunna.[78] These personalities have pursued rather an independent position toward other authorities, including those in power, and have relied on the network of their students and followers through which they have been able to mobilize thousands or tens of thousands of supporters willing to protect their leader.[79] Some of these respected personalities, such as Alauddin Mansur in Kara-Suu, have used their authority to support the policies of the state.[80] Others—such religious figures exist in every southern region, including Jalalabad, Suzak, Osh, Kara-Suu, and so on—have sometimes entered into conflict with the muftiate and by extension with the attempts of the state to control religious issues.

For example, in the Kara-Suu region, Momammad Rafik Kamalov, a relative of Abduvali Qori, who had served for twenty years as the imam of the largest mosque in the region, was popular for his willingness to address political issues, including the situation in Uzbekistan. Reportedly four thousand to five thousand people attended his Friday sermons and he could boast ten thousand supporters. In 2006 Mohammad Rafik was killed in an operation conducted by the special services, after having allegedly been involved in terrorist activity against the Kyrgyz police and the state, as well as having cooperated with the Islamic Movement of Turkestan, the successor organization of the IMU (CXW 2006). His son, Rashod Kamalov, replaced his father as imam of the Al-Sarakhsiy mosque in Kara-Suu and has been imprisoned on several occasions since then.[81]

New Islamic groups in the Kyrgyz Ferghana Valley from abroad have mostly not sought to engage in the conflict with other religious authorities and the government. The Tablighi Jama'at (Proselytizing Society) was a revivalist movement founded in 1926 in India that spread to Central Asia after the dissolution of the Soviet Union. Inspired by the teachings of its founder, based on a dream, its proponents traveled in groups and visited communities to carry out the *dawa* (the call, the invitation to the faith), imploring Muslims to join God on a house-to-house mission by claiming: "We must make God the center of our lives and set aside human things." The movement has forbidden political discussion and it has been registered with the muftiate and its office of the *dawa/davaat*.[82] In a few areas of southern Kyrgyzstan, Wahhabi communities have reportedly established economic "solidarity groups" that consist of simple credit unions with the provision for members to work together on collective enterprises (ICG 2003a, 29).

Hizb-ut-Tahrir's Practice and Discourse

In comparison with other local actors, Muslims who have associated themselves with or sympathized with the HBT in the Kyrgyz Ferghana Valley have often acted as if they were free, as if they had not subjugated themselves to other existing sources of authority in their individual contexts.

Initially, the group members focused on study and learning with the aim to generate a deeper awareness of Islamic culture in informal circles. One member, Yodorbek, after being arrested for distributing the group's leaflets at the Kara-Suu market in 2012, stated: "A friend of mine named

Saidkamal asked me over to his house to discuss work. . . . We had a conversation about religion, in which it was said that many Muslims are not living according to Sharia Law" (Kamalov 2012). Another member explained in 2007: "Hizb disseminates ideas. It organizes lessons for interested people and teaches them in cells (*halqa*)." According to this member: "If there is no Internet, we distribute leaflets, for example. You know, there are gatherings in villages, when people get together and eat rice pilaf, for example. We distribute ideas there. The means of distribution are not important. Ideas are important. For different places, we have different ways to disseminate them" (Saidazimova 2007).

Over time, the HBT's proponents have also sought to interact with society publicly, with the goal of making the society adopt the party's ideas as their own. One member in Osh province explained: "We conduct a political struggle; our task is not to build the state ourselves, but to explain to people how to build the state." Another from Kara-Suu said: "We don't call on people to join Hizb now, we explain to people what the [Koran] says, what we should do. It is not compulsory to be a member of Hizb; some aren't Hizb members, but all know Hizb ideas" (ICG 2003a, 6, 21). One sympathizer in Jalalabad summarized: "The basis of [HBT] is that current society finds itself in circumstances similar to those in which the Prophet Mohammad lived in Mecca. It is the obligation of all Muslims to work toward the creation of the kind of conditions that ruled at the time when the Prophet established Islamic rule in Medina."[83]

For example, members have staged demonstrations in defense of their imprisoned fellows and used the trials and the release of those detained to expose the moral shortcomings of the ruling elite (McGlinchey 2009, 20). According to a member from Kara-Suu, more people showed up at his trial and subsequent release than visited him on the birth of his children (ICG 2003a, 23). The mayor of Osh, Melis Myrzakmatov, described how "citizens are often grouped together in the community to protest against such negative phenomena in society as corruption, unemployment, prostitution" (Kutueva 2011).

In some villages of the Kyrgyz Ferghana Valley, HBT members have instituted their own order based on the example of the Prophet Muhammad. This has involved eliminating alcohol and boasting that the imam be able to leave the safe in their mosque unlocked without the fear that someone will attempt to steal the money, in contrast to the experience in areas under the authority of the government.[84] This has also happened in towns such as Osh, where the mayor has claimed: "Members of [HBT] have their own mosques and communities and the population even knows them and drinks tea with them."[85]

On the occasion of elections, group members have publicly refused to participate in them. In Osh in 2005, for example, Ulugbek Ruziyev was arrested for the possession of a leaflet titled, *A Ruling on Participation in Parliamentary Elections according to Sharia*, which called on Muslims to boycott elections if candidates did not meet seven requirements. According to Dilyor Jumaboyev, a member of the HBT:

> A candidate must . . . openly disavow the Western capitalist system and all other *kufr* [unbelief] systems. Second, [a candidate] must openly announce his intention to change kufr systems and create Islamic ones instead. Third, they must take their programs from Allah's book [the Koran] and his messenger's *Sunnah* [the second major source of jurisprudence in Islam after the Koran]. Fourth, they must announce that the parliament will be used as a pulpit to propagate Islam. Fifth, they must separate themselves from other candidates who support kufr systems. The sixth requirement is not to collaborate with or bow down before official authorities. The seventh requirement is that the [secular] candidate's program must propagate the aforementioned ideas among the people. (Saidazimova 2005)

Prior to the presidential elections in 2011, party members affixed posters on poles in Jalalabad claiming that to participate in the elections was haram.[86] The HBT proponents have also called for people to ignore other public events promoted by the government. For example, the party has inveighed against the celebration of International Women's Day, claiming that Klara Tsetkin, who invented the March 8 holiday, was herself a prostitute.[87] In some cases the party members even scared the police by threatening a curse in the eyes of God and an adverse reaction from the community stating that: "If you struggle fiercely against us, the *imam* won't come to your house" (ICG 2003a, 29). With their lives being ruled by the objective of becoming the group that "invites to the good, orders what is right and forbids what is evil," the party's followers have not been afraid of potential punishment at the hands of state officials.[88]

For HBT members in the Kyrgyz Ferghana Valley the existing policies and what they conceptualized as "politics" altogether became only a plot aimed at weakening the Muslim community.[89] Among young people, the group members have argued that "During the time of the Soviet Union they built socialism; you saw how unsustainable it was; there was a collapse. Now you have democracy, but what good does this democracy give you? Nothing good. This is all Western."[90] In prisons, where the HBT has worked, some of the party proponents have claimed that there is a need for sharia "because there are no rules if there is a democracy. And we will adopt sharia, everyone will listen to sharia, and finally there will be order."[91] In 2011, a party sympathizer who used to work for a human rights organization even stated: "I was in Warsaw for training on human rights; they say it is universal, but democracy was invented by people. In this I agree with Hizb-ut-Tahrir that only Islam can be [the blueprint for social order]."[92]

Since the beginning, the HBT's claims and activities have been actively opposed on both informal and formal levels in the Kyrgyz Ferghana Valley. Among the local Islamic authorities and elders, the ideas of HBT are perceived as being confused and un-Islamic.[93] On a formal level, the muftiate adopted and distributed a fatwa against HBT in 2002 and instructed the imams to speak out against the party during their Friday prayers (ICG 2003a, 38). More recently, the muftiate and the Ministry of Interior have also organized events in the Kyrgyz Ferghana Valley in which mullahs, analysts, and psychologists have addressed young audiences to teach them the differences between Islam and extremism (Kamalov 2012). In one such seminar, for example, one of the major Islamic authorities in the south, Alauddin Mansur, proclaimed that those who set up political parties were politicians and not Muslims.[94] The discourse of the muftiate and religious figures under its command also focused on explaining that the Prophet Mohammad did not charge Muslims with establishing a caliphate at any cost. As one state official has argued:

> The Prophet Muhammad never said that when he died his followers should build a caliphate; there is nothing like this. On the contrary, after the last hajj when he returned to Medina, his aide asked him how we would live, encouraging him to name someone to rule for him. He replied that they themselves should choose, from among their own number. And when asked what it would be like, he said that the best time was during his time, their time, and that it would become worse and worse thereafter. He stated that they would be persecuted as believers. The aide asked him how they should live. He answered that they should pray at home; he did not say they should take up the sword and fight. No, he said that they should pray at home, and if it were not possible to pray at home, they should go to the mountains and herd sheep, and there in the middle of mountains they should live and pray. He did not tell them to undertake jihad, to kill and establish a *caliphate*. And not a single extremist could say anything against this argument,

and in the Koran there is nothing that says that followers should only live in a caliphate.[95]

The state has also charged the alleged and real members of the HBT with offenses of separatism and extremism and has sentenced them to prison terms.[96]

Nonetheless, the movement has continued to find sympathizers across society—among the young, the unemployed, business people, educated people, and those working within the state apparatus.[97] Furthermore, for those Muslims associated with or sympathizing with the idea of the HBT, the group has remained the only real authority on Islam. As a party sympathizer in Jalalabad argues:

> There are the old [religious authorities], but they do not recognize them here. There was one authority in Suzak, he was 103 years old. He died and left a son, who is now the authority in Suzak. They have their own ones in Jalalabad. They are in general new leaders who already know the Arabic language, who truly more or less have an understanding. And now there is a particular authority, a single, even real, power . . . it is the party of [HBT]. And they are the real authority, the real people, in my opinion. Even if they asked me what is the party of Kyrgyzstan, I would say only [HBT], the other parties are nothing.[98]

No Need for Politics

This chapter has discussed the groups and communities in the Ferghana Valley, in both the Soviet and post-Soviet periods, for which the ideas of Mujaddidiya and Hizb-ut-Tahrir have been important. Specifically, the chapter has placed the practices and rhetoric of the two movements within the local contexts of the Uzbek and the Kyrgyz Ferghana Valley, along with the approaches of other religious and social authorities engaged in promoting Islam.

The chapter has argued that when compared with other actors, who have either accepted the status quo, challenged the official Muslim establishment, or worked for the regime, those who have associated themselves with the Mujaddidiya group and Hizb-ut-Tahrir have often acted as if they were free, that is, as if they had not subjugated themselves to other existing sources of authority in their individual contexts. For those Muslims who have sympathized with or supported these groups there has been a delegitimization of not only local authority but also state power and its official Muslim representation. Furthermore, the chapter has argued that the diverse political contexts in which the groups operate, and the arguments that the local authorities or ruling regimes and official Muslim representation have used against them, have not prevented the two groups from making the existing forms of social and religious authority, including the state, appear unnecessary.

This chapter suggests that in future the role of "radical Islam" in the Ferghana Valley should be approached from another perspective, beyond current state-driven or policy-driven imperatives. This is warranted irrespective of how radical Islam has been conceptualized in Central Asia or the nature of the scholarly discourse so far—be it as Islamic resurgence, a current of Islamic activism that gives priority to political action, the by-product of a failed state, or a threat to secularism. Specifically, it might be approached from an individual's viewpoint concerning the need for "politics" and deliberate rejection of existing forms of social and religious authority, including that of the state regimes.

PART II

A VIEW FROM ABOVE

ISLAM AND THE STATE
IN CENTRAL ASIA

CHAPTER FOUR

Engineering Islam

Uzbek State Policies of Control

David Abramson and Noah Tucker

S oon after Uzbekistan became independent in 1991, its government led by President Islam Karimov acknowledged Islam as an integral component of national identity (Khalid 2007, 132). The public recognition of Islam as part and parcel of national identity and state interests has allowed and at times even encouraged growth in religious practices and symbols, and that growth in turn prompts new efforts to control them. This dynamic has fostered multiple and contradictory analyses of the role of Islam in contemporary Uzbek society. On the one hand, Islam's growing presence in public discourse creates the impression that Uzbekistan, including the state, is becoming increasingly religious, perhaps more than is actually the case. On the other hand, the self-proclaimed secular Uzbek state's attempts at social control, including how Muslims express their religiosity, have become so extensive that in many ways they recall the Stalinist period. Yet regime-led operations to monitor, limit, and ultimately engineer Muslim religiosity at a time when Uzbek citizens are increasingly embracing Islam as an integral part of their identity forces the state to engage with religion in more and more spheres of social life, drawing it farther away from its Soviet secular roots.

Religious observance and interest in Islam has grown steadily in Uzbekistan since 1991, but under conditions of increasing state-organized supervision and regulation. In the 1970s and 1980s the Soviet security apparatus continued to monitor religious activity to ensure it did not become a mobilizing force against the state. Having destroyed most of the institutions of independent religious authority in the first decades of Soviet rule, the late Soviet state tolerated religion, provided it did not undercut touted socialist progress. This relatively laissez-faire approach yielded to new forms of control in Uzbekistan's post-Soviet period of independence.

Growing popular interest in Islam can be assessed in several ways. Mosque attendance has increased along with the number of mosques built since independence. Since generally only men are allowed to visit mosques (Ferghana.ru, August 17, 2009), it is important to look at other indicators as well. Visits to saint shrines and other sacred sites have also increased (Abramson and Karimov 2007). The availability of previously and sometimes still banned religious items on sale in stores that advertise halal food, religious clothing, and Islamic literature and their use in social spheres is further evidence (Cleek 2012; Institute for War and Peace Reporting 2012). Moreover, as people explore their religious identity, they often engage, and challenge, state institutions, which in turn respond with policies justified as protecting state interests. This exploration ranges from donning headscarves in schools and broadcasting religious content in the media to studying Islam abroad and establishing business associations based partly on Islamic principles. State responses are often inconsistent, confusing, and brutal. Gradually, however, these myriad engagements have forced state actors to improvise and elaborate rules and restrictions as well as to establish institutions to train new generations of religious leaders committed to supporting the political status quo. Intermittently enforced bans on headscarves and beards in public institutions, the sale of religious clothing, strict controls over publishing, media, and advertising halal food are just some of the most widely reported restrictions (Bayram 2011).

These policies also impede discussions about Islamic authenticity, morality in political and economic spheres, and right and wrong religious practices from dominating public discourse or even being broached at all. In their place, however, a state-controlled discourse that exaggerates the threat of extremism has stunted Islamic intellectual development and created an environment in which thousands of people have been imprisoned under brutal conditions. State-controlled Islamic practice and accompanying corruption has alienated many Muslims from the very institutions the Karimov regime has tried to control (Fergananews.com, February 15, 2012). Rather than resign themselves to heavy-handed, state-promoted Islam that fails to address the deeply personal and infinite range of issues that makes religion meaningful, many Muslims turn to alternative sources of Islamic authority such as nonclerical religious leaders—from celebrity voices like the journalist and poet Hayrullo Hamidov to local folk healers—and the Internet, which both facilitates access to religious perspectives from abroad and preserves the messages of many homegrown teachers the Uzbek government long ago banned or repressed. As this chapter demonstrates, these sources often address the kind of moral questions many people ask of religion.

We do not see this turn to non–state-sponsored institutions as necessarily an indication of what scholars of religion in the former Soviet Union have for decades characterized as unofficial, parallel, or underground Islam. We draw on Gupta's (1995) and others' theorization of the state as institutional sites of interaction wherein individuals invoke state interests for many reasons, including as a justification for promoting and protecting personal interests. These sites include state institutions such as government ministries, state security, and universities, but they also include weddings and other life-cycle events where neighborhood (*mahalla*) committees, religious leaders, or others are "expected" to take responsibility and to be held accountable for the actions of the group. These myriad engagements with "the state" and how people negotiate them collectively contribute to the formulation of policies regarding Islam and secular life when they come to the attention of government officials. Of course, accountable individuals often seek to avoid such attention, for reasons and in ways we shall describe below.

This chapter examines the interaction between newly emergent forms of Islamic expression and state responses. These forms of expression, while enacted in Uzbekistan by Uzbekistani Muslims, are also influenced by global Islamic trends. State institutions, especially security agencies, try to limit, isolate, appropriate, or co-opt "external" influences and unofficial domestic developments with the overarching goal of regime preservation. In presenting this range of phenomena, we argue that the Uzbek government does not uniformly repress Islamic practice; rather, it cherry-picks policies that prevent Islam from becoming a legitimate competitor to state authority while also using religious discourse and ritual to suppress public speech and assembly that is potentially critical or otherwise subversive of the state. This select tolerance affords Islam an important, but highly circumscribed, role in the public sphere. In conjunction with this, state policies rigorously police attempts by religious advocates to promote reformist visions of Islam. We posit that policies designed to regulate religious social interaction are developed to ensure social control for the purpose of regime stability and self-preservation, the same primary goal that informs authoritarian regulation of so many other areas of life in Uzbekistan.

The increasingly popular use of Islamic discourse to address areas of life previously framed in secular cultural terms engages state interests and, consequently, the attention of the anointed guardians of the state, the security services. Growth of interest in Islam has forced the state to engage uncomfortably and awkwardly with religious practice since independence, drawing local institutions—from the mahalla to secular universities—into the formulation of a web of regulations and restrictions that are difficult to enforce without the often unwelcome involvement of the pervasive National Security Service (NSS). Even where security or other representatives of the state are not present, fear of potential interference by the ubiquitous state security and police services compels people to take into account and consider whether and how to act in accordance with state interests.

While fear of the state informs some of these considerations, people also draw on a range of other strategies and interests, including the calculated use of "state" interests to pursue personal agendas, religious or otherwise, deliberate subversion of, and even relative disregard for state interests (Gupta 1995). In writing on the politics of everyday life under Stalin, Stephen Kotkin (1995, 21–22) notes "one resists, without necessarily rejecting, by assessing, making tolerable, and, in some cases, even turning to one's advantage the situation one is confronted with."

This uneasy dynamic has led Olcott (2012) and others to claim that Islamists are successfully imposing their will on the state. Islamists are forcing state institutions to accept, grudgingly or unknowingly, positions on Islam that are leading to the desecularization of Uzbek state and society and a shift toward Salafism. Salafist, or puritanical, interpretations of Islam challenge state claims of what constitutes authentic Uzbek Islam. Olcott has also argued that efforts to outflank Salafist claims about what Uzbek society should be like have led to an increase in the use of Islamically framed arguments in secular spheres—on national television or in the courtroom, as we will discuss below. Olcott (2012, 207–13) views this as evidence of creeping Salafism. The muftiate often directs Islamic clergy to deliver moral messages against practices such as homosexuality, lavish weddings, Valentine's Day, religious study abroad, rock music, Internet use, and tattoos (Jonikhonov 2011; Tashkent Channel Two 2011; Tashkent Turkiston 2011; Uralov 2012). That religious leaders are now authorized to comment on such a wide range of social issues is new to Uzbekistan and contributes to the impression that Islam is gradually taking over the state. Yet, the government's flirtation with Sufism as Uzbek nationalism's "Islam of choice" is most likely designed to forestall other forms of Islam taking root in society.

Is Islam, Salafist or otherwise, capturing the state? As we discuss below, this clerical mobilization often occurs when the Uzbek state decides to undermine representatives of secular, and sometimes foreign-supported, nongovernmental organizations whose programs and educational campaigns (involving HIV/AIDS, homosexuality, the Internet, elements of Western popular culture) the Uzbek regime believes are its sole prerogative. This gives the impression that Islamic morality is directing state policy and clergy are playing an outsized role in addressing social issues. However, more often than not, the regime appears to be sending mixed messages. Not only do religiously spearheaded campaigns against particular Western or alien practices come and go, but the president's own eldest daughter, Gulnora, played an outsized role in reclaiming many of these issues on secular terms by sponsoring very public events on promoting the Internet, HIV awareness, and circumcision ceremonies (e.g., Kumkova 2012) as well as promoting Western-style culture by recording her own pop music, starring in often racy music videos, and allowing otherwise banned Halloween costume parties at nightclubs she owned (RFE/RL November 22, 2012; Uznews 2012, 2013). This double standard was likely intended to convey not that the daughter of the president is morally superior, but that she was untouchable due to her relationship to the president and that elites and the populace alike should get used to it. Her subsequent fall from favor gave her father the opportunity to demonstrate that even his daughter could not act with impunity. Above all it sends a message about who is authorized to speak and think freely and who is not. Many who have joined the discussion of these issues from either a secular or a religious perspective have found themselves on the wrong side of the line as the state or its local representatives shift course abruptly in whichever direction they feel preserves that primary goal of regime stability.

The following discussion shows that while state security represses certain kinds of religious expression, religious and local authorities are encouraged to promote select Islamic values and practices, especially if they silence criticism of the Karimov regime. For example, local security organs view secular funerals as more threatening than standard religious ones. As we shall discuss below, efforts to control weddings are more complex, in which secular weddings are promoted over Islamic ones, provided they are small in size. We shall also see how neighborhood (mahalla) leaders play an important local role in reinterpreting state positions, including by invoking Uzbek cultural spiritual values and traditions as beneficial to individuals, families, and their community, while seeking to keep security services at a distance.

Religion Policies or Social Control?

The Karimov regime's approach to Islam is illustrative of its strategies for managing and preventing dissent, which currently focus on control of public discourse and message dissemination. This control includes efforts in many spheres of life to restrict who can speak publicly, the content of public speech, and the size of public gatherings. Public, here, can mean either a crowd of strangers or a large group of acquaintances. Given the collective nature of much religious practice, state control clearly extends to Muslim behavior not only in mosques but also at numerous key life-cycle events that are imbued with Islamic meaning and take place at private homes and community spaces often within neighborhoods. These include weddings, funerals, circumcisions, and many memorial ceremonies that mark periods of time following death, collectively referred to in Uzbek as *to'is*.

Most Uzbeks attend dozens of such life-cycle events in a year and the number of guests range from several hundred to thousands. Given their social, economic, and religious importance in most people's lives—numerous scholars have documented this elsewhere—they are prominent occasions where people reaffirm and negotiate social relationships, values, and identity. McBrien (2006) demonstrates how young women in Kyrgyzstan learn about and experiment with religion at "new" Islamic weddings (as opposed to "traditional" secular ones). It is not uncommon to find that people, often strangers welcomed by the hosts, attend weddings to hear a sermon, especially when a popular imam officiates. McBrien notes that people attend such gatherings to hear popular imams who use the occasions to communicate to large crowds outside of the restricted setting of the Friday mosque, where sermons are either heavily censored or prescripted by the Spiritual Administration of Uzbekistan (muftiate) in Tashkent for mass delivery.

On September 10, 2012, the mayor of Tashkent Rakhmonbek Usmanov issued a decree limiting to one hundred the number of guests who could attend weddings, funerals, and other ritual ceremonies, as well as stipulating the hours when such events could occur and specifying that individuals officiating and performing at such events will have to register with the Ministry of Justice. His explicit reason was that weddings had become so large and exorbitant that many people depleted their life savings and even went into debt to marry off their children (RFE/RL 2012a). State officials all the way up the hierarchy to the president have periodically used this argument against lavish weddings since the 1990s (zakonuz.narod.ru 1998; uzdaily September 10, 2012). But there are probably also unstated reasons behind these pronouncements, depending on the regime's political needs at the time, including limiting public displays of wealth or the size of audiences listening to religious messages that have not been preapproved by the state.

At the neighborhood level, mahalla committee leaders might question why a family has chosen to have an Islamic-style wedding, in which men and women are segregated, alcohol, music, and dancing typically are absent, and therefore expenditures are substantially lower. Officials from the community and members of the security service are known selectively to discourage parents or other relatives from opting for Islamic weddings for their children, asking, "Why don't you want to have a normal wedding and celebrate this momentous occasion?" (fergananews.com April 7, 2012). Consequently, Islamic weddings are recast as somber affairs that are devoid of the enjoyment expected of a wedding celebration. In contrast to funerals, discussed below, the turn toward Islamic weddings is viewed as extreme, even as an indicator of extremist religious views, and hence dangerous. While we do not know how widespread this trend is, the economic savings alone must be an important incentive (Expert Working Group 2012; fergananews.com April 7, 2012).

Local officials are more likely to exert pressure on a family whose child has worked or studied abroad for an extended period of time and returned more religiously observant than when he or she left or than the level the family is accustomed to (Expert Working Group 2012; fergananews.com April 7, 2012). These circumstances are increasingly common, given the large number of migrant laborers from Uzbekistan who travel abroad for work, regardless of whether the bride or groom has lived in Russia or in a majority Muslim country like Turkey or Pakistan. Such shifts in religious practice when they occur raise red flags for security officials and, separately, mahalla committees embedded in neighborhoods in addition to the increased attention from state security that travel abroad attracts. Anyone who has studied religion abroad without prior permission from state officials is faced with intense scrutiny and questioning by the NSS upon returning to Uzbekistan. While some students try to conceal religious study in countries like Egypt and Turkey by traveling through Russia on the pretense of being a migrant laborer, it does not always escape the eye of the NSS, which uses informants embedded in Uzbek communities abroad to "out" those with an active interest in Islam, including those who make the *hajj* (Abramson 2010; Bayram 2011; Expert Working Group 2012).

Thus, state security organs deem Islamic weddings as well as large secular ones as potential threats. Consequently, state policies and security practices pressure people toward smaller, nonreligious weddings that are more affordable, avoid displays of excess, limit the size of public gatherings, and do not provide religious figures a platform to preach or usurp state channels to propagate moral behavior.

Mahalla committee leaders also actively seek to influence the form of funeral ceremonies, but in some cases promote an Islamic model. In 2010, a famous Uzbek filmmaker, Malik Kayumov, died while visiting relatives in Moscow. After his body was repatriated to Tashkent for burial, officials denied the large crowd of people who came to honor Kayumov the right to have a civil memorial service (*grazhdanskaia panikhida*). Instead an Islamic one (*janoza*) was held (youtube 2010). According to a news article (uznews. net, April 30, 2010), a friend surmised that the Uzbek National Security Service wanted to avoid a civil funeral, which usually entails numerous eulogies by friends and colleagues and it would be difficult for the NSS to monitor the content. Islamic funeral ceremonies in Uzbekistan typically are brief affairs, involving a short prayer recited by an imam. Of course, the wishes of the deceased and relatives are not necessarily taken into account, resulting in a religious ceremony for an individual who might have eschewed religion his entire life in a way consistent with Soviet socialist values commonly shared by members of the Uzbek intelligentsia.

A similar case, involving a less famous individual, gives us a more detailed sense of the extent of Uzbek state intrusiveness. In 2007, family members asked a close colleague of a prominent and religiously unobservant Tatar academic who had just died to organize a civil funeral for her at her courtyard home. On the day of the event, leaders of the mahalla where she resided approached the colleague and asked about the funeral arrangements. When he explained that there was going to be a civil service, the mahalla elders urged him not to do this, suggesting that a simple Islamic service that "gets it over with quickly" would suffice. When colleagues resisted, the elders began to seize control of the arrangements, segregating the sexes by herding female members of the household and guests inside the house to view the proceedings through the windows and allowing men to remain in the courtyard. Confusion reigned while eulogists battled with mahalla leaders for control of the proceedings and stole opportunities to praise the achievements of the deceased (personal communication 2012).

What are mahalla leaders afraid of in such circumstances and why would security organs take such measures, if only behind the scenes, to push an Islamic form of memorial service? While mahalla leaders might justify the pressure in terms of a preference for religious piety over secularity, it is more likely that they want to limit the possibility that spontaneous speech in front of a large crowd might reflect badly on them. Since independence, the mahalla in Uzbekistan has shifted increasingly from a community to an administrative unit of the state. Fear of drawing the attention of the NSS is pervasive. What if word got out that people were making speeches critical of the state, or in the case of a civil funeral, by eulogizing the deceased's life, praised the Soviet past at the expense of or as a critique of present-day Uzbekistan? Mahalla leaders do not want to bring the state into their community any more than necessary. They appear to be serving the interests of the state, yet they also seek to keep the state at a distance. Thus, the imposition of Islamic funerals on even unobservant Muslims leads to the unintended consequence of promoting Islamic practice. Not only does an Islamic funeral become the politically safe option, it becomes the explicit justification for it—"We are Uzbeks, therefore Muslims, and should honor the deceased with our own tradition, which is Islam"—strengthens the identity bond between nation and Islam in a society where religious observance is growing.

The Persistent Problem of Independent Voices: Media and the Public Discourse

Outside of local community institutions, the state and its agents have been forced to react to the many ways Islamic voices are increasingly a part of the broader public discourse. Just as at the community level, the state has developed a strategy of attempting to proscribe certain voices while authorizing others who will reliably craft messages that fit the regime's interests. So while the strategy employed to regulate media and the public discourse has included familiar repressive measures against voices deemed to threaten social control, new media technologies and sustained popular interest in these voices and the Islamic themes they raise have made it impossible to eliminate them and their perspectives entirely. This has prompted the state to promote its own "trusted" speakers on new and old media to try to ensure that Islamic perspectives conform to state interests, sometimes even promoting them over secular voices when viewed as a means to silence criticism of the Karimov regime and promote perpetuation of the status quo.

The Soviet Union and later independent Uzbekistan used very similar measures to closely monitor religious publishing, sermons, and education.

But then as now, popular and independent-minded imams gained broad followings beyond their local communities through underground samizdat media production. From the late Soviet period, the most common form of independent religious media was the cassette tape. Official condemnation seems to have done relatively little to limit access to or the popularity of the recorded sermons by imams who have been long repressed or eliminated, expanding the ability of interested listeners to interact with these charismatic reformers across state-constructed or -monitored barriers with relative ease (Frank and Mamatov 2006).

As Internet access and use has steadily increased, samizdat production has shifted to the Internet and MP3s. Uzbek government censors (Kendzior 2012) have failed to keep pace with tech-savvy young Muslims, who continue to distribute in some cases the same banned sermons from the early 1990s that still have popular resonance. These are distributed in increasingly innovative and technologically sophisticated ways, including by hacking neutral third-party sites hosted in the United States or Europe and uploading content invisible to the sites' regular users but easily accessible with a direct link. More often, though, interested Internet users protect the content and the safety of others accessing it by copying it endlessly across a broad variety of free media archive sites around the world, loading the banned reformist sermons onto sites dedicated to pop music and sometimes even videos of scantily clad performers, hiding the files among "general interest" content that would not trip the various blocks and Internet firewalls inside Uzbekistan (Kendzior 2012).

Some independent imams, like the late Sheikh Muhammad Sodiq Muhammad Yusuf (1952–2015) and his circle, leaped past the physicality of cassette tapes and rapidly adapted traditional teachings to the Internet. Muhammad Sodiq's followers run a sophisticated Internet portal, Islom.uz with content available in four languages and a rapidly growing list of subsites dedicated to specific "consumer" demographics. A wide variety of basic religious educational and cultural material is posted with professional graphic design layouts, photographs, audio and video materials, and hundreds of articles geared toward increasing religious education and awareness among laypeople of the place of religion in their everyday lives. Popular material from this site is reproduced across the Internet on blogs and file-sharing sites. The site importantly also includes a Fatvo (fatwa) forum, where readers from around the world submitted hundreds of questions for the sheikh asking for a religious opinion or theological interpretation on things both profound and mundane that he appears to have answered personally.

One of the most successful religious new media entrepreneurs is a protégé of Sheikh Muhammad Sodiq's media enterprise, the popular journalist, poet, and sports commentator Hayrullo Hamidov. Though Hamidov was repressed by the Uzbek government in 2010 and sentenced to six years in prison, these same new media production and distribution techniques have made it next to impossible for the state to effectively curtail the continued spread of his teaching, poems, and essays. An engaging and quietly charismatic figure, Hamidov (2007) transitioned a successful career as a sports journalist into a series of projects that brought a religious perspective to everyday life and sensitive social issues that government-approved media outlets refused to discuss.

The ease with which Hamidov could move from sports to poetry to social problems like prostitution, corruption, or human trafficking across radio, video, and print make him perhaps unique at present, but it is likely that even when his voice was silenced in prison, other talented young religiously minded media figures took on similar roles. Faced with the emerging threat of the Islamic state and messages from Uzbek-led groups fighting in the conflict in Syria and Iraq, the Uzbek government made the unprecedented decision to release Hamidov early in February 2015. Shortly after his release, he began a partnership with one of the country's most popular entertainment Web sites, Sayyod.uz, urging other young Uzbek Muslims to understand that the Islamic state is a heretical group that does not speak for their faith (Hamidov 2015; Ozodlik 2015). Hamidov's pre- and post-imprisonment careers are evidence that the Uzbekistani government recognizes that as a generation emerges that never knew the repression and limitations of the Soviet period, they, like their counterparts across the rest of the Muslim world, will begin to engage with religious teaching outside the walls of the mosque and look to figures like Hamidov for their understanding of how Islam shapes their identity and their everyday lives (Mandaville 2005).

As this Islamicization of the public sphere grows, the state is faced with the dilemma of how it can control independent voices speaking from a religious perspective (Eickelman 2003). The strategy that the Karimov government has adopted is a mixed one—it stifles some voices like Hamidov's when they seem beyond control, but it adopts Islamic rhetoric and practices and instrumentalizes these to its own ends in others. Following the same strategy it uses to control and shape religious discourse in brick-and-mortar mosques and in the bazaar, the Uzbek NSS shows increasing interest in limiting new media discourse to voices and forums it feels it can strictly police and control, attempting to limit and curtail any discussion that happens outside its direct observation or strays from preapproved themes. New media make it much more difficult for them to control and police this space effectively, leaving them few options other than to try to control which individuals are allowed to produce content that will be viewed by a large audience. This gives trusted figures like the disciples of Muhammad Sodiq Muhammad Yusuf considerable leeway as long as they are willing to use their influence on behalf of government objectives from time to time, and motivates the government to physically eliminate those whose opinions or actions are deemed less predictable.

State Use of Religious TV Programming: Love Your President! Be Content with Bread! (Or Allah Will Give You a Disease . . .)

The state-sponsored religious establishment has in recent years also attempted to use nontraditional media to spread religious messages that serve the government's own purposes. This tactic seems to have been used increasingly since the Andijan events in 2005. The state-owned Uzbek Television First Channel has regularly produced a program called *Hidoyat Sari* (Toward guidance) for over a decade (Tashkent Mulkdor 2004). This innovative process has created, or attempted to create, the first government-sanctioned religious media celebrity in Uzbekistan, the head imam of Tashkent Anvar Qori Tursunov. It is unclear what the viewership for the programs is or how they are received by a wider audience, but Tursunov's program is remarkable for its religious content among a broadcast lineup that is otherwise overwhelmingly dedicated to stale, predictable "traditional Uzbek" music or dancing, innocuous soap-opera-style entertainment, or heavily propagandized news programs and documentaries.

Hidoyat Sari is also remarkable for the extent to which it mirrors the heavily propagandized content from other shows with a religious flavor. The program is frequently used as a platform to warn viewers against "foreign influences," extol the virtues of the Uzbek government, the personal guidance and wisdom of President Karimov, and to urge viewers to give thanks to God that they are lucky enough to have such a just and prudent leader. The extent to which the government openly uses Tursunov and Islam as a tool for its own agendas cannot fail to be both frustrating and embarrassing for Muslims who tune in for actual religious guidance from one of the country's highest ranking ulema. Some programs condemn anyone for being unhappy with the status quo, for wanting something to eat other than bread, and for failing in the eyes of God to love their president as much as they love their parents. One episode even went so outrageously far as to hint (through another speaker, not Tursunov) that dissatisfaction with the status quo might cause God to curse people with diseases like tuberculosis (Tashkent Channel One 2009).

This increasing mobilization of religious imagery and hodgepodge theological prevarication in the government-controlled media is something new, and seems to represent a trend in which the Uzbek state increasingly and incautiously attempts to bend and mold Islam for its own purposes. The transparent pandering to government talking points and the theological acrobatics required to do it, however, likely severely limit the popular appeal of such programs among religiously minded Uzbeks and may only make the government's puppet clerics a more convenient target for their reformist rivals.

Criticism? Blasphemy!

Over the past several years the Uzbek government has also increasingly deployed a "religious values" discourse to justify blatant abuses of human rights and attacks against vocal critics of the status quo. While much of the language focuses on "our common morals" or "national traditions," religious figures and specific Muslim religious language have been used by state-controlled media and state courts to punish activists and critics and to warn the public of "foreign influences" that the government inevitably connects to any implied criticism or discussion of serious social problems. In combination with other media campaigns and speeches that warn the public against the evils that may lurk in animated films, cell phones, and the Internet, these messages attempt to use hot-button issues to stir up a conservative and increasingly religious population against "foreign enemies" who supposedly want to impose anti-Muslim and immoral values on Uzbek society.

The two prominent cases from recent years, those of the AIDS activist Maksim Popov and the well-known photographer and filmmaker Umida Ahmedova, show remarkable similarities in the content of the government's accusations and the propaganda campaigns that accompanied Ahmedova's case in the national media. Both were accused of "slandering the Uzbek people," "undermining the psychological and moral development of young people," "promoting perversion" and "failing to accurately represent reality," but also, in a new twist "contradicting Islamic values."

Popov, whose case has drawn much less international attention, was sentenced to seven years in prison primarily for distributing a Russian-language educational pamphlet published in Kazakhstan that offered information about AIDS prevention and the dangers of drug abuse. At his trial, the prosecution accused him of "perverting underage youth" and "promoting homosexuality and prostitution." At least one high-ranking cleric was brought to testify against him, (un)ironically accusing him of violating religious values in a secular court, and the expert witnesses used by the prosecution accused him of slandering the Uzbek nation by simply acknowledging that prostitution, homosexuality, and sexually transmitted diseases existed as social issues in Uzbekistan (Chilanzar District Court 2009; Ianovskaia April 27, 2010).

Umida Ahmedova's photographs of Uzbeks in their everyday lives and several short ethnographic films on women's social issues in Uzbek society had gained international recognition in Europe and Russia, bringing much more public attention to her case. Religious symbols were deployed very overtly by the state during her trial, though there is little to no mention of religion in her artwork. Two representatives of the Committee on Religious Affairs were brought to testify against her, but they seemed at a loss in their testimony to explain how her work supposedly offended Islam (Sharipov, Schkovorodyuk et al. 2009; Volosovich February 15, 2010).

As if someone were unsatisfied with their performance, the judge himself read a special opinion in addition to her verdict. He accused Ahmedova of betraying her religion, and compared her photographs of what appeared to be impoverished Uzbek communities to blasphemy along the lines of drawing cartoons of the Prophet Muhammad. In both his supplement and a scathingly critical article published in a Tashkent newspaper, Ahmedova was explicitly connected to unnamed "foreign powers" who want to undermine Uzbekistan's public image and her work was blamed for promoting drug abuse, perverting young people, and promoting gay marriage (Makhmudov 2010). These criticisms are particularly canned, since unlike Popov's activism, her work has no mention at all of homosexuality or drugs in its content (e.g., Akhmedova and Karpov 2008).

In reality neither Popov's activism nor Ahmedova's art made any commentary at all about the morals or traditions of the Uzbek people, much less Islamic issues. Ahmedova's work drew attention to real and acute social problems like gender inequality, poverty, and social obstacles faced by women whose intimate private lives are policed and controlled by their whole community. While it would seem that she would draw the most criticism for the latter, genuinely controversial issue, the vast majority of the "expert panel conclusions" written for her trial and the testimony given during the process focused on a book of her photographs that were allegedly "doctored" to make Uzbekistan look impoverished and underdeveloped. As if taking a page directly from Stalin, the underlying point to most of the "expert panel" criticism was that her art failed to portray new buildings and happy people in Uzbekistan (Sharipov, Schkovorodyuk et al. August 5, 2009).

The Uzbek government appears to believe it can deflect public discontent with social and economic issues by co-opting popular anger arising from conservative social mores or revivalist religious sentiments. More recently, for example, Uzbekistani state television produced a documentary accusing citizens who had sought asylum in Norway of combining participation in Islamic extremist groups with "homosexual activities" (Atayeva 2014; O'zbekistan Telekanali 2014). These campaigns seem perhaps dangerous, especially given the Karimov administration's famous aversion to popular anger and protest and the fact that Tashkent authorities blamed homophobic Islamic extremists for the 2009 murder of the Ilhom Theater director Mark Weil, one of the very few openly gay public celebrities in Uzbekistan. Even though the government seems much less than willing to deal with angry crowds or the social divisions that these campaigns may come to highlight in a religiously diverse population, they seem surprisingly unafraid to co-opt these issues if only to create the impression that the state is a moral authority.

Ensuring a "Captive Audience": Social and Economic Consequences?

The state's often contradictory attempts to police and engineer the emerging Islamic public sphere may have broader social and economic consequences. Hayrullo Hamidov's own popularity, for example, is not significant enough to make his supporters a dangerously unsatisfied demographic. But his powerful patron and teacher, Muhammad Sodiq Muhammad Yusuf, was by some assessments the single most important religious figure in Uzbekistan. According to occasional reports from his relatives and poems and letters from him that they published, Hamidov was treated exceptionally well in prison and given an unprecedented amount of freedom for someone convicted on such serious charges (Hamidov 2011). Muhammad Sodiq publicly used his influence to protect Hamidov in a limited way (Ferghananews.com April 29, 2010), and this unusual leniency may reflect that (although it may also reflect his own popularity and the state's cautiousness about making him a public martyr figure). These quasi-independent Islamic leaders have an uneasy live-and-let-live cooperative agreement with the state.

More broadly, if the Uzbek state continues to persecute young and popular teachers like Hamidov who increasingly bring Islam out of the mosque and into everyday lives in a way that younger Uzbeks can relate to, their ability to influence religious discourse will likely continue to decrease. By offering as competition only highly scripted propagandized programs like Anvar Qori Tursunov's broadcasts, they will find it even more difficult to control religious messaging and may find that the older-generation clerics that they sponsor have increasingly little influence over the way people think about Islam. Ultimately this is likely to be good for religious freedom, but it may prompt the Uzbek government to continue even harsher repressive measures as they sense control over religious discourse slipping away.

An example of this type of intensification is a campaign the Uzbek government has engaged in since 2008 against young men it calls "Nurchilar," whom they accuse of being followers of the Turkish theologian Said Nursi and members of a foreign-funded organization based in Turkey. The trials and the media campaigns that accompany them openly distort Nursi's theology and claim that the peaceful, spiritualist Nurcu movement is a terrorist organization.

In reality, the campaign consistently targets former students of the Turkish-Uzbek high schools run by the Fethullah Gülen movement throughout Central Asia and Turkey and even in the United States. The schools in Uzbekistan were considered elite educational institutions and were highly competitive until the government shut them down in 1999, likely as a result of a foreign relations flap with Turkey. Graduates of these schools were multilingual, ambitious, and often the best and brightest in their communities (Balci 2003; Peuch 2004). Many of those arrested in the campaign had gone on to study abroad in Turkey, the United Kingdom, or the United States in co-sponsored exchange programs and were frequently upwardly mobile, religiously active middle-class or elite young entrepreneurs and professionals who maintained and leveraged their international professional networks (Ferghananews.com February 17, 2009; Sadriddin 2009).

The government's transparent campaign to repress upwardly mobile young men who are religiously active further hurts its already deeply strained credibility as an interpreter of what constitutes "religious extremism." This is all the more true given that Said Nursi's work has been widely available in Uzbekistan since independence and was until very recently published in the country with the full approval of the Uzbek government.

The work of more obscure local religious figures like Akrom Yuldashev was easier to distort, but the wide availability of Nursi's work and his reputation as one of the most prominent moderate Muslim theologians of the twentieth century make this campaign particularly controversial. Combined with the excellent reputation of the Turkish-Uzbek schools and the high standing many of the repressed young men had in their communities, this campaign appears to have potentially more serious popular repercussions than the ones against localized groups like Akromiya or socially marginalized ones like the Jehovah's Witnesses.

The Next Generation

Approximately 60 percent of Uzbekistan's population is too young to remember the effects of Soviet policies on religious life (United Nations Population Division 2011). Consequently, despite hearing about it from older generations, mostly in piecemeal fashion, the attitudes, identity, and assumptions of Uzbeks thirty years of age and younger have been shaped largely by recent, dramatically different phenomena, such as the state's embrace of Islam as an integral part of Uzbek identity, a less restrictive environment for Muslims in Russia as experienced by millions of Uzbek labor migrants, and opportunities to engage with Muslims throughout the world, including in countries where Soviet citizens were prohibited from traveling. For example, youth expectations of Muslim leaders' knowledge of the Koran and ability to apply Islamic teachings to everyday questions are likely higher. As early as the mid-1990s, crowds of worshippers, at least at some of the more popular Friday mosques in Tashkent, mobbed imams with questions about how to live one's life (personal communication 1994). Belief in God, weekly or daily prayer, and participation in rituals such as fasting during the month of Ramadan are more widely taken for granted and expected in some communities, even if people do not participate to the same degree. Unlike in the Soviet period, it is widely understood that an individual has gone to the mosque if he is absent from work midday on Friday (personal communication 2006).

Meaningful polling on politically sensitive topics like Islam is virtually impossible in Uzbekistan and very little qualitative research on generational attitudes and religious knowledge has been conducted. Nevertheless, we can learn something from state policies that target Islamic education, such as state-sponsored training and placement programs for new Muslim clerics. Martha Olcott (2012) documents the limited education made available to train new imams to staff and lead the country's burgeoning number of mosques and Muslim communities.

Since independence, the Uzbek government has invested large amounts of money in building up an Islamic infrastructure. While far from meeting the needs of the country's population, so far the government has established a governmental Religious Affairs Committee, its own spiritual establishment (muftiate), a secular Islamic University, eight madrasas for men and two for women, and an Islamic Institute for training imams. Under evolving regulations, madrasa graduates can become deputy imams, but graduates of the Islamic Institute can be certified to work as full imams. It is fair to say that the Uzbek government has done more than any of its Central Asian neighbors to develop educational opportunities for training future Islamic leaders and to preserve and win recognition for Uzbekistan's Islamic heritage sites (ISESCO 2007). Kyrgyzstan and Tajikistan not only have fewer resources than Uzbekistan, but instability in both countries has made policies concerning religion a lower priority. This is not to say that all the above institutions do not exist in Kyrgyzstan and Tajikistan. They do, but their regulation and incorporation into a comprehensive state plan on religious education have been comparatively sporadic and lax.

In the Soviet and early postindependence periods Islamic education was not standardized. Building on current standards, the government is gradually replacing the previous generation of imams with younger men who have graduated from state institutions, including with degrees in non-religious subjects from secular institutions. Meanwhile, the government wants imams to have more than a narrow theological education and be able to counter articulately extremist or unorthodox views (as defined by the state) when they arise in their community. In addition to these qualifications, the government has increasingly imposed restrictions on imams. Not only does the muftiate draft the content of sermons, but imams are also required to get permission from the local NSS office to travel outside their home region (personal communication 2012).

The success of this program has been mixed. In some cases, the new training is welcome. Elsewhere, new imams face community resistance because their training often is politically charged and does not meet the spiritual needs of a community. In a mosque near Namangan, a freshly minted and newly appointed imam communicated his zero tolerance for extremist views, urging members to be as vigilant as he in eliminating it from the community. Half of the community, mostly older members who were used to a different and less aggressive style, took offense and switched to a different mosque (personal communication 2011). More frequently, younger mosque attendees are more likely to be unsatisfied with state-trained imams. While older community members might be content with an imam who can lead the Friday prayer, younger Muslims have higher expectations, especially those looking for guidance and spiritual healing, such as in marital and family relations, unemployment, or other financial difficulties.

The Limits of State Control

The Karimov regime has been particularly vigilant in propagandizing against perceived internal and external threats to its authority and stability. In reaction to the Arab Spring in 2011, the government mobilized messages targeting youth (Tashkent Channel One February 14, 2011; Tashkent Channel Two 2011). The growing role of political Islam in a number of Arab Spring countries (politically in Egypt, Tunisia, and militantly in Yemen and Syria) heightened the regime's concern and steered it toward restricting forums, usually online, where religious messages are most likely to be heard. In general, the government has put a lot of energy into blocking religious Web sites that propagate Islamic messages it considers threatening while also mobilizing newly trained young clerics to communicate its own messages (islom.uz 2013; maxala.org 2012).

Currently, the regime's effort to provide young imams with secular and theological training in state institutions demonstrates an interest in cultivating a cohort of compliant clerics just knowledgeable enough about world events, such as the Arab Spring, to help articulate why that is not the path Uzbekistan should take (uzmetronom 2012). In a televised speech on the eve of Independence Day 2012, Karimov exhorted religious leaders to make citizens aware of the dangers of the Arab Spring from a religious perspective (BBC Monitoring 2012); by October the muftiate kicked off a national workshop for imams to brief them on the government's talking points (Committee on Religious Affairs 2012). In November these imams delivered an officially crafted sermon simultaneously from every *minbar* (pulpit) in the country, warning that the wave of democratic reform in the Middle East was in fact an anti-Muslim plot, reminding them that dissension (*fitna*) is a grave sin in Islam and claiming that "[The] 'Arab Spring' crises have not brought peace, calm, or better lives to any of the places that have been their victims. On the contrary, the 'Arab Spring' has turned into the 'Arab Oppression.' . . . We, the Muslim sons of this land, are society's conscientious [*ongli*] and active members. Protecting peace and calm in our country—and recognizing the value [*qadr*] of the blessing of peace—we are obligated to ceaselessly give praise to our Creator for this great blessing Allah has given us (Office of Muslim Affairs 2012).

This response places centralized control of religious messages largely in the hands of the muftiate, where the talking points can be reliably dictated by politics or even by the president himself, as in this case. But it also relies on government-trained, young, and loyal imams in communities throughout the country and authorizes them, and their listeners, to discuss political questions and world events from a religious perspective. As we argued above, this approach does not always work, especially when it advocates for preserving the status quo. And when it does not, it potentially drives alienated Muslims elsewhere. Furthermore, this push toward more "worldly" clerics could also undermine the regime's simultaneous efforts to limit the kind of Islamic knowledge available by creating a cohort of religious leaders who demand more than their predecessors.

We have also argued that interest in Islam continues to grow, due in no small part to expanding Internet access and social media participation and to the millions of migrant laborers who travel abroad. State policies of control whose repression prevents religious institutions increasingly from meeting people's needs and expectations drive some to satisfy those needs "underground." "Underground" can mean radical or extremist groups for those who believe that violence is the only route to effect change. Much more often, however, Central Asian Muslims turn to other forms of spiritual authority, often outside the mosque and madrasa, where religious practice is so far less regulated or its regulation is less intrusive. If underground Islam means anything in a police state where there is no organized political opposition, it realistically refers to access to spiritual and moral guidance from alternative authorities such as spiritual healers (*folbins*), saint shrines, and other sacred sites, which do not rely on state-controlled clergy and which have not yet or only minimally been subjected to state regulation (Peshkova 2009; Rasanayagam 2010). There scholars have found a burgeoning use of private sites such as homes wherein the use of "traditional" healing practices are imbued with Islamic meaning. We can expect that state regulations will eventually address these practices too, perhaps by using a combination of Soviet-style secular arguments to declare them ineffective or not modern and post-Soviet methods of mobilizing religious leaders to claim they are un-Islamic.

CHAPTER FIVE

Subversives and Saints

Sufism and the State in Central Asia

Emily O'Dell

During the imperial Russian conquest and the Soviet period, state authorities considered Sufism a threat and thus an ideology that needed to be controlled and destroyed. In response to armed Sufi resistance movements against state attempts to control and define Islam, the tsars and the Soviets both weakened the influence and public presence of Sufism in Central Asia by directing religious officials to issue fatwas against Sufism, placing Sufis under strict surveillance, and stripping Sufi endowments of their wealth. The detention, deportation, and execution of a large number of Sufi sheikhs led to a decline in the visibility and quality of Sufi leadership and scholarship. While the tsars and Soviets branded Sufis as radical extremists, the independent Central Asian states that emerged after the collapse of the Soviet Union in 1991 reversed course and embraced the cultural, historical, and spiritual aspects of Sufism and local traditions (in conjunction with Hanafi jurisprudence) as integral to their national identities and national security.

At a time when Sufi history, monuments, and practices are under assault around the Muslim world (O'Dell 2013), Sufism in Central Asia has been transformed from an enemy of the state to an indispensable ally of the state in combating Islamic "extremism." With "orthodoxy" and "extremism" having been redefined by state-sanctioned Islamic boards in the post-Soviet period,[1] the state promotion of Sufism in Central Asia serves today as a reclamation of precolonial history, a restoration of justice from the Soviet past, and a political vehicle to combat political and religious resistance to the power and legitimacy of the state itself.

Supporting Sufism in the Post-Soviet Period

After the collapse of the Soviet Union, Central Asia became more open to a variety of Islamic influences through Muslim missionaries, satellite dishes, and religious literature. Consequently, fear of radicalization or contamination by "foreign" interpretations of Islam has dominated national and religious legislation in Central Asia since independence. Mirroring the Russian Federation's promotion of Sufism and local traditions in Chechnya to combat political opposition and religious extremism, the religious boards of Central Asia chose after independence to promote a "national" Islam based on Hanafi jurisprudence, Sufi principles, and local folk traditions. Any Islamic beliefs, practices, or ideologies that fall outside of this redefined orthodoxy are interpreted as threats to the mandates and authority of the state.

It is not possible to give one clear definition of Sufism, though many notable Sufis throughout the centuries have tried. However, for the purpose of this research, it is possible and necessary to define the acceptable contours of Sufi practice in Central Asia today as understood and articulated by state religious authorities. In my interviews with state-sanctioned ulema throughout Central Asia over the past several years, "correct" Sufism has repeatedly been defined as the esoteric dimension and inner practices of Islam that enable Muslims to purify their hearts from imperfections and refine their outer characters. According to today's current ulema, Sufism can be practiced individually without the supervision of a guide or the support of a group. Acceptable methods for purifying the heart of all negative characteristics—a time-honored Sufi goal and tradition—include reciting the *shahada* or the ninety-nine names of God with prayer beads (*tesbih*), visiting the tombs of legendary Sufis for inspiration, and consciously modifying one's outer behavior. While visiting the shrines of notable Sufis out of respect for their pious lives is considered permissible by today's ulema in Central Asia, directly praying to these figures is highly discouraged. While public Sufi gatherings (*zikr*) are not desirable, small private gatherings in homes that incorporate chanting and singing are in fact permitted. Though initiation with a Sufi teacher is allowed, it is not considered necessary for practicing Sufism. Though many religious authorities in Central Asia are themselves Sufi sheikhs, the emergence of "charismatic" Sufi leaders with large numbers of followers is strongly discouraged. These official articulations of Sufism are seen as being compatible with Hanafi jurisprudence.

Post-Soviet fatwas on Sufism issued through post-Soviet religious boards and state-approved imams are complete reversals of fatwas from the Soviet period that set out to discredit and destroy Sufism. For instance, the chief imam of Almaty, Kulmuhammad Mahanbet, posted a fatwa on his Web site supporting Sufism, with a caveat: "You can visit a historic site or a tomb of outstanding people only for teaching or edification. Do not bow down to them."[2] While doing field research in Kyrgyzstan, I found a book called *Sufism* (written and published by the muftiate in Russian and Kyrgyz) for sale at the Central Mosque of Bishkek and various mosques in Osh. This book provides a thorough explanation of the acceptable parameters of Sufi practice. Considering that the promotion of Sufism in Central Asia is correlated with the shift in jurisprudential orientation in the Caucasus, it is no surprise that official religious opinions on Sufism from Russia and Central Asia share similar judicial interpretations and articulations. The chief imam of Russia, when asked if Sufism is innovation or polytheism, replied: "Sufism is a desire to worship God consciously—it is the improvement of one's moral qualities, when one tries to understand oneself in the context of eternity, and to create within and around himself an atmosphere of faith and religious practice. Sufism is definitely not polytheism." While official religious opinions in Central Asia are not strictly enforced or followed,[3] they reveal a great deal about the state production of post-Soviet religious knowledge and the current acceptable contours of Sufi practice and philosophy in the region.

The promotion of Sufism at the state level in Central Asia is by no means a carte blanche for any and all Sufi activity. Sufi zikrs rarely if ever occur in public, and Sufi adherents are hesitant to share the extent and nature of their Sufi devotion to both domestic and international sheikhs. However, at a time when Sufi practices and "spaces" are currently under attack around the Middle East and Southeast Asia by Salafi-inspired groups, the efforts of Central Asian governments since independence (long before the "war on terror") to safeguard and promote Sufi heritage should be viewed as an essential measure necessary to protect cultural heritage and local practices, and not merely as a manipulative and paranoid ploy to stamp out Islamic and political dissent, as many have charged. Nevertheless, the embrace of Sufism by governmental and religious authorities in Central Asia still has the potential to backfire, as it has recently in the Caucasus.

While *partokratiia* in the Caucasus initially viewed Sufi sheikhs as dangerous rivals after the collapse of the Soviet Union,[4] they soon sought the support of the Sufis to delegitimize Wahhabism.[5] Though Sufi sheikhs were initially reluctant to cooperate with governmental authorities, they agreed to enter the political arena out of concern that fighters returning from Afghanistan would attack them. In 1992, the leadership of the Spiritual Board of Muslims of Dagestan (Dukhovnoe upravlenie musul'man Dagestana, DUMD) was given to Said Afandi Chirkeisky,[6] the head of both the Naqshbandi and Shadhili religious orders in Dagestan. In the period between the two Russian–Chechen wars (1996–99), authorities in Moscow gave preferential treatment to Sufi leaders to oppose Wahhabi volunteers who came from Arab countries to the Caucasus during the war of 1994–96 (Gammer 2005, 839). Russia also renovated numerous shrines of Sufi sheikhs throughout Chechnya,[7] and agreed to fund an Islamic institution in Grozny named after the Sufi "pacifist" Kunta-Haji Kishiev.[8] Russian attempts to co-opt Sufi leadership into the state structure backfired with the assassination on August 28, 2012, of Said Afandi Chirkeisky and five of his followers by a female suicide bomber. Though Chirkeisky was a widely revered Sufi leader, his frequent criticism of Wahhabism and his alignment with the regime had long made him a prime assassination target as a perceived collaborator.[9]

While the post-Soviet promotion of Sufism at the state level can be explained as one dimension of a cultural revival, a nationalist agenda, and a political strategy, it may also be understood from the perspective of trauma and social memory (Garagozov 2005). The history of Sufism in Central Asia under the tsars and the Soviets was defined by an array of traumatic events (liquidation of Sufi endowments and the assassination of many Sufi sheikhs), which only intensified anti-Russian/colonial sentiments in the region among Sufi adherents. The privileging of local and cultural genealogies (epitomized by Sufi and folk "heroes") in the post-Soviet period has helped to transform the region's politically traumatic past to a culturally rich and heroic one. The embrace of Sufism and Hanafi jurisprudence as "national" inheritances from the region's precolonial past has allowed Central Asian religious authorities to reject the influence of foreign religious actors or ideologies (e.g., Wahhabis) and the Soviet suppression of Sufism, while simultaneously promoting religious boards patterned on those from tsarist and Soviet times and enacting policies inspired by those of the Russians in the Caucasus. The creation and reclamation of these "national" memories (Antze and Lambek 1997, vii) has allowed post-Soviet regimes to reengineer the region's precolonial Sufi heroes and local spiritual inheritances to fit the political demands of the national project and meet the perceived social and religious needs of citizens.

While the religious boards of the Central Asia Republics share many of the same features of governance and Islamic law, their promotion of Sufism and Hanafi jurisprudence differs in several respects. In the following section, which surveys the state promotion of Sufism in Uzbekistan, Tajikistan, and Turkmenistan, the "politics of the dead" in each of these republics is more than just a cosmetic shift in jurisprudential orientation toward the Hanafi *madhhab* informed by Sufism and local traditions. In using the "dead" of the past to validate the new order of the present, each religious council has had to reconfigure language, ethnicity, education, and space to conform new religious prerogatives to the national project. Translation, heritage preservation, and archaeology have all contributed to the promotion of historical and national myths of origin to create and maintain a group identity separate from the region's Soviet past. The ongoing debate between the official religious authorities and those who oppose Sufism is as much a contest between dueling madhhabs about the applications of Islamic law, as it is a fight over who controls the past along with its memory and interpretation in the present.

Heroes, Healers, and Heritage: Promoting Sufism in Uzbekistan

Uzbekistan's state promotion of Sufism since independence is reminiscent of the Russian Federation's strategy of promoting Sufism at the state level in the Caucasus. Immediately after the dissolution of the Soviet Union in August 1991, Uzbekistan's president Islam Karimov (the previous first secretary of the former Uzbek Communist Party) embraced the Sufi masters buried in Uzbekistan, along with Timur and Pahlavon Mahmud, as the forefathers of the modern nation-state, and framed Sufism as an antidote to religious extremism and terrorism. As in the Soviet period, the newly independent government assumed control over the muftiate and Islamic clergy in Uzbekistan (Polat 2000, 50). While the Islamic establishment in Uzbekistan during the Soviet period denounced Uzbek superstitions, shrine visitation, and excessive mourning at funerals,[10] Sufism in the post-Soviet era has been stylized as a fundamental aspect of the "altin meros" or the "golden heritage" of Uzbekistan. The ruling authorities' embrace and promotion of Sufi philosophy and practices has reversed centuries of persecution against Sufism and local traditions in Central Asia and given more visibility to women's leadership in spirituality, to healing modalities used to mitigate the effects of illness and disability, and to the preservation of Islamic material culture in Central Asia.

The celebration of medieval Sufi "saints" connected to the territory of modern-day Uzbekistan has served as a cornerstone of the nation-building agenda (Zarcone 1995). Since independence, Uzbekistan has sponsored countrywide celebrations to mark the birthdays of legendary Sufi leaders,[11] such as Bahauddin Naqshband, Khoja Ubaydallah Ahrar, Muhammad al-Hakim al-Tirmidhi, Ahmad Yasawi, and Abd al-Khaliq Ghijduvani.[12] In September 1993, President Karimov and the state mufti, Abdullah Mukhtar Khan, publicly celebrated the 675th anniversary of the birth of Bahauddin Naqshband at his shrine complex in Bukhara. In 2003, for the 900th birthday anniversary of Abd al-Khaliq Ghijduvani, a master of the Khwajagan-Naqshbandi Sufi order, the *imam khatib* of the great mosque of Bukhara, Abdulghafur Razzoq Bukhoriy, published *Tariqatga yo'llanma* (A guide to the Sufi path). While Uzbekistan has focused its reconstruction of Sufi identity on the Naqshbandi Sufi order, President Karimov has not limited his endorsement of Sufism to the Naqshbandi Sufi order—even though many of the highest religious administrators identify as adherents of the Naqshbandi Sufi order. For instance, the year 1994 was named the "Year of Yasawi," after the eleventh-century Sufi master Sheikh Ahmad Yasawi (buried in Turkistan, Kazakhstan), who was the subject of academic conferences that same year in Uzbekistan, Kazakhstan, and Turkmenistan. Uzbekistan has also promoted the famous fifteenth-century Naqshbandi Sufi poet and administrator, Alisher Navoi, as an ideal state administrator who ruled with Sufi morals and without any conflict of ideology with the state. President Karimov frequently asks young Uzbeks to combine their steadfast "Uzbekness" (*özbeklik*) with Sufi humanistic ideals from the past.[13] By celebrating and commemorating the lives of these medieval Sufi saints and writers, Uzbekistan's state authorities have made these historical figures the bedrock of the nation's spiritual, philosophic, historical, and poetic pasts.

The Timurid period has served as an idealized past on which Uzbekistan has built new national narratives and venerated medieval Islamic traditions exemplified by the Naqshbandi Sufi order (Hegarty 1995). The Naqshbandi tradition in Uzbekistan is conceptualized as a truly Turkic *tariqa*, even though Bahauddin Naqshband wrote his mystical works in Persian. In the post-Soviet period, Uzbek writers, such as Arif Usman (1993), have argued that the Naqshbandi Sufi order should be considered a purely Turkic Sufi order. Thus, the state's refashioning of Sufism and local traditions into a national Islam has engendered remappings of history, ethnicity, and language.

The Uzbek promotion of Sufism has reconfigured precolonial Sufi narratives into coherent national narratives through translation and literature.

Since independence, there has been an increase in the publishing of Sufi literature in Uzbekistan and throughout Central Asia. The state endorsement of Sufism has encouraged the translation of works from Persian and Arabic into Uzbek, such as classical biographies of Zangi Ota and Bahauddin Naqshband. Because Stalin ordered all references in Sufi literature to God or the Prophet Muhammad and his caliphs to be purged, these censored terms have been reinserted in new publications of mystical poetry by Yasawi, Mashrab, and Navoi. Books about Bahauddin Naqshband and Najmuddin Kubra, in addition to the 2004 translation of Alisher Navoi's *The Language of the Birds* into modern Uzbek, can be found at numerous bookstores throughout Uzbekistan. Pamphlets on Sufism written in Uzbek are distributed in mosques, bazaars, and shrines. Nevertheless, there has not been an infusion of foreign materials on Sufism; on the contrary, the most prolific authors on Sufism in Uzbekistan are Uzbek, such as the poet Sadriddin Salim Bukhari,[14] and academic Najmiddin Komilov—an adviser to President Karimov on religious and cultural issues.

The Uzbek promotion of Sufism has led to different public spaces being rebranded and renamed. In 1991, Karimov had the avenue formerly known as "Lenin Street" renamed Bahauddin Naqshbandi Prospect. The Uzbek government also advertises its promotion of Sufism with signage, including billboards with quotations from Bahauddin Naqshband, and signs erected at the tombs of "saints" in both Uzbekistan and Karakalpakstan describing their pious lives and cultural relevance. In Uzbekistan, radio has also been used to spread Sufi ideals and Sufi philosophy.[15] There are similar live programs in several provincial centers, including a popular program in the city of Urgench that broadcasts discussions of Sufi poetry. The radio broadcast of Sufi programs on Sufi masters such as al-Ghazzali and Bahauddin Naqshband creates a path for Sufism to penetrate the walls of shops, cars, and homes—sacralizing such space with Sufi poetry and philosophy.

Sufism is taught today at Bukhara's Mir-Arab madrasa, the largest religious teaching establishment in Central Asia, and courses such as "The Spiritual Heritage of Uzbekistan" and "Uzbekistan's Own Way to Independence and Progress" have been woven into the curricula of schools and madrasas. Despite restrictions on teaching Sufism outside official institutions of learning, Sufi teachers, such as Khaja Ahmadjon Makhdum Khanafi-Naqshbandi Mujaddidi (a Naqshbandi sheikh),[16] Ghulom-ota Normat (a Yasawi sheikh),[17] and Dowud-khon (a Qadiri sheikh),[18] transmit their Sufi knowledge in hujras, as in Soviet times. While doing research on Sufism in Bukhara, I was fortunate to meet with a Sufi sheikh and professor at

Bukhara's Mir-Arab madrasa, who expressed his unconditional support for the state's endorsement of Sufism, and informed me that Sufism is taught as a separate subject at the madrasa. Despite the pedagogical support for Sufism in religious education, Uzbek authorities are unwilling to open the *khanaqah* (Sufi monastery) at the shrine of Bahauddin Naqshband, despite the pleas of members of the Naqshbandi Sufi order. Perhaps because a khanaqah devoted to Sufi instruction and experiential knowledge could lead to powerful and influential Sufi teachers with hundreds of followers, the state has prevented formal and public Sufi communities from being formed.

Due to its inclusive nature, Sufism has long been a refuge for those who are on the periphery of society, such as the ill, disabled, and poor. In post-Soviet societies in Central Asia, Uzbek women have been active as healers (Fathi 2010), drawing their healing practices from both shamanism and Sufism (Sultanova 2010). Because Sufism and local traditions have been invited out from behind the shadows of the Soviet period, the healing power of women is once again on display and available in the public sphere at home and abroad. The film *Habiba* (about a Naqshbandi female healer in Uzbekistan whose beliefs and healing rituals draw on Sufism and shamanism) is often screened in introductory courses on Islam and gender in the United States. Because many of these female healers endeavor to heal patients who have mental illness and physical disabilities, mental illness and disability are afforded more visibility in the public eye and local communities.

The post-Soviet celebration of women in Uzbekistan as religious teachers has allowed women in the public sphere to honor important medieval Sufi figures, transmit spiritual knowledge, and adjudicate Islamic law. *Otinchalar*, female religious teachers, provided the bulk of women's education in Central Asia until the Jadidists framed them as carriers of a primitive and superstitious past—a sentiment with which the Soviet "modernists" agreed. In the post-Soviet period, great importance has been placed on otinchalar, who are praised by the state as "progressive" female teachers of spiritual and worldly knowledge (see Ibrohimov et al. 1996, 89). Otinchalar usually come from families linked to a distinct Sufi lineage. Called *ustozim* (my master) by their disciples, otinchalar conduct ceremonies to honor dead Sufi masters, interpret Islamic law, and mediate conflicts within families.[19] Paralleling the initiation process of shamans, traditional otinchalar are "called" by God through divine messages delivered by prophets, Sufi saints, and ancestors in mystical dreams, or by virtue of a miraculous recovery from a severe illness—whether physical or mental. While such a divine election grants the otinchalar their spiritual authority, they also are expected to know Koran, hadith, and Islamic law.[20]

Several of the ceremonies conducted by the otinchalar in Bukhara are dedicated to specific Sufi saints. Spiritual gatherings attended by women in Bukhara are rooted in both Sufi and local folk traditions (Sultanova 2000, 534–35). One of most unique and exclusive rituals for otinchalar to oversee in Bukhara is the Xatm-i yozdehom, a ceremony performed by women to honor Sheikh 'Abd al Qadir al-Jilani, the founder of the Qadiriyya tariqa, and other Sufi saints revered in Central Asia.[21] In fact, two special ritual occasions in Uzbekistan revolve around the commemoration of the lives of two notable Sufi women—Bibi Seshanba and Bibi Mushkulkushod, who were both relatives of Bahauddin Naqshband (Andreev 1927; Sukhareva 1960). In their honor, the Koran is recited, and selections from books about their pious lives are read. These ceremonies that blend together the "memory" of male and female Sufi saints with the ritual power of local practices provide opportunities for women to have spiritual leadership roles, while simultaneously building community and group identity around rituals that were forced underground in Soviet times (see Kramer 2001, 373).

When I was doing research on Sufism in Bukhara, I was invited to attend an all-female ceremony led by a *dastarhanji*,[22] an organizer of ritual events for the *mahalla*, and a Naqshbandi otin, who leads a weekly zikr gathering for women. After the otin placed a piece of paper with Koranic verses written in ink into a bowl of water, she asked each woman to drink from the bowl for spiritual strength and healing. She also placed four lit candles, a stick of fragrant herb (*issrik*), packs of tea, a mirror, and an even number of sweets and bread on a tablecloth stretched out on the floor. A bowl of milk was passed around three times to all the women in order for each woman to make a wish. After these ritual preparations, a seated Sufi zikr and prayers were offered for the soul of Bahauddin Naqshband, his relatives, and his lineage. Despite governmental support for these types of gatherings, some female spiritual teachers in Central Asia denounce Sufism and local healing practices as heretical innovations.

Throughout Uzbekistan, the post-Soviet renovation and visitation of Sufi spaces and shrines illustrates how a shift in Islamic jurisprudence and religious policy affects the preservation and presentation of material culture and cultural heritage.[23] Today, shrine pilgrimage and the beliefs underlying it play a prime role in religious expression in Uzbekistan, and help to create a communal religious identity in line with the ideals of the national project. Whereas the Soviets used Sheikh Naqshband's mausoleum as a silk factory and storehouse for fertilizer, President Karimov reopened the complex in 1991, and restored other popular shrine complexes, such as those of Shah-i Zinda, Abu Mansur al-Moturidi, Khoja Ahrar, Imam Muhammad ibn Ismail al-Bukhari, and Mahdumi A'zam. Uzbekistan has also allowed Sufis from outside of its borders to help restore its Sufi spaces, such as the shrine of Mir Khulal—which had fallen into ruin under the Soviets, but was rebuilt with the help of *murids* from Pakistan following the Naqshbandi Sufi order.[24] Some of the most popular shrines include those of Bahauddin Naqshband, Khoja Ahrar, Mahdumi A'zam, Sayid-ota, Eshon Buva Avlie, and various disappearing saints (*gayib*) like Goib-ota in the Kattakurgan region of Samarkand. Female saints such as the shrine of Bibi Aysha in the south of the Samarkand province are also popular, as are shrines connected to Khidr, who is seen as a source of good luck and a patron to workers and travelers (Chvir 2006). In addition to sanctioning these Sufi spaces as legitimate spaces of religious practices, Uzbekistan also tacitly gives approval to the "local practices" that take place at these shrines.

Uzbeks visit shrines for blessings (*baraka*) related to fertility, marriage, exams, and business deals. A saint's tomb is seen as a space of intercession where blessings can be obtained through pilgrimage and shrine rituals (Radtke 2002). Many people visit Sufi shrines to obtain a sacred talisman, which may take the form of paper with religious formulas on it from the Koran intended to cure illness or bring good luck. At most shrines, pilgrims tie textile bands of cloth around trees or bushes for good luck, and to leave their wish behind at the shrine. At the shrine of Bahauddin Naqshband, pilgrims walk three times around the shriveled remains of a tree mystically linked with the founder of the order. While these ritualistic practices are considered permissible by state religious authorities, there are limits. For instance, a sign at Shah-i Zinda instructs visitors not to appeal to the deceased for intercession, but to pray directly to God instead.

Unfortunately, most research on religious ritual and practice in Uzbekistan fails to include the Autonomous Republic of Karakalpakstan. While I was doing research on Sufism in Uzbekistan, I had the opportunity to travel to Karakalpakstan to survey the current state of Sufi shrine pilgrimage and rituals. The largest and most popular Sufi complex that I visited was the Sultan Uwais-bobo mausoleum complex in the To'rtkul district of Karakalpakstan, where a new cultural center dedicated to Sultan Uwais bin 'Amir al-Qarani was being built.[25] Uwais al-Qarani was a pious camel shepherd from the village of Qaran in Yemen in whose name a Sufi tariqa later developed (Baldick 1993). His initiation onto the path of Islam through visionary experiences with the Prophet Muhammad later became a template for Sufi initiation in a number of different Sufi orders. Many current scholars have not heard of his shrine in Central Asia, even though in the 1920s and 1930s it was one of the most popular pilgrim destinations in Central Asia (until its closure in the 1960s). The mausoleum, which ostensibly dates to the ninth century CE, was reopened during perestroika and restored after the collapse of the Soviet Union.

When I visited the mausoleum of Uwais al-Qarani, it was very crowded with pilgrims circumambulating both the shrine and the large rectangular pool filled with fish near the steps that lead up to the mausoleum. Similar to other Sufi shrines in Uzbekistan, the life story of this revered Sufi saint is inscribed on large, colorful posters in the first courtyard of the shrine. Pilgrims also visit a mountaintop above his shrine to view impressions on the ground believed to have been formed by al-Qarani's knees and feet. Thus, this shrine complex that commemorates a Sufi revered by numerous Sufi orders around the world as one of the first practitioners of Sufism weaves together the memory of a Sufi saint from Yemen with local practices connected to the sacred water below his shrine and "imprinted" landscape above it.

While Uzbekistan has made commendable efforts to preserve and protect its Sufi heritage—which is often framed as "national" heritage (*meros*)—the Sufi history promoted by the government has been diluted and divorced from its tormented modern context in Central Asia. In the state's official Sufi discourse on radio, television, in print, and on the signs posted at shrines, there is little to no mention of the horrendous repression that Sufis suffered, or of the resistance movements they led against the tsars and Soviets. Sufi sheikhs and the history of armed Sufi resistance are rarely mentioned as having been the most organized and feared source of resistance to tsarist and Soviet rule. Thus, the history of Sufism memorialized in Uzbekistan is one sanitized of Sufi violence.[26] Uzbekistan's decision not to include the oppression of the Sufis and their armed resistance against imperial and Soviet powers in official state discourse reinforces the notion of Sufis as eternal "pacifists" and "peacemakers" who do not pose an inherent threat to the stability of the state.

Sufism in Uzbekistan today is not exempt from being viewed as a possible threat to the political, religious, and social order. In his publications *Tasavvuf 1: Yoki Komil Inson Ahloqi* (Sufism 1: The virtues of the perfect man) and *Tasavvuf 2: Tavhid Asrori* (Sufism 2: The secrets of unity), Najmiddin Komilov, a senior Uzbek official who has written widely about Sufism, articulates a distinction between "correct" Sufism and "incorrect"

Sufism. "Correct" Sufism is thought to aid the development of human-kind, whereas "incorrect" Sufism results in religious extremism. Kamilov believes that the promotion of Sufism, and in particular the Naqshbandi Sufi order, allows the Uzbek people and even its army to be stronger and more prepared to defend the homeland against Wahhabism.

Religious policies under the Soviet period attempted to destroy the classic institution of the transmission of spiritual knowledge from *pir* to murid (between Sufi master and disciple),[27] and Uzbek religious officials have not tried to resurrect or encourage the charismatic authority of Sufi sheikhs. As a result, Sufism in Uzbekistan today is defined less by the intimate and loyal ties forged between a teacher and student and more by the national "ethos" believed to lie in the pious lives of the saints, and the spiritual principles espoused in their poetry. Nevertheless, as Sufi practices and spaces have come under attack in Africa, the Middle East, and Southeast Asia, it is notable that Uzbekistan has taken such bold steps to protect its cultural heritage and local traditions, regardless of any underlying political intentions.

The promotion of Sufism in Uzbekistan is not limited to a local audience, as it also serves as a convenient tool for foreign policy and foreign tourism. Uzbekistan has welcomed foreign policy experts, religious pilgrims, and international tourists to the country's Sufi shrines. President Karimov's embrace of Sufism to combat politicized Islamic movements has received a boost of support from the United States War on Terror. The Uzbek government has strengthened its relationship to the United States by promoting Sufism as an integral weapon against terrorism and suppressed religious groups like Hizb-ut-Tahrir. The Uzbek government maintains close contacts with the Islamic Supreme Council of America, which represents followers of the Naqshbandi order in the United States and is presided over by Sheikh Muhammad Hisham Kabbani, the deputy leader of the Naqshbandi Haqqani Sufi order (who has participated in numerous United States government and policy initiatives on Islam). For instance, Kabbani was a keynote discussant, along with Bernard Lewis, for a Nixon Center conference and report written to encourage United States policymakers to support "indigenous revivals" of Sufism in Central Asia to "deflect some of the increasing criticism from Muslims that the war on terror is purposely directed at destroying Islam" (Baran 2004, 6). The embrace of Sufism and preservation of Sufi spaces have helped Uzbekistan secure more funding and resources as a public partner in the War on Terror. The absence of strictly hierarchical Sufi orders led by sheikhs with charismatic authority allows the Uzbek state to sponsor Sufism as a spiritual set of ideas and practices divorced from any institutions or individuals that might post a challenge to the authority of the state.

The Persian Past and "Peaceful" Present: Sufism in Tajikistan

Similar to neighboring Uzbekistan, Tajikistan's government and religious authorities contend that the best Islamic jurisprudential position and remedy against extremism is the promotion of Hanafi jurisprudence coupled with Naqshbandi Sufism. In fact, as Tim Epkenhans notes (chapter 8, this volume), Tajikistan declared the year 2009 as "the year of Abu Hanifah," the founder of the Hanafi brand of Islam. Through its embrace of Hanafi jurisprudence and Sufi philosophy, Tajikistan's government has sought to keep Tajikistan's "national" brand of Islam protected from outside Islamic influences that may threaten the nation's cultural and religious heritage. While authorities in Tajikistan, including the president, extol the historical and cultural significance of Sufi shrines and saints in the media and in literature, Tajikistan has not been as aggressive as Uzbekistan in presenting itself as the chief sponsor of local traditions associated with the shrines, in patrolling the transmission of Sufism through *murid–murshid* relations, or in marketing its Sufi heritage for tourist and foreign policy consumption.

The transition away from communism in Tajikistan differed from that of the other Central Asian republics because of the brutal civil war (1992–97) that followed independence. While the Tajik civil war is often cited as evidence of the destabilizing potential of Islamic political activism (Akbarzadeh 1996; Atkin 1992; Lynch 2001; Nourzhanov 2005; Rubin 1993), the political vacuum and crisis in Tajikistan after the fall of the Soviet Union was related to a variety of factors, such as ethnic conflict, regionalism, and warring elites. Tajikistan remains the only Central Asian republic that permits Islamic parties to participate in the political process—an agreement that was reached at the end of the civil war. Though Islam provides only a partial explanation of the devastating civil war, Tajik political authorities often use the war as an example of the danger Islam poses if left unmonitored. Thus, while other Central Asian governments warn about the potential danger of wrong or undesirable interpretations of Islam (Wahhabism) to destabilize the state, Tajikistan has its own recent armed conflict to use and frame as a cautionary tale.

Many of the most visible religious figures in Tajikistan in the post-Soviet period, as in the Soviet period, descend from influential Sufi dynasties. In 1988, as glasnost finally reached the borders of Tajikistan, local mullahs separated from the official muftiate for Central Asia (known by the Russian acronym, SADUM), and elected their own chief mufti—Hoji Akbar Turajonzoda, who had been the former qazi qalon of Tajikistan (the country's highest Islamic imam) in the last years of the Soviet Union. Hoji Akbar Turajonzoda (b. 1947), the spiritual chief of the Tajik opposition during the civil war, belongs to the Qadiri Sufi order. His father, Ishan Turajan, is the murid of a famous pir from Kurgan-Teppe, Hazrat Ishan Khalliljan. In the purges of the 1940s, many members of the Turajonzoda family were sent to Siberia. The ones who survived returned to Tajikistan after Stalin's death. After independence, Turajonzoda threw his support behind the Islamic Renaissance Party (IRP), which teamed up with the democratic opposition to oust the Communist regime in Dushanbe in 1992 and form a coalition government. Nevertheless, Communist supporters, backed by Russia and Uzbekistan, fought back, and eventually the leaders of the coalition, including Turajonzoda, were forced to flee as the fighting intensified.

Sufis were on both sides of the barricades during Tajikistan's civil war. Despite Turajonzoda's involvement in the civil war, many of Tajikistan's leading Sufis were reluctant to involve themselves in political activity, and some vocally condemned the civil war. For example, Hajji Ismail Pir Muhammadzadah, a Naqshbandi sheikh and the imam of the mosque in the Ghissar region of Tajikistan, vocally opposed the civil war in Tajikistan, and actively spoke out against the involvement of spiritual leaders in that war. Abd al-Wahhab Zadah Qahhari Ismail was also against the war in Tajikistan, and especially against participation in the war by people of faith. After Turajonzoda fled to Afghanistan, he was replaced as mufti in February 1993 by Fatullah Khan Sharifzade,[28] a fellow Sufi, and the son of a Naqshbandi pir, Damullah Mohamed Sharif Hissar. Throughout his tenure as chief mufti, Sharifzade served as a devoted supporter of the government of President Emomali Rahmon, and opposed attempts by some members of the IRP to install a pro-Islamic regime. He was assassinated on January 21, 1996, by unknown gunmen at his home in the Hissar region. Turajonzoda was allowed to return to Tajikistan after he and other opposition figures were amnestied as part of the agreement that ended the civil war. He has served as the former qazi-kalon (1988–93), deputy prime minister (1999–2005) and senator (2005–10) of Tajikistan's Upper House (Majlisi milli).

As the current leader of the opposition, Turajonzada does not profess to be a Sufi sheikh, but he does legitimize his religious authority by emphasizing that he descends from a noble family of *ishans*. Throughout the history of Tajikistan, the ishans of various Sufi orders have exerted a profound influence on the daily life of the people, and they continue to be popular. Today, many prominent religious figures in Tajikistan identify as Sufis, such as Ishan Turajan, Ishani Abdulhaliljon, and Ishani Nuriddin—who are all followers of the Qadiriyya tariqa. Notable public figures who are followers of the Naqshbandi tariqa include Domullo Mukhammadi, Domullo Hikmatullo, and Makhsumi Ismoil. In the post-Soviet period in Tajikistan, it has been politically advantageous for religious specialists to identify as belonging to a Sufi or ishan lineage, whereas in the Soviet period such affiliations and genealogies were underplayed and discouraged.

Unlike in Uzbekistan, Tajik nationals did not write most of the books for sale on Sufism in Tajikistan.[29] When I surveyed the bookstores that surround the central mosque of Dushanbe, the Yakub Charkhi mosque (named after the most famous Naqshbandi Sufi saint buried in Tajikistan), I found a number of books on Sufism, yet none of them were written by a modern Tajik author. On the contrary, I found books written in Persian and Arabic by notable medieval Sufis, such as Mevlana Jalaluddin Rumi al Balkhi, Ibn Arabi, al-Ghazzali, Bahauddin Naqshband, and Abu Hamid Mohammad al-Ghazzali. Currently, there are no restrictions on the publication of Sufi literature or the importation of Sufi literature from other countries such as Iran. Nevertheless, all the books sold at these bookstores are checked and approved by governmental authorities. Over the past several years, Tajikistan has been receiving new editions of *diwans* (poetry collections) and Sufi texts from Iran—a trend that is likely to continue with the increasing attention being paid to Persian language and poetry. While some sheikhs in Tajikistan have published their own writings in newspaper and magazine articles, such writings are not currently available at these bookstores.

As in other Central Asian states, Tajikistan's political and religious authorities have publicly supported shrine pilgrimage as a "national" form of Islamic practice that preserves tradition and curbs undesired Islamist trends. Unlike in Uzbekistan, shrines in Tajikistan are not all uniformly marked or explained by government signage. The country is dotted with innumerable Sufi shrines, especially in the three major oblasts of Badakhshan, Kulab, and Soghd. The most prominent shrines in Tajikistan are largely dedicated to early Islamic figures, such as Hazrat Ali and Khalid Bin Walid at Hissar, and Sufi saints from the twelfth to sixteenth centuries. The capital Dushanbe contains the popular shrine of Yaqub Charkhi, Tajikistan's most famous Naqshbandi sheikh and a student of Bahauddin Naqshband.

The state's promotion and preservation of Sufi history can be seen explicitly at the shrine of Sayyid Ali Hamadani in Kulab, which borders

Afghanistan in the south of Tajikistan. Even though he is buried in Kulab, Sayyid Ali Hamadani is revered throughout Tajikistan, and even appears on the 10 somoni banknote. After the conclusion of the civil war, the Tajik government, with the support of the Iranian government, renovated the shrine. During this preservation and renovation process, the government accorded this Sayyid the status of a "national saint." The government also dedicated a museum to him in front of his shrine, which contains abundant literature on his life and philosophy in the form of books and manuscripts published from different parts of the region including India, Pakistan, and Iran. The government's investment in renovating this shrine and building this museum to a national saint illustrates its commitment to promoting the Sufi pilgrimage and history.

The practice of shrine visitation in Tajikistan is distinct from the other Central Asian Republics in one important respect. Shrines in the autonomous oblast of Gorno-Badakhshan are linked to Ismailism, a branch of Shia Islam and the primary religious orientation of the Pamir region. As a result, Tajikistan has hundreds of shrines that incorporate Shia Islamic practices and pre-Islamic symbols (such as animal horns and special stones). In Gorno-Badakhshan, shrines are dedicated to Ismaili pirs, *khalifas*, and revered Sufis, along with early figures of Islam, such as Muhammad Baqir and Hazret Ali. As in neighboring countries, shrines in Badakhshan tend to be connected to "sacred" and "healing" aspects of the landscape, such as holy trees, hot thermal springs, unusual rock formations, and the footsteps of early Islamic figures. Because shrines in Badakhshan are an essential aspect of Ismaili religiosity and community identity, many of the shrines were rebuilt after the civil war, or are in the process of being restored. From Badakhshan, shared sacred lineages and shrines trespass the borders of Afghanistan, Pakistan, and China. Jo-Ann Gross is one of the few Western scholars to study the shrines of Tajikistan. In her research on two of the more important Ismaili shrines of the region—which are located in Shughnon in Afghanistan—she has found a wide variety of accepted narratives and practices (Gross 2013). With the reopening of relations with the global Ismaili community after independence, made possible in large part from significant support from the Agha Khan, the Shia Imami Ismaili Tariqah and Religious Education Committee has gradually been regulating Ismaili practice. As a result, the rituals and practices at these shrines are becoming more standardized over time.

Tajikistan's promotion of Sufism at the state level transcends and trespasses international borders. In July 2011, the Tajikistan ambassador to India, Syed Baig, urged the people of Jammu and Kashmir to embrace Sufism and propagate peace and brotherhood at an International Sufi Conference in Srinagar. The public visibility and embrace of Sufism in Tajikistan extends to Tajik-dominated areas in Afghanistan, such as Balkh and Mazar-i Sharif, where Sufism is once again being practiced without fear of reprisal by the Taliban. When I journeyed from Tajikistan to Balkh, Kunduz, and Mazar-i Sharif in Afghanistan to research the visible resurgence of Sufism in the north, a significant number of Afghans of all ages were making public pilgrimages to the region's medieval Sufi shrines. In Afghanistan today, many Sufi shrines have detailed signs posted attesting to the piety and blessings of the Sufi saints buried there, as the Afghan government has chosen to promote and use Sufis as mediators with the Taliban. In Balkh, just as throughout Central Asia, I saw many Afghan pilgrims tie pieces of fabric to bushes surrounding the shrines, circumambulate the tombs three times, and hammer nails into sacred trees to make a wish. At the house believed by Afghans to have belonged to Mevlana Jalaluddin Rumi's father in Balkh (though Rumi was likely from Vakhsh in Tajikistan), my Afghan hosts prayed (along with some local children) for the soul of the legendary Persian poet. Sufism in Afghanistan, however, is not confined to the Tajik- and Uzbek-dominated north. Zikrs of the Naqshbandi, Qadariyya, and Chishtiyya also take place each week in the capital of Kabul.

Sufism is also currently being promoted in Islamic education and pedagogy in Tajikistan.[30] The Islam promoted in government-run schools is infused with Sufi philosophy, in an attempt to counter Islamic extremism and produce perfected human beings. While conducting research on the pedagogy used to teach Sufism at the Islamic University in Dushanbe (the country's only religious institution of higher learning), I spoke with Nabotov Zainiddin, an esteemed and knowledgeable professor of Sufism. He is also the author of the main Sufi textbook that he uses for his Sufism course—which surveys the history of all the major Sufi orders in Central Asia. Zainiddin believes that students must learn the history of Sufism for theological purposes, as well as for their own personal spiritual development. In his opinion, Sufism is the path that can help to polish the heart from imperfections, promote local and international peace, and help each Muslim in striving to become an *insan kamil* (a perfected human being). With Zainiddin, I had the opportunity to visit Naqshbandi and Qadiri sheikhs outside of Dushanbe and witness them conducting initiations, leading zikr, and providing guidance and education.[31]

The Islamic University in Dushanbe has also participated in implementing a curriculum to promote the Sufi tenets of tolerance and peace. Nabotov Zainiddin is one of several professors in Tajikistan and Kyrgyzstan, along with his colleague Saodat Davlatova, who has taught the "Religious Identity, Islam and Peace Building in Central Asia" curriculum created by the University of Peace in 2007 for students, clerics, secularists, nongovernmental organizations, and administrators in Tajikistan and Kyrgyzstan to promote peace building by bridging the attitudinal gaps between secular and Islamic education in Islamic societies threatened with religious and other identity-based conflicts. As the curriculum of the Islamic University is controlled by the government, the offering of such courses indicates that the state is committed to promoting Sufism at the highest levels of Islamic education. In addition to state-sponsored Islamic education, the Soviet legacy of underground education continues in the living sheikhs teaching Sufism in Tajikistan today. For instance, Abd al-Wahhab Zadah Qahhari Ismail, a Qadiriyya sheikh and the imam of a mosque in the Vakhdat region, south of Dushanbe, studied Sufism with the grandfather of Khoja Akbar Turajonzoda, the former deputy prime minister and chief mufti of Tajikistan.

As the only Persian-speaking Central Asian Republic, the practice and promotion of Sufism in Tajikistan differs in several significant ways from the other republics. Sufi literature in Tajikistan is often sold in the original Persian, and Tajik authorities maintain close relations with Iran on matters of shared cultural heritage. Iran has contributed to the "revival" of Sufism in Tajikistan by exporting Persian Sufi literature and restoring Tajik shrines. Because of its geography, many remote shrines remain out of the reach or concern of the government. Due to Tajikistan's location, Sufi practices and local traditions there are linked to similar sacred practices in neighboring China, Afghanistan, and Pakistan. Because of its significant Ismaili population, shrines in Badakhshan are an essential component of Shia community identity and religious legitimacy in Central Asia. While the government of Tajikistan reversed course as did the other Central Asian republics after independence to embrace Hanafi jurisprudence and Sufism, the practice of Sufi rituals and local traditions is more varied because of the country's geography, location, and Shia population.

Restoring Historical Justice and Sufi Heritage in Turkmenistan

As in Uzbekistan and Tajikistan, Turkmenistan's political and religious authorities chose to endorse Sufism as integral to Turkmenistan's identity and practice of Islam after independence. From the state's perspective, as articulated by former president Saparmurat Niyazov (1990–2006) in his book *Rukhnama*, Islam in Turkmenistan is an unusual blend of Sufi mysticism, Sunni Islam, shamanism, and Zoroastrianism. While Turkmenistan promotes Sufism at the state level like Uzbekistan and Tajikistan, Niyazov went one step farther by publishing numerous writings that convey his own personal, spiritual, and emotional connection to Sufis from the past, and his own participation in the practice of shrine visitation. Nevertheless, Sufi practice today largely consists of shrine visitation, insofar as the mystical tradition of spiritual teachings being transmitted and embedded in a hierarchy of sheikhs is virtually nonexistent in Turkmenistan.[32]

Islam is one of the prime indicators of social self-identification in Turkmenistan (Safronov 2000, 79). Traditionally, even before the Soviet period, teachers of Sufi orders, or ishans, played a more influential role than the ulema (Muslim scholars) in Turkmenistan. Because the independent Turkmen tribes lacked Muslim *kadis* to judge cases in accordance with Islamic law, sharia held influence only in the sphere of family law, and was mainly invoked by mullahs at birth, circumcision, marriage, and funeral ceremonies. Today, knowledge about Islamic law in Turkmenistan is much less than knowledge of tribal customary law (*adat*). While new religious institutions, such as religious schools and mosques, were built after the fall of the Soviet Union with financial support from Saudi Arabia, Kuwait, and Turkey, very few Turkmen attend prayers at the mosques, even though some imams offer instruction in Arabic, Koran, and hadith.[33] Due to the lack of attendance at mosques—which are closely monitored—throughout Turkmenistan, shrines offer a dynamic space within which religious and spiritual discourse can take place in a less monitored environment. Without competing voices of religious authority, due to both strict state control and the legacy of Soviet policies against Islamic education and practice, the state-sanctioned form of "national" Islam in Turkmenistan, which promotes Sufi rituals and practices as national traditions, remains dominant and largely uncontested in the public sphere.

While the Islamic clergy in Turkmenistan are under the control of the state authorities, Turkmenistan does not have a Council of Ulema, as do the other Central Asian Republics. Because knowledge of Islam after independence was weak (Safronov 2000, 84–85), many Turkmen are unfamiliar with basic Islamic principles. Furthermore, unlike in other Central Asian republics, neither the Council on Religious Affairs nor the grand mufti issue fatwas. Currently, the highest ranking religious officials in Turkmenistan are: Charygeldi Seryayev, the chairman of the Council on

Religious Affairs under the president of Turkmenistan, Yalkap Hojagul-yev, grand mufti of Turkmenistan, and Gurbanberdi Nursahatov, deputy chairman of the Council on Religious Affairs. All official religious activity in Turkmenistan is overseen and monitored by the Council on Religious Affairs, which is composed of both Islamic clerics and representatives of the Russian Orthodox Church. The council also runs the Muslim Religious Board, which chooses and supervises all the clerics in the country. Clerics who desire to become official clergy must be selected by the state and educated at an official religious institution.[34] Turkmenistan is unique among its Central Asian counterparts because the mufti does not issue fatwas for public dissemination.

One significant difference between the practice and legislation of religion in Turkmenistan is the foundational text on which post-Soviet Turkmen identity is constructed. The *Rukhnama* presents a "history" for the nation based on the region's medieval past. Niyazov had passages from the *Rukhnama* inscribed alongside passages from the Koran on the walls and minarets of the Turkmenbashi Ruhy Mosque in his hometown of Gypjak. The inscription above the main arch of this mosque reads: "*Rukhnama* is a holy book, the Qur'an is Allah's book." The *Rukhnama* was more omnipresent under Niyazov than it is today. Since coming to power in 2007, President Berdimuhamedov has gradually phased out the *Rukhnama*, and is reported to be writing his own sacred book for the nation.

The situation in Turkmenistan with regard to religion and the clerical establishment has changed somewhat from the time of Niyazov, when all imams had to repeat an oath of loyalty to the "fatherland" and the president after each daily prayer. In fact, in February 2000, an elderly imam, Hoja Ahmed Orazgylych, was arrested for comments he made about Niyazov's religious requirements. Further, Orazgylych's translation of the Koran was attacked by Turkmen authorities, who had all copies of the translation burned before sending him into internal exile and demolishing his home and its adjacent mosque in Ashgabat. Another notable conflict between the muftiate and the secular authorities happened in 2002, when Turkmenistan's chief mufti, Nasrullah ibn Ibadullah, objected to having passages from the *Rukhnama* inscribed alongside passages from the Koran on the outside of the mosque. Mufti Nasrullah ibn Ibadullah was arrested, convicted of plotting to kill the president, and sentenced to jail for twenty-two years. Today, religious clerics are monitored by the state, and essentially do not function on their own without state approval. The lack of an independent clergy in Turkmenistan gives more legitimacy to the power and accessibility of deceased saints at the shrines who are appealed to for healing, hope, intercession, and inspiration.

During the Soviet period, all but four mosques in Turkmenistan were destroyed or turned into museums of atheism. In the absence of these larger religious structures and communal sites of religious authority or instruction, local shrines became the true centers of religious life, and they have remained a prime feature of religious practice, ritual, and identity in Turkmenistan. The veneration of shrines, which are generally tombs connected with Sufi saints, pre-Islamic deities, mythical personages, and tribal ancestors, continues to play a central role in the public performance of religious ritual and pilgrimage in Turkmenistan today. Niyazov (2005) framed his campaign to restore these shrines as a national duty to restore historical justice and to provide current and future generations of Turkmen with the invaluable heritage of their ancestors. Turkmenistan has a rich history of shrine visitation, and the government has gone to great lengths to restore and preserve their architectural and cultural heritage. In addition, foreign archaeologists and conservation preservationists, including myself, have been allowed to help restore Sufi heritage and shrines in places like Merv.

In recent years, many articles have appeared in state-sponsored Turkmen-language newspapers and journals celebrating the country's tradition of pilgrimage, and detailing the histories of specific shrines and the holy people to whom they are dedicated. Nevertheless, it is virtually impossible to purchase any reading materials on Sufism, other than Niyazov's publications (which make frequent reference to various Sufi saints and shrines). In the state media, and in the opinions of many Turkmen, pilgrimage (*zïyarat*) is part of a more expansive tradition and concept known as *hatïra*, which translates as "respect" or "honor," and is used to refer to honoring and paying respect to one's ancestors. Niyazov officially acknowledged zïyarat as a dutiful expression of patriotism and an essential aspect of being Turkmen. Niyazov (2005, 24) was self-consciously aware of his project to use memory and the past for the sake of national pride, noting that "memory of the past is not just a stock of historical knowledge for us: it is a moral pivot, a cornerstone of our patriotism to identify ourselves as a single nation with the feeling of proper pride that is typical of a large family of peoples." Thus, this "sacred" practice or ritual has been promoted and framed as an integral component of Turkmen identity, within the context of ancestor worship.

After independence, Niyazov fostered the Sufi tradition and incorporated it into the regime's larger nation-building project. In his poem

Konya-Urgench, he lauds the "three hundred and sixty saints" of Konya Urgench, and says that Konya Urgench is "like Mecca for the Turkmen." He begins the poem by saying that he himself has "come on a pilgrimage" to Konya Urgench to visit these holy and venerated shrines. Thus, he proudly proclaims his own position as "pilgrim" to the "saints." Further, in *Konya-Urgench* (2006), Niyazov pays homage to the "dervishes and explorers, who traveled around the world, opened the way to friendship and fraternity, by broadening societies' horizon of thought," in bringing Islam to Turkmenistan. In the *Rukhnama*, he lauds the many saints from Central Asia, and equates their healing breath with the fertile land of Turkmenistan, writing: "Like the breath of Gorkut Ata, Hoja Ahmet Yasawi, Bahauddin Naqshbandi, Najmedin Kubra, Salar Baba, and Mane Baba, this fertile and flowerful land is a remedy for thousands of ailments and problems" (Niyazov 2005, 78–79). Sufis are celebrated and commemorated for extending the reach of Islam in Central Asia, and their monuments are embraced as signs of a "national" architecture, even though they predate the nation by several hundred centuries.

Niyazov considered the shrine of Nejmeddin Kubra (1145–1221), which he called "a second Mecca for Muslims" (2005, 26), to be a source of patriotism for the nation because of Kubra's death at the hands of Mongol invaders in 1221 (when he died with 360 of his followers). About his tomb, as well as the adjoining tombs of Sultan Ali, Piryar Veli, and Jamilijan, the favorite disciple of Nejmeddin Kubra, Niyazov (2005, 94–95) writes, "today, many centuries later, these four shrines represent a stable symbol of courage, inflexible will, unity and love for motherland of the revived Turkmen people, now passing through flight of spiritual revival and [our] cultural prime." Thus, these saints are framed not only as ancestors of the nation but also as proud patriots whose courage and love paved the way for the "motherland" to realize its spiritual and cultural potential. When I visited the shrine of Nejmeddin Kubra in Konya-Urgench, dozens of pilgrims of all ages were visiting the shrine for blessings related to school, marriage, and fertility. Regardless of how these medieval saints are reconfigured to fit the national project, these shrines continue to serve as important centers of hope and healing for those who visit them.

As in other parts of Central Asia, many "holy figures" in Turkmenistan are connected to local rock features and other sacred landscapes. Some saints or mythical ancestor spirits are believed to have split particular rocks, turned melons into stone, or disappeared into the centers of caves. For instance, when I visited the shrine of Parau Bibi, I was told by local pilgrims that the beautiful girl after whom the shrine was named had been swallowed up by the mountain after she refused to be handed over to the town's enemies. Within the sacred topography of Turkmenistan, pilgrims enact folk traditions informed by shamanistic rituals in their pilgrimages to both Sufi shrines and sacred landscapes (Safronov 2000, 74). Like many other Muslims in Central Asia, Turkmen often tie rags and small object to branches of trees and bushes at shrines and holy sites. These strips, called *alem*, *mata*, or *bolegi*, signify a wish or appeal made to a particular saint or ancestor.

Pilgrims may visit a shrine to make a wish for the future or to give thanks for a wish that was fulfilled in the past by the saint, such as the conception of a child (Privratsky 2001, 160). At the shrine of Qyz Bibi, I found the trunk and branches of a giant tree completely covered in pieces of fabric in hopes that the dreams left behind might come true. At the shrine of Najmeddin Kubra in Konya-Urgench, I witnessed several teenage pilgrims balancing "sacred" stones on their fingers to see if they would magically spin. When I was working on restoring the shrine of Ibn Zayd at Merv, I noticed that a number of pacifiers and tiny cloth cribs had been affixed to a "sacred" dead tree near the shrine by those hoping to conceive. At the "horn cemetery" in Nokhur, on the border with Iran, I was able to photograph roughly one hundred gravestones topped with horns—a legacy of the region's shamanistic past—and inscribed in Arabic, Russian, and Turkmen. Horns similarly adorn the entrance of Parau Bibi's shrine. Because Turkmenbashi deemed the region's Zoroastrian history and shamanic past as prime ingredients of Islamic identity and practice in the present, these visible symbols of the region's pre-Islamic past are encouraged and preserved, whereas in other parts of the Muslim world they would be deemed "heretical" and thus be destroyed.

Pilgrimage in the post-Soviet period in Turkmenistan is encouraged to embrace local communal practices, celebrate the region's cultural heritage, and perform Islamic devotion. Pilgrimages were subversive under the Soviets (Bennigsen and Wimbush 1986; Subtelny 1989), and while some Muslims still made visits to local shrines, many instead honored "holy" people by praying to and for them in private, as "public" Islam was the target of the antireligious policies (Privratsky 2001, 188). Today, Turkmen hold special meals at shrines, given in the memory of the saint, and recite the Koran for saints and ancestor spirits (Privratsky 2001, 18). These sites serve as spaces in which vulnerability—from physical illness, mental illness, disability, and fertility (Tyson 1997, 28)—is expressed and healing is sought. These personal wishes to both ancestors and Sufi saints weave together the tangible and intangible worlds of the community. These Sufi shrines are places of transaction where local customs are passed down, Koran is learned, wishes are made, and communal identity is enacted and reinforced. Thus, these sacred spaces mediate the physical and spiritual worlds, and pilgrims visit them to attend to and heal the spiritual self, as well as the mind and body.

While governmental authorities in Turkmenistan extol the historical and cultural significance of Sufi shrines and saints in the media and literature, Turkmenistan has not been as eager as Uzbekistan to co-opt shrines and present itself as the chief sponsor of traditions associated with the shrines. These holy sites continue to provide those who visit them with a sacred place in which to practice their devotion, to appeal for help (especially with regard to infertility and medical problems), to receive a spiritual blessing from the saint, and to express both their religious and national identities. These shrine complexes—some large enough to accommodate several hundred pilgrims at once—simultaneously satisfy the spiritual and cultural needs of pilgrims and serve as local displays of national and cultural pride. Niyazov (2005, 76) notes in the *Rukhnama* that the vault of Qyz Bibi in Merv, the mausoleum of Mohammed bin Zeyd, and the mosque of Hodja Yusuf Hamadani all "embrace the national signs of Turkmen architecture." Since Turkmenistan's independence, Niyazov was explicit about reclaiming the Sufi heritage found within Turkmenistan's borders, and these shrines continue today to be popular places of devotion.

In addition to promoting Sufism in the *Rukhnama* and other literature, Niyazov arranged for the reconstruction of the mosque and mausoleum complexes, such as that of the twelfth-century Sufi scholar, Hodja Yosef Hamadani, one of the most important shrines in Turkmenistan (which remained open during the Soviet period). He called for these unique monuments, connected intimately with the history of the nation, to be valued and preserved, unlike in the Soviet period when they were "undeservedly forgotten and did not receive proper attention" (Niyazov 2005, 95). Today, the shrine of Hamadani in Merv is so popular that I noticed grease from the hands of pilgrims who touched the shrine while circumambulating it has created a stain around the middle of the shrine. The local practices of Turkmen pilgrims change the landscape and shrines themselves with the traces of their presence they leave behind. Another problem I encountered while working to preserve Sufi shrines in Merv was that pilgrims who erected "praying" stones next to the shrine had taken the stones out of the shrine itself to enact this practice (a shamanistic-inspired local tradition).

Thus, a number of stones from the Sufi shrines in Merv, such as at the shrine of Ibn Zayd, where busloads of visitors from the local sanatorium travel for healing, have been removed in the service of "enacting" these local practices. While local practices help build communal identity, they can also lead to the destruction of cultural heritage at the same time.

It would be a mistake to assume that these sites are praised only as sites of exploitation for the national project, for Turkmenbashi also appealed to the spiritual nature of these sites in his defense and restoration of them. With regard to Kubra's tomb, he said, "let this sacred monument serve forever our people as a stronghold of spirituality and a symbol of unfading memory of ancestors' greatness" (Niyazov 2005, 96). While Turkmenbashi's writing is often ridiculed for being the bizarre musings of a megalomaniac dictator, these reductive analyses often overlook the spiritual dimension and justification of his national project. In the *Rukhnama*, he writes: "spirituality is the life's origin formula" for "all the ways begin with spirituality—if we want to have united nations we must unite them spiritually." Further, he stated that his task was "not only to preserve these monuments, but to reconstruct special atmosphere of high spirituality which bore these architectural masterpieces" (Niyazov 2005, 95). Thus, Turkmenbashi went beyond just lauding these shrines for their national or patriotic importance, by invoking the spiritual philosophy and environment that helped to give rise to the holy people venerated at these shrines.

Following in the footsteps of former president Niyazov, current president Berdimuhamedov publicly encourages pilgrimage to the country's shrines, and the government even provides free accommodation for pilgrims in some circumstances. The government sent a sponsored group of Turkmen pilgrims to visit the shrine of Sufi leader and poet-philosopher Magtymguly Pyragy (1733–97) and his father Azadi in the village of Aktokay in Iran's Golestan province, which borders Turkmenistan. In 2009, citing fears concerning the spread of swine flu that were echoed by the religious boards of other Central Asian republics, Turkmenistan barred Muslim pilgrims from going on hajj to Mecca, and instead encouraged them to visit thirty-eight sacred sites across Turkmenistan, even though most of the sites had historical or cultural, rather than religious, significance. In fact, the government often forbids many of its citizens to go on pilgrimage to Mecca, but organizes (in its place) a tour of all the shrines in the country as an alternative. Thus, shrine pilgrimage in Turkmenistan has essentially been privileged by the state as equal (or even superior to) the pilgrimage required by every Muslim to Mecca before he or she dies.

In Turkmenistan, notable women of the past are remembered in sacred spaces, regardless of whether or not they are buried there, and shrines also serve as a prime space to confront issues of the body, specifically conception and pregnancy. At the Turabeg Khanum Mausoleum in Konya Urgench, which is named after the wife of the Golden Horde ruler of Khorezm, Qutlugh Timur (ruled 1321–33), women crawl down into the central crypt to tie pieces of fabric to two wooden boards and make a wish. Even though there is no evidence that Turabeg Khanum was ever buried in this structure, which was restored between 1983 and 1993 (and work was done on its inner dome between 1999 and 2000), this shrine is engendered as a "female" space, and the crypt is a central place where women gather to make a wish—usually for a child. At Kyrk Molla, a semicircular hill located at the same site as the Turabeg Khanum Mausoleum, women roll down the hill in hopes that this ritual will get them pregnant. While this ritual derives from the region's pre-Islamic past, there are no prohibitions about women using their own bodies at the shrine—either by rolling down hills or stepping through bowing branches of sacred trees—to help their bodies generate new life. Thus, these sites of "death" are also framed as generative spaces, which can aid in conception.

The inclusion of shaman-inspired healing is not limited to the Sufi shrines: female healers assert their spiritual authority and knowledge by using local healing modalities to treat patients. When I visited a local female healer in Merv, I encountered a line of women waiting to be healed on my way out the door. Many of the women had brought with them sick children to be healed. The healer combined Koranic recitation with pre-Islamic healing practices, such as spitting, divining from touch, massage, and cupping. The synthesis of local practices and Sufism is not limited only to shrine visitation, and female traditional healers are believed to be endowed with special spiritual powers that allow them to move between the physical and spiritual worlds.

State support for Sufism and local practices in Turkmenistan differs from the promotion of Sufism in the other Central Asian Republics in several respects. First, Turkmenistan is unique because the supreme mufti does not issue fatwas. Second, after the fall of the Soviet Union, Niyazov articulated and disseminated the "national" Islam of Turkmenistan through his *Rukhnama* to provide "spiritual guidance to the nation" by weaving together his own autobiography, a revisionist history of his country, praise of Sufi saints, and the poetry of Sufis like Magtymguly Pyragy. More than any other leader in Central Asia, Niyazov celebrated his country's pre-Islamic past, and framed traditions derived from Zoroastrianism and shamanism as integral to the practice of Islam.

The Future of Sufism in Central Asia

Post-Soviet religious laws and fatwas in Central Asia aimed at asserting the supremacy of Hanafi jurisprudence and Sufism over Hanbali and Shafi'i jurisprudence are products of an ongoing heated theological debate between different *madhhab* (schools of Islamic jurisprudence) that began during the early Soviet period. The shift in state policy toward Hanafi jurisprudence and Sufism after independence in Central Asia was motivated by political, cultural, national, and religious considerations. During perestroika, in the wake of the Soviet incursion into Afghanistan and the revolution in Iran, an alliance developed between Sufi and Soviet authorities in the Caucasus against the threat of Salafi veterans of foreign and domestic conflicts instigating an armed struggle against Soviet rule and the "unorthodox" practices, practitioners, and spaces of Sufism. After the fall of the Soviet Union, this strategic shift in alliance was diffused throughout Central Asia, and newly minted religious boards, founded on the same hierarchical structure of SADUM, redefined "orthodoxy" in favor of Hanafi jurisprudence and Sufism to promote "nationalized" forms of Islam "purified" of foreign influence. Since independence, the state promotion of Sufism and "national" traditions has sought to "restore historical justice" and disempower schools of jurisprudential thinking that are seen as incompatible with state security, national identity, cultural memory, and heritage preservation.

Seeking to reverse tsarist and Soviet policies that criminalized Sufism and local traditions, while simultaneously disarming the secularly defined religious realm from becoming fertile ground for politicization, governments throughout Central Asia since independence have strived to promote shrine visitation, and to disseminate Sufi history and philosophy in literature, the media, and education. While this shift in state policy and theology illustrates how post-Soviet authorities are reproducing and shaping Islamic jurisprudence, nationalism, and cultural identity from above, the fact that many Muslims in Central Asia do not even hear about the fatwas being issued or outright ignore them suggests that Islamic practice in Central Asia is not easily penetrated or shaped by state structures. Similarly, in the Soviet period, fatwas against shrine visitation did not end this popular practice. The jurisprudential authority of religious authorities in Central Asia is not fashioned by the state to be coercive, as these fatwas are not strictly enforced. While the proliferation of "unofficial" religious authorities in the landscape of Central Asia and the shrinking realm of the authority of "official" authorities is by no means a new phenomenon, new forms of communication in the post-Soviet period, such as the Internet, are allowing more opportunities for local religious actors and globalized authority figures who claim the right to speak about Islamic law in authoritative ways to get their voices heard and disseminated in Central Asia.

Though Sufism is supported at the state level in post-Soviet Central Asia, the relationship between the state and Sufism is by no means homogeneous or uniform. Uzbekistan is unique for putting considerable effort into marketing Sufi shrines and history for local, tourist, and foreign-policy consumption. The encouragement of women spiritual authorities and healers to practice in public in Uzbekistan stands in contrast to Tajikistan, where women are feared to be prime suspects of indoctrinating children into "radicalism," and in Turkmenistan, where all acceptable religious authority must lie with state authorities, and the dead Sufi saints of the past. Tajikistan is unique for the number of Sufi sheikhs who continue to transmit Sufi knowledge as a "living" tradition one-on-one from their homes throughout the country. In Turkmenistan, Niyazov's writings are unique for emphasizing the national "duty" to "restore historical justice" and "give the invaluable heritage" of ancestors to the present and future generations of Turkmen; further, his proud positioning of himself as "pilgrim" to shrines renovated by his government gives the strongest endorsement of any leader to the national "duty" of visiting the great Sufi masters of the past. Thus, while governments across Central Asia promote Hanafi jurisprudence and Sufism, the cultural dimensions, local enactments, and governmental supervision of Sufism and local traditions take different forms.

What remains to be seen is whether Central Asia's two decades of promoting Sufism and Hanafi jurisprudence at the state level will continue to prevent Sufi heritage from coming under attack in Central Asia, and whether the threat of such a backlash from the security vacuum in Afghanistan will provoke these governments to encourage a more open and public version of Sufism to emerge. Maintaining security and preserving the region's cultural heritage may depend on political and religious liberalization, if the tsarist and Soviet trend of alienated religious groups taking up arms to oppose the state control of Islam in Central Asia is not to be repeated.

CHAPTER SIX

Unregistered

Gray Spaces in the Soviet Regulation of Islam

Eren Murat Tasar

In 1988, at the eclipse of Soviet power, a bureaucrat in the government's Council for Religious Affairs (CRA) cautioned Kyrgyzstan's Council of Ministers that "the vestiges of patriarchal-tribal traditions have not been erased among the population, in large part thanks to the unregistered functionaries of the Muslim cult."[1] This lament echoed long-standing unease within the Party-state about the legal status of the many unregistered, or illegal, Islamic religious figures, whose ranks far outnumbered those of the officially recognized Central Asian muftiate (commonly known by the Russian acronym SADUM).[2] It also evinces the widespread resignation among religious policymakers that seventy-five years of atheistic cultivation had effected too little change in the lives of many Soviet Muslims, due to the state's inability to neutralize the machinations of religious figures lacking legal registration.

As a source of consternation and worry for the leadership, one might have expected the issue of the unregistered to elicit a comprehensive political, legal, and administrative response. Yet at no point in Soviet history did this take place. Instead, the unregistered constituted a permanently unresolved gray space in the state's regulation of Islam. This remained the case even during heightened periods of high-level xenophobia concerning the Muslim population's political reliability, such as Khrushchev's antireligious campaign (1959–64) and the early years of the Soviet occupation of Afghanistan. Why did the senior leadership never develop a consistent strategy for dealing with the unregistered? As this chapter will demonstrate, the absence of any provision in Stalin's religious reforms of 1943–44 for enforcing the registration requirement on Muslim "clergy" was to blame. The reforms clearly specified the requirements for registration, without offering any guidance on how to deter, let alone punish, violators. This omission, which speaks to the wartime Stalinist state's hesitation regarding the use of repression in law enforcement, became the subject of fierce official debate for the remaining five decades of the country's history.

Though at first glance a matter of legal wording and administrative regulation, the Party-state's posture toward the unregistered reflected profound official disagreement concerning the direction society should take after the Second World War. Because postwar officialdom repudiated the antireligious violence of the late 1920s and 1930s (as well as mass repression more generally), attention turned to alternative strategies that might best deter unregistered figures from providing religious "services" to the population. At stake was fundamental unease concerning the relationship between Bolshevik ideology and the sanctity of Soviet law. Religious policymakers, all of them Communists, had to juggle two conflicting obligations: the Bolshevik requirement to struggle with religion, and the Soviet requirement to promote rule of law and Socialist legality, including the right to freedom of conscience guaranteed by the 1936 Stalin Constitution. Consequently, a rift emerged in official circles concerning how much coercion the state might employ to enforce the registration requirement on Muslim figures.

This rift became especially pronounced in Soviet Central Asia for two reasons. First, because the region had the largest concentration of Muslims in the Soviet Union, the sheer scope of unregistered activity rendered any attempt to assert total control over Islam problematic. Second, unlike other Muslim areas of the former Russian Empire, Central Asia did not have its own Muslim Spiritual Assembly (or muftiate) until 1943. Both social realities and historical precedent thus militated against effective regulation in the religious sphere. Bureaucrats in religious policymaking circles directly confronted the challenge of fulfilling the demands of Bolshevik ideology and Soviet legislation on the ground. Through an analysis of Soviet policies toward the unregistered in Central Asia over five decades, this chapter argues that the postwar Party-state's indecision in fact signaled tacit acceptance that no solution existed. Official policies envisioned but one modest goal: to retard the growth of unregistered Muslim life.

The Unregistered and "Gray Spaces"

This may seem an unusual attitude for an avowedly atheist state to adopt, but Soviet policies toward the unregistered bear close comparison to other, much better known "gray spaces" in the Party-state's policy implementation. By gray spaces I mean the many gaps distancing the Soviet state's pretensions to total control over high-profile policy areas from its limited capacity to enforce such control on the ground. Perhaps the most famous, and ubiquitous, of these gray spaces was the underground economy, which even in the most repressive periods constituted an important part of everyday life, and perhaps played a crucial role in the regime's very survival.[3] State policies toward alcohol, another prominent gray space, mirror treatment of the unregistered most closely of all: the more "revolutionary" periods of Soviet history, such as the late 1920s and the early Gorbachev years, witnessed centralized campaigns against both alcohol and religion (White 1996, 25), while the "statist" Party-state under Brezhnev established commissions within local government to police both policy areas (Tarschys 1993, 18).

Gray areas varied dramatically in character, but all posed a single dilemma for law enforcement officials: only by restoring those punitive functions exercised by the state during the Great Terror could they create a climate of sufficient fear to deter "practitioners" in meaningful numbers. The postwar state's unwillingness to use such tactics confined the struggle with the black market, alcoholism, the alcohol trade, polygyny, the veil, unregistered religious practitioners, and many other gray areas to the realm of propaganda and disciplinary action against individual violators.

The scholarly literature on religion in the Soviet Union has generally assigned the Soviet state a higher degree of efficiency in dealing with the unregistered than it could legitimately claim, while the social history literature has largely eschewed discussion of religion. For this reason the unregistered issue has, to date, not been discussed in terms of gray spaces such as the black market. Yet the unregistered offer an excellent example of an ideologically unacceptable phenomenon that the state had no choice but to tolerate in some measure. This was a necessary consequence of its own policies toward religion. In bureaucratic parlance, the "unregistered" technically referred to all religious figures lacking registration from the state. The term could be applied to a diverse array of characters, ranging from female Islamic scholars and community leaders (varyingly called *tin* and *abysta*) to shamans and sorcerers. In practice, however, the term most often referred to prayer leaders (imams), readers of the call to prayer (*muazzin, sufi, sopu*), and, most especially, religious figures who lacked permanent status in a stationary mosque. These mullahs (often termed "wandering" mullahs) conducted ceremonies for a fee, including prayer readings at major life-cycle milestones (name-giving ceremonies, circumcision) and recitation of the Koran during Ramadan (*xatm-qur'an*). It goes without saying that the unregistered can be treated as a cohesive category only from the Soviet state's perspective.

The Party-state's unregistered problem was largely a Muslim one because of the preponderance of itinerant figures and because prayers could be performed just about anywhere. Russian Orthodox Christianity, whose adherents vastly outnumbered Muslims in the Soviet Union, also had unregistered figures and sites, but these revolved almost entirely around stationary holy sites such as shrines, or at least were understood that way in official parlance, and therefore lent themselves to restriction more facilely.[4] Followers of smaller Protestant groups such as the Jehovah's Witnesses arguably resembled Islam in the ease with which they circumvented Soviet restrictions. Because the state banned their activities entirely, however, it viewed such groups as a political, rather than legal or administrative, obstacle (Baran 2014). No religion other than Islam posed a challenge of comparable scope.

As their designation suggests, the unregistered violated the spirit, if not the letter, of Soviet religious legislation because they lacked the registration documents provided by the state to SADUM employees alone. Stalin's religious reforms of 1943–44 entailed the establishment of four officially sanctioned Islamic organizations (here referred to as muftiates) and a government bureaucracy, the Council for the Affairs of Religious Cults (CARC), to supervise their affairs. Both CARC's founding charter and three laws proclaimed by the Soviet government in the period 1944–46 clarified the procedures for registering legal mosques and staff under SADUM's control (Ro'i 2000, 20–22). Remarkably, however, no law explicitly forbade the existence of unregistered religious societies.[5] Religious policymakers were therefore left to interpret the senior leadership's posture toward the unregistered by making inferences from Party decrees.[6] Herein rested the basic ambiguity. In the absence of any central or historical guidance, the question of what to do about the unregistered remained perpetually open to ideologically informed debate depending on the political climate of a given year and the individual bureaucrat's orientation. Until the Brezhnevian Party-state effected a widespread systematization of religious policy in the 1970s, this ambiguity also gave local government significant leverage in restricting, or ignoring, religious groups. Thus, the unregistered constituted a substantial gray space in Soviet religious policy, insofar as the vast majority of Muslim life took place beyond the handful of legal mosques.

This inability to concertedly assault practices that the Party had always regarded with extreme unease illustrates the difficulty of balancing ideological considerations with a commitment to the rule of law. The choice between broad-based regulation and a campaign-style shock attack against a given social evil always generated vociferous debate in official circles. Only the country's senior leadership could resolve these internal bureaucratic conflicts, by signaling its preference for one line or the other. The following sections demonstrate that Soviet treatment of the unregistered progressed in precisely this fashion through three distinct stages. From the 1943–44 religious reforms until 1958, bureaucrats favoring a posture of moderation and leniency toward illegal Muslim life in the name of the rule of law held the upper hand in religious policymaking circles. With the onset of Khrushchev's antireligious campaign of 1959–64, their opponents advocating a harder line emerged victorious. Finally, in the 1970s, the Party-state combined both approaches into a restrictive, but consistent, pattern of regulation, largely involving the assessment of fines on a relatively small number of individuals. This outcome signified tacit acceptance that the unregistered were a permanent feature of Muslim life.

The Moderate Line: Ignoring the Unregistered, 1943-1958

The years following Stalin's religious reforms witnessed the rise of a constituency within the Party-state calling for moderation toward religion, including the unregistered. These bureaucrats, based primarily within CARC, argued that strict adherence to Soviet laws respecting freedom of conscience would, with time, convince God-fearing Soviet citizens of the moral superiority of communism. As more people abandoned religion and turned to atheism, they believed, popular demand for functions performed by unregistered religious figures would also decline. Rather than extralegal coercion, fines, and imprisonment, the best weapon in the antireligious struggle was effective propaganda concerning the parasitic role of religion in society. The predominance of this line led to an explosion in unregistered activity throughout Central Asia during the 1940s and 1950s.

Such an unlikely posture toward religion from within the Party resulted from two aspects of political life in the postwar Soviet Union, and indeed would have been unthinkable at any other point until the late

1980s. First, though perfectly willing to target specific groups in extralegal fashion, the postwar state remained wary of mass repression as a tool for advancing policy objectives; late Stalinist officialdom did not undertake any campaigns against large segments of the population in the fashion of the Cultural Revolution or Great Terror. Second, by all accounts, the dictator exhibited little or no interest in religion after approving his 1943–44 reforms. In this situation, lower-level bureaucrats determined the course of religious policy during Stalin's final years of life, while the period from 1953 to 1958 saw confused debate within the senior echelons concerning what his legacy actually meant for religion in the Soviet Union. Only in late 1958 did Khrushchev successfully characterize this late and post-Stalinist indifference toward religion as a criminal betrayal of Bolshevism.

A moderate line toward the unregistered crystallized within CARC gradually from the mid-1940s to the early 1950s in response to conditions on the ground. When the council appointed its first representatives to the Central Asian republics in 1945–46, they encountered nearly unresolvable policy challenges: tens of thousands of Central Asian men were returning from the Nazi front to a region that had witnessed virtually no regulation of religion since the late 1930s. In these conditions, the silence of Stalin's religious reforms concerning enforcement of the registration requirement left CARC bureaucrats in a quandary.

All concerned recognized the need for some kind of solution. The council's representative in Kyrgyzstan, Hakim Akhtiamov, expressed bewilderment at the state of religious affairs in his first report to Moscow, noting that "all of our districts, major settlements and often even small villages feature individuals whom the people call 'mullas' but whose primary activities impact society as a whole, i.e., collective farmers, artisans and workers. . . . To prohibit this is inexpedient and impossible."[7] Akhtiamov recognized that only by injecting a major official presence into the everyday affairs of mosques could the state assert dominance in Muslim life. Within a year he had forwarded a list of one hundred illegally operating Friday mosques in southern Kyrgyzstan's urban centers to his superiors in the capital, yet received no response as to how he should proceed.[8] His suggestion to register these mosques as a means of lending religious policy some semblance of order similarly elicited only silence.[9] At stake was a growing and seemingly unresolvable gap between the scope of organized religious activity (in the form of illegal mosques and mullahs performing ceremonies in communities) and the limited number of houses of worship and personnel the state was willing to register.[10]

Moscow's silence on these issues stemmed not from indifference, but rather from confusion. Chaired by a former KGB colonel, CARC's headquarters in the capital held responsibility for formulating, and securing senior approval of, all aspects of religious policymaking, including the critical question of how to deal with unregistered prayer houses and religious figures.[11] CARC transmitted no clear guidance to its republican representatives concerning the unregistered because the Soviet Union Council of Ministers itself offered no such guidance. The second half of the 1940s therefore represents a period of experimentation during which religious policymakers felt remarkably unconstrained in proposing solutions for regulating and restricting the unregistered.

On the ground, the default solution became taxation. CARC bureaucrats reasoned that if they lacked official backing to imprison or otherwise punish unregistered religious figures, they could deter unregistered activity by assessing the legally mandated tax for priests. Unfortunately, religious policymakers lacked the authority to directly tax anybody. They therefore had to compile lists of names and addresses of unregistered figures in a given locale, forward them to the local provincial tax department (OblFin), and hope that inspectors would follow through by visiting the home of each unregistered figure. The available documentation suggests that in most cases, tax officials ignored these lists.[12] Even in instances where the financial authorities proved responsive to data about unregistered figures, it was unclear how much tax the figures should pay: a slew of relevant decrees issued by various government departments in the mid-1940s created a critical ambiguity.[13] Bureaucrats such as Akhtiamov argued that unregistered Muslim figures should pay the tax of 130–150 rubles assessed on priests in the Russian Orthodox Church. They reasoned that this amount, which a priest in the church hierarchy might presumably cover with assistance from parish members and the Church itself, would prove overwhelmingly burdensome and punitive to the typical unregistered imam or mullah; in general, these figures worked as collective farmers and did not derive the majority of their income from providing religious "services." Unfortunately for CARC, the laws also opened a loophole that allowed certain religious figures to qualify as "rural" clergy; this entitled the taxpayer to expend the low rate of twenty rubles assessed on most artisans and craftsmen.[14] Worse still, not a single one of these laws made any distinction between registered and unregistered.[15] From the bureaucrats' perspective, the clearest indication of this policy's failure was that unregistered figures who paid these taxes openly stated that the tax receipts legitimized and legalized their activity.[16]

Time and time again, the bureaucrats found their efforts to impose some sort of control over the unregistered thwarted. With the country's senior leadership largely uninterested in religion, political will did not exist to enforce the registration requirement through any function exercised by the state, such as imprisonment, taxation, or even widespread intimidation. What little antireligious activism did occur during the 1940s resulted solely from the zeal of individual local government officials. In these conditions, by the end of the 1940s an argument began to emerge within CARC (and CA-ROC) that the best way to handle the unregistered problem was to ignore it.

An attitude of laissez faire toward the unregistered appeared clearly within the council's Central Asian ranks by the early 1950s, well before the now famous CPSU Central Committee Decree of November 1954 castigating Party members who "place any Soviet citizen under political suspicion [simply] because of his religious beliefs."[17] This emerged, for example, in the case of an ethnically Turkish *eshon* in southern Kyrgyzstan, who promised to stop "spreading the *eshon* worldview" after the council's provincial representative cornered him at home.[18] In short order he received a reprimand from Akhtiamov, who noted that although the eshon "cannot engage in spiritual activity as a cult functionary without official registration," the deputy had behaved "erroneously" by showing up at his front door. "With such methods you can only compromise yourself before the clergy and believers, as a result of which you will no longer have the ability to study the religiosity of the population."[19] When the same deputy reported the existence of an illegal mosque that had held prayers without disruption since 1924, neither he nor Akhtiamov took any action.[20] In Jeti-Oguz district, Issyk-Kul province, CARC's representative Madylov engaged an eighty-five-year-old religious figure named Toktobayev in conversation, suggesting that as an "unregistered mulla" he violated the law. Toktobayev brazenly replied that "he is a mulla, he does not hide it and never has, and pays an annual tax of one hundred fifty rubles and [therefore] will not abandon his spiritual activities." Neither the representative, nor the bureaucrats in Frunze and Moscow receiving his report, took any subsequent action.[21] This also applied to the case of Soken Tagayev, a widely revered unregistered religious figure in the province.[22] When another "wandering mullah" in Issyk-Kul begged the functionary to grant him registration, promising "to give all the donations coming from believers to the state," Madylov merely replied that the government had no need for the believers' money.[23]

CARC's apparatus in Tajikistan and Uzbekistan applied the same approach. The Uzbekistan representative "specifically told his oblast' *up-*

olnomochennye [provincial representatives] that those groups which did not apply to register might continue functioning." All correspondence concerning the gathering of intelligence about unregistered figures "was to be accompanied by cautions against administrative measures, particularly closure" of mosques (Ro'i 2000, 306–7). By mid-decade this attitude had become the rule in Tajikistan. The representatives took no action upon learning of the popularity of a shaman, Romulo Salomad, and a sorcerer, Muhammad Ominxon, in Shahrinov district.[24] This was likewise the case with Akrom to'ra eshon, a shaman specializing in women's infertility who roamed the Kyrgyz settlements spanning the mountainous border of Kyrgyzstan and Tajikistan's Badakhshon province.[25] CARC's deputy in Badakhshon lamented to a registered *khalifa* that "unregistered khalifas have started injecting energy into such practices" as *dakhvati fano* (an Ismaili funeral rite) but also stated that "those rituals that are necessary for the believers must be performed."[26] In fact, he had a list of the names of 174 Ismaili unregistered khalifas.[27] As in countless other instances in CARC's annals from the three republics—especially in reports on shrines—the bureaucrats exhibited an almost academic interest in uncovering information about unregistered figures without taking any subsequent action. This points to general acceptance that any major steps toward curtailing unregistered religious life would prove neither feasible nor even desirable.

By 1958, Akhtiamov exhibited no hesitation in providing ideological justification for the council's inaction toward the unregistered throughout the prior decade. At a forum in Moscow, he stated that "administrative intervention should not be permitted in reference to unregistered religious life [*v otnoshenii nezaregistrirovannoi tserkvi*], since such interference can engender nothing but harm."[28] As Akhtiamov explained to one of his deputies, this reasoning rested on the constitutional principle of freedom of conscience guaranteed to all Soviet citizens. "In the context of freedom of conscience," he elaborated, "we cannot limit [unregistered] activity since, in many cases, religions require congregational observance of the cult."[29] When given a choice between carrying out the antireligious struggle and respecting the rule of law, Akhtiamov argued that the latter must take precedence. This argument represented formal elaboration of a policy that, in 1958, the council had been implementing for the better part of a decade.

Though CARC adopted a hands-off approach and pushed local government to do the same, it bears emphasizing that the public proscription on religion remained intact, above all for Party members. The moderate climate of the 1950s did not temporarily transform Soviet Central Asia into a liberal democracy: Central Asian Muslims aspiring to any kind of career needed to observe religious practices with discretion.[30] Such a climate most certainly did, however, offer breathing room to a society that had experienced the Great Terror less than two decades earlier. That one could, with relative ease and little fear of retaliation, call on an unregistered mullah, abysta, or otin to perform life-cycle ceremonies, testifies to the unprecedented official flexibility toward Islam in this era.

The council's moderate line thus resolved the problem of the unregistered by ignoring it on the ground and formally questioning the need for registration in the first place. In other words, religious policymakers all but signaled that no solution existed. Given the Party's history of combating religion, however, such a position could not remain tenable for long.

The Hard Line: Campaigning against the Unregistered, 1959-1964

CARC successfully advanced this line for much of the 1950s because political will to tackle religion did not exist in the country. Yet by the mid-1950s such zeal was gathering tangible traction among antireligious hard-liners. They watched in dismay as the politics of moderation brought official restrictions on religion to their lowest levels since the 1920s. Stalin's successor as Party leader, Nikita Khrushchev (1894–1971), successfully capitalized on their frustration to solidify his own legitimacy by launching a new antireligious campaign, which largely consisted in an attack on the unregistered. This strategy formed part of Khrushchev's broader characterization of Stalin as a traitor to the Bolshevik struggle. He pointed to the council's policies of the 1940s and 1950s as evidence of late and post-Stalinist lethargy in the ideological fight to build communism.

Khrushchev despised religion. "In God's name, they hide their individual criminal antisocial misdeeds," he thundered at the clergy, calling on the Party to "expose their actions and show people the sole path to moral and spiritual liberation."[31] But he refused to resort to the methods employed by Stalin during the Great Terror. Where Stalin had glorified an all-powerful state as a vehicle for cleansing society of obstacles to communism, Khrushchev sought to restore what he viewed as the early Bolsheviks' success in arousing the masses against injustice.[32] Where the late dictator had encouraged systematic roundups of religious figures regardless of registration status, Khrushchev was content to make the clergy uncomfortable by letting local government decide where, when, and who to strike. Social change could entail some violence, but needed to come from the bottom up.

Notwithstanding his energetic antireligious rhetoric, Khrushchev's options were limited. A return to Stalinist mass repression remained beyond question. The state could (and did) dramatically restrict the legal religious organizations' finances and activities, yet never questioned their central role in postwar religious policy, let alone their existence.[33] Moreover, Khrushchev relied on the four muftiates, most especially SADUM, as instruments of Soviet public diplomacy to the Muslim world. Over the course of the 1960s the muftiate established ties with organizations in over fifty countries.[34] By default, then, the unregistered became the largest and most expedient target of the new antireligious campaign.

Like their moderate predecessors, however, hard-line religious policymakers under Khrushchev found no solution to the unregistered issue. Unwilling to arrest or even fine religious figures on a massive scale, while largely lacking the capacity to ensure consistent local implementation of antireligious policies, they, too, tacitly accepted that illegal religious life would remain a permanent feature of the Soviet landscape. Instead of trying to eliminate particular elements of religious life that had thrived during the 1950s, the campaign sought to make an example out of a handful of religious figures and practices. Policymakers hoped that strategic, highly symbolic punitive action would resonate among the faithful, most especially within the ranks of unregistered religious figures.

A good illustration is the campaign-era crackdown on the holy mountain known as the Throne of Solomon.[35] The most popular holy site in the five republics in the 1940s and 1950s, the mountain attracted as many as 100,000 pilgrims on 'Eid ul-Adha in 1954 and 1955.[36] Situated at the center of the southern Kyrgyz city of Osh, the mountain's thousands of pilgrims were assisted in their devotions by dozens of dynastic shrine keepers, known as sheikhs, who lived in homes directly adjacent to the site.[37] These sheikhs performed rites on the mountain and in their homes. They lacked registration and bore no connection to SADUM. Official efforts to shut these figures out of Central Asia's most popular holy site offer critical insight into the methodology and underlying assumptions of the campaign-era assault on the unregistered.

Local authorities appeared committed to seeing the crackdown through. In Osh and throughout Central Asia, a flurry of heightened antireligious rhetoric and promises of administrative action followed issuance of a CPSU Central Committee decree, "On Measures to Stop Pilgrimages to So-called 'Holy Places,'" dated November 28, 1958.[38] On April 10, 1959, the Osh city government announced a number of administrative measures "on the basis of numerous demands made at community gatherings." These included transforming the summit into a touristic panorama site complete with a statue of Lenin, and requesting that the police block access to the dynastic sheikhs. Those who attempted to furtively enter the mountain "should be exiled to the outskirts of the city in an administrative fashion." The authorities also obliged the city works department to take over the cemetery at the Throne of Solomon, which at that point was completely managed by the sheikhs.[39] Moreover, the city government handed Abdulloxon Ravati, a historical mosque at the mountain's base, to the Osh Pedagogical Institute for use as classroom space on June 12, 1961.[40]

Yet few of these promises to clamp down on the unregistered were actually implemented. During Muslim holidays in 1963, the authorities attempted to post voluntary security guards (*druzhinniki*) around the shrine. Thanks to this effort, there were no pilgrims or sheikhs at the White House for the very first time on 'Eid ul-Adha in 1963.[41] Although the pilgrims could not make it to the summit, they brushed off the guards and instead headed to the cemetery at the foot of the mountain, in numbers approaching ten thousand people.[42] One can only assume that the patrol volunteers looked on helplessly from the mountain's higher elevations, upon the throngs of Muslims performing rites below. During the following year, 1964, the voluntary guards proved even more ineffective. When it emerged that "social controls" would only be in place around the shrine till noon on 'Eid ul-Adha, the crowds waited until afternoon to descend on the shrine, en masse.[43] Such an outcome reveals that the campaign's fierce rhetoric often disguised the absence of any real program for cracking down on religion.

For some unregistered figures the campaign engendered a need for stealth that had not existed before. This would become a common feature of unregistered activity in the Brezhnev years. Take the case of one elderly mendicant present on the mountain for an extended period in 1963. Aware that local government had eyes and ears everywhere, he left his white robe on the ground and walked away, monitoring it from afar. CARC's representative observed that "some people left bread [on the robe] and others left money after reciting some kind of prayer. It all happened so fast that within 30 minutes or so a huge mound of bread and a lot of money had accumulated." It later emerged that the old man had been watching the representative "hidden in the crowd."[44] Where a climate of fear did exist, the unregistered could thus avail themselves of half-hearted state surveillance mechanisms.

Yet defiance appears to have been a more common response from the site's unregistered figures. Most of these dynastic sheikhs suffered little more than a slap on the wrist throughout these years. The plans to administratively exile them, a phenomenon observed in other parts of Central Asia, never materialized. At the outset of the antireligious campaign, they engaged in violent scuffles with unspecified individuals (probably SADUM employees) who attempted to forcefully remove them from the mountain.[45] On May 23, 1961, the neighborhood committee of the area immediately surrounding the mountain conducted an inspection at the house of an unregistered sheikh, Mamaniyaz Abdulazizov. When they confronted him about the presence of pilgrims from Andijan at his residence, he replied: "This is our season. We have always welcomed guests and will continue to. Do as you like."[46] This reception of "guests," consisting of the recitation of prayers and performance of rites for pilgrims inside the sheikhs' homes, continued in full swing during Muslim holidays and the pilgrimage-intensive summer months of 1963.[47] Remarkably, in 1961 the shrine's "chief sheikh" enjoyed employment at the city works department, "guarding" the cemetery directly beneath the Throne of Solomon.[48] If administrative exile, arrest, taxation, or humiliation of some sort ever occurred in reference to these figures at the shrine, the documentation makes no record of it.[49]

The campaign's sporadic implementation at the Throne of Solomon reveals three core characteristics of policy toward the unregistered during these years. First, central policymakers lacked the capacity to ensure that local officials implemented antireligious policies the way their authors intended them. This is explained by the fact that the country's senior leadership had largely recused itself from religious affairs since the Great Terror. Chains of communication and supervision between local government and the very top echelons (i.e., the CPSU Central Committee) were, at least in religious matters, long dormant at the time of the campaign's inauguration. Second, even under Khrushchev, antireligious activism lacked the high profile it had enjoyed during earlier revolutionary episodes, such as the Cultural Revolution. Local government in Central Asia continued to prioritize agriculture, and, from the early 1950s onward, cotton production figures, over ideological matters such as religion.

Third, and most important, the Khrushchevian Party-state aspired not to wipe out unregistered religious life, but merely to slow its growth. The unpredictable, haphazard nature of enforcement observed at the Throne of Solomon, as well as the absence of any follow-through, characterized the campaign more generally, with the aim of sending a message to all unregistered figures by making an example of a handful of figures. This demonstrates that the bureaucrats did not consider it within their power to restrict all or even most religious life to the auspices of legal organizations.

These factors could, of course, translate into more dramatic intervention than observed at the Throne of Solomon. All depended on the relative zeal or indifference of local government officials. For example, a particularly ugly crackdown took place at the nearby shrine of Shoh Fozil on 'Eid ul-Adha in 1959, when members of the KGB branch in Uzbekistan's Namangan province crossed into Kyrgyzstan and, in sight of thousands of pilgrims, humiliated, excoriated, and confiscated the belongings of several unregistered sheikhs.[50] At another shrine and holy spring in the neighboring Kyrgyz city of Jalalabat, Hazrat Ayub, almost all the sheikhs were fired from their positions at the health resort located on the site, which they had all but operated independently during the 1950s.[51] Taxation also emerged as a widespread punitive mechanism for deterring unlucky unregistered figures detected by zealous bureaucrats, with the amounts assessed astronomically exceeding the legally mandated norms of the 1940s and 1950s.[52] Unregistered figures who experienced these measures clearly fared worse out of the campaign years than the sheikhs at the Throne of Solomon, yet from a policy implementation perspective the underlying principle remained the same. The campaign's strategy was to deliver swift, dramatic blows against targeted sites, communities, and individuals, with no mechanism in place for ensuring that they did not resume playing a role in religious practice at some point in the future.

Unsurprisingly, the campaign failed to eliminate, or even to retard, unregistered activity in Muslim communities, bequeathing the search for a comprehensive solution to bureaucrats appointed by Brezhnev. It is perhaps telling that many elderly Central Asians today recall the antireligious climate of the Great Terror (which some remember from their early childhoods), or the tense climate in which religion was often practiced in the 1970s–1980s, but have little or no recollection of Khrushchev's antireligious campaign. Muslims experienced its impact only in those localities where bureaucrats chose to implement it. For Khrushchev's successors, the key lesson was that a meaningful assault on religion was no longer viable.

Combining the Moderate and Hard Lines: Regulating the Unregistered, 1970s–1980s

In the early 1970s policymakers combined what they deemed the most effective policies of both the moderate period and the campaign years.

This fusion of two very different policymaking perspectives enhanced bureaucratic control over religion through a complex mechanism for monitoring and restricting unregistered figures without prohibiting them from facilitating religious practices. Pragmatism and an emphasis on pursuing attainable objectives guided official behavior during these years. Two constraints informed this posture. First, the struggle with religion could not be abandoned totally, since it rested at the core of the Party's identity. Second, the Brezhnevian Party-state asserted legitimacy by repudiating the "hare-brained" scheming that it accused Khrushchev of promoting. Brezhnevian policymakers reasoned that his reforms in all areas, including religion, had brought the country nothing but chaos instead of tangible, measurable results.

Policies toward the unregistered during the Brezhnev years followed a model of supervised autonomy or managed chaos, mirroring those applied toward other gray spaces. This approach evolved in parallel with the emergence of what Alexei Yurchak (2006, 126–57) has termed "deterritorialized milieux," or autonomous spaces permitted by the state in which citizens could craft individual moralities and worldviews. Much as the post-1964 Party-state progressively accepted a citizenry that crafted its own identity and lifestyle without official surveillance, so too did it identify certain ideologically unpalatable social phenomena as no longer meriting concerted pressure, and even demanding some measure of bureaucratic regulation (in varying degrees of formality). The preponderance and centrality of unregistered figures in Muslim communities in Brezhnevian Central Asia are but one reflection of the same rationale underpinning the black market's renaissance during the 1970s–1980s (Goldman 1983). An equilibrium between autonomy from state regulation and some degree of official supervision and involvement is the hallmark of gray spaces during the Brezhnev era.

In these circumstances, much of the ideological hue coloring discussion of the unregistered in previous decades disappeared overnight. Instead of looking to a chiliastic solution in the future days of mature communism, policymakers sought to find a permanent, and all-but-legal, niche for a phenomenon that could never fully be legalized for ideological reasons. This attempt consisted in an array of measures falling within two umbrellas of official activity. First, the dramatic punitive measures of the campaign years were diluted significantly in severity but applied to a larger number of people, with draconian punishments going only to individuals deemed guilty of the most reprehensible and fanatical excesses. Second, a new mechanism of "attaching" unregistered figures to registered mosques signaled a move toward tacitly legalizing illegal practitioners. Both approaches reveal that the religious policymakers of the 1970s–1980s sought not to eliminate or intimidate, but rather to regulate, the unregistered. Regulation replaced retaliation as the underlying principle.

A major bureaucratic reform heralded this new approach. Responsibility for dealing with the unregistered was transferred from CARC to "assistance commissions" (*komissii sodeistviia*) housed within city and district governments. Unsuccessfully introduced during the campaign years to stimulate popular mobilization and grassroots participation in the antireligious struggle, they were meant to gather intelligence, engage in propaganda, and track violations of the law by religious figures.[53] From the late 1960s into the 1970s, the state channeled substantial resources to create such commissions and consolidate existing ones.[54] Four hundred such commissions emerged in Kyrgyzstan in 1967 alone.[55] They became the primary vehicle through which policymakers implemented their new regulatory framework for monitoring and managing the unregistered.

For the first time in Soviet history, responsibility for the unregistered now rested with a single department of local government. But rather than use their authority to track down and punish large numbers of people, the commissions devoted almost all their resources to "prophylactic measures" (*profilakticheskie mery*), warnings issued verbally or in writing. As the deputy head of government in Uzbekistan's Xorazm province explained, the commissions considered prophylaxis a first step by default. "Measures aimed at stopping the activity of the unregistered clergy" would, first, "consist of individual prophylactic discussions," followed by "cultivation and explanatory work among the population and clergy, administrative measures and taxation, and, finally, criminal prosecution for a number of malicious violators of Socialist legality."[56]

Prophylactic measures constituted the most frequent course of action, preferred over other, more severe, methods. The commissions coordinated the activities of numerous local agencies to ensure that prophylactic measures affected as many figures as possible. A 1982 report noted that the assistance commissions received "active help in the conduct of cultivation and prophylactic-warning work" from a host of local bodies: "the administrative commissions; commissions for the affairs of the underaged; street, neighborhood, and quarter committees; parent committees in a number of cases (involving the coercion of children into the observance of religion); volunteer people's guards [*druzhiny*], comrade's courts, and so on."[57] While relying on the full organizational armory of both Party and government to penetrate unregistered religious life more broadly than ever before, the assistance commissions thus exhibited little of the zeal often associated with antireligious hard-liners. Their main interest was in consistency and stability.

When prophylaxis failed to deter practitioners sufficiently in the commissions' view, the next step was usually punitive taxation. The application of taxation under Brezhnev reflected a hybrid of the moderate and hard-line approaches. In the 1940s and 1950s, bureaucrats had assessed a moderate tax on large numbers of unregistered figures with some pretense of legal justification, however murky. During the campaign years, by contrast, a small number of unlucky figures paid astronomically high taxes (or, more accurately, fines) to serve as an example to the unregistered as a whole. The hybrid approach retained the punitive rationale behind taxation by making the average tax the equivalent of several months salary.[58] However, the extremely low priority assigned to taxation by local government led to a revival of the moderate period's relaxed climate.

In the late 1960s, religious policymakers found themselves echoing the lament of the postwar years, complaining of lackluster efforts by local financial organs to take action against unregistered figures, even after receipt of detailed lists of the unregistered in a given area.[59] In Kyrgyzstan, for example, the council presented the republican Ministry of Finance with information about 312 illegal figures, only 82 of whom underwent taxation. In 1971 the ministry received a list of 89 figures, but exonerated 43.[60] The representative in Tajikistan reported in 1977 that local financial organs continued to ignore instructions from the Soviet Union Ministry of Finance on this question.[61] As a result instances of punitive taxation remained modest in scope: 39 mullahs were taxed in Uzbekistan's Karakalpak republic in 1977;[62] in 1982, 26 underwent taxation in Xorazm province and 53 in Surxondaryo.[63] The figure for all of Tajikistan in 1980 came to only 30 people.[64] These numbers do not support a trend toward increased or decreased taxation in the long term. Rather, they suggest the application of taxes as a standardized affair, perhaps not as mundane as a speeding ticket, but hardly matching the description of what one might term repression.

The evidence concerning prophylaxis, taxation, and other measures applied against the unregistered, supports one conclusion. The Party-state of the 1970s and 1980s possessed the intelligence and physical capacity to seriously intimidate a substantial number of unregistered figures through punitive action and/or imprisonment. But it did not. Instead, it permitted the unregistered to practice in a climate of some tension.

Even as the bureaucrats considered how traditional enforcement mechanisms, such as warnings and taxation, might be deployed more broadly and less dramatically, they embarked on a truly dramatic recalibration of their approach to the unregistered, namely, the reform known as "attachment" (*prikreplenie*) of unregistered figures to a SADUM-operated mosque. Attachment represented the formalization of a trend that had been gaining traction since the late 1960s in the state's approach toward gray spaces. Dispensing with the fantasy that it could eradicate the unregistered entirely, CARC and the assistance commissions endeavored to introduce some marginal measure of bureaucratization into their relations with the unregistered, while tacitly acknowledging that much religious life would continue to occur beyond their control. This approach of supervised autonomy or managed chaos entailed official resignation to the permanent preponderance of lightly managed areas as part of a larger, effectively controlled social fabric. Put metaphorically, a pyramid of blocks could contain certain hollow units without posing a threat to the integrity of the whole structure.

Attachment started out experimentally in 1976 and became a stable feature of the state's management of mosques thereafter.[65] At the initiative of the Committee for Religious Affairs, or CRA (as CARC was known after 1964) in Moscow, the republican representatives began directing assistance commissions to grant verbal permission to unregistered mullahs to perform the funeral rite. Technically, this would only occur in areas lacking a registered mosque.[66] Two considerations drove the bureaucrats to embrace this option. First and foremost, these attached figures would "commence work toward cessation of the activities of their unregistered colleagues." In this sense, one could speak of it as a "method for putting the network of religious societies in order."[67] Second, they could offer intelligence about religious life in outlying areas where neither the muftiate nor the council had any presence.[68] As table 6.1 demonstrates, the practice became quite widespread in Kyrgyzstan. Not only did these attached unregistered figures exceed their registered counterparts in number, they also brought in much more money from the population. During the 1970s and 1980s Kyrgyzstan's thirty-three registered mosques had between thirty-four and thirty-nine employees, meaning that even in the attachment program's very beginning they were vastly outnumbered by unregistered figures attached to their mosques.[69] If one considers that attached figures constituted but a small fraction of the total unregistered, one can fathom why this issue was always destined to remain a gray area. One official put it best when he explained that the idea's origins and popularity "emerged from an assessment of the religious situation on the ground [*iskhodia iz*

Table 6.1. Attachment in Kyrgyzstan

1976	1978	1980	1982	1984	1986	1990
2	75	250	296	320	321	275

Source: KRBMA 2597/2s/125/120-1 (January 16, 1986).

ucheta real'noi religioznoi obstanovki]."[70] In granting large numbers of people a fraction of the privileges and rights given to SADUM employees, the bureaucrats felt they were both strengthening the muftiate's authority and increasing their supervisory capacity in the landscape. Attachment presupposed the ongoing existence of illegal religious life.[71]

The assistance commissions' activities in the areas of prophylaxis and attachment reflected a systematic bureaucratization of state regulation and monitoring of the unregistered. This new model of regulation succeeded in large part because it avoided the excesses of previous policymaking periods. The moderate-liners of the 1940s and 1950s had generated a vicious backlash within the Party by identifying freedom of conscience as one of the antireligious struggle's core principles. Khrushchevian hard-liners had ventured to the opposite extreme by attempting to assault an aspect of religious life that flourished in every Central Asian community. By contrast, the Party-state of the 1970s and 1980s abandoned any pretense of trying to wipe out the unregistered, while maintaining a consistent and increasingly systematic struggle with religion through propaganda at the workplace, school, and internal Party discipline. For this reason, Central Asian Muslims were more likely to receive exposure to antireligious propaganda in their youth in the 1970s–80s than at any other point in Soviet history, but less likely to experience overtly offensive state intervention into their personal lives and communities on religious grounds. This solution acknowledged the concerns of both the moderate and hard-line impulses in the history of Soviet religious policy.

What this looked like on the ground is apparent from Vera Exnerova's impeccably researched article in this volume. She conducted interviews with religious figures in present-day Uzbekistan who studied with unregistered jurisconsults in the Brezhnev era and after. Her research makes clear that the authorities were aware of the whereabouts of many prominent teachers operating illegal *hujra*s but largely refrained from harassing them. Exnerova's work describes a large, vibrant network of illegal Islamic education whose demise the authorities could have facilitated with ease. That no such official crackdown occurred demonstrates that the state accepted unregistered religion as something permanent.

That religious policymakers regarded this model as a success is clear from their response to the greatest external shock to the Soviet regulation of Islam during these decades, the occupation of Afghanistan. The 1979 invasion, and to a lesser extent the Islamic Revolution in Iran during the preceding year, generated considerable consternation concerning the domestic threat posed by Islam, especially among influential academic circles in Moscow. This environment of fear led to a number of CPSU Central Committee decrees directly referencing the unregistered, including, "On initiatives to thwart attempts by the enemy to employ the 'Islamic Factor' in a way hostile to the interests of the Soviet Union" (November 25, 1981), and "On isolating the reactionary segment of the Muslim clergy" (April 5, 1983).[72] The CRA responded to this concern at the central, all-Union level not by launching a new campaign on the unregistered but, instead, reinforcing existing policies and suggesting that no basis existed for concern. A 1981 inspection team from the CRA in Moscow, for example, reported that local government in Tajikistan's Qurghon Tappa province was taking no action against the unregistered. "This situation is all the more alarming because the province lies on the border [with Afghanistan] and, in connection with the recent activation of Islam overseas, all kinds of negative phenomena might emerge in the context of an almost complete absence of control over trends in religious life." Yet in spite of outlining the situation in such stark terms, the team only recommended that the local assistance commissions get more organized.[73] When the Institute of Scientific Atheism under the CPSU Central Committee dispatched a "special brigade, including staff members of the CRA" to conduct "selective surveying [*anketirovaniia*]" about the population's attitude toward unregistered Sufi masters, they could only report back "that Shiism and its transmission through ishano-muridic formations did not find support in the past, not only among ordinary Muslims but also among the rank-and-file Islamic clergy."[74] The CRA's representatives in Central Asia responded to CPSU decrees expressing fear of the unregistered "by bringing the network of [unregistered] religious organizations in order and consolidating control over the implementation of legislation concerning religious cults."[75] Bureaucrats on the ground rejected any suggestion that Central Asia's unregistered figures posed a political threat to the Soviet state, and offered further justification for the assistance commissions' central role.

During the 1970s–1980s, bureaucrats staffing the CRA and hundreds of assistance commissions became the first religious policymakers to offer the unregistered a permanent niche in Soviet society. Unregistered activity took place in a climate of some tension and even fear, yet, with the right degree of caution and acumen, most practitioners could fulfill the roles demanded by their communities unhindered. Hence the unusual combination during these decades of a powerful Party-state seemingly passionate about fighting religion, and a Muslim population that continued, overwhelmingly, to observe an array of Islamic practices through the offices of myriad community-based, unregistered practitioners.

Gray Spaces and the Soviet System

Stalin's wartime reforms bequeathed to postwar policymakers a flawed and ultimately unworkable blueprint for containing religion through legal religious organizations. The unregistered remained too numerous, and too central to the religious practice of most Muslims, to tackle through any strategy but mass violence. Constrained by its unwillingness to restore the tactics of the Great Terror, the Party-state approached this significant gray space in its regulation of Islam from different angles, first by ignoring the unregistered, then by attacking them haphazardly. After Khrushchev's ouster, the state relegated ideological considerations to secondary status and pursued a policy of regulating and closely monitoring unregistered figures. Religious policymakers formulated and implemented their new religious policy cognizant that a significant gray space rested at its center. This was the most effective and logical means of balancing the Party's tradition of antireligious activism with an underlying drive for political and social stability.

Treating the unregistered as one of many major gray spaces in the Soviet system, rather than simply as a laughable failing of state policies toward Islam, forces historians to rethink long-standing assumptions about the repressive climate in which Islam was supposedly practiced during the Brezhnev years. The existence, and experience of engaging with, gray spaces had profound implications for how Soviet citizens understood their relationship to the state. Ordinary people often did not perceive gray spaces as exceptions to the Soviet system. Rather, these spaces *were* the system insofar as they played a significant and perhaps preeminent role in shaping the experience of being Soviet. Unregistered practitioners facilitated a stable, normative experience of being Muslim in Soviet conditions, largely free of onerous state meddling. From this perspective the preponderance of unregistered figures in Central Asia throughout the postwar decades explains both why the Soviet Party-state never had a "Muslim problem" in the region and, more broadly, why it enjoyed and continues to claim ongoing legitimacy in the five republics.

Unsurprisingly, this powerful and complex legacy has profound implications for the landscape of relations between Islam and state across Central Asia today. These relations have experienced more tension in the era of independence than at any point since Khrushchev's antireligious campaign. This is perhaps ironic given that none of the region's post-Soviet governments espouse scientific atheism, but it is in fact an unsurprising outcome. With independence thrust upon them overnight, the post-Soviet governments of Central Asia could no longer accept the Brezhnevian reconciliation of the hard and moderate lines. Such a hybrid approach could only work in the context of a powerful state that did not believe Islam posed an immediate security threat. In contrast, Central Asia's new post-Soviet rulers experienced a major crisis of confidence as the period from the late 1980s to the early 1990s saw a rise in ethnic violence, economic deprivation, and religious tension throughout the region. From this perspective their abandonment of much of the Soviet legacy of tolerating unregistered figures makes perfect sense.

Many unregistered figures, however, saw no reason to cast aside the modus vivendi developed under the Soviets. By the end of the 1980s, already, isolated Muslim communities in the towns of the Farg'ona Valley (especially Andijan, Namangan, and Qo'qon) had all but declared open independence from official religious institutions in matters of religious dogma and mosque management. This constituted a logical trajectory for any Soviet gray space in the conditions of glasnost and perestroika. (By 1990–91, the mafia-run black market had effectively supplanted official structures as the country's functioning economy.) The late Party-state may have been willing to tolerate this status quo, but its Central Asian successors were not. Thus relations between the independent state and the unregistered after 1991 very much started on the wrong foot, featuring a profound disconnect between a population that had grown accustomed to lax controls on religion, and a nervous, newly empowered elite that now viewed Islam as a potential threat to its fragile authority. It thus seems that although the Soviet state has vanished, the gray spaces its policies created will last well into the future.

PART III

A VIEW FROM WITHIN

SOURCES OF RELIGIOUS AUTHORITY
IN CENTRAL ASIA

CHAPTER SEVEN

The Ascendance of Orthodoxy

Nation Building and Religious Pluralism in Central Asia

Noor O'Neill Borbieva

It was a sunny Friday afternoon during *orozo* (Ramadan) in July 2013. The streets around the main mosque in downtown Bishkek were filled with cars and pedestrians, many of them men with skullcaps and rolled up prayer rugs. They streamed into the main entrance, past beggars and rows of tables covered with books, DVDs, Zamzam water,[1] and prayer beads. Around the corner, women ducked between the mosque complex and the Islamic University's main building to a discreet entrance at the back of the main prayer hall and gingerly navigated the piles of shoes strewn around a small covered porch abutting the back door. The room was hot and stuffy, despite its high ceilings and tall windows. About halfway down the room's length, a tall wood partition divided the room in half, leaving the far side obscured. As women entered, an authoritative woman ran among the rows, finding small spaces for newcomers.

I tied my veil more carefully over my hair and surrendered myself to the flow of the crowd, finding a small square of floor in the middle of the group. There must have been at least 150 women seated in the space when I entered, many of them doing prostrations while waiting for the *khutba* (sermon). I had barely sat down before the khutba began. Although it was in Kyrgyz, a language in which I have conducted many years of fieldwork, the distortion of the microphone and the rustling of the crowd prevented me from understanding anything but isolated words. Happily, the call to prayer was easy to distinguish. Women jumped up to begin prayer, quickly sitting down after stern admonishment from the woman who had earlier been directing them to their places. The call to prayer ended and finally it was time to pray. After the short, two-*reket* (prostration) *juma namaz* (congregation prayer), there was a rush for the door, as women hurried to find their shoes and leave.

Those who did not make it out in the initial rush discovered that goings-on were not over. Instead, they were enthusiastically invited to stay for *daavat*, religious instruction, by the same authoritative woman. "Come, form a circle, let's get started," she called out. The women gathered close around her. She stood holding a book and a stack of papers and launched into a long lecture, only occasionally glancing at her materials.

The *daavatchy* started with a discussion of how to maximize the spiritual benefit (*soop*) from fasting. She was careful to define Arabic words that might be unfamiliar to newcomers and skillfully mixed Islamic theology and scripture with Kyrgyz slang, familiar sayings (*makals*), and entertaining observations about Kyrgyz culture. She talked about Islamic history, recounting life stories of Judeo-Christian prophets, early heroes of Islam, and famous Central Asian scholars. She emphasized the importance of the five daily prayers (*namaz*) and reciting the Koran and talked through a list of reprehensible acts, which included disrespecting parents, gossiping, and drinking alcohol. I left reluctantly after an hour and a half, drawn away by another commitment. Although she showed no signs of slowing down, I felt I had heard enough to understand her central message: Central Asian Muslims should educate themselves about their religion—about the beliefs and practices it prescribes and about its history. Her references to prophets, scholars, and Central Asia's historical ties to the Hanafi school of Sunni Islam reminded her audience that historically, not only was Islam important to Central Asia, but Central Asia was important to Islam.

The striking image of the main mosque in Bishkek filled with women and the themes of the daavatchy's lesson are part of a broader story of Islamic revival in Central Asia, extensively documented in recent ethnography (Bellér-Hann 2001; Louw 2007; McBrien 2006, 2009; Montgomery 2007; Privratsky 2001; Rasanayagam 2010; Roberts 2007; Schwab 2015; Stephan 2006). These accounts describe the revival from many ethnographic points of view, but common themes include the reliance of this revival on scriptural sources of knowledge, its connections to foreign—particularly Arab—centers of Islam, and its tense relationship with what are described as distinctively Central Asian understandings of Islam. These accounts often link the revival to broader, conservative trends across the Islamic world (L. Ahmed 2011; Kolig 2012; Meijer 2009; Roy 2004). Although the global context is important, my focus here is the local story. I do not discount the role foreign knowledge and global trends play, but I argue that Central Asian Islam must also be understood by attending to Central Asian histories.

My account draws on a variety of sources, including historical scholarship, ethnography (conducted by myself and others), and locally produced books, newspapers, recordings, and other media. In studying these sources, I focus on the relationship between power and religion, particularly the way shifts in the locus of power over the course of the pre-Soviet, Soviet, and independent periods have changed the way Islam is understood and lived. I follow Talal Asad, who rejects the notion that religion is a universal human domain, "a distinctive space of human practice and belief which cannot be reduced to any other" (Asad 1993, 27) and views it instead as a culturally constructed category, shaped and defined through the workings of power (Asad 1993, 29; 2003). My description of Central Asian Islam seeks, in Asad's words, "to understand the historical conditions that enable the production and maintenance of specific discursive traditions, or their transformation— and the efforts of practitioners to achieve coherence" (Asad 1986, 17).

Islam in Pre-Soviet Central Asia

Central Asia became part of the Muslim world early in the history of Islam. Arab armies reached Transoxiana, the heartland of Central Asia, by the early eighth century. In the centuries that followed, the region became a cosmopolitan center of Islamic learning and a crossroads of vast trade networks that connected the extremes of the Muslim world. At the same time, the productive tension between Turkic and Persian cultures and the settled and nomadic ways of life maintained diverse approaches to spirituality, and to the extent that the region could be described as "Islamic," Islam was less a discreet, uniform tradition than a multifunctioning set of practices and institutions that touched many domains of life and was informed by a decentralization of religious authority.

In "The Idea of an Anthropology of Islam," Talal Asad suggested studying Islam as a "tradition," by which he means not a shared set of beliefs and practices, but a collection of competing discourses. These discourses often disagree, but are similar in that they relate practices to a distinctively Islamic past, present, and future (Asad 1986, 14). Because of the intense diversity of

Central Asian Islam, I go one step farther, constructing Central Asian Islam as several traditions, each of which comprises numerous competing discourses. In my discussion I address three particularly influential traditions: the scholarly tradition (shariat), Sufi orders (*tariqat*), and customary practice (*urp-adat*).[2] Although I offer descriptions of the practices and institutions commonly associated with them, I do so not to reduce them to practices and institutions but to illustrate that each tradition has a distinctive way of producing, transmitting, and recognizing authoritative religious knowledge.

Religious authority in the scholarly tradition, the realm of the ulema (religious scholars; singular, *alim*), was based on an individual's expertise in a vast textual tradition. Once an alim's expertise was established, he could work as a cleric, *qazy* (judge), or teacher. Young men who aspired to become members of the ulema studied in urban colleges, or madrasas, where they slowly worked through a core curriculum of Koranic commentaries by local scholars (students did not typically study the Koran or Hadiths) (Khalid 1998, 33). Although texts were ostensibly the object of study, most of the instruction occurred orally; groups of students read through a text together, one passage at a time, guided by a scholar who was part of a line of transmission of knowledge about the text that stretched back to the author of the text and who lectured on the meaning of the text. Upon completing study of the text, a student received an *ijaza*, or license, which identified him as having received the transmission and allowed him to teach the given text. In this way, the tradition both emphasized the importance of literacy and textual sources of knowledge and "was marked with a profound distrust of the ability of the text to convey the author's intention" (Khalid 1998, 29).

The influence of this tradition was felt far beyond urban centers. Even in rural areas, boys studied in elementary schools called *maktabs*, where clerics taught them the Arabic alphabet and a rich curriculum of religious and literary texts. Beginning texts addressed the importance of doing God's will and the basics of Islam, while more advanced texts introduced literary classics by the region's most famous poets (Shahrani 1991).[3] Although students acquired minimal functional literacy, familiarity with these texts gave them the ability to fulfill the ritual obligations (such as namaz) that indexed them as respectable members of their communities. The harsh, authoritative style of instruction, which included corporal punishment, instilled in children proper deference to teachers, elders, and the sacred texts of Islam (Keller 2007, 251; Khalid 1998, 20–21; Shahrani 1991).

One source of this tradition's power, then, was the ulema's expertise in a textual tradition Central Asians were taught to revere. Another source of their power was financial. The ulema controlled a vast system of endowments, or *waqfs*, which among other things funded the upkeep of religious buildings and provided scholarship money to madrasa students. Together, these sources of power gave the ulema considerable independence from the political leadership and allowed them to run schools, mosques, and courts without interference (Khalid 2007, 27; Lapidus 1996). At the best of times, the ulema benefited from strong political leaders who maintained security and order and funded religious endowments. Political rulers who were tempted to challenge the ulema often realized that their own popularity depended, in part, on their willingness to patronize scholarly institutions and visibly uphold the morals and norms defined and defended by the tradition (Khalid 2007, 27–33).

Coexisting with the scholarly tradition were Sufi orders, called tariqats (Khalid 1998, 32; Louw 2007, 44–45; Shahrani 1984, 32; Sultanova 2011). These groups were led by charismatic teachers, called *pirs* or *ishan*. Sufi leaders ranged from radical pirs, who promoted deviant behavior and were accused of heresy, to conservative pirs, who adhered closely to the norms taught by the ulema and welcomed ulema into their brotherhoods. Pirs attracted followers not with their erudition but with their charisma and their expertise in experiential forms of spiritual learning. The Sufi orders represented a more inspirational manifestation of Islam, "instilling beliefs and attitudes in an existential rather than purely cognitive and didactic manner" (Schubel 1999, 73).

In some eras, the ulema discouraged or even condemned certain Sufi practices on the grounds that they were *bidayat*, or innovation (i.e., not validated by scripture and therefore suspect). Of particular concern to scholars was shrine pilgrimage (*zïyarat*). Popular pirs were venerated as saints after their deaths, and their tombs became pilgrimage destinations. More than zïyarat itself, ulema wanted to discourage certain practices associated with zïyarat, including ritual lamentations and praying to saints for intercession (Babadzhanov 2004, 165). These efforts generally failed because of the tariqats' popularity (Babadzhanov 2004, 155). Despite these disagreements, it is important not to overstate the tension between these traditions. Works by the greatest Sufi poets were central to the maktab curriculum (Shahrani 1991) and many religious scholars were also members of Sufi orders (Khalid 1998, 32).

The third tradition, urp-adat, comprised domestic, mortuary, and other customary observances that reinforced key Central Asian values such as family, hospitality, and reciprocity. Some of these practices, such as circumcision, marriage, and burial rites, were informed by shariat Islam if not directly officiated by the ulema. Others, such as visiting *mazars* (holy sites, including Sufi shrines and natural formations, such as springs and waterfalls) in pursuit of health, prosperity, and fertility, were influenced by the Sufi tradition. Still others, such as rituals honoring the ancestors, healing rituals, and various life-cycle rituals, drew on Islamic vocabularies and symbols but had a distant relationship, if any, to formal Islamic knowledge. They were valued because they fostered community solidarity, linked everyday life to a broader Islamic moral order, and indexed Central Asian lineages and landscapes as part of the *dar ul-Islam* (Aitpaeva 2009a, 2009b; Aitpaeva, Aldakeeva, and Egemberdieva 2010; Aitpaeva, Egemberdieva, and Toktogulova 2007; DeWeese 1994; Privratsky 2001). Knowledge about these practices was rarely written down, but rather stored in the collective memory of communities and families and transmitted orally from elder to younger.

These three traditions, each with its own sources of legitimacy and understandings of religious authority, coexisted in Central Asian communities and individual lives. Muslim Central Asians could attend Friday mosque prayers, go to a shariat court to solve a property dispute, frequent a Sufi lodge, and recite the Koran for ancestors at the Thursday night meal, without censure (Khalid 1998, 32; Lapidus 1996, 14–15). The traditions thrived together because Central Asians of the pre-Soviet era understood that authoritative religious knowledge could come from a variety of sources: an imam, a qazy, a pir, an elder, a poem, even a dream. This comfort with decentralized religious authority would change with the advent of Russian colonialism and the Soviet era. After this shift, state power increased dramatically, limiting what Clifford Geertz has called the "scope" of religion (1968, 112), and changing the standards used to judge the legitimacy of religious knowledge.[4]

Islam during the Soviet Era

Much has been written about the profound changes to Central Asian Islam that occurred during the Soviet era (Keller 2001; Ro'i 2000; Saroyan 1997). The Soviet regime was a self-consciously modernizing power, and it viewed the pervasive spirituality and power of religious institutions in Central Asian society as obstacles to its agenda. Early Bolshevik leaders attacked all three traditions. The regime weakened the scholarly tradition by seizing its financial resources, imprisoning and/or killing ulema, and reassigning many of the tradition's functions to the state (e.g., education, the court system, social welfare).⁵ The regime killed or imprisoned Sufi leaders, effectively breaking chains of oral knowledge transmission and initiation that stretched back centuries (Schubel 1999, 73–74). Urp-adat came under attack when the regime identified and condemned a number of popular practices on the grounds that they were economically exploitative. They called these practices *byt* crimes, crimes of custom.

During and after the Second World War, these attacks eased, and surviving ulema across the Soviet Union asked the regime to set up official spiritual directorates modeled after institutions set up by the tsarist empire (Ro'i 2000, 100–103). The regime, realizing its attacks on revered experts and institutions was hurting its popularity in Muslim regions, gave in, and several directorates were set up, including the officially recognized Central Asian muftiate (commonly known by the Russian acronym SADUM).⁶ Under SADUM's guidance, a handful of mosques and madrasas reopened and clergy were accredited.⁷ SADUM was given permission to publish a limited number of books and periodicals and issue fatwas, authoritative decrees about religious practice that have no legal force but to the faithful represent a source of guidance regarding proper practice and belief.

Studies of these publications and fatwas suggest that SADUM clerics were sincerely committed to preserving Islamic spirituality in the face of atheist encroachment, but to do so they were willing to offer unconventional, "accommodationist" rulings such as excusing Muslims from prayer and fasting if the observances prevented them from fulfilling their work responsibilities, or allowing Muslims in the military to eat pork (Ro'i 2000, 140, 464; Saroyan 1997, 44, 68). At the same time, they were more likely to cite scriptural sources, with the implication that many of their rulings were quite restrictive compared to those of earlier scholars. These strict rulings included fatwas against customary practices such as large wedding feasts and certain mazar rites on the grounds that they were bidayat.

The ulema's newfound interest in scripture, as opposed to reliance on local commentaries, was a significant shift from the pre-Soviet era. One reason for this shift was the political context; many of the traditional practices rejected in scripturalist Islam were considered exploitative and/or superstitious by Soviet authorities. Another reason for the shift may have been Arab influence. Soviet ulema enjoyed unusual freedom to travel and some of them spent time in the Arab world (Babadzhanov 2004, 170). They also appear to have received a steady volume of Arabic religious texts from the region, including scripturalist-leaning Salafi texts (Babadzhanov 2004, 164). A third reason may have been the residual influence of the Jadid movement, a short-lived modernizing movement in Central Asia that advocated both embracing scientific knowledge and a purification of Islam, in the sense of a return to scripture (Khalid 1998; 2007). Whatever the reasons, SADUM's rejection of practices that had routinely been accepted as legitimate by pre-Soviet ulema caused consternation among the populace and even among registered clerics (Babadzhanov 2004, 164–65; Babadzhanov and Kamilov 2001, 202; Ro'i 2000, 147; Saroyan 1997, 50).

The Sufi tradition suffered a drastic reduction in its popularity, visibility, and legitimacy (Ro'i 2000, 385–93; Schubel 1999). Shrine pilgrimage continued but many pirs had been killed or exiled in the early attacks, devastating a tradition that depended on the oral transmission of knowledge from pir to murid. Some tariqats survived but because SADUM viewed them as competitors and the regime viewed them as a potential source of anti-Soviet mobilization, they remained illegal and were forced to operate underground (Babadzhanov 2004, 163; Ro'i 2000, 385–93; Tasar, chapter 6, this volume).

If Soviet efforts undermined the power of the scholarly and Sufi traditions, they inadvertently increased the power and importance of urp-adat, which became the main if not only outlet for many individuals' and families' spiritual energies (Babadzhanov 2004, 159; Kuchumkulova 2007, 166; Privratsky 2001; Ro'i 2000, 462; Tett 1994). Soviet antireligion campaigns encouraged families and individuals to confine ritual observances to the private sphere, but there they persisted. Obligatory practices, such as namaz and orozo, increasingly became associated with the domestic sphere and were resolutely preserved by elders and women (Ro'i 2000, 441, 454; Tett 1994). Even Communist Party members allowed religious observances to go on at home, and some practices, such as circumcision and burial rites, were observed by nearly 100 percent of the Muslim populace (Khazanov 1994, 151; Kuchumkulova 2007, 166; Privratsky 2001, 96–97; Ro'i 2000, 456–57).

One reason urp-adat became so important had nothing to do with religious conviction and everything to do with Soviet "nationalities policy." With the goal of creating a unified Soviet populace, the regime, somewhat counterintuitively, promoted a classification system that assigned every citizen to one of dozens of ethnic groups (*natsional'nosti*). The creation of this classification system was informed by indigenous understandings of identity as rooted in kinship, language, way of life (e.g., sedentary/nomadic), occupation, religion, and region of origin, but the categories were consolidated and institutionalized in unfamiliar ways (Hirsch 2005; Shahrani 1984, 34–35). In Central Asia, many ethnic groups were recognized as "Muslim." By allowing religion to inform the construction of ethnic categories, the Soviets inadvertently intensified Central Asians' identification with Islam. Even the most unobservant members of "Muslim" ethnic groups understood that Islam was a part of their identity and that taking pride in their ethnic identity (which Soviet propaganda encouraged them to do) implied taking pride in their Muslim heritage.[8]

Many scholars who write about religion in Central Asia argue, mistakenly, that the link between religion and ethnic identity, fostered by the nationalities policy, divested Islam of spiritual significance and reduced it to "an element of national and cultural identity" (Rasanayagam 2006b, 377; see also Khalid 2003, 2007, 98, 107; McBrien 2006, 344; McBrien and Pelkmans 2008, 88; Ro'i 1995). Although the aggressive promotion of socialist atheism together with the social costs of religious observance dampened religious fervor among many classes,[9] these processes reduced the scope of Islam in people's lives but not its spiritual significance. The regime secularized society in the sense not of getting rid of religion but demarcating religion as a discreet domain (with particular functions) that was distinguishable from other domains (and their functions).

This process of differentiation was linked to the first of several key changes in spirituality evident by the end of the Soviet era: The Soviet regime expanded state power by taking control of social domains that had earlier been controlled by "religious" interests. Where once education, the court system, and the redistribution of wealth in the interests of social welfare had all been directed by the ulema, they were now directed by the state. Where once Central Asians celebrated the joys of community and shared cultural heritage in Sufi brotherhoods and at life-cycle rituals and mazars, now young comrades could do so at state-sponsored houses of culture and national holiday events such as parades.

The increase of state power and the limitation of religion to a confined domain contributed to a second key change: the objectification of Islam. In pre-Soviet Central Asia, as in much of the Muslim world before the modern era, the practices, beliefs, texts, societies, and individuals modern observers might label "Islamic" were not necessarily so identified. As Dale Eickelman and James Piscatori have argued (1996), Islam tended to be so organically embedded in social contexts that many Muslims would not have spoken of Islam as a discreet category. Only in response to modernizing trends, such as state socialism, has Islam become objectified, meaning it becomes possible to identify Islam as "a self-contained system" that its believers could "distinguish from other belief systems" (Eickelman and Piscatori 1996, 38; see also Saroyan 1997, 57–58).[10]

A third key change was the destruction of the Sufi tradition. Although the Sufi tradition is now being revived in some regions, particularly where states view it as useful to their nationalist projects (e.g., Louw 2007, 48–49; Sultanova 2011), in general, Sufism lost its power to mediate between other spiritual traditions. In the pre-Soviet era, Sufi orders' trust in oral transmission and experiential learning had tempered the formality of the scholarly tradition, possibly reinforcing the latter's healthy distrust of textual knowledge; at the other extreme, Sufi orders' associations with popular saints and shrines had allowed them to serve as conduits for formal knowledge about proper forms of worship, thereby legitimizing many customary practices.

The loss of the Sufi orders led to the fourth key change: the polarization of constructions of religious authority. Where once there had been productive disagreement among and within all three religious traditions regarding what sources of knowledge were acceptable, by the end of the Soviet era there was a relatively narrow understanding of legitimate authority in the scholarly tradition. Always conscious of state interests, the ulema produced relatively consistent directives, drawing on a small corpus of scriptural (and scripturalist texts).[11] At the other extreme, the privatization of customary practice meant that not only were practices diverse, but so were ideas regarding what constituted legitimate knowledge about the practices. For knowledge about the practices each community (or family) depended on its own respected elders, few of whom had any formal education (Aitpaeva and Egemberdieva 2010). When these practices became visible after independence, their popularity, diversity, and distance from any formal sources of Islamic knowledge made them obvious targets for aggressive attacks by a new generation of state-aligned Islamic scholars.

Religious Revival

My discussion of the postindependence era focuses on Kyrgyzstan, which I have been visiting since 1997. In this small and relatively poor and unstable nation, citizens have witnessed a rapid expansion of religious infrastructure and a visible increase in public religiosity (ICG 2003b, 2009b; Kuchumkulova 2007; McBrien 2006a, 2006b, 2009; Montgomery 2007; Ro'i and Wainer 2009; USDS 2013). Although Kyrgyzstani citizens still enjoy more religious freedom than citizens of other Central Asian republics,[12] religious freedom decreased precipitously after a restrictive Law on Religion was passed in 2009. The law raises the number of members necessary for registering a religious group from ten to two hundred, prohibits aggressive proselytism with the goal of converting citizens, prohibits the participation of minors in proselytism, and requires all religious literature to be examined by the state (USDS 2013, 2). Since then, the Almazbek Atambayev administration (in power since 2011) has criticized constitutional clauses establishing the freedom of religion and threatened to add further restrictions to the Law on Religion.

Restrictions on religious activity are enforced by the State Commission for Religious Affairs (SCRA), which registers religious organizations and monitors all religious activity. SCRA denies registration to groups it deems represent "a threat to national security, social stability, interethnic and interdenominational harmony, public order, health, or morality" (USDS 2013, 3). Associations that do not register cannot conduct business as legal entities and are subject to fines and other punishments. International monitors report that many religious groups that are refused registration have seen their members harassed and their property confiscated. Foreign religious workers have also been denied registration and threatened with the revocation of their visas or even deportation (Bayram and Kinahan 2014).

It is no secret that these regulations are designed to limit the activity of all religious groups other than those associated with Orthodox Christianity and official Islam. By "official Islam," I refer to any activity that is overseen by the Spiritual Directorate of Kyrgyzstan Muslims, or Muftiate. The Muftiate was modeled after republic-wide bodies established during the Gorbachev era to replace the original multirepublic directorates. It was founded in 1993 and began operations in 1996 when a *kurultay* (conference) of Muslim leaders elected the first mufti and members of the Ulema Council, which monitors the Muftiate. Not unlike scholarly Islam of earlier eras, the Muftiate derives its power in part from the religious expertise of its representatives, many of whom have studied in the Middle East. The Muftiate also has considerable financial resources. It receives donations from congregants and foreign organizations and governments and allocates these funds to services for the faithful, including the expansion of religious infrastructure.[13] It also controls the profitable Office of the Hajj, which distributes visas and sells travel packages to those interested in performing the hajj.

The extent to which the Muftiate's religious capital and financial resources translate into actual independence from the state is unclear, but probably limited. Although technically independent, the Muftiate remains deeply dependent on the state in a symbolic sense, since its jurisdiction is coterminous with state borders. In material terms, the Muftiate depends on the state to uphold its status as Kyrgyzstan's only authority on Islam.

Thanks to state control, only the Muftiate has the right to license Islamic clerics and daavatchys, approve the curricula used at Islamic educational institutions, dictate Friday khutbas, issue fatwas, and approve (or ban) books on Islam for publication (USDS 2013, 7). Absent state control, the Muftiate would surely have to compete with a variety of other Islamic authorities.[14]

While the state would not like the Muftiate to grow so popular as to become a threat, it has an interest in protecting the Muftiate's legitimacy. The state depends on the Muftiate to define and promote a theologically sound form of Islam among Kyrgyzstan's devout that diverts support away from the extremist, political Islamic groups the state views as a threat.[15] The Muftiate does this mostly willingly; throughout its publications, the Muftiate offers arguments against "extremist" Islam, that is, groups with political goals. It also explicitly promotes patriotism and Kyrgyz nationalism.[16]

Although the Muftiate would probably prefer to see its popularity lead to more independence, bad behavior on the part of its officials has prevented it from achieving this. Financial scandals involving the Office of the Hajj and public conflicts with outspoken imams have called attention to political favoritism and corruption in the institution and led to the resignation of top officials, including several muftis (McGlinchey 2009; ReliefWeb 2007; RFE/RL 2011b, 2012b; Sagynova 2006). In the wake of the most recent scandal, the Atambayev administration intensified its oversight, insisting that the Muftiate increase reporting of its activities (especially its finances) and involve state officials, including law enforcement officials, in the credentialing of clerics. In an unusual example of state interference in matters of doctrine, the Atambayev administration directed that the Muftiate appoint clerics only from among those who adhere to the Hanafi school of Islam (Bayram and Kinahan 2014, 2). These new efforts are clearly less a response to the Muftiate's growing popularity than a manifestation of the state's concern about the directorate's failures.

Official Islam

Despite these tribulations, the Muftiate enjoys unparalleled influence over Islam in today's Kyrgyzstan. The sheer number of the faithful that attend Friday services and the widespread availability of the Muftiate's literature ensure that whatever the faithful think about the institution, its interpretation of Islam is very influential. Examples from this literature confirm that the Muftiate views itself as the institution most responsible for shaping the Islamic revival in the republic. As such, it prioritizes the following goals:

(1) communicating the basic beliefs and practices of Islam; (2) establishing the Koran and Hadiths as the ultimate sources of authoritative knowledge about Islam and familiarizing the faithful with the language and structure of these texts; (3) orienting the faithful toward the goal of unquestioningly doing God's will in order to achieve safety in the afterlife;[17] and (4) reinforcing the historical connection between Central Asia and Islam. In the discussion below, I draw on textual and ethnographic sources to illustrate the first three of these goals.[18]

The ideas expressed in the first three goals are central themes in introductory books for children and adults. A children's picture book, *Requirements of Faith and Islam*, is simply a list of the beliefs and practices required in Islam (accompanied by colorful pictures that include Kyrgyz ethnic iconography) (Ibraev 2013). The required beliefs are belief in Allah, the angels, the holy books (the Bible and the Koran), the prophets, the afterlife, and fate. The required practices are the five pillars, which the book attributes to Imam Bukhari, the early compiler of a major collection of Hadiths and native of Bukhara (in modern-day Uzbekistan). Two other picture books for children include this information as well as stories from the Koran and Hadiths, information about the Prophet, the basics of namaz, and a few short Hadiths "for memorization" (Chotonov 2006; Seidalieva 2012). A manual for teachers of school-aged children, called *A Book of Conduct and Morals for Muslim Children* (Abdylda uulu and Chotonov 2002), begins with a discussion of the central tenets of Islam (belief in the oneness of God, belief in the Prophet, belief in the Koran, belief in the Day of Judgment, and the importance of the five pillars) and includes detailed descriptions of how to observe namaz. The second half is a translation of an Arabic text, "Conduct and Morals in Islam" (unattributed). At the end of the first half, a discussion of desirable personal qualities includes extensive quotations from scripture and ends with the following words:

> You are required to fulfill the obligations [*parz-mildetter*] required by God [*Allah taala*]. If you do so, God will protect you from the suffering of death and hell. Stay away from all those things that God has forbidden, run away from those corrupt things that your body wants, and always remember God. In this way you will protect yourself from devils [*shaitandar*]. (Abdylda uulu and Chotonov 2002, 38)

A pamphlet for women titled "Why Must I Wear Hijab?!!!" includes the following passage:

> God [*Allah Taala*] has told us which things are useful, which things are harmful to us. . . . God [*Allah*] says this in the Qur'an: "Have We not . . . guided him on the two highways [Kyrgyz adds, "good and bad"]?" (The Land, verse 10)[19]. God has warned us about the good and the bad, but only some people have chosen the correct path, the path of obeying God's commands and avoiding that which God has prohibited. (Ryskulov and Möküyeva 2012, 11)

The pamphlet is structured as a series of questions and answers, allowing the writers to acknowledge and respond to common objections. One question states, "What kind of good will I receive from wearing hijab?" The authors respond, "Wearing *hijab*, like *namaz* and *orozo*, is considered *parz*. It is God's command. Instead of discussing the things God has commanded, saying I like this one or don't like that one, we must try to adopt them all immediately" (Ryskulov and Möküyeva 2012, 18). In other words, do not assess God's commands in terms of the personal benefits they offer. God's will must be obeyed without question.

A common message in texts and sermons is that those who want to practice correctly must learn to distinguish between different categories of actions. This was the subject of a lecture I observed at the Islamic University in 2004. The female speaker told her audience of women, "Remember, first we need to do the obligatory actions [*parz*]. These are the things God has ordered us to do. Next, we can do *sünnöt*. *Sünnöt* are the things the Prophet did." She then offered an example, applying this knowledge to a practical question many members of her audience faced: deciding how strictly to cover.

> There are two forms of covering. There is *hijab* and there is *nikab*, which is covering everything except the eyes. *Nikab* is *parz* only for the prophet's wives. For all other women, it is *sünnöt*. Of course if we do it, we earn spiritual reward [*soop*], but it is not required, and we need to make sure we are fulfilling all our other *parz* first. If I wear *nikab* but commit sin, what is the use of my *nikab*? Worry first about avoiding sin and fulfilling your *parz*. Only if you are sure about these things, can you think about *nikab*.

In her field site in southern Kyrgyzstan, Julie McBrien observed similar consciousness raising among the devout, who had started to distinguish between traditional and "sunnati" weddings. Traditional weddings include loud music, dancing, mixing of the sexes, display of the bride, and alcohol, elements considered sinful by the devout. Sunnati weddings leave out these sinful elements and instead often feature a lecture by a daavatchy (McBrien 2006b).

Another common message in these texts is that the faithful should be proactive in seeking information about Islam. In the hijab pamphlet, a questioner protests that she lacks a "deep [*tereng*]" understanding of shariat, and that this prevents her from adopting hijab. The authors respond, "This is not an excuse, because we are living in the technologically and scientifically advanced twenty-first century. If you look for the information you need, it is in books and audio and video cassettes; if you desire you will even find it on the internet" (Ryskulov and Möküyeva 2012, 18).

This concern that ignorance leads to incorrect practice is evident in an extended example I take from an article written by a Muftiate official. The official describes visiting the village of his relatives to attend a funeral (Abdyldaev 2003). He reports that although he saw less drunkenness than he had seen during earlier visits, other aspects of the funeral did not conform to Islamic law. For example, the grieving family had slaughtered several animals to provide food for many guests. The official points out to his hosts that these excessive expenditures "do not conform to *shariyat* [*shariyatta mynday jokko*]." The villagers are surprised and ask for clarification. The visitor explains that in Islam this is considered a hardship for the bereaved family, and that food should instead be brought to the grieving family by neighbors and friends.

Later, someone asks why sometimes the Koran is recited once for the dead and sometimes many times.[20] The Muftiate official responds, "The Mufti issued a *fatva* that the Qur'an should be recited only once at the grave during a funeral, and we must obey the Mufti's *fatva* [*fatvaga moyun sunushubuz kerek*]." The interlocutor responds, "But in the past, wasn't the Qur'an also recited for all the dead [*jalpy ölüktörgö da okylchu emes bele*]? Why won't you do this anymore?" The visitor asks, "Do you know how to recite the Qur'an?" "No," answers the man. "For the relatives of the dead, reciting the Qur'an is done in a specific place and in a particular way," says the visitor. "Instead of offering excuses like you must go and recite the Qur'an for everyone in the graveyard, why don't you gather up your sons and grandsons and recite the Qur'an for your own deceased in the proper way?" To this question, the narrator recounts, the man could offer no response [*unchukpai kaldy*].

Discursive Competition

Beyond the immediate sphere of official Islam, Kyrgyzstani Muslims' spiritual sensibilities remain deeply informed by urp-adat, which connects spiritual desires to local cultures, landscapes, and genealogies. In contrast to official Islam's focus on the individual and the status of his/her actions in the eyes of God, urp-adat dictates communal observances and individual observances that facilitate "the maintenance of human life in a communal setting" (DeWeese 1994, 36).[21] Official Islam demands a lot, but information about these demands is clear, consistent, and widely available. Urp-adat, in contrast, is inconsistent in its demands and reasoning. If the diverse discourses that form the tradition of customary practice share anything, it is the awareness that its practices are the focus of attacks by representatives of official Islam. As the following discussion shows, Kyrgyzstani Muslims who engage with and reproduce the tradition of customary practice must incorporate into the tradition's defining discourses explicit defenses against official Islam's attacks

Most Kyrgyzstani Muslims revere Islamic scripture and recognize the scholarly expertise of the representatives of official Islam, but they question many of the tradition's demanding dictates. For example, official Islam teaches that namaz, the five-time daily prayer, is required of all adult Muslims. In many communities, however, popular consensus has maintained since the Soviet era that namaz is best postponed until an individual is advanced in years because of the difficulty young and middle-aged people face in balancing careers and family life with spiritual commitments. Some Kyrgyzstani Muslims told me it is actually worse to begin praying and stop than never to begin at all, and they use this to justify delaying prayer until retirement. Other Kyrgyzstani Muslims I knew enthusiastically embraced a modified version of namaz; mostly single, working mothers, they could not fit in the full five prayers, but were vigilant in saying the morning prayer, and found comfort in knowing that in doing so they were fulfilling God's will.[22]

Whereas official Islam prescribes practices that are conspicuous and public, such as wearing hijab or attending juma namaz, many Kyrgyzstani faithful remain suspicious of public displays of piety and argue that official Islam's emphasis on public religious expression encouraged dishonesty and hypocrisy. This perspective, sometimes offered in the form of stories or aphorisms, was related to the conviction—common among Kyrgyzstani Muslims—that inner goodness (particularly as measured by the honesty, generosity, and humility one applies to one's social involvements) is what matters, and that public behavior is not a reliable indicator of inner goodness. One story I heard on several occasions told of two men who had died and were facing God's judgment. The first, a drunkard, had never prayed.

As he awaited judgment, his heart was overcome by despair and fear. "Why did I ignore my religious duties?" he lamented, sure that he would never be accepted into heaven. The second, a pious man who had never missed a prayer, stood fearlessly as his soul was weighed on the great scale, confident that God would accept him into heaven. The judgment surprised them both: the drunkard, for his sincere humility, went to heaven; the pious man, for his hubris in thinking he could predict God's will, was sent to hell.

Official Islam is aware of these objections and offers a number of stock responses. One response agrees that hypocrisy (*munafyk*) is a form of wrong doing (*zulum*) and reminds the faithful that correct attitude, particularly sincerity (*ikhlas*), is as much a condition of an act's acceptance (*kabyl aluu*) by God as correct form (Jalilov 2014, 40; Narmatov 2011, lecture 1). An alternative response reminds the faithful that sincerity—or any combination of good personal qualities—is not enough to secure God's favor. One must also fulfill all parz. In the hijab pamphlet, a questioner says she heard Islam teaches that as long as the heart is pure (*taza*) the individual is pure. The writers respond:

> The goal [*maksat*] of a pen is to write. If it writes, it is useful, if it does not write, it is not useful. Similarly, the duty [*mildet*] of a clock is to show the correct time. If the clock does not show the correct time, it is not useful. From that we understand that the body's duty is to bow and prostrate [*sajda, ruku kylyy*] to Allah, to avoid those things that are prohibited by Allah, to do Allah's commands, to do just work. Only when the body does these things, can the body be considered corrected [*ongolgon*]. If the body does not do these things, it is incorrect. If you say your heart is pure but you do not obey Allah's commands [*Allahtyn buiruktaryn atkaruudan alys bolsong*], you are lying to yourself. (Ryskulov and Möküyeva 2012, 6–7)

In her field site, many of McBrien's informants defended traditional weddings on the basis that these observances were more authentic, and that the sunnati weddings of official Islam represented "a deformation" of their culture and "an affront" to their way of life (McBrien 2006b, 349). Official Islam responds that these local practices, however storied, are not authorized by scripture. Many popular practices associated with weddings, funerals, and holiday celebrations other than the two Islamic holidays (*Orozo Ait* and *Kurman Ait*) are rejected as bidayat in fatwas, publications, and sermons (see, e.g., Jalilov 2014, 84–92; McBrien 2006b, 348). As the Abdyldaev article illustrates, official clerics are often willing to offer additional justification for the rejection of these practices (2003). Abdyldaev, for example, notes that expensive funeral feasts that involve slaughtering many animals are a hardship for the bereaved family (see also Ashimova 2002). Official clerics also describe ritual weeping (ökürüü) and ritual lament songs (*koshoks*) as both bidayat and unnecessary emotional burdens (Kuchumkulova 2007, 233). Kuchumkulova counters that official criticisms of popular Kyrgyz mortuary practices ignore the communal benefits of these practices. For example, in her village, slaughtering many animals for a funeral feast was an important form of wealth redistribution. If a family was poor, wealthy relatives stepped in to help sponsor the feast, and the observance ensured the good health of all (Kuchumkulova 2007, 262, 268). Prohibitions against the singing of koshoks, she points out, ignore their power to console those who are grieving (237). Elsewhere, I have described how pious women I knew resisted official Islam's rulings against wedding exchanges, preferring to continue observing these practices so as not to create tension in their community (Borbieva 2012b).

Perhaps the most versatile and devastating argument used against customary practices is the charge of *shirk* (idolatry), meaning a practice depends on belief in the supernatural power of agents other than God. Visiting psychics (*közü achyks*) or shamans (*bakshys*), whose power is believed to come from spirits (*jinns*) and devils (*shaitans*) is popular, but condemned as shirk by official clerics. One former mufti quotes the Prophet's words from a Hadith, "Whoever goes to a psychic and believes what he is told becomes an unbeliever [*kaapyr*] in the eyes of the Prophet and the Qur'an" (Jalilov 2014, 26; see also Myrzabekov 2004). The popular practice of displaying protective amulets called *tumars* is also considered shirk, because the person displaying the tumar puts his faith in the tumar rather than God. Finally, praying to ancestors or historical figures is rejected as shirk. An article titled "We Do Not Worship Manas; We Are Proud of Manas," from the Muftiate's Web site, warned readers that praying to Manas, the hero of Kyrgyz epic poetry, is a form of shirk. "No matter to what level a hero has reached, he does not merit worship. Because worship is only due to the Creator."[23]

Official Islam's dependence on the shirk argument calls attention to a profound difference in the way these two traditions understand the divine. In official Islam, divine power is transcendent and largely inaccessible. One can develop trust in God (*tavakkul*), pray that God will come to one's aid (*duba kyluu*), and do good deeds to acquire soop (such as reciting the Koran), but these must be done with the understanding that God's favor is never guaranteed. Many customary practices, in contrast, suggest that divine power is close and accessible; it can infuse objects in the landscape and be manipulated by gifted individuals. This distinction is particularly interesting when applied to scripture. Belief in the Koran as the uncreated word of God is a central tenet of Islamic faith, but for official Islam, the Koran is holy only as a repository of divine knowledge. Many customary practices, in contrast, ascribe divine power to the physical object of scripture.[24] Thus, even if many tumars are, in fact, triangles of leather in which verses of the Koran have been sewn, official Islam still considers trusting them to be shirk. Salamat-eje, a Kyrgyz woman who came of age in the late 1960s, offered this reflection on the way Kyrgyz Muslims in the village venerated the physical manifestation of scripture: "Normal people thought they shouldn't read the Qur'an, that only *moldos* [clerics] should read the Qur'an and interpret it and that the Qur'an should only be in a mosque. It was that holy to them. They were afraid of it. If someone held out the Qur'an to them and said 'touch it,' they would be startled and refuse. No one even wanted to know what the Qur'an meant. If something was in Arabic, everyone respected it; we thought it must be holy and we recited it because it was *soop*."

In my experience, when Kyrgyzstani Muslims defend customary practices against the charge of shirk, they often do not question the sinfulness of shirk but rather the validity of the accusation vis-à-vis the practice in question. A mazar guardian in Talas tells a group of Kyrgyz ethnographers that in praying at the mazars, Kyrgyz "are not praying to the stones and the streams, but they are asking for Allah's blessings at these sites and believe these are places where the connection between God and human beings is stronger" (Aitpaeva 2009a, 232). Similarly, Salamat-eje described to me a practice she had been taught by her elders: at the first sliver of the new moon, she was to go outside, bow to the moon, and express her wishes (*tilek aituu*). When challenged by her pious teenage daughters that the practice was shirk because it was a form of worshipping nature (*jaratylyshka bash iyüü*), she countered, "This is not about worshipping nature. This is about respecting nature [*jaratylyshty syiloo*]." The fact that Kyrgyz faithful make discursive distinctions such as worshipping versus respecting, or praying *to* an object versus asking for Allah's blessing *at* an object, is arguably a testament to the power of the official discourse. If the commission of bidayat can often be excused on the basis of ignorance, official Islam teaches that any Muslim with a minimum understanding of her faith should have an intuitive understanding of what is shirk and not, and even those who are quite distant from official Islam seem to have taken this to heart.[25]

Knowledge and Power

I have long known Salamat-eje, who I introduced above, to be a spiritual woman. She recites the Koran for her ancestors on Thursday nights, prays at local mazars, does not drink alcohol, and fasts when her health permits. She had long resisted adopting namaz, even as a number of her friends started to pray, because she was critical of the hypocrisy that often accompanies public piety. On a recent visit to Kyrgyzstan, however, she told me that she had finally started to pray. Excitedly, I asked her how she liked doing the prayer and if it was having a positive effect (*taasir*) on her. She brushed off my question, saying simply, "It is an obligation [*parz*], a duty [*mildet*]. You have to do it."

I wanted to ask her more questions; I wanted to get her to tell me why, how she had learned the prayer, and what it meant to her. I wanted to analyze her answer for signs of the Muftiate's discourses as filtered through her devout friends or to confirm she was acting on guidance from farther back in time—a mother, a grandmother, a village moldo who had told her she, too, would pray when she became an elder—but the tone of her voice and her simple, evasive words left me speechless. She had told me all I needed to know, she seemed to be saying. Her ability to answer my question while not answering my question—a verbal ruse I felt she had used on me many times before—was an expression of quiet, determined power that both frustrated the curiosity of this foreign researcher and gave me reasons to hope that Central Asians will not relinquish control of their spiritual traditions so easily. As much as official Islam wants to use the trauma of the Soviet era to delegitimize Kyrgyzstani Muslims' spiritual intuitions, many of the faithful I knew were not so easily persuaded. Even if many of them have adopted the practices that official Islam teaches are obligatory, they do so on their own terms, as Salamat-eje seemed to do.

Olivier Roy argues that in many faiths, but particularly Islam, global migrations and other modern trends have led to a shift from "religion" to "religiosity" (Roy 2004; see also Dialmy 2007, 65). In Roy's understanding, "religion" exists where faith is organically embedded in particular cultures and their landscapes. In religion, authoritative knowledge has multiple and diverse sources, including habit, community consensus, and communally recognized authorities, such as elders. "Religiosity," in contrast, insists that faith is independent from culture, community, and place. In religiosity, authority is narrowed, located in a small collection of mobile texts that have legitimacy anywhere and in anyone's hands. Dale Eickelman offers a similar account of changing understandings of religious authority, but where Roy links the shift to global migrations, Eickelman links it to rising literacy rates and the expansion of print capitalism. In the Arab world, he says, these changes have allowed the faithful to depend less on communal, oral forms of religious knowledge and more on textual practices of reading, questioning, and citation. The result is a narrowed understanding of religious authority, intolerance for contradiction, and a shift from viewing scripture as symbolic to viewing scripture as a source of knowledge (Eickelman 1992; see also L. Brenner 2001; S. Brenner 1996; Horvatich 1994). A number of scholars attribute these changes to colonialism. According to this argument, the loss of identity, moral certainty, and political and economic stability associated with postcolonialism make scripturalist Islam's certainties more appealing (e.g., Ahmed 1992; Ismail 2004; Turner 1994, 84).

These ideas are helpful in understanding the Kyrgyzstani context. Where top Muftiate officials have degrees from Saudi Arabia or Egypt and religious texts translated from Arabic and Turkish are available in every village bazaar, it is no surprise that many Kyrgyzstani Muslims find unique, local understandings of Islam less compelling than discourses defined in a limited, accessible corpus of texts and shared with Muslims all across the world. Central Asia, like the Arab world, has benefited from an extraordinary democratization of education. The literacy rate in Central Asia rose from about 5 percent in 1917 to nearly universal by the 1970s (Sievers 2003, 53). When the official leadership tells the faithful that legitimate answers to their spiritual questions can be found in texts (and in published interpretations of those texts by recognized experts), they are speaking to a literate public that has long valued textual sources over collective memory and oral traditions. While it is true that colonialism has shaped Kyrgyzstani spirituality, the postcolonialism argument may be the least helpful here. Remember that for many Kyrgyzstanis, official Islam threatens cherished sources of stability and certainty when it attacks urp-adat, which they turn to as a source of communal solidarity, identity, and existential comfort. My argument, then, is that while reflecting on broader trends in the Muslim world contributes to an understanding of contemporary Central Asia, equally (if not more) useful is attending to local histories and trajectories.

The changes in Kyrgyzstani Islam since the pre-Soviet era cannot be explained solely with reference to globalization, modernization, transnationalism, jihadism, or some other generalizing rubric. The changes in Kyrgyzstani Islam are the products of unique and dramatic shifts in the nature of state power during the Soviet and post-Soviet eras. Pre-Soviet

Central Asian spirituality was diverse. It included multiple Islamic discourses that engaged in constructive competition; they disagreed in ways that ultimately reinforced each other's power. This, in turn, allowed them to counterbalance ever-ambitious political leaders. Colonization, beginning with the Russian occupation and intensifying during the Soviet era, disrupted this balance, giving more power to the state and legitimizing a narrowed understanding of authority according to which discursive disagreement is threatening.

Independence brought further changes. Although the Soviet balance of power was largely maintained, economic instability weakened the state, forcing it to look for new ways to expand its control. One form of control it has turned to increasingly is control of religion. The state believes that by limiting religious diversity it prevents the emergence of religious ideologies that might challenge its power, and by repressing unpopular minority faiths it pleases its majority constituency: mainstream Orthodox and Muslim citizens. On both counts, it protects its own power and engages the help of the Muftiate. The state knows that its Muslim-majority population feels entitled to the freedom to worship and learn about Islam, so the state supports, protects, and (when necessary) controls the spiritual directorate. This close association empowers the Muftiate but imprints its discourses with the intolerance of disagreement and suspicion of rival sources of authority that is a mark of the post-Soviet authoritarian state.

Kyrgyzstanis respond to these pressures in diverse ways. Many Kyrgyzstanis find the Muftiate's interpretation of Islam to be compelling, and they appreciate the widespread availability of Islamic literature. Others want to become better Muslims as measured by the official discourse, but the high level of dedication this demands leaves them content to be, simply, "bad" Muslims (e.g., Montgomery 2007, 355–56). Salamat-eje's response falls somewhere between these responses. Others renounce Islam entirely to join other faiths or embrace a more resolute atheism (e.g., Borbieva 2012a). Still others draw on non-Muslim histories to create new faiths (e.g., Sarygulov 2001). The question that occupies me most as an observer of religious life in Kyrgyzstan, particularly after reflecting on the historical changes in state power, is whether the revival will continue to be a local story, or whether foreign influences and global trends will take advantage of a weak state to overwhelm whatever remains authentically Central Asian about Kyrgyzstani Islam.

CHAPTER EIGHT

Islam, Religious Elites, and the State in Post-Civil War Tajikistan

Tim Epkenhans

Since its rise to power in 1992, Tajikistan's authoritarian government under President Emomali Rahmon has cultivated notoriously difficult relations with "Islam" as the majority religion of Tajikistan's population and with Muslim religious leaders.[1] The legacy of the Soviet Union, its disintegration and the successive civil war (1992–97) still influences perceptions of "Islam" among the dominating political elite in the remote and mountainous Central Asian country. The government and parts of the urban civil society cultivated discourses that hold Islamic concepts of political and social order as well as the ubiquitous "Islamic fundamentalism" (*islomgaroi*) responsible for the outbreak of the civil war in 1992. Thus, public observance of Islamic religious practice—especially in urban Tajikistan—was considered by government officials and urban civil society representatives as intractable and a challenge to the government's nation-building project. The government of President Rahmon thinks of the Tajik nation rather in terms of ethnicity (race), language, and a carefully selected historical memory in which "Islam" was largely excluded (Laruelle 2007). Despite official politics and repressive actions against religious communities, Islam in its many variations has regained a vital, dynamic, and public place in Tajikistan's society. Over the past decade, religious specialists have become visible public figures courted by the media, lay religious communities, and even politicians as moral, social, and religious authorities within the Tajik society.[2] The public observance of Islamic religious practices (prayer, mosque attendance, rites of passage, pilgrimage) and the adoption of an Islamic habitus (language, dress code, diet) have significantly increased among a younger generation of Tajik Muslims.[3] At the same time, government strategies about how to either contain or embrace "Islam" remain inconsistent and ambiguous. While some officials in the presidential administration view Islam as an essential challenge to their conception of a Tajik nation (and their authoritarian rule), others have supported the idea of integrating Islam into the national narrative of independent and post–civil war Tajikistan and by (re)gaining "ownership" over the definition of what "Islam" should mean in the Tajik society.[4] Especially the official announcement of 2009 as the "Year of Imomi A'zam" commemorating the founder of the Hanafi law school in Islam, Abu Hanifa (d. 767 CE), had a brief but significant impact, since it opened the discursive space in Tajikistan and officially sanctioned Islam as part of the Tajik national identity. Simultaneously, the government has tried to increase its institutional and judicial control over religious associations by implementing a set of laws and restructuring the Department for Religious Affairs (DRA, Kumitai oid ba korhoi din) as well as the quasi-state religious administration, the High Council of Tajikistan's Ulema (Šuroi olii Ulamoi Tojikiston).[5] In addition, the government continues to denounce any form of social and political discontent—especially in the country's marginalized eastern regions—as a manifestation of "Islamic radicalism and fundamentalism" eventually trying to fit its alleged security challenges into the agenda of potential international donors, however without addressing central concerns, namely, corruption and the concentration of power in the hands of a few. Since Tajikistan's security forces do not operate transparently or under any democratically legitimized control, officials manage to manipulate the media, population, and eventually the international community on the extent of the security challenge posed by radical groups (Heathershaw and Montgomery 2014).

Despite official projections of a glorious past and present by the president and his entourage, for the majority of Tajiks the present signifies a daily struggle with economic deprivation, exploitation as labor migrants, violence in the country's periphery, endemic corruption, a collapsing education and health-care system, political and social marginalization as well as the absence of the rule of law.[6] The government's orchestration of "virtual politics" (Heathershaw 2009; Wilson 2005) and national identity are more and more measured by reality and dismissed by large parts of the population. Islam with its strong appeal to "justice" and "rule of law" crystallized in the politically charged concept of sharia as the quintessential idea of Islamic law and a legitimate social order offers an alternative version to official narratives of Tajik national identity, polity, and culture. Islam in this context is a maker of cultural "authenticity" and genuine "morality" transcending the Soviet legacy as well as the complex post-Soviet disorder (Hallaq 2009; Louw 2007; Rasanayagam 2010).

In this chapter, I argue that a consolidation of Tajikistan's religious field has taken place since the mid-2000s following a period of "revival" and "mutation" between the 1950s and 1990s.[7] Consolidation in this context means (1) that religious specialists have reemerged as public figures, (2) that public observation as well as social acceptance of Islamic practices and rituals has significantly increased especially among a younger generation of Tajiks, (3) that the discussion in Tajikistan's public sphere about the significance of religion in society and state has intensified, and (4) that the government has adopted (even though inconsistently and reluctantly) a more accommodating approach to religion—however, not out of benign considerations of religious freedom but with the ultimate intention to control the religious field.

The consolidation has also increased the interaction of religious specialists with the larger social space (economy and politics), that is, religious specialists are not limited to their immediate religious function (and field), but are active in adjacent fields as well. Quasi-government institutions, such as the High Council of Ulema, interfere frequently and attempt to extend control over the religious personnel in Tajikistan, however, with limited impact: financial resources are modest, influential and popular religious authorities refuse to get publicly involved with the High Council of Ulema or even disregard its decrees (see below). Administrative practices—conducted usually in coordination with the DRA—such as the registration of mosques and the appointment of an *imam khatib*,[8] were often negotiated within the specific local context and not according to the (admittedly vaguely formulated) law on religious associations (Jumhurii Tojikiston 1998). The government's ambiguous policy regarding Islam has worsened tensions between the state and the society and has alienated religious groups and individuals who generally operate within the limitations of Tajikistan's constitution and the civil law. At the same time, the process of consolidation and the increased *public* social interaction of religious specialists with the larger social space have increased the competition among the religious specialists.

Already in Soviet times, research on Islam in Tajikistan was operating with a set of categories such as "official" or "parallel" Islam while evaluating religious authorities (or more precisely their agenda) as "moderate," "radical," and so forth. Abdullo Rahnamo (2009, 195–208), who has positioned himself in recent years as one of the central academic authorities on Islam in Tajikistan, distinguishes between three categories of religious specialists in Tajikistan, the official ulema (*ruhaniyoni rasmi*) who are integrated into the official, state-sponsored institutions, the traditional ulema (*ruhaniyoni sunnati*), who are according to Rahnamo quietist and apolitical, and finally the political (*siyosi*) or reformist (*islohtalab*) ulema. However, the categorization of religious authorities as "official," "reformist," "parallel," or "political" has been repeatedly criticized for its limited analytical value, which neglects the dynamics within the religious field (Epkenhans 2011; Rasanayagam 2006a; Saroyan 1994). Does "official" indicate the legal status of a religious specialist as registered with the authorities (the DRA and High Council) and does it imply that he also shares the political agenda of Tajikistan's government? Likewise, categories such as "traditional" or "reformist" are too vague to possess explanatory power and refer to very different constituents of a religious specialist's interaction with the wider social space. For instance, the religious agenda of the overwhelming majority of Tajikistan religious specialists is rooted in the larger Hanafi Sunni Islamic "tradition" while discourses of an Islamic "reform" (*isloh*) are limited to a few urban lay religious intellectuals and activists. Religious specialists, such as Hoji Akbar Turajonzoda, are both "traditional" *and* "reformist" since they struggle to reestablish a more normative understanding of Hanafi Sunni religious *tradition* as well as to *reform* the institutional structure regulating Islam in Tajikistan. Simultaneously, lay religious communities expect religious specialists to provide "authentic" religious advice to very tangible daily problems and grievances, which often implies a flexible (or *reformist*) approach to the larger religious tradition.

The Soviet categorization of "official," "unofficial," or "parallel" was facilitated by corresponding discourses among the academic establishment in Oriental Studies (Klimovič 1965; Tasar, chapter 6, this volume) and reveals more about the Soviet administrative and discursive practice than about the religious agenda of given religious specialists. Furthermore, it neglects the interaction, dynamics, and commonalities among religious specialists of different provenance within the religious field. This is not to deny the importance of official registration (or the demonstrative refusal to register and the denial of registration) with the Soviet and post-Soviet authorities.[9]

Local communities—represented by their (in)formal elites—nominate, for instance, imam khatibs (who run the important Friday mosques), but the final authority to appoint an imam khatib is with the DRA as stipulated in the Religious Association Law since 2009 (Jumhurii Tojikiston 2009, §11, 6). Until the implementation of the new law, the appointment was negotiated rather informally between the High Council of Ulema, the DRA, and local communities. The local government was often reluctant to reject a disagreeable candidate bluntly and negotiated rather unconventional solutions with local communities in order to avoid open conflict.[10] With the new Law on Religion, this has changed. The registration process has been carried out more formally in recent years and, among others, Abdullo Rahnamo has been active in the official examination of imam khatibs on behalf of the DRA and the High Council of Ulema, thus judging and evaluating their religious capital and their loyalty to the government.[11] Rahnamo's involvement echoes Devin DeWeese's (2002, 310) statement, that one of the "strange ironies of Soviet history [is] that the Communist Party and the Soviet academic establishment [in Oriental studies] were essentially allied with the official Islamic clergy (not to mention fundamentalists abroad) in adopting a 'rigorist' interpretation of what constituted 'real' Islam." Certainly, Rahnamo is not an isolated case where research is intermingled with a political agenda and research on contemporary Islam in Central Asia (but not only there) always has an intrinsic political dimension influencing the various discourses on Muslim communities and eventually shaping the political agenda of the regional governments as well as the international community.

The Religious Field and Religious Capital
in Contemporary Tajikistan

Rather than referring to categories of "official" or "parallel," I apply Pierre Bourdieu's concept of the religious field (*champ religieux*) for the analysis of the contemporary religious elites in Tajikistan. Bourdieu's concept is particularly productive since it provides a model for processes within the religious field but also the interaction of religious specialists (in the Islamic context: ulema) with the larger society (i.e., other fields). According to Bourdieu the religious field is a structured and contested social space with specific rules, power relations, and distinctive forms of reproduction in which religious specialists generate religious capital, that is, charisma, "secret" spiritual knowledge (for instance, transmitted through mystical lineages and Sufi orders), the "correct" interpretation of religious sources and a concept of a religiously legitimized social order) that corresponds to specific expectations and needs of the religious lay community or the wider society. Eventually the accumulation and representation (habitus) of religious capital by the religious specialists reveal the specific dynamics of power relations within the field (Bourdieu 1971; 2011, 30–91). An important aspect of Bourdieu's concept is the interaction between the various fields (religious, economic, political, arts, education) as well as the disposition of symbolic capital from one field to another (for instance, how religious capital is valued in the economic or political fields). Thus, religious specialists should not be portrayed exclusively within the religious field but also as actors in other fields. Eventually, Bourdieu's categories might help to detach the discourse on Islam in Central Asia from the established categories.

Mapping the religious field in Tajikistan and identifying the most influential religious authorities and—perhaps more important—their religious agenda are to some extent a discretionary affair due to the heterogeneity of the religious field and the lack of empirical data.[12] This chapter does not fill the gap of empirical data but presents some conceptual thoughts on the dynamics within the religious field, the forms of religious capital within the Tajik context, the interaction with the larger social space, and eventually the interference by Tajikistan's government in religious affairs.

The majority of religious specialists in Tajikistan claim affiliation with a Sufi order, mostly by descent from an influential Sufi lineage such as the Naqshbandior Qadiriyya. Honorific titles such as *išon* (ishan), *pir*, *maxsum*, or *šayx* (sheikh) indicate their claim and reference to a *silsila*, a mystical genealogy. In particular the claim to a specific, often locally entrenched genealogy generates a significant form of religious capital among local communities. However, seventy years of Soviet antireligious persecution and the profound social transformation (urbanization, industrialization, and education) changed the social landscapes of Central Asia and repressed Sufism in the public space. Despite the ubiquitous reference to Sufism by religious specialists in contemporary Tajikistan, there is no tangible debate about the intrinsic teachings and practices of the mystical dimensions of Islam, thus Sufism in Tajikistan is not institutionalized and associated with particular beliefs and practices, but rooted in genealogies and a local social environment.[13] The genealogy—here relationship between the teacher (*murshid*) and the student (*murid*)—is also important for the transmission of religious knowledge and therefore symbolic religious capital: memorizing the Koran, mastering the central religious sources, and having a knowledge of Arabic (or at least an able pretense of it) and the canon of classical Persian poetry framed in a particular personal transmission. All major religious specialists emphasize their relation to and initiation by a popular religious authority, such as Mulloxoja, Mullo Baroti Sovetskiy, *eshoni* Turajon, *domlo* Hindustani, or Sangi Kulula. Personally transmitted religious knowledge and initiation constitutes a more important form of symbolic capital than a formal education.[14]

While genealogy and religious knowledge constitute the most important form of religious capital, the formal position a religious specialist occupies, for instance, as imam khatib of one of the 314 registered Friday mosques in Tajikistan, generates symbolic capital as well and allows a given religious specialist to address his congregation publicly during the Friday prayer (*namozi jum'a*).[15] The majority of the prominent religious authorities who recur frequently in the media are (or were) appointed imam khatib of a major regional Friday mosque, such as maxsumi Pir Ismoil Muhammadzoda (aka Ismoil Abdulloev, imam khatib of the Muhammad Rasulluloh Friday mosque in Hisor), Huseyn Musozoda (imam khatib of the prestigious Šayx (Sheikh) Maslihatdin Friday mosque in central Khujand), Ibodullo Kalonov (or Kalonzoda, imam khatib of the Nuri Islom Friday mosque in Khujand), or Hoji Mirzo Ibronov (the former imam khatib of the Hiloli Ahmar Friday mosque in Kulob). The contemporary imam khatibs and officials in the religious administration are predominantly from a generation born in the 1950s. An older generation (born in the 1920s and 1930s), such as domullo Muhammadi Qumsangiri (Panj),[16] has retired from offices or lives reclusively, such as domullo Hikmatullo in the Qarategin Valley. Importantly, none of the popular religious authorities openly supports the Islamic Revival Party of Tajikistan (Hizbi nahzati islomii Tojikiston, IRPT).

One of the most prominent contemporary religious personalities in Tajikistan is the former *qozi-kalon* (1988–93), deputy prime minister (1999–2005), and senator (2005–10) of Tajikistan's Upper House (Majlisi milli), Hoji Akbar Turajonzoda. Although since his resignation as senator in 2010 he has not occupied any public office, he is highly visible in the Tajik media, and his brothers Nuriddinjon (who is a leading Qadiriyya sheikh in the region) and Mahmudjon run the Xalifa Abdulkarim Friday mosque in Vahdat (Epkenhans 2011, 85).[17] The activities of the three Turajon brothers are relatively well-documented through the media, their publications, and their Web sites. In addition, I refer to Pir Ismoil Muhammadzoda (Hisor) as a representative of the religious field in Tajikistan. Although the

Turajon brothers and Pir Ismoil are contenders in the religious field, at the same time, they are businessmen with vested economic interests and also leading authorities in two of the main Sufi brotherhoods in Tajikistan, the Naqshbandi (Pir Ismoil) and Qadiriyya (Turajon brothers) with extended networks of followers or aspirants (murid).[18]

The Turajon brothers capitalize on the religious charisma (or sanctity, *karomot*) of their father eshoni Muhammadrafi' Turajon (1934–2005). Similarly, Pir Ismoil derives his popularity from his father Sangi Kulula (1884–1968), a highly popular and venerated Naqshbandi sheikh in the Kulob area with extended networks of followers in Afghanistan and Uzbekistan.[19] His son, Pir Ismoil, virtually "inherited" his father's murid networks in the larger Kulob area and is today very well connected to the dominating "Kulobi" elite in Tajikistan. And he does not hesitate to put Naqshbandi principles such as *khalvat dar anjoman* (reclusion within society) and *dil ba yoru dast ba kor* (the heart with God and the hand at work) into public practice.[20] Pir Ismoil has accepted several businessmen and politicians as his murids who provide certain services for him as their murshid (spiritual leader). Next to monetary contributions (for instance to maintain Pir Ismoil's Friday mosque or for public works), murids offer voluntary work for their murshid who reciprocates with religious services (especially for the Muslim rites of passage) and simultaneously includes his murids in his patronage networks.[21] Interestingly, Pir Ismoil is not particularly renowned for his impeccable knowledge of the Islamic disciplines, but for his talent as a brilliant reciter of classical Persian poetry, which often conveys ethical and moral advice (*pand* or *nasihat*) and which he embeds in the larger "Islamicate" (Marshall Hodgson) tradition. Accordingly, he presents himself as a skillful equestrian in an Iranian-Islamic tradition of masculinity/manliness (*javonmardi*).

In general, there is a reciprocal benefit for both, murid and murshid: through his religious capital and particular habitus, Pir Ismoil occupies the position of a moral authority among local communities in his area of influence. His intimate associations with the dominating elite (which he exhibits publicly) legitimizes the social stratification and power relations within the Tajik society and the elite's (often predatory) business activities. However, a nexus between ulema and business (*bazaar*) is a common phenomenon in Islamic societies (and not only there) (Moaddel 2005). Thus, businessmen and politicians use their status as murids of Pir Ismoil to generate legitimacy and local support for their activities. Simultaneously, Pir Ismoil is able to pursue his own vested business interests—agriculture, trade, horse breeding, and so forth—unchallenged, despite an extremely unfavorable business climate in Tajikistan. However, Pir Ismoil also acts as an agent for disfranchised local communities mediating in conflicts with elites, thus establishing (his concept of) social order and patronage networks.

Hoji Akbar Turajonzoda (2006, 156–57) likewise refers to the larger Iranian-Islamic cultural tradition in his writings and scathingly ridicules contemporary Tajik poets and writers who romanticize the pre-Islamic past; these are merely people who might know about "national culture [*farhangi milli*]" abstractly from encyclopedic works but who have never understood or sympathized with the "real" national culture and have never shared its weltanschauung (*jahonbini*), morals (*ahloq*), and way of life (*shevai zinidigi*). At the same time, he does not hesitate to concede his significant business interests and income. Turajonzoda owns the cotton processing factory Paxta and most of the arable land suitable for cotton cultivation in the Vahdat district (until 2003 Kofarnihon) east of Dushanbe. The processing plant offers favorable conditions for the local cotton farmers, above all no-interest loans for the purchase of fertilizers, pesticides, seeds, and diesel bypassing the ruinous futurists.[22] Thus, Turajonzoda reinforces his religious capital (and that of his family) by presenting himself as a successful businessman with a strong social and moral consciousness offering decent wages to his employees as well as transparent and fair business relations with his clients—local farmers in his constituency. Implicitly, his orchestration of business ethics and morals has generated additional tensions with the dominating elites—and perhaps marks one of the central differences between him and Pir Ismoil. Since his early career in the religious field, Turajonzoda has always been an ambitious and fairly independent player in the political field as well (Epkenhans 2011). In recent years he has repeatedly criticized the government for its politics and hinted that he would run for office again. However, the government has launched a campaign to discredit Turajonzoda insinuating that he was a KGB agent and eventually that he and his brothers are Shiite Muslims (see below).[23]

This is not to say that Pir Ismoil is a "traditional" or apolitical religious specialist—on the contrary—his Kulobi provenance and entanglement with the dominating elites, his patronage networks, and his vested business interests make him a political actor in Tajikistan's society providing legitimacy to the current political system in Tajikistan. Pir Ismoil's call to the public that "a mosque is the place for worship and not for politics [*masjid joi ibodat ast, na joi siyosat*]" should therefore not be understood as an expression of his being an "apolitical" or a "traditionalist" religious specialist, but as an intrinsically political statement supporting the regime's agenda.[24]

Turajonzoda and Pir Ismoil are particular but not uncommon actors in Tajikistan's religious field. Both have—as do other religious specialists in Tajikistan—vested economic interests, both act as agents of marginalized communities, and both have contributed with their religious agenda to the consolidation of the religious field in Tajikistan—although the "economic" taxation of symbolic capital in this chapter might create the impression that the particular religious agendas of Pir Ismoil or Turajonzoda only rank second for positioning them in the religious field.[25] In fact, Pir Ismoil and Turajonzoda (as well as his brothers) are highly popular among lay religious communities *because* of their religious agenda and for their advice on everyday affairs, usually called *amr ba ma'ruf*—commanding right—in the Islamic tradition.

Commanding Right and Forbidding Wrong

A central concern of Pir Ismoil, Hoji Mirzo, the Turajon brothers, and most of the prominent religious specialists in Tajikistan refers to one of the central tenets of Islam: "commanding right and forbidding wrong" (*amr bi 'l-ma'ruf va nahy az munkar* in Sura 3:104–10) in the form of advice and counsel (*pandu nasihat*). As Michael Cook (2000) has shown in his seminal study, this tenet has multiple dimensions within the Islamic traditions, addressing religious praxis (*ibodot*), central dogma (*aqida*), and in general the question of how to lead a life agreeable to God. Moreover, all religious authorities surveyed in Tajikistan emphasize the social and moral implications of *amr ba ma'ruf*, that is, the implementation of social order and a just economic system. The ulema bears the responsibility for reminding the society about how to command right, while politicians or rulers should actively struggle for the public interest (*maslaha*) of the Islamic community, as allegedly Abu Hanifa specified: "Putting things right (*taghyir*) with the hand is for the political authorities (*umara'*), with the tongue for the schol- ars (*'ulama*), and in (or with) the heart for the common people (*'amma*)" (Cook 2000, 309).

In recent years, the term amr ba ma'ruf (or *amri ma'ruf*) has become a synonym in Tajikistan for advice given by religious specialists. Prominent religious authorities who operate a Friday mosque, such as Nuriddinjon (until 2011) in Vahdat, Pir Ismoil in Hisor, and Hoji Mirzo in Kulob, give advice either after or before the Friday prayer. Their assistants collect and sort out questions submitted by the congregation, the selected questions are read out and answered publicly by the imam khatib. In case the imam khatib wants to address a specific topic, he might "manipulate" a corresponding question or "encourage" his followers to ask the "right" question. Regularly, the *suol va javob* or *posuxi pursisho* ("questions and answers" or "answers to questions") are recorded on audio or video DVDs and distributed in front of mosques and in bazaars throughout Tajikistan.[26]

A relatively new phenomenon in Tajikistan is the "Islamic" Internet, which has expanded rapidly in recent years and offers unprecedented features in the communication and dissemination of Islamic principles and beliefs. Islamic weblogs in Tajik discuss a plethora of related issues, and several religious authorities have established Web sites in order to reach out beyond their Friday mosques, in particular to the significant number of Tajik labor migrants in Russia and elsewhere. Web sites offer audio and video recordings of amri ma'ruf as well as other religious events as downloads in mobile phone compatible formats. Likewise, the Web site of the IRPT (www.nahzat.tj) offers various religious advice (nasihat) as well as downloadable copies of their weekly newspaper (*Najot*) and monthly magazine (*Safinai umed*).[27] The Turajon brothers Nuriddinjon, Mahmudjon, and Hoji Akbar Turajonzoda are perhaps the Internet pioneers of Tajikistan's religious field in maintaining a popular Web site (www.turajon.org), a Facebook account (www.facebook.com/turajon), and a YouTube channel (www.youtube.com/turajoncom) with some 200 hours of video material. The Web sites offer biographies of the three brothers and their father, eshoni Turajon, publications on a broad range of Islamic traditions, video and audio downloads. The Web site also hosts a large online archive on legal and moral advice (suol va javob) with 1,084 questions addressed to the three Turajon brothers between 2010 and August 2012.[28] Table 8.1 provides an overview and shows the distribution of topics between the three brothers.

The Internet has gradually changed the patterns of interaction between the religious specialists and their followers because the questions are usually submitted anonymously. Thus taboo topics regarding, for instance, sexuality, are much more explicitly addressed than in personal communication. The Internet is restricted and expensive in Tajikistan, the government frequently shuts down Web sites (including social media platforms such as Facebook and Odnoklassniki), often citing technical problems and maintenance (Nozimova and Epkenhans 2013).

Table 8.1. Distribution of Topics among the Turajon Brothers

Discipline (Category)	Nuriddinjon	Turajonzoda	Mahmudjon
aqida (Arabic for "belief," "dogmatic theology")	30	11	7
hajj (pilgrimage to Mecca)	6	2	–
tahorat (ablution)	38	14	28
zakat (alms, charity)	17	4	16
muomalahoi moli (economic affairs)	25	23	9
namaz (prayer)	192	61	173
nikoh va taloq (marriage and divorce)	82	38	52
gunagun (miscellaneous)	29	14	22
ruza (fasting during Ramadan)	60 (joint *fatwa* by the three brothers)		
qism baroi zanon (section for women)	83	14	34
Subtotal (*ruza* included in Nuriddinjon)	562	181	341
Grand total	1,084		

In the case of the Turajon Web site, the suol va javob are grouped in ten subsections. The largest number of questions by far are related to the ibodot, the regulation of ritual practice and worship (57 percent), while the "social law" (*mu'omalot*) is addressed in some 25 percent of the cases.[29] The ibodot-related questions deal predominantly with practical issues and the correct performance of the formal prayer (*namoz* or *salot*) and the supplication (*duo*), the ritual purification (*tahorat, ghosl, tayammom*), the pilgrimage to Mecca (hajj) as well as aspects of fasting during Ramadan (*ruza*). The answers of Nuriddinjon, Turajonzoda, and Mahmudjon are unspectacular and delimit their religious agenda firmly within a normative Sunni Hanafi scholarly tradition.

The most interesting parts of the archive, however, are the miscellaneous (*gunagun*) and the section for women (*qism baroi zanon*) because these sections allow conclusions about the social relevance and embedment of religious specialists within the Tajik society. Both sections cover mundane, but often very personal and intimate issues, especially family affairs (domestic violence, youth, marital life, polygamy), general moral conduct within the local community, social problems (unemployment), health issues, drug abuse, sexuality, and—above all—the dramatic impact of labor migration. Since independence, the former Soviet claim to gender equality has yielded to the domination of men in a highly paternalistic society. Young women in particular face increasing discrimination and inequality in education and access to the labor market as well as with regard to individual liberties. Moreover, the long-term consequences of labor migration and the absence of two-thirds of the population of working-age men in Tajikistan's patriarchal society on families, local communities, and in particular the status of women are not yet foreseeable (Hegland 2010; Khushkadamova 2010; Nozimova and Epkenhans 2013).

The questions submitted by women carefully reflect these conflicts within the Tajik society and indicate the intrinsically social and political dimension of amri ma'ruf, especially since *public* religious elites are exclusively men. Tajikistan's media and public take no notice of female religious specialists (usually called *bibi-otun, bibi-xanum,* or *bibi-xalifa*) who offer specific religious services for women (Stephan 2010), and in a controversial decision the High Council of Tajikistan Ulema banned women from attending mosque services in 2004.[30] The IRPT has promoted the participation of women in the party and the two media outlets, *Najot* and *Safinai Umed,* frequently present the IRPT's conception regarding the role of women in society, which generally satisfies a conservative urban electorate.[31] The IRPT supports in particular the legal equality of women in society and equal access to education, but leaves no doubts that motherhood, devotion to family life, and submission to her husband is the actual purpose of a woman's life. Similarly, the three Turajon brothers advance a rather conservative view on the role of women in society, but approach the issue from an Islamic-judicial point of view, arguing that the inequality of women in the contemporary Tajik society is related to weak state institutions and a fundamental misinterpretation of Islamic legal provisions by local communities without proper religious guidance. According to Turajonzoda (2011, 16–27), normative Hanafi Sunni law guarantees perfect equality between men and women and therefore social order within a society. Consequently, Nuriddinjon and Turajonzoda present themselves as "modern ulema" (*ulamoi muasir*) who have a refined understanding of the social landscapes in Tajikistan (including female ones) and the role of Islam in society. For instance, Faxima from Mastčoh asks eshoni Nuriddinjon in February 2011, whether it is permitted to go on the hajj as a single woman without men. Nuriddinjon replies that "a woman should conduct the hajj with male relatives. . . . But modern ulema give women permission to go on the hajj in case the women are alone in their community and there is no threat of dissent." Nuriddinjon also defied the 2004 decree by the High Council of Ulema and publicly invited women to attend religious services at his Xalifa Abdulkarim Friday mosque.

The Turajon brothers represent a balanced conservative position. They clearly explicate that women share the same dignity as men and that Islam—compared to other religions—genuinely liberated and enlightened women. Out of consideration for their conservative and predominately male audience, however, they set limits to the demand for emancipation and equality. In various sermons, Nuriddinjon admonished his female audience, that they should respect their husbands as "teachers" (*muollim*) of the family and support them.[32]

The recorded and written amri ma'ruf circulating in Tajikistan need a far more thorough analysis, which is beyond the scope of this chapter. Furthermore, there is insufficient data on the relevance of amri ma'ruf in everyday life and the social composition of the questioners. However, incidental narratives—the (inevitable) taxi driver who listens nonstop to religious recordings, interviews, personal observation—and disparate data on the numbers of Web site visitors cautiously support the impression that amri ma'ruf has transcended beyond the immediate religious dimension to the social and political spheres by offering tangible advice for central grievances in Tajikistan's contemporary society. Advice given by religious specialists is perceived by parts of the population as genuinely "authentic" and "credible" and this seems to be valid also for a younger generation as the popularity of "Islamic" ring tones and applications for mobile phones demonstrates. Furthermore, the current trend among religious authorities and intellectuals to reconcile the Islamic with the Iranian/Tajik heritage should be considered within the wider political context as an alternative, inclusive version of Tajikistan's national identity in contrast to the exclusive government-sponsored one.

Obviously, the issue of authenticity and credibility constitutes a serious challenge to Tajikistan's political elite and their authoritarian rule. This is demonstrated in a letter of August 2010 from Abdurahim Holiqov, the former chairman of the DRA,[33] to President Rahmon. Holiqov expresses his concerns regarding the enormous influence exerted by religious specialists (here *mulloho*) through their audio and video recordings on a younger generation of Tajiks.[34] He recommends challenging the religious specialists' hegemony in the definition of morals (*axloq*) and values (*arzešho*) by intensifying government propaganda, for instance by producing television plays with popular actors based on spiritually (*ma'navi*) valuable texts of the "national" literary tradition, such as Mavlana Jaloliddin Balxi's (aka Rumi) *Bahoristan* and *Masnavii ma'navi* (thirteenth century), Sa'di's *Bustan* (thirteenth century), the *Nasihatnoma* of Kaykavus (eleventh century), and finally the *Zaxirat-ul-mulk* of Mir Sayid Alii Hamadoni (fourteenth/fifteenth centuries). Eventually, he explicates that suppression of politicization of Islam (*siyosišavi*) is the most important responsibility of the government. However, in order to succeed, the government has to challenge malicious (*gharaznok*) groups on two dimensions, morals (axloq) and belief (*e'teqod*). Holiqov's letter indicates disagreements within the political elite of Tajikistan about how to counter the increasing popularity of religious specialists and their projections of "authentic" identity. While religious specialists who refer to a narrow, exclusively Islamic tradition (for instance those who are labeled as "Salafi") can be easily portrayed as representatives of an "other," "foreign," or "alien" Islam, those religious specialists who have either integrated—or reconciled—the religious and cultural traditions (for instance, the Iranian-Islamic synthesis) directly challenge the official, regime-sponsored narratives of the Tajik nation at root and are difficult to marginalize or brand as the "Other."

Official Identity Politics

In August 1996, a year before the end of the civil war, Rahmon gave a programmatic speech titled "The Tajiks in the Mirror of History" (Tojikon dar oinai ta'rix) (Rahmon[ov] 2002, 3–12). In his speech Rahmon establishes *the* official Tajik national narrative: "It is known to all, that the Tajiks are genuine Aryans [*oriyoiasl*], and from ancient times the original inhabitants [*sokinoni asli*] of Central Asia" (4). Rahmon describes the Tajiks as peace-loving, altruistic, united, honest, and cultured people who established with the Somonid Dynasty, a sophisticated Tajik polity rich in cultural finesse in the tenth century CE. The peaceful Tajiks, however, did not anticipate the viciousness of their neighbors (the Turks—*turkho*), who repeatedly plundered and eventually occupied the homeland of the Tajiks, destroying their first polity and quasi-parasitically establishing their own statehood based on the Tajik model.

Rahmon's historical narrative, which is largely a reinterpretation of the Soviet-era repertoire of historical narratives (Yountchi 2011), was initially based on three constituent historical themes: first, the Aryan ethnic origin of the Tajiks (see figure 8.1), second, the "completion" (*tashakkul*) of the Ta-

FIGURE 8.1. Tajikistan (Khujand), 2001. Rahmon: "The Aryan civilization is the spiritual cradle of mankind."

jik nation during the Somonid reign—in order to distance the Tajiks from the Iranians—and third, the promotion of Zoroastrianism as the authentic religion of the Tajiks (Rahmon[ov] 2002, 10–14). While the idea of introducing Zoroastrianism as the officially sanctioned religion was abandoned quickly,[35] the "Aryan" origin and the glorification of the Somonids remain the central elements of the official construction of Tajik identity. Reviewing the state history textbook, Helge Blakkisrud and Shahnoza Nozimova conclude that Islam "is suspiciously absent" (2010, 185). Indeed, chapters dealing with Islam reveal a highly essentialist concept: Islam is portrayed as intellectually rather unsophisticated and as an independent and unalterable variable disconnected from the fundamental social, political, and cultural developments of the Tajik society. Furthermore, textbooks imply that Islam is not part of the Tajik Self, but an Arabic/Uzbek Other, a religion alien to the Tajiks imposed on them by the Arab invasion in the eighth century. The lengthy description of the Somonids as the first Tajik polity is completely silent on their contribution to the Islamization of Central Asia and the Islamic civilization as such (Ghafurov 1998; Ne'matov 2003; Xojaev 2002; Ya'qubov 2001). Eventually, the construction of an explicitly secular national identity by an authoritarian regime is not a unique feature of Tajikistan. The Pahlavi Dynasty in Iran (1925–79) invested significant resources in promoting a secular national identity referring to the pre-Islamic

Iranian history, the dynastic continuity since the Achaemenid Empire (500 BCE), and the alleged Aryan origins of the Iranians (Ansari 2012).

Despite the "virtual" character of politics in Tajikistan, this does not mean that identity politics are generally based on empty symbolism. Identity politics are rather an idiom in which dominant elites express their conception of "moral" values, social order, and "justice" as well as the relationship between state and society—echoing Antonio Gramsci's statement that state power needs not only coercion but also persuasion. The Rahmon government continuously emphasizes the secular (*dunyavi*) character of the Tajik state and statehood (*davlatdori*) (Rahmon 2002). The constant affirmation of secularism and atheism is related to the Soviet habitus among Tajikistan's contemporary political elite. However, the emphasis on secularism is not only rooted in a Soviet habitus. First, Rahmon and his entourage have experienced the capacity of religious authorities to mobilize people in the late 1980s and early 1990s. Especially Turajonzoda demonstrated how an independent and politically self-conscious qozi-kalon was able to emerge as a vital political actor in Tajikistan. At the same time, ideological slogans of the Soviet Union were exposed as performative rituals devoid of any meaning (Karim 1997; Yurchak 2006). Second, the political elite—predominantly from the CPT—of the late 1980s and early 1990s continuously depicted the heterogeneous opposition as Islamic fundamentalists or with a popular pejorative term as *vovchiks* (Karim 1997, 456; Nasriddinov 1995, 15).[36] Although some actors in the government faction (such as the notorious Sangak Safarov or Haydar Sharifov) referred to Islamic modes of legitimation for their actions,[37] it became obvious during the civil war and in particular after the peace agreement in 1997, that Rahmon's administration would not be able to claim "ownership" over Islam. His 1996 speech on the origins of the Tajiks was drafted in anticipation of the integration of the IRPT after a peace agreement. With the exclusion of "Islam" as part of the Tajiks' identity, Rahmon assigns to the IRPT the role of not only a political opposition but also a cultural one. Third, despite Rahmon's frequent assertions of building a democratic government based on the rule of law, the dominant elites have demonstrated a stronger intention to extract resources and dismantle the state, severely restricting the capacity to deal with the post-Soviet transformation process (Ganev 2005). Islam reconstructed by religious specialists in Tajikistan strongly postulates justice and good governance (amri ma'ruf and *maslahat*), whereas secularism in the understanding of post-Soviet rulers is largely restricted to the separation of religion and state without any subtle values and ideological subtext. Furthermore, prominent religious authorities portray Islam within the larger Persian and Islamicate cultural tradition as an "authentic" concept of Tajik identity *and* social order. While in their amri ma'ruf imam khatibs address tangible grievances in the Tajik society and offer practical but nonetheless culturally "authentic" solutions, government projections of a particular national identity are largely disconnected from everyday realities in Tajikistan.

A Change in Strategy? The Year of Imomi A'zam

In 2007 Tajikistan's government declared 2009 as the Year of Imomi A'zam (Abu Hanifa) indicating a sudden change in strategy by embracing Islam as part of Tajikistan's cultural heritage and identity. Previous commemoration years, such as the controversial year 2006 as the Year of Aryan Civilization (*soli tamadduni oriyoi*), usually reflected the paradigms of official identity politics. According to observers, officials in the presidential administration developed the idea in order to regain ownership of Islam in the Tajik society. The initiative of including Islam was accompanied by measures to increase control over religious associations and by redrafting the Law on Religion and by instructing the law enforcement agencies to increase their pressure on religious communities.

Reportedly, Rahmon liked the idea since it gave him the opportunity to stage himself abroad and at home as a benevolent Islamic ruler, obviously with the intention to attract foreign investors from Islamic countries, such as Qatar, and to enhance his standing in the Organization for Islamic Cooperation (OIC). Accordingly, Dushanbe was elevated to the "Capital of Islamic Culture" in 2010 and posters of Rahmon appeared praising the moral value of prayer (see figure 8.2), and in November 2011 he headed the foundation stone ceremony for the construction of Central Asia's largest Friday mosque in Dushanbe.[38] Although Rahmon did not craft the book on the Year of Imomi A'zam himself, he outlined the significance of Abu Hanifa in a lengthy article in the government mouthpiece *Jumhuriyat*.[39] Rahmon presents his vision of Abu Hanifa in terms of Tajikistan's civil war experience and the strong state as guarantor of peace and stability: "The experience of the years of civil disturbance in Tajikistan indicate, that in case the fundament of state is weakened, the level of treason and dishonorable, immoral behavior against the people increases" (Rahmon 2009, 1). Rahmon concedes that the Koran is a source of advice and counsel, commanding justice (*insof*), fraternalism (*barodari*), as well as tolerance (*tahammulpaziri*), which is also a central topic in Abu Hanifa's writings.

FIGURE 8.2. Tajikistan (Khujand), 2010. Rahmon: "Humanity flourishes with prayer."

However, Rahmon specifies that Abu Hanifa was first and foremost a Tajik merchant (*tojir*) and not merely a religious scholar, thus he was predominantly concerned with justice and fairness (*adlu qist*) in commerce (*bazaar*) and less in the political or social system (Rahmon 2009, 2).[40] Consequently, Rahmon "de-Islamicizes" Abu Hanifa by integrating him into the larger Persian literary heritage of Rudaki or Kaykavus Ibn Iskander,[41] and by presenting his oeuvre as a "mirror of princes" (*andarz* or *pandu nasihat*) genre without any religious content. In Rahmon's version of Abu Hanifa, the founder of the Hanafi law school admonishes his followers to show respect (*ehtirom*) toward the ruler (*podshoh*), to accept one's position in society, and to attend to one's duty (Rahmon 2009, 6), thus legitimizing the existing political and social order. These qualities, Rahmon continues, are needed for the "cultural reconstruction" (*bozsozii farhangi*) of post–civil war Tajikistan (Rahmon 2009, 7).

Despite Rahmon's effort to neglect Abu Hanifa as an imminent Islamic scholar, his intervention, as well as various events during 2009 celebrating Abu Hanifa,[42] opened space for a string of publications calling for a stronger integration of Islam into the official representation of Tajikistan (Rahnamo 2008, 2009; Markazi islomshinosi 2009). However, among government officials enthusiasm to reintegrate Islam into daily political practice and the narrative of Tajik identity was muted and already critically reviewed during 2009. Perhaps Tajik officials and Rahmon himself realized that a demonstrative reference to alleged Islamic values and principles in foreign policymaking does not overcome considerations of realpolitik. In addition officials complained about the lack of coordination and resources, the limited institutional capacity on the level of the DRA and High Council of Ulema, and conflicting strategies regarding how to implement the new policy.[43] Perhaps, a good example of the inconsistencies and disagreements is evident in the development of a textbook on Islam. In 2008 the Ministry of Education launched pilot classes on religious instruction from the sixth grade on, replacing the Soviet-style seventh-grade class on world religions (Rahimzoda and Axmadov 2000). However, the textbook for the new class, *Principles of Islamic Knowledge* (Asoshoi ma'rifati Islomi), was severely criticized by some religious authorities as well as government officials and the few copies that circulated in 2009 were withdrawn silently.[44] Despite the commemoration of Abu Hanifa and Rahmon's brief rapprochement with religion in 2009, the overall government policy regarding religion and religious association remained hostile or at least ambiguous. In any case, the Rahmon administration obviously has larger ambitions to reinvent Tajikistan and Tajik society. The inclusion of Islam was only a short episode and the government returned to its conceptualization of "Islam" as external to their conception of an "authentic" Tajik identity. While the intellectual struggle for the "hearts and minds" of the Muslim communities in Tajikistan was suspended, the government resorted to control and manipulation through laws and government institutions.

A Cultural Revolution? Regulating Traditions and Religion by Law

During glasnost the "rule of law," constitutional order, and legality already constituted an important issue among political actors in Tajikistan. Accordingly, all factions in the civil war claimed to defend the constitutional order while denouncing their opponents' policies as "unconstitutional" (*ghayrqanuni*) and illegal (Kenjaev 1993; Rahmon 2002). Rahmon, for instance, continuously orchestrates himself as the champion of constitutional law (*hoquqbonyod*) and order in his public announcements legitimizing his accession to political power mainly in legalistic terms, and therefore his consolidation of power was accompanied by writing and rewriting of the legal codes. Relevant for this analysis are three laws that were implemented between 2007 and 2011: The "Law on Regulating Traditions, Festivities and Ceremonies" (Jumhurii Tojikiston 2007), the "Law on the Freedom of Conscience and Religious Associations" (2009), and finally the "Law on the Responsibility of the Father and Mother in the Education and Up-bringing of a Child" (2011). In 2007 the government used the legislature to pass a law on regulating traditions, festivities, and ceremonies to impose severe restrictions on the format of religious rites of passage.[45] The law on traditions offers in addition a reading of the government's conception of norms, morals, and values that it imposes on the population. Unsurprisingly, this imagination does not differ from President Rahmon's earlier characterization of the genuine qualities of the Aryans: sobriety, frugality, discipline, and a sense of unity and reason. Considering the tremendous contradiction between the elites' public lavishness (Rahmon sports a white Bentley convertible in parades) and their projection of proper national conduct, segments of Tajikistan's urban population have succumbed to an increasing cynicism, calling the law a "cultural revolution" that infringes on the freedom of assembly and gives local officials a pretense for intruding into privacy. A year later and after several years of discussions, Tajikistan's parliament passed a new religious association law with a highly intrusive character allowing the DRA to interfere directly in the internal affairs of religious associations, including substantive evaluation of the merits of a religion (Epkenhans 2010, 324–27; OSCE/ODIHR 2008). The 2011 law on parental responsibilities has a similar intention. The central directive bans youth under the age of eighteen from attending public prayers in mosques and imposes a curfew on youth from 10:00 p.m. to 6:00 a.m. in summer and from 8:00 p.m. to 6:00 a.m. in winter (Jumhurii Tojikiston 2011, §4). Furthermore, parents are accountable for teaching their children to "respect their homeland [*ehterom ba vatan*], the law [*qanun*], and national values [*arzeshoi melli*] (§8). Characteristic of post-Soviet Tajik legislative texts is the vagueness and ambiguity of language, which allows highly arbitrary implementation of the laws.

Control and Manipulation: Government Institutions and Islam

The severe restrictions and government intrusion into the private affairs of its citizens—despite the international conventions to which Tajikistan acceded after 1992—inherently follow Soviet patterns of regulatory politics and the two central government agencies administering Islam are part of the Soviet institutional legacy in Central Asia, the DRA, and the High Council of Tajikistan's Ulema. The institutional setup of the DRA has changed several times over the past decade reflecting dissent and inconclusiveness in the presidential administration. Until 2006, the DRA operated as a state committee under the presidential administration with branch offices at the regional *viloyat* (oblast) level. The DRA's chairman was considered to hold the rank of a minister. Between 2006 and 2010, the DRA was restructured as a department in the Ministry of Culture. In 2010 the DRA was again reassigned to the powerful presidential administration.[46] The DRA is generally responsible for the implementation of the religious association law, and thus all religious groups and associations have to register with the DRA and submit their bylaws and regulations for approval (Epkenhans 2010, 323–30). Under the chairman Abdurahim Holiqov (in office from May 2010 to February 2015), the DRA has intensified its coordination with the High Council of Ulema, the quasi-state administration for Islamic affairs. The council is a successor to the official muftiate for Central Asia during the Soviet period (commonly known by the Russian acronym, SADUM[47]) and to the republican *qoziyot* until 1996 (Saroyan 1994). As DeWeese (2002, 306) remarks both SADUM and qoziyot were structures of "Soviet life that became 'indigenized' and assimilated into Islamic religious life, and not only as a means of control—though they are certainly used in that way by many of the post-Soviet governments but as part of the local assumptions and expectations regarding the ways in which religious affairs are to be recognized and regulated."

Between 1996 and 2010 the council under the leadership of Amanullo Nematov was a relatively unimportant and indiscernible institution with few competences and little influence on dynamics in the religious field. This has changed perceptibly with the appointment of the council's new chairman Mukarram Abdulqodirzoda in 2010, which came as a surprise to most observers.[48] With Abdulqodirzoda a more interventionist and disputatious personality assumed the position of council chairman and in coordination with the DRA's chairman Holiqov (who was appointed a few months earlier) the council emerged as a belligerent and aggressive actor in the religious field, obviously with the government directive to recapture control over the religious field and contain insubordinate and independent religious authorities. Informed observers of Tajikistan's politics agree that Rahmon has been less engaged in the micromanagement of political affairs in recent years. Instead, the presidential administration seems to formulate the general political directives while the various institutions and department—sometimes in a competitive setting—implement the directives according to their interpretation. Thus, the realignment of the DRA and its increased cooperation with the High Council for Ulema has to be seen in this particular context.

Accordingly, the DRA and High Council of Ulema replaced several imam khatibs, reorganized the Islamic University,[49] and increased control over the nineteen Islamic secondary schools (madrasas) in Tajikistan. Simultaneously, it established an examination board for imam khatibs (in which Abdullo Rahnamo is involved) and issued a list of suitable topics for Friday sermon (*khutba*). An official representative of the DRA declared that the khutba should be limited to a maximum fifteen minutes of offering advice (*pand*) as well as commanding right (*amri maʿruf*). As suitable topics the DRA representative singled out "respect for father and mother, friendship, and comradeship [*dustivu rafoqat*] and not to lie,"[50] and attached a list of sixty mandatory khutba subjects. Furthermore, the High Council introduced a salary for the imam khatibs and even issued a distinct standardized dress code.

Most spectacular, however, was Abdulqodirzoda's decision to confront Turajonzoda and his brother ešoni Nuriddinjon, arguably the most prominent actors in Tajikistan's religious field. The conflict commenced gradually with a formal complaint against Turajonzoda for failing to submit his essay "The Place of Women in Islam" (2011) to the High Council for official approval and escalated when Abdulqodirzoda accused Nuriddinjon of instigating religious hatred by celebrating the Shiite religious festival of *ašura* in December 2011.[51] Although a successive court case between Abdulqodirzoda and the Turajon brothers was decided in the latters' favor, the High Council nonetheless closed the Xalifa Abbdulkarim Friday mosque in Vahdat and eventually demoted the mosque to a regular five-times-daily-prayer mosque (still its current status as of July 2015). The conflict between Abdulqodirzoda and the Turajon brothers received an immense media response—especially considering Tajikistan's restrictive public sphere. *Millat, Ozodagon, Faraj, Paykon,* and *Asia Plus* reported in detail about the dispute with little sympathies for the High Council and its chairman. The IRPT's weekly *Najot* even called Abdulqodirzoda's actions against the Turajonzoda brothers "malicious and conspiring [*gharanok va fitnaangez*],"[52] and demanded a fundamental reform of the High Council of Tajikistan's Ulema, which should transform the institution to an independent representative of Tajikistan's ulema.

Abdulqodirzoda certainly did not confront the Turajon family without approval by the presidential administration. However, there is perhaps another motivation for his aggressive approach: Abdulqodirzoda—as a former official in the DRA—has little symbolic capital at his disposal within the religious field. He is not affiliated with a prominent religious family, he has no significant circle of students and followers, and he certainly lacks the particular charisma of religious authorities such as Turajonzoda, Nuriddinjon, or Pir Ismoil. Thus, by confronting the Turajon family, he obviously intended to demonstrate his determination to occupy a central position within the religious field of contemporary Tajikistan. Furthermore, Turajonzoda has repeatedly recommended reforming the High Council of Ulema by restoring its independence (like the qoziyot he organized between 1988 and 1992). Because Turajonzoda was formerly the popular though not undisputed qozi-kalon, his statements carry some weight and challenge Abdulqodirzoda's authority. Finally, the rumors about Turajonzoda's affiliation with the KGB in 2009 as well as the campaign by the DRA and the High Council against him and his family has to be seen in the wider political context of Tajikistan, in particular the presidential elections in November 2013. Turajonzoda has frequently been tipped by the Tajik media as a potential candidate running for various offices, including that of president. While he used to comment on these reports equivocally, leaving the door open for a candidacy, he repudiated any further political ambitions in May 2012.[53] The concerted negative campaign against him and his family by the government-controlled media and the High Council of Ulema certainly influenced his decision.

The public conflict between the High Council and the Turajon brothers illustrates the increasingly confrontational policy of the government regarding Islam and religious authorities in Tajikistan. However, it also shows that the private media have regained a more influential position among Tajikistan's general public and that it will be increasingly difficult for the government to impose its interpretation of social and political dynamics on the public.

The Limits of Consolidation

In the past decade religious specialists have been able to consolidate the religious field in Tajikistan despite challenges by radical Islamic groups and continuous interference by an authoritarian government, which envisions Tajikistan as a "secular" nation united by race and historical destiny. The process of consolidation in the religious field is multifaceted. Religious specialists have assertively resumed the religious, ethical, and social guidance of lay Muslim communities and have "invested" their symbolic capital in the economic and political fields. Religious specialists present their advice (nasihat) as "authentic" and entrenched in the Islamic *and* Iranian (or better: Tajik) cultural heritage as well as embedded in the modern social imaginaries of Muslims in Tajikistan. Religious specialists, such as the three Turajon brothers and Pir Ismoil, have represented their religious, social, and cultural agendas assertively in recent years and have challenged—intentionally or not—core elements of the nation-building project of Tajikistan's authoritarian government. They also address central social grievances in the Tajik society and represent a concept of common good (maslahat), which either legitimizes the existing social and political order (Pir Ismoil) or (carefully) outlines alternative social practices alleviating the social inequalities in Tajikistan (Turajonzoda). In either case, however, the conventional classification of religious specialists as "parallel," "official," "traditionalist," or "reformist," as suggested by the Soviet-era literature on Islam and recently for Tajikistan by Abdullo Rahnamo, inadequately reflects the complexities of the religious field in Tajikistan and in particular their relationship with the political field and the larger society. Perhaps, Bourdieu's model of a religious field (including the categories of habitus and symbolic capital) can offer an alternative framework for understanding some societal roles and functions of religious specialists in Tajikistan, for the analysis of the spiritual dimensions of Islam—the "enchanted modern" (Deeb 2006)—Bourdieu's model is certainly less applicable.

The process of consolidation is not irreversible. Over past years, the government has struggled to establish its authority over the religious field by restructuring "official," quasi-government Islamic institutions and by sanctioning a more interventionist approach. Despite an inconsistent strategy, limited personal and financial resources, and at times a rapid change of mind by the dominating elites, the High Council of Ulema has gradually had success in assuming more regulatory responsibilities (in cooperation with the DRA) regarding the operation of the Islamic University in Dushanbe, the contentious examination of imam khatibs, and the general implementation of the religious association law. Additionally, the High Council under Abdulqodirzoda seems to have reemerged as an institution that lay Muslims address for legal counseling.[54] Interestingly, alleged radical or extremist Islamic groups, such as the notorious Hizb-ut-Tahrir, which throughout the 2000s was presented as the ubiquitous danger in Tajikistan and Central Asia, have become largely irrelevant for the High Council or the DRA, perhaps an indication that the construction of danger discourses in Central Asia is dubious (Heathershaw and Megoran 2011; Heathershaw and Montgomery 2014). Instead and for the above-mentioned reasons, both institutions focus on the "mainstream" religious specialists in Tajikistan.

Considering the heterogeneity and diversity of the religious field and the strategies of religious specialists to evade official directives, and also the limited resources (financially as well as intellectually) invested by government agencies in controlling Islam, the interventions by the government in the religious field might generate additional tension in a society exposed to the complex and difficult challenges of social, economic, and cultural transformation.

CHAPTER NINE

When Religion Resorts to Violence

Explaining the Spatial Variation in Religious-Based Mobilization in Kyrgyzstan

Alisher Khamidov

In the early 1990s, a time when the newly independent states of Soviet Central Asia grappled with economic turmoil and political turbulence, scholars and journalists made ominous predictions about the role of religion in Central Asia. Freed from Soviet control, as some observers claimed, Islam would emerge as a potent political force capable of mobilizing masses and toppling post-Soviet Communist elites (Allsworth 1989; Haghayeghi 1996; Voll 1994). To substantiate such dire predictions, observers pointed to a staggering rise in the level of religiosity among Central Asians in the early 1990s (Botobekov 2001),[1] the arrival of various religious denominations, including radical ones, in the region, and growing ties between Central Asian Muslims and religious communities in Afghanistan, Iran, and Pakistan (Lubin and Rubin 1999).

As Tim Epkenhans (chapter 8, this volume) demonstrates, religion proved its capacity to serve as a mobilizing force in the 1993–97 civil war in Tajikistan when Islamic opposition locked horns with the post-Soviet secular authorities. Militants belonging to the Islamic Movement of Uzbekistan (IMU) were also driven by their religious credo when they infiltrated the Kyrgyz and Uzbek sections of the Ferghana Valley in the summer of 1999 and 2000, respectively.[2] Nevertheless, the dire prediction that the entire region would be engulfed by Islamic mobilization has failed to materialize. With the exception of Tajikistan, Central Asia witnessed neither large scale religious mobilization nor an alliance between the religious and secular opposition groups. Observant citizens stood aloof from the tumultuous developments such as the May 2005 Andijan uprising in Uzbekistan and the two popular uprisings (March 2005 and April 2010) in Kyrgyzstan. In general, religious-based protests, when they erupted in some parts of the region, were small in size, narrow in geographic scope (they occurred in some geographic locales but not in others), and weak in organization.

This chapter addresses two questions arising from the above observations about religion and politics in Central Asia: First, what explains the seemingly timid role of religion in Central Asian politics? And second, why has tension between the secular state and religious communities been more pronounced in some geographic areas than in others? In other words, why have some Muslim communities in some Central Asian corners chosen to challenge the state in a more direct and violent manner while similarly aggrieved communities have chosen to pursue peaceful means of resolving disputes with the authorities?

Scholars of Central Asia have paid some attention to the theme of tension between secular states and Muslim communities. In particular, four schools of thought can be identified in the literature. According to the first school, tension is caused by the secular state's exclusion or marginalization of Muslims, a process exacerbated by the perceived anti-Muslim bias in the foreign and domestic security policies of secular governments (Rashid 2002). A second explanation is that tension is the work of global extremist groups espousing the creation/restoration of an Islamic caliphate (Naumkin 2005). The third view is that the conflict between religion and state disguises unresolved interethnic problems in some secular countries.[3] And finally, the tension between state and religion is depicted by some observers as part of a broader trend—a clash of Western and Muslim civilizations (Huntington 1993).

Though this work does not deny the relevance of these explanations, it posits that repressive policies of central governments, ethnic animosities, unsanctioned activities of such radical organizations as Hizb-ut-Tahrir (HBT) or the IMU might be necessary but not sufficient catalysts for head-on confrontations between secular states and religious communities in Central Asia. Furthermore, while the above-mentioned explanations may provide answers to why tension exists between the state and religion, they give an insufficient account of why violent confrontations are more pronounced in some areas than in others.

I look past these theories to advance a more nuanced explanation. I argue that spatial variation in tensions between the secular state and religion is decidedly a result of local politics. In more precise terms, I argue that in villages and towns in Central Asia where localism ties and Soviet-era informal dispute-resolution arrangements bind local government officials with members of religious communities, various conflict triggers (such as agitation by radical groups, discriminatory and repressive state policies toward religion, or the plight of coreligionists in other parts of the country or the world) are unlikely to provoke violent confrontation between the state and religious communities. In regions where local informal ties and Soviet-era dispute-resolution arrangements become weak or are damaged, the external triggers are likely to provoke head-on collision between the secular state organs and religious communities.

Methodological Issues

My explanation pays attention to the intricate three-way interaction among the central state, local power brokers, and members of Muslim communities. One piece is not adequate to explain the complex nature of this interaction. I demonstrate the utility of my proposition by examining the contemporary period in Kyrgyzstan, with a specific focus on two southern towns—Nookat and Kara-Suu—during the period from March 2005 to 2009.

Three factors explain the choice of Kyrgyzstan between 2005 and 2009 as the focus of this study. First, the period under investigation was marked by leadership and policy continuity. In the aftermath of the March 2005 Tulip Revolution, which toppled his authoritarian predecessor, former president Kurmanbek Bakiev promised to expand political freedoms (including religious rights) of Kyrgyz citizens. As Bakiev's policies grew more authoritarian in subsequent years, however, Kyrgyz citizens witnessed a gradual erosion of their political freedoms, including their right to worship.

Second, there had been a geographic variation in the level of tensions between the state and religion during the selected period. In the northern part of the country, protests against the government's growing stranglehold over religious affairs remained nonviolent. For example, in July 2006, Mutaqallim, an organization promoting Muslim women's rights, collected thirty thousand signatures in support of a petition that urged the authorities to allow Muslim women to be photographed in headscarves for national passports. In spring 2007, the Congress of Kyrgyzstan's Muslims, another Muslim organization, issued a petition protesting the decision of the Ministry of Internal Affairs to ban the public prayer of Muslims on Eid-al-Fitr, a holiday celebrating the end of the holy month of Ramadan, in the central square of Bishkek. In early 2008, residents of a small village in the mountainous Naryn region organized picketing, demanding that the local authorities evict a Kyrgyz family that converted to Christianity.

In the southern part of the country, however, the Bakiev government's increasing efforts to "tame" religion had resulted in a direct violent confrontation between Kyrgyz security forces and pious residents. On October 1, 2008, several hundred local residents of Nookat clashed with Kyrgyz police after the authorities banned the public celebration of Orozo-Ayt (Eid-al-Fitr), a Muslim holiday marking the end of Ramadan. A campaign of indiscriminate arrests, which the police conducted after the riot, targeted alleged members of HBT, a banned organization in Kyrgyzstan, whom officials accused of provoking public disturbances. Based on tenuous evidence, authorities prosecuted and sentenced thirty-two Nookat residents to lengthy prison terms for fomenting the unrest, causing an outcry from both local and international human rights groups (Ponomarev 2009).

The third reason has to do with the ease of access to informants. Despite growing authoritarianism under President Bakiev, Kyrgyzstan, with its more democratic and pluralistic history, offered a permissive environment for researchers to investigate political and religious activism. Although authorities continuously harassed their political opponents and pious residents suspected of membership in banned Islamic groups, they seldom punished scholars and investigators who studied political opposition and banned Islamic activism.

The rationale for selecting Nookat and Kara-Suu was straightforward. The two towns are located in the same Osh region, and they share many socioeconomic and demographic features. Populated by large ethnic Uzbek minority communities, both towns have the status of *raion* centers. Between 1991 and 2005, both towns witnessed gradual economic decline, popular migration, and a religious revival. Nevertheless, their communities' responses to government Orozo-Ayt restrictions differed. In Nookat, the government's strict policy led to rioting. Meanwhile, Kara-Suu did not witness riots over government Orozo-Ayt restrictions. The case of Kara-Suu is important because it is representative of other cases such as Aravan, Uzgen, and Osh.

I relied on a variety of sources to collect data. Government agencies, human rights organizations, and journalists produced a variety of reports providing often conflicting accounts of what happened in Nookat in early November 2008. I also relied extensively on my fieldwork in several South Kyrgyzstan towns. From May to November 2009, I conducted eighty-five semistructured interviews with ordinary community representatives, clerics, nongovernmental organization (NGO) representatives, journalists, and government officials in Aravan, Nookat, Uzgen, Kara-Suu, Osh, and Bishkek. In October 2011 and February 2012, I conducted twenty-five follow-up semistructured interviews with human rights activists, clerics, and government officials in

Kara-Suu, Aravan, Osh, and Bishkek. In July 2012, I interviewed three individuals in Nookat who spent time in prison for taking part in the Nookat events but who were subsequently amnestied and released by the Kyrgyz provisional government in May 2010, a month after the April 2010 uprising.

Contending Views on Tension between the Secular State and Religion

Various theories have been advanced to explain conflicts between the secular state and religious communities in Central Asia. According to one such theory, Central Asia is home to a tolerant and traditional version of Islam and thus foreign extremist groups such as HBT are chiefly responsible for religious militancy in the region (Botobekov 2001). Though popular with security officials, this theory is not convincing. For example, nearly all the Nookat riot participants were the town's natives and not foreigners.[4] Moreover, HBT has consistently refused to accept responsibility for violent conflicts between the state and religious communities, claiming that any such accusations were a "Western plot" to weaken Muslim unity in Kyrgyzstan.[5]

As suggested by HBT's allegation, conflicts between the secular state and Muslim communities are seen by some observers as the sign of a growing "civilizational" rift between the West and the Islamic world.[6] The "clash of civilization" thesis may be appealing to some observers,[7] but it has limited explanatory power if applied to Kyrgyzstan. To be sure, the United States has maintained military facilities in Central Asia as part of the United States-led military campaign in Afghanistan, but there was no evidence that United States military presence instigated the Andijan uprising in May 2005 or the Nookat riot in October 2008. Troublingly for the theory, many ordinary Muslims in Andijan, Kara-Suu, Nookat, and other parts of Central Asia viewed the Andijan uprising and the Nookat riot as local incidents and not as events that were part of the broader rivalry between the West and the Muslim world.[8]

The third explanation emphasizes the importance of state repression as a catalyst for Muslim mobilization (McGlinchey 2004). Across Central Asia, as this view posits, the ruling regimes have sought to limit political participation of citizens and cracked down on opposition groups, including religious-based political groups, fueling public discontent and creating new recruits for extremist ideologies. For example, in his study on Muslim mobilization in Uzbekistan and Kyrgyzstan, Eric McGlinchey, a United States scholar, suggests that "Islamist movements in Central Asia are first and foremost a response to local authoritarian rule: the more authoritarian the state, the more pronounced political Islam will be in society" (McGlinchey 2004).

The proposition that state repression is a chief factor behind Muslim mobilization has a degree of relevance. At first glance, the Kyrgyz government's restrictions on Orozo-Ayt appeared to be a catalyst for the Nookat events. This explanation, however, has a number of limitations. First, it provides insufficient answers to the spatial variation in Muslim mobilization in Southern Kyrgyzstan. In other words, one would expect that the Kyrgyz government's decision on Orozo-Ayt would cause similar protests or riots in Kara-Suu, Aravan, and Uzgen, whose residents share socio-economic and demographic characteristics with communities in Nookat. Second, if state repression provokes Muslim mobilization, authoritarian countries such as Turkmenistan (where the state uses repressive measures to control its sizable Muslim population) would be likely to emerge as the site of frequent Muslim protests. Just the opposite has proved true: Muslim protests have been virtually absent in Turkmenistan, indicating that state repression may actually deter Muslims from engaging in protests.

The fourth view is that ethnic tension and ethnic differences may account for the geographic variation in religious mobilization. The nomadic past of the Kyrgyz, as some Central Asian scholars claim, means that they take a less formal approach to Islam than the Uzbeks and Tajiks (Tabyshalieva 2000). Other observers have suggested that the real and perceived discrimination against Kyrgyzstani Uzbeks has pushed them to join banned Islamic groups. The "ethnic explanation" has a degree of relevance. Indeed, the majority of protesters in Nookat were ethnically Uzbek. This explanation, however, cannot explain why the Nookat protest, as well as other events related to religious demands, attracted observant Muslims from both the Uzbek and Kyrgyz communities.[9] The fact that the increasing numbers of ethnic Kyrgyz, Kazakhs, and Uyghurs have joined banned Islamic groups such as HBT in recent years further undermines this explanation.

In sum, the explanations presented above provide insufficient answers to the research questions, necessitating a new explanation. Below, I describe the details of a new approach to the study of Islamic mobilization in Kyrgyzstan that seeks to provide sufficient answers and presents a more nuanced portrayal of religious-based protests in Central Asia.

Importance of Soviet-era Dispute-Resolution Institutions and Muslim Politics

In contrast to the various explanations considered thus far, this chapter claims that informal dispute-resolution structures and arrangements involving local officials, power brokers, and communities impact the propensity of religion to be used as a mobilizing force in Kyrgyzstan. This section describes what these arrangements are, how they emerged, and what role they play.

To understand how Central Asian secular authorities interact with religious communities, it is necessary to pay close attention to the Soviet-era period of Central Asian history. Local dispute-resolution institutions constitute an important but poorly examined legacy of Soviet rule in Central Asia. These institutions were designed by Moscow policymakers to help local officials deal with religious citizens' demands and grievances. At the local level, Soviet policymakers created a tiered system of religious control that, in some way, emulated the internal organization of the Communist Party.

In every village and raion center, the Soviet authorities created *sovet mestnykh ullama*, or councils of local clerics. Consisting of *kazy* (a representative of the central muftiate), *imam khatib* (the chief imam of the central mosque), and ordinary mosque imams, such local clerical councils were tasked to deal with day-to-day administration of matters relating to religious practices of pious residents. Clerical councils also carried out fatwas, religious injunctions of Sredneaziatskoe dukhovnoe upravlenie musul'man (SADUM), the Tashkent-based official muftiate for Central Asia, which oversaw these councils through its regional affiliates in the provincial centers. Although local clerical councils were formally subordinated to the muftiate representatives in the provincial centers, *raikom* (raion branch of the Communist Party) and raion branches of the Soviet KGB supervised the work of clerics through raikom departments for propaganda and agitation.[10]

To be sure, a myriad of issues caused tension between the state and religion during the Soviet period. As Eren Murat Tasar (chapter 6, this volume) amply demonstrates, in the last three decades of Soviet rule, when Moscow seemingly managed to rein over religious dissent in Central Asia, tensions between the Soviet state and believers arose because of the proliferation of unregistered mosques and seminaries, widespread practices of private tutoring of religion in *hujras* (private rooms or cells, often used for prayer), and unsanctioned proselytizing by so-called unofficial imams, clerics who earned respect from local communities for their knowledge of Islam but lacked official credentials from the muftiate.

Local officials and state-designated clerics demonstrated remarkable adeptness at resolving thorny issues in relations between the state and religion. When divisive issues arose (accounting for public donations to mosques, eradicating activities by unofficial imams, cracking down on private tutoring of Islam), local clerical councils would hold a meeting, debate the issue, and adopt a decision that would be accepted by involved clerics and community members. If the matters were not resolved at the clerical level, raikom officials and deputies of the *raisovet* (raion council members) would get involved. If neither local clerics nor officials were able to resolve the matters at hand, a raion branch of the KGB would intervene. Given its political weight in the former Soviet Union, the KGB's pronouncements on local religious issues were taken by local officials and residents as the most authoritative judgments.[11]

Bounded by kinship and localism obligations, clerics and officials strove to avoid unwanted attention from the central authorities. Local Communist Party officials regularly sent upbeat reports on how they were successful in their efforts to reduce the number of unregistered mosques and hujras and to identify and punish unofficial clerics (Ro'i 2000). In their turn, unofficial clerics kept a low public profile to shield local officials from the central government's punitive organs such as the police and state prosecutors.

Such informal pacts between local officials and clerics often stemmed from practical reasons. Because local government officials were often understaffed and overworked, they had a particular interest in using the influence and resources of Muslim clerics (Roy 2000). Meanwhile, cooperation with local officials allowed Muslim clerics to gain protection from the central state's repressive organs and survive the campaign of reprisals directed against clergy (Ro'i 2000). Informal arrangements also provided religious groups with informal venues and opportunities to negotiate, amend, and even reverse central decisions and policies that adversely affected religious practices.

Although Soviet rulers in Moscow were aware of local officials' informal arrangements with their constituents, they often condoned such practices (Roy 2000). The Soviet authorities routinely relied on clerics to help mobilize citizens for various goals in Central Asia: fighting the Nazis during the Great Patriotic War in the early 1940s, implementing massive agricultural campaigns in the 1960s, struggling for world peace in the 1970s, and supporting perestroika policies in the late 1980s.

Changes in State-Religion Relations in Kyrgyzstan since 1991

After Kyrgyzstan and the other Central Asian republics gained independence in 1991, their citizens witnessed significant changes in the domain of religious practices. Amid the relaxation of state controls, Islam moved swiftly from private corners to the public realm in the early 1990s. As Central Asia opened up to the outside world, the number of mosques and seminaries quadrupled while various religious groups established a foothold in various corners of the region. Taking advantage of new political freedoms, former "unofficial" clerics emerged from their hidden hujras and became vocal and officially recognized voices in their communities. In many areas of Central Asia, formerly unofficial imams also presided over local efforts to reinstate religion's pre-Soviet role in public life.[12]

With the rise of religion in public life, the number of thorny issues causing tension between officials and clerics has multiplied. Even before the IMU infiltrated South Kyrgyzstan in both the summer of 1999 and 2000, all the Central Asian governments had identified Islamic radicalism and militancy as top security threats. The regional governments' punitive campaigns to stem unsanctioned religious activism specifically targeted HBT, causing a widespread outcry not only from the country's Muslims but also from local and international human rights defenders. In addition to radical Islam, other issues that have emerged as highly divisive across Central Asia include management of the hajj (the Muslim pilgrimage to Mecca), hijab (headscarves), and private religious education for children.

Despite the spike in the number of disputes between the state and religion, Soviet-era approaches to dealing with religion have largely remained intact. Secularism, separation of state from religion, and state control of religious affairs—three contradictory legacies of seventy years of Soviet rule—have continued to define state–religion relations across Central Asia. Central Asian republics' constitutions all declare the secular character of the country, guarantee the freedom of worship, and affirm the separation of state and religion. Despite these provisions, the states continue to meddle in religious affairs through the State Agencies on Religious Affairs and through their informal control of muftiates, or the Supreme Muslim Spiritual Boards.

At the local level, Soviet-era institutions of religious control and dispute resolution are still at the crux of small village and town politics across the region. Heads of raion administrations and *ail okomtu* (local governments), deputies of raion and local councils, school directors, heads of *mahalla* and *kvartal'nye komitety* (neighborhood committees), members of councils or courts of *aksakals* (elders), and some NGO representatives replaced Soviet party activists in the leadership positions, but the rationale is the same: help the state control and mobilize citizens. In Kyrgyzstan, for example, local officials and clerics have played key roles in securing popular backing for incumbent leaders during elections.[13] Authorities in Bishkek have also relied on local officials and clerics to *immobilize* citizens in cases when popular mobilization threatened the interests of the ruling regime (Orozbekova 2009).

Why do local officials and clerics continue to help the state and how do they mobilize or immobilize citizens in Kyrgyzstan? A mixed policy of incentives and punishments by Bishkek is what drives local officials and clerics. Pliant officials and clerics receive various perks such as job promotions, tax relief, financial concessions, state contracts, and cheap property in sought-after areas.[14] Less-yielding officials and clerics have had to deal with an array of central state bureaucratic weapons, including the prosecutor's office, courts, and financial police.[15]

Local officials and state-friendly clerics have relied on similar mechanisms of incentives and punishments in their dealings with ordinary community members. When *raziasnitel'nye raboty* among constituents (consciousness-raising campaigns that usually involve exerting peer pressure and invoking traditional respect for authority, kinship, and localism ties) produce few results, local officials and clerics rely on the local bureaucratic apparatus. Local officials use the assistance of tax police, local *kommendaturas* (which enlist young men for active military service), passport-issuing desks, and the land and property registration service to ensure community members' compliance.[16]

For all their outward support of Bishkek, local officials, just as their Soviet predecessors, sometimes flout central government's directives concerning religious affairs. For example, central authorities in Bishkek require local governments to identify and report to security services anyone suspected of having links to HBT and other radical groups. But local officials prefer to try local solutions aimed at keeping suspected HBT activists in check, rather than reporting them to the police. The alleged Islamists, after all, are their neighbors, relatives, and constituents. As one local official in Kara-Suu admitted: "If someone turns out to be a[n] [HBT] member, we try to resolve this problem with the help of the mahalla [local neighborhood council]. We rely on pressure from parents, relatives, and aksakals [elders] to force these young people to abandon dangerous thoughts. Usually they [HBT members] listen to us. Seeing a community member go to prison on religious extremism charges makes everyone in [the] community unhappy."[17]

Localism and kinship obligations compel local officials, clerics, and ordinary community members to observe an informal code of conduct. One such rule is to share information. For example, heads of kvartal'nye komitety are often informed about visitors to their communities (whether guests and relatives of community members or foreign donors) before such visits take place.[18] The second requirement is to avoid unwanted attention from the central authorities. For example, in late 2008, when the prosecutor's office initiated several lawsuits against local government officials in Aravan town for improperly distributing land plots to build a new mosque, an Aravan native who was widely believed to have tipped off the prosecutors, was ostracized by friends, relatives, neighbors, and local officials.[19]

Third, the local codes of conduct proscribe unsanctioned popular mobilization because such events can attract the attention of police and the security service. The early June 2009 arrest of Abdulwohid Isabaev, an Aravan resident, on charges of belonging to HBT, is a case in point. Isabaev's friends and sympathizers organized a protest on the first day of the court hearing, but they dispersed the next day when the father of the arrested pleaded with the protesters to disperse. As it became evident in subsequent days, the judge, an Aravan native, promised the arrested man's family to impose a lighter sentence on their son if the protesters dispersed.[20] Isabaev was subsequently given a one-year suspended sentence and released from prison.

In certain circumstances Soviet-era local dispute-resolution institutions and informal codes of conduct fail to prevent unsanctioned mobilization by disenchanted citizenry. In some cases, the central state can adopt an unpopular policy without consulting with local government activists and giving them enough time to conduct community outreach activities. In other cases, suspecting local officials of leniency in enforcing state policies, including directives against Islamic radicals, the authorities in Bishkek can send the police and National Security Service (Kyrgyz SNB, successor of the KGB) to investigate alleged wrongdoings, thus crippling the ability of local officials to influence local politics. For example, the legal investigation against a group of Aravan local officials who were accused of impropriety in distributing land plots for the mosque affected their work by forcing them to spend an extensive amount of time with the investigators.[21]

There are also cases when local institutions of dispute resolution and popular mobilization can be captured by local elites who pursue their own narrow interests. For example, in early 2002, supporters of Azimbek Beknazarov, a jailed politician, managed to use local government structures and local networks in marshaling popular support during their nonviolent campaign to release Beknazarov in early 2002 (Radnitz 2005). And finally, personal antipathies among local officials and community members may also hamper the work of local dispute-resolution institutions.[22]

Having described the role of Soviet-era institutions of religious control and conflict-resolution institutions in local politics, I now turn to the discussion of how they influenced events in Nookat and Kara-Suu in late 2008, a period when the government's approach toward religion became increasingly intrusive. Before proceeding to that task, it is important to start with an overview of state–mosque relations in Kyrgyzstan and the

series of events that prompted the Kyrgyz government to adopt the Orozo-
Ayt restrictions in late 2008.

Prelude to Nookat: Brief Overview of State-Mosque Relations in Kyrgyzstan, 1989-2008

In the early years of independence, Kyrgyzstan continued the liberal approach to religion that was initiated by Moscow's perestroika policies in
the late 1990s. As a result, the number of mosques, madrasas, and seminaries quadrupled in the early years of independence, and various kinds of
religious missionaries established a presence throughout the country (ICG
2003b). Nevertheless, a series of events in the late 1990s and early 2000s—
specifically, the IMU's infiltration of South Kyrgyzstan in 1999 and 2000,
and a rise in the public visibility of HBT—ushered in a more restrictive set
of government policies.

Having seized political power as a result of the March 2005 Tulip Revolution, President Bakiev promised to introduce wide-reaching democratic
changes. His administration, however, adopted a harsher government
approach to dealing with religious militancy. In July 2006, the Kyrgyz
SNB signed an agreement with the Uzbek Security Service on conducting
joint antiterrorist operations and broadening intelligence cooperation. Immediately after the cementing of the Uzbek–Kyrgyz antiterrorist alliance,
Kyrgyz security forces engaged in hundreds of search-and-seizure operations in which they arrested dozens of HBT members. Security officials
contended that the raids led to the recovery of explosives and propaganda
material published by extremist organizations and disrupted terror cells
that were supposedly plotting future attacks.[23]

In connection with the crackdown, Kyrgyz and Uzbek security forces
carried out several controversial shootings of suspected Islamic militants,
including the popular imam Muhammadrafiq Kamalov on August 6,
2006. Kamalov, the imam of a mosque in Kara-Suu, was noted for holding
comparatively liberal religious views; he permitted members of the underground radical group, HBT, to worship at his mosque, even though he
publicly disagreed with the organization's stated aim of reestablishing an
Islamic caliphate in Central Asia.[24]

Hardening government policy toward religion continued in 2008. In
February 2008, the State Agency for Religious Affairs submitted to Parliament a new law on religion, which imposed stricter rules on registration
of mosques and seminaries. Registering a new mosque required the signa-

tures of two hundred people; previous legislation required only ten. Clerics had to go through periodic exams to establish their theological/ideological reliability; the previous law made no mention of periodic clerical exams. The law also prohibited private religious tutoring, the unsanctioned distribution of religious materials, and proselytizing. In addition, it banned mosques from admitting children.

In July 2008, the Kyrgyz government adopted an "interdepartmental plan on the prevention of religious extremism and fundamentalism," which enhanced the ability of officials to control spiritual life.[25] Claiming that HBT was using various holidays such as Orozo-Ayt to advance its ideology in South Kyrgyzstan,[26] the document instructed local governments to take measures that would prevent HBT from using the festivities to advance its goals.[27]

When Things Go Wrong: Evidence from Nookat

On September 25, 2008, when Adaham Isakov and Manas Isakov, two leaders of an "initiative group" representing Nookat's Muslim communities, approached local officials to obtain a permit to hold public festivities honoring Orozo-Ayt, they received a negative reply. Abdygany Aliev, *akim* (head) of the raion administration, and Jalil Atambaev, chief of the Nookat police, told the group's leaders to distribute the public funds that the group collected for the holiday among local charities. The group leaders were told to celebrate the holiday in the privacy of their homes and not in the central square as the organizers had requested. The official response was puzzling to many ordinary Nookat residents; in previous years, local officials were active participants in the festivities associated with the Muslim holiday.

On September 27, when the initiative group leaders visited Aliev again, he informed them that the raion administration had no jurisdiction over venues for public celebrations. Ergeshaly Shanazarov, the head of the Gulistan *ail-okmotu*, the local municipality that was in charge of the central square, told the initiative group's leaders that the central square was reserved for the celebration of Senior Citizens Day celebrated on October 1. Disturbed by the Muslim initiative group's incessant visits and phone calls, the akim Aliev called a gathering of local officials where it was agreed that the public festivities would take place at the central stadium and not in the central square (Ponomarev 2009). This compromise solution, which emerged after a lengthy debate, seemingly satisfied a majority of the meeting participants, including the police and the SNB.[28]

Things took an unpredictable turn on October 1, the celebration day, when festive groups of Nookat residents found out that the stadium had been closed, and police troops that had arrived in Nookat the previous night from Osh demanded that everyone leave the venue. In response to the police action, a large crowd of Nookat residents gathered in the central square, demanding a meeting with Aliev. Addressing the crowd, Aliev, the chief of Nookat traffic police, and a muftiate representative who happened to be in Nookat that day, urged everyone to disperse, but without providing an explanation for the police actions and the change of plans.[29] A scuffle between police and some protesters provoked a riot during which protesters threw stones at the police and the government building. In the course of the rioting that lasted less than two hours, several police officers and a dozen local residents were injured, and the government building was partially damaged.

The Nookat residents paid a heavy price for the riot. In the immediate aftermath, authorities in Bishkek fired Aliev and suspended several raion officials. In subsequent days, the police and the SNB, carrying out a campaign of indiscriminate arrests in Nookat, detained and harassed hundreds of residents, often on trumped-up charges.[30] An extremely dubious and uncharacteristically hasty court hearing followed shortly and led to the sentencing of thirty-two of the accused, including Adaham Isakov and Manas Isakov, to lengthy terms in prison. The state's handling of the Nookat caused an outcry from civil society organizations.[31]

Given the costs of the Nookat events, why did the local authorities and power brokers fail to prevent the riot? It should be remembered from the section on theory that local officials use local dispute-resolution institutions to prevent unsanctioned protests, and that under certain circumstances, local officials are unable to activate such mechanisms. The following section provides a detailed account of these circumstances.

Tense Relations among Local Officials

The rivalry between the raion administration and the police played a key role in the outbreak of the Nookat riot. The Nookat police chiefs viewed Adaham Isakov and Manas Isakov as the agents of HBT and the decision on Orozo-Ayt as an unnecessary concession to the banned Islamic group.[32] On September 30, Azamat Jumamatov, a police officer of the Nookat *deviaty otdel*, a police department in charge of combating religious extremism, had sent a report to his superiors at the Osh oblast UVD, the provincial

branch of the Ministry of the Interior, describing the connivance of local authorities and requesting additional police detachments (Ponomarev
2009). The Osh UVD had granted the request.[33] Thus, the tension among
local officials meant that central officials became aware of local problems
and decided to intervene.

Various factors accounted for the tension between the raion administration on the one hand and the police and the SNB branches on the other.
First, officials representing these three agencies operated in different environments and faced divergent incentives. While the Nookat police and the
local branch of the SNB were subordinated to the Ministry of the Interior
and the central SNB directorate, the raion administration officials are an-
swerable to the assembly of raion deputies—the oblast leadership. According to several Nookat residents, police chief Atambaev was personally tied
to Janysh Bakiev, President Bakiev's younger brother who was in charge of
Kyrgyzstan's security services in 2007–10. Atambaev's ties to Janysh Bakiev
are supported by circumstantial evidence. He reportedly received a distinction for handling the aftermath of the riot, and he continued to serve
as Nookat's police chief until July 2009.[34] He was not fired from the police
even when his subordinate killed a Nookat journalist in 2009, a development that caused a scandal in Bishkek. Atambaev was quietly transferred
to Osh where he assumed control over the police of the Osh International
Airport, a lucrative spot for many police officers.[35]

Second, Aliev admitted that there was personal antipathy in his relations with Atambaev, though he refused to provide details.[36] Zahidzhan
Abidzhanov, Aliev's deputy, did not hide his contempt for Atambaev,
saying that he was an outsider and a careerist.[37] Atambaev's antipathy for
Abidzhanov became apparent on October 1, 2008, when he sent a report to
his superiors in Osh, claiming that Abidzhanov was inciting the crowds
to engage in violent actions, a charge that Abidzhanov had to refute in
Kyrgyz courts in subsequent weeks.[38]

The rivalry between the raion administration officials and the police meant
that information sharing was flawed. The police failed to inform the raion
administration about their late September 2008 reports to their superiors and
the decision to close off the holiday venue on October 1. As Aliev himself
admitted, he found out about the police decision to cancel the festivities only
on the morning of October 1, at a time "when I was shaving and thinking
about the speech that I would give at the Orozo-Ayt celebration."[39] After
his numerous attempts to reach Atambaev by telephone failed that morning,
Aliev rushed to the building of the raion administration to find the crowds

of disgruntled residents. As Aliev recalled: "When I got there, I found that Atambaev and [the] police were inside the building. . . . He [Atambaev] told me that things ha[d] gotten out of control and that [the] police w[ere] in command [of the raion]. He told me to follow his order . . . otherwise I would be punished by Bishkek. . . . I had to obey. . . . What else could I do?"[40]

Disruption of Local Dispute-Resolution Institutions

Relations between local officials and communities were also marked by tension. Aliev had a reputation as a good akim in Nookat, but as an ethnic Kyrgyz from a village in a remote corner of the Nookat raion, he lacked crucial localism and kinship ties with Nookat residents, many of whom are ethnically Uzbek. As a result, Aliev had little control over the crowds of angry Nookat residents on October 1. In the absence of credible information, many Nookat residents saw him as a liar.[41] Ergeshaly Shanazarov, the head of the Gulistan ail-okmot and an ethnic Uzbek, was distrusted by the town's observant Muslims because of his secular lifestyle and his penchant for toeing the central government's line.[42]

Strains in relations between state-backed clerics and Muslim communities contributed to the Nookat events. Disagreements on Orozo-Ayt within the Nookat Muslim communities reflected the deeper ideological rivalry between state-affiliated clerics and "unofficial" imams.[43] State-affiliated clerics have toed the government line, supported "traditional Islam," a version of Islam that combines religious practices with local traditions, and opposed various banned groups. "Unofficial" imams have taken a different approach, criticizing close ties between officials and clerics, making consistent calls for purifying Islam of *bidayats* (innovations) associated with local traditions, and allowing members of banned Islamic groups in their mosques.

The Nookat Muslim initiative group, whose members had reputations as "unofficial" clerics, failed to use the established dispute-resolution mechanisms, a development that deepened animosities among local officials. For one thing, the initiative group of Muslims refused to resolve the matter at the council of local ulema; the group's leaders decided to take the issue straight to the akim of the raion, a move that caused consternation on the part of the police and the SNB.[44] The Nookat clerics' failure to resolve the dispute through the council of local ulema combined with the Nookat raion officials' decision to overrule the objections of the police and the SNB meant that the local-level dispute-resolution mechanisms were disrupted, thus increasing the likelihood of a violent confrontation.

State Policy Adopted in a Swift Manner without Consultation with Local Officials

The cancellation of the Orozo-Ayt celebration caught Nookat's local officials by surprise. Believing that the compromise solution achieved on September 29 would be upheld, influential local officials and power brokers were out of town. Like many Nookat residents, they were surprised to find out that the stadium was cordoned off by the police on the morning of October 1. And upon arriving at the central square, they were also astonished to learn that the akim had changed his mind, and that control was transferred to the police and the SNB. In the absence of any information and leadership and in an atmosphere of chaos, many local officials simply did not know what to do.[45]

When the riot broke out, local officials, community leaders, and informal power brokers immediately sought to disperse the belligerent crowds made up of youths. Abidzhanov, Aliev's deputy, made phone calls to members of the raion council who were away, urging them to rush to the central square and calm the protesters.[46] He then enlisted several informal youth leaders with whom he had preexisting ties to convince crowds of youths to disperse. Soip-qori, a respected Nookat cleric who once served as the muftiate's representative for the Osh oblast, abruptly left Osh (where he was on business). When he arrived in Nookat, he persuaded the police to open the stadium and then managed to convince approximately three hundred youths to leave the protest site and resume festivities at the stadium.[47] Other members of the local activists (*mestnyi aktiv*)—school directors, teachers, NGO representatives, local businessmen, and mosque imams—all worked together to calm the crowds.[48] Largely due to the efforts of local community leaders (and not to police action), the situation had stabilized by the afternoon of October 1.[49]

When Things Work: Evidence from Kara-Suu

In contrast to the example of Nookat, the events in Kara-Suu demonstrate that when local officials and power brokers activate local dispute-resolution mechanisms in due time, the prospects for religious-based riots are low. The discussion that follows presents how, faced with an unpopular government policy to implement, the Kara-Suu local officials and clerics devised a clever and original way to prevent the outbreak of popular protest over the Orozo-Ayt restrictions.

Despite being a small town of twenty thousand people located twenty-three kilometers to the northeast of Osh, Kara-Suu is among the bustling spots in Central Asia. During the Soviet period, the town served as an important transit point in the regional railway system. With the collapse of the Soviet Union and the subsequent decline of the railway networks in the 1990s, the town continued to flourish thanks to the Kara-Suu bazaar, one of the largest markets in Central Asia that specializes in trade with China. Home to famous theologians such as Alawuddin Mansoor (who translated the Koran into Uzbek in the early 1990s), Muhamadrafiq Kamalov (a popular imam who was assassinated in 2006), and Sadykjan Kamalov (former head of Kyrgyzstan's muftiate and director of the Osh-based Islamic Center), Kara-Suu is also considered a center of piety and Islamic learning in the Ferghana Valley.

In late September 2008, when rumors began to spread in Kara-Suu that the central government had banned the celebration of Orozo-Ayt, groups of residents flocked to the local municipality for an explanation. Akhmad Rakhimov, the town's mayor, was visibly disturbed by such visits because he did not know what to tell his visitors. The mayor did not admit this, but apparently he did not receive instructions from Bishkek that proscribed the public celebration of the holiday on October 1, 2008.[50] To clarify the matter for himself, the mayor met with the SNB chief for the Kara-Suu raion. Following the meeting, Rakhimov called a gathering of the town's local officials where it was decided that the mayor's office would be in charge of combined festivities for Orozo-Ayt and the Senior Citizens Day.[51] The mayor then asked members of the Kara-Suu town council to go throughout the town to ensure that everyone got the message.

The festivities on October 1 were conducted at the Kara-Suu central park in "an atmosphere of friendliness and good neighborliness."[52] The event, which featured speeches by local officials and communal eating of *plov*, a traditional Uzbek dish, had brought together a majority of the town's local officials, aksakals, and imams of state-affiliated mosques. The SNB and police chiefs attended the event as well. Though some alleged HBT members were also present, they kept a low profile. There was no police crackdown or provocation by various unsanctioned groups.

In contrast to the riot in Nookat, how and why did local officials in Kara-Suu manage to avert popular protests over the central government's Orozo-Ayt restrictions? The findings from the Kara-Suu case are as follows: first, relations among local officials were marked by collaboration, a condition that prevented unwanted central government intervention; second, key local officials were connected to community members through personal, kinship, and localism ties, which enhanced their capacity to influence local residents; and third, before adopting restrictions on Orozo-Ayt, there were consultations among local officials, a condition that enhanced the ability of local officials and power brokers to use local conflict-resolution mechanisms well in advance. Each of these factors deserves separate attention.

Collaboration among Local Officials

In contrast to Nookat, where the head of the local administration had a troubled relationship with the chiefs of the local police and SNB branches, the Kara-Suu mayor maintained direct channels of communication with the local branches of the SNB and the Ministry of the Interior. The close collaboration was, in part, a direct consequence of the August 2006 assassination of Muhammadrafiq Kamalov by Kyrgyz and Uzbek special security forces. The central-state-sanctioned assassination had galvanized Kara-Suu residents and put enormous pressure on local officials. Seeking to prevent popular protests against the central government, local officials had doubled their efforts to strengthen dispute-resolution mechanisms in the months and years that followed Kamalov's assassination.[53]

In the aftermath of Kamalov's assassination, local officials paid special attention to cultivating personal ties with one another. As the mayor's assistant recalled, "the SNB chief is not a native [of Nookat], but he is an understanding and smart guy. . . . He cooperated with our office in good faith."[54] At the mayor's invitation, the SNB and the police attended all meetings held by the Nookat town officials regarding the Orozo-Ayt celebrations. Cooperation with the SNB was crucial for the mayor's office because the SNB chief provided the mayor with valuable information about Bishkek's seriousness regarding Orozo-Ayt and the negative repercussions from not complying with the central directive.[55]

The SNB chief also advised the mayor's office to take over the planning and implementation of the public festivities.[56] This advice played a key role in satisfying the requirements of the central government in Bishkek and the demands of observant Kara-Suu Muslims. As the Kara-Suu mayor's assistant claimed, "we [the mayor's office] served as the main sponsor for the festivities. But the funding came from ordinary residents, including the *biradar* (brotherhood) networks." The mayor's assistant privately hinted that the term *biradar* networks referred to HBT.[57]

In Nookat, Aliev, the head of the raion, was perceived as an outsider.

In contrast, the mayor of Kara-Suu was seen by many as one of Kara-Suu's best sons. The mayor came from a well-respected Uzbek family (his father also served as the mayor before him). Apart from being the city's chief, Rakhimov also enjoyed a reputation as a *palvan*, or wrestler, who had won several national and Central Asian wrestling competitions in the past. To be sure, the mayor had some political opponents in Kara-Suu, but he also had significant support from various corners.[58] The Nookat martial arts school and its students, founded by the mayor, provided "muscle support" for the mayor's initiatives when required. As Rakhimov himself proudly claimed, he was elected with more than 70 percent of the vote.

Rakhimov claimed that, unlike officials in Bishkek, local government employees live among their constituents and are linked through family and ethnic ties. "When I walk to my office in the morning," he said, "I recognize every person on my way. One is a neighbor; another is a former classmate. In a small town like ours, people know each other and help each other.[59] The mayor asserted that the fact that he was a Kara-Suu native and a popular mayor meant that his decisions were accepted by a majority of residents as legitimate.

Local Officials Used Dispute-Resolution Institutions Well in Advance

Unlike its Nookat counterpart, the Kara-Suu local council not only consisted of local officials, school directors, and heads of kvartal'nye komitety but also included clerics, businesspeople, and influential local residents—some of whom were either secret sympathizers or actual HBT activists. As Sobir Akhmedov, the Kara-Suu mayor's right-hand man and the head of the council of Kara-Suu's sixteen neighborhood bloc committees, claimed, in choosing people for the Kara-Suu local council, what counted was not one's membership in political parties, but one's reputation as an honest and active citizen.[60]

Local officials were able to activate local dispute-resolution mechanisms long before the holiday. To ensure the success of his plan, the mayor enlisted the backing of influential people in town—famous theologians such as Alawuddin Mansoor, Sodikzhon Kamalov, and Rashot Kamalov. On September 27–29, the mayor himself held meetings with imams of each mosque and respected community members to ensure that everyone was "on the same page" regarding the mayor's Orozo-Ayt celebration decree. As the mayor claimed, the theologians not only endorsed his plan but also sought to gain backing for the plan from the town's Muslims after traditional Friday prayers and in private meetings with mahalla elders and various community leaders.

Support from respected clerics was only part of the town leadership's strategy. The council of aksakals and the sixteen kvartal'nye komitety, which controlled much of community life in Kara-Suu, played a key role in enlisting popular support for the mayor's Orozo-Ayt celebration plan. As Sabirov recalled, his colleagues at the council of the elderly and neighborhood bloc committees visited "almost every household." When Kara-Suu mestnyi aktiv approached them, all imams, both state-affiliated and independent, agreed that there was no need for the public celebration of Orozo-Ayt. As Sabirov claimed, many HBT members also agreed with the mayor's plan because "they all respect the mayor and us." HBT activists in Kara-Suu claimed it was not simply their "respect for the mayor" that was a factor, the party's Kara-Suu activists obtained information about the government's provocation from their sympathizers in the Kara-Suu branch of the SNB.[61]

In sum, embroiled in divisions and competition, Kara-Suu officials' counterparts in Nookat were unable to prevent a violent encounter between central government forces and residents. In contrast, more cohesive Kara-Suu authorities chose a plan of action that not only satisfied the authorities in Bishkek but also enlisted the support of Kara-Suu communities, a condition that helped them to avert protests or a potential violent clash.

The Central Role of Local Ties

This chapter has sought to fill in an important gap in the study of Central Asian societies. Students of the region have devoted considerable attention to the study of tension between the state and religious communities, but have failed to explain the spatial variation in Muslim mobilization. This study has demonstrated that violent confrontations between the state and religion are not necessarily a result of political repression, ethnic discrimination, foreign involvement, or a clash of civilizations. The main claim of the chapter is that informal arrangements between local officials and communities, which emerged during the Soviet period, are crucial to understanding the nature of religious-based protests in Kyrgyzstan and other parts of Central Asia.

As the Kyrgyz government sought to tighten controls over religion in 2008, this approach placed Kara-Suu and Nookat local officials in a bind. The authorities in Nookat chose to toe the central line in implementing an unpopular policy on Orozo-Ayt, a decision that paved the way for a violent encounter between the central government forces and residents. In contrast, when given an unpopular policy to implement, well-connected local officials and power brokers in Kara-Suu found an ingenious way of accommodating both the central government and local communities and relied on their local influence to immobilize communities, thus averting a potentially violent clash between local residents and the central state's security forces.

There are four implications of these findings. The first is related to the effects of the Soviet past on post-Soviet Central Asian republics. As time goes by, there is a tendency among some scholars to diminish or even dismiss the influence of the Soviet-era period on contemporary politics in Central Asia. This study has demonstrated that some Soviet structures and informal rules of political behavior are still relevant. Just as their Soviet predecessors, central officials continue to enlist the support of local power brokers.

The second implication concerns the nature of the state in Central Asia. Observers tend to present the state as a monolithic entity by paying scant attention to differences in the policy approaches of government agencies and the personal incentives of officials (e.g., ICG 2003b). As this study has highlighted, the central state and local government officials operate in different environments and have different incentives. Bishkek authorities require local governments to implement central policies even when such policies are unpopular with local communities. Meanwhile, personal connections and kinship obligations often encourage local officials to go easy on their communities.

The third implication is that Muslim communities and groups are not monolithic. In the international and Central Asia media, HBT is often presented as a "fast-growing radical group" that poses an imminent threat to regional security.[62] The reality is far more complex. In recent years, Central Asia has been the site of fierce ideological and theological competition. As Muslim activists pursue a global agenda of building closer ties with their coreligionists abroad, as this study has highlighted, often their primary allegiance is not to the global Muslim *ummah* (or community) but to their relatives, neighbors, and friends who live next door.

The fourth implication concerns the study of informal institutions and identities in Central Asia. Clannishness, tribalism, regionalism, and localism are often depicted by government officials and some scholars in a negative light. This study does not deny that informal structures tend to undermine some central state policies. But the study also shows that under certain circumstances, informal structures can play a powerful role in mitigating conflict. In Nookat, local officials' capacity to influence protest was hampered by internecine rivalry and the central state's punitive actions. In Kara-Suu, localism ties and dispute-resolution mechanisms averted a potentially bloody clash.

PART IV

A VIEW FROM OUTSIDE

INTERNATIONAL ISLAM
AND CENTRAL ASIA

CHAPTER TEN

The Localization of the Transnational Tablighi Jama'at Network in Kyrgyzstan

Mukaram Toktogulova

There are six people: two young Kyrgyz men and two young women, a five-year-old girl and me in the car that is driving us from Karakol, a small town in the Issyk Kul region of Kyrgyzstan, to Talap village. Two women sitting in the back seat are clothed in long black dresses, wear a hijab on their heads, and cover their faces with a black veil (in accordance with *purdah*, or the principles of gender segregation); a girl is in a white dress and white hijab, which covers her head and neck. To my surprise, Fatima (names are changed), one of the women in the car, whom I met yesterday in Karakol, where I had come to do fieldwork on Tablighi Jama'at (TJ), and who had invited me to join this trip, completely ignored my attempts to communicate with her, turning her face away from me and looking straight ahead. Both women look straight ahead and keep a silence that is rarely broken, except by a girl who asked for something from her mother, who replied in whispers, not letting others hear her voice.

Men are also clothed in an unusual way. The first of them, Abdullah, a thirty-two-year-old Kyrgyz man is driving the car. He wears long gray Pakistani-style clothing (*shalwar kameez*), and skullcap on his head. Another man, Suleiman, who is twenty-six, is clothed in the same way but in white. Both of them wear long beards. Suleiman is listening to an inspirational religious speech (*bayan*) on his mobile device about how the

Prophet suffered in the struggle for faith. We all listen to that speech, and every time the Prophet's name is mentioned, everyone except me and the small girl, repeat the ritualistic phrase—*Sallalahu aleihu wa sallam*. These two families, who are known in Kyrgyzstan as *davatchys* (the local name for Tablighi activists) are going on a *zïyarat* (welcoming) tour to one of the villages of the Jeti Oguz province of Issyk Kul,[1] where a group of Dungan davatchys from Tokmok is conducting a preaching tour (*masturat davit*). One of the davatchys suggested that I join the Tablighi journey, when I met him at the mosque the day before and introduced my research goals. I was expected to learn about their experience by observing the preaching tours and to get a "realistic" picture of Tablighi activities because he was unhappy about how the local media misinterpret their practices and connect them with extremist groups.

When we approached one of the bazaars on the way, Abdullah asked his wife what foods they like to buy for women preachers, turning his face in another direction to avoid eye contact with a woman, a ritual known among Tablighi Jama'at activists as lowering one's gaze in front of women (*kozdu saktoo*). Fatima wrote her suggestions on a piece of paper and gave it to her husband. The two men left the car to buy food for the preachers (davatchys) from Tokmok. After they left Fatima looked at me to ask if I am OK with such a long trip. It was the first time she looked at me and started talking. I asked why they were silent on the journey.

This is a rule (*tartip*) that a woman is not allowed to speak in the presence of another man, except her husband, and her close male relatives—brother, father, son. A woman's voice is also *aurat* (a part of the body that should be hidden), because a woman's voice is soft, beautiful and that's why it can attract a man, leading him to bad thoughts and actions. For instance, only four men could talk and see our Fatima ene [she referred to the Prophet's daughter Fatima as a mother, a Kyrgyz style of referring to respected women]: her father, husband, and two sons. Men also follow the tartip [rules of behavior] avoiding eye contact and face to face communication with other women. These rules help them to deal with *nafs* [ego], that can lead men to bad actions; instead man should concentrate his thoughts on *kalima*, repeating it, or listen to bayan and focus on the content of bayan, this is the way to control nafs for men, they also should avoid worldly talks (*dunionun sozu*), which attracts people's attention to worldly matters—the material side of life, disturbing them from faith. That's why on the way our husbands didn't talk very much, and concentrated on bayan.

When the men returned from the bazaar with bread, melon, and vegetables, we continued on our way.[2]

People like Abdulla and Suleiman, are well-known as Muslim preachers (davatchys) in Kyrgyzstan. Everyone can see them near the mosque, when after Friday prayer they leave the Central Mosque in small groups for their preaching tours, *davat*—the local name for *haruj* (Ar.)—or when they come to someone's house, knock on the door, and ask to renew kalima, inviting adult male Muslim fellows to the mosque to listen to an inspirational religious talk (bayan).

According to the report of the Davat Department of the Spiritual Administration of Muslims (Muftiate) in 2011, 8813 davatchys conducted forty days of preaching tours in Kyrgyzstan. The number of Tablighi activists increases sharply if we include davatchys who made international tours to other countries, to annual congregations (*markazes*) in India, Bangladesh, and Pakistan as well as those who did three-day, fifteen-day, and four-month preaching tours and welcoming tours. The number increases too if we include the number of female Tablighi activists, known as *masturat*, who make up a significant part of the Tablighi Jama'at Network (TJN) in Kyrgyzstan. Female Tablighis are actively involved in TJN preaching activities through weekly female teaching sessions (*taalim*) and preaching tours conducted by women accompanied by their husbands or male relatives (*masturat davat*), which usually last three, fifteen, or forty days.

Davatchys in Kyrgyzstan represent the global Tablighi Jama'at Network, which reached Central Asia, including Kyrgyzstan in the 1990s, after the collapse of the Soviet Union. The transnational TJN plays a large role in recovering religious practices among Kyrgyzstani "post-Soviet Muslims," who were distanced from Islam as result of the influence of "scientific atheism" under the Soviets (Shahrani 1994) and contributes significantly to the "re-Islamization" process, in which different local and international actors and the state are involved. The term "re-Islamization" refers to the recovery of religious practices among Muslims in Kyrgyzstan by different local and international actors, including the transnational Tablighi Jama'at missionary movement, which introduces new practices in society and teaches new ways of leading a pious life, which other scholars have described as the "Sunnaization" of Islamic practices (Metcalf 1996). Learning and focusing on the Prophet's sunnahs, Tablighi activists in Kyrgyzstan contribute to the shift from "traditional"—here meaning the mixture of Islamic and cultural traditional customs that continued during the Soviet era—to orthodox Islam, the main tendency of the re-Islamization process in Kyrgyzstan.

Using the term "re-Islamization," I am also aware of its problematic aspects, which may misleadingly suggest that in the Soviet Union Islam was lost, or that what we had there was not Islam. By "re-Islamization" I refer to the recovery of Islamic practices among Muslims in the country—previous familiar Islamic practices that were "domesticated"—as well as new practices introduced by global Islamic movements without labeling them "correct /not correct" or "Islamic/un-Islamic." Instead this chapter discusses the localization of the TJN in Kyrgyzstan, meaning how universal features of global TJN are adapted to the local sociocultural and political context.

Localization is a significant part of any type of globalization. In our case even "alternative globalization" (Reetz 2010), which already signifies its distinctive features in opposition to western globalization, also requires another level of adaptation in every new context, modifying its universal features to local demands. The need for localization is dictated by large sociocultural, religious, and historical differences between the local culture and what global TJ activists bring to that culture. The differences between these two sides create difficulties in the integration of local Muslims into the global network. "Alien look," "alien style of communication," and "alien behavior or practice" became central issues debated in the discourses around TJ in Kyrgyzstan. To overcome these difficulties TJ activists develop linguistic, sociocultural, and religious adaptive strategies that enable the TJ global movement to be localized in Kyrgyzstan. In this chapter I discuss what makes Tablighi activists "alien" as well as how they modify universal features of the TJN to respond to local demands.

This chapter is based on ethnographic materials that I collected in 2008 fieldwork in Kyrgyzstan, in 2012 in Bishkek, Osh, Talas, Karakol, and Jeti Oguz. In Bashy, I interviewed twenty-four male and twelve female Tablighis and attended female teaching sessions (*taalim*). These materials are used to provide the reader with a detailed picture of global and local features of Tablighi practices in Kyrgyzstan, including haruj, davat, bayan, *zïyarat*, and taalim. Other sources collected in the field present personal stories, Tablighi narratives, metaphors, and symbols to provide insight into the reflexivity of Tablighi actors, which demonstrate the personalization of religious practice among Kyrgyzstani Muslims. This chapter includes information on female Tablighi practices that are not covered in recent articles on TJ in Kyrgyzstan (Balci 2010; Nasridinov and Ismailbekova 2012) but are a significant part of the TJN and play a key role in the networking processes of Tablighi Jama'at in Kyrgyzstan, where Tablighi women contribute significantly to bringing religion to families and society, by preaching Islam among women and children. In this chapter, I also discuss the relationship between the state and Tablighi Jama'at in Kyrgyzstan, which reveals a complex interconnectedness of globalization, politics, socioeconomic, and cultural aspects.

Brief History of Tablighi Jama'at and Its Universal Principles

TJ originated as a missionary movement in India in 1926 under the leadership of the Islamic scholar Maulana Muhammad IIyas Kandehlavi (1885–1944) "as a response to the rise of the Hindu proselytizing movement" (Reetz 2009b, 293). Under the influence of British colonization Muslims in India stopped observing the obligatory Islamic rituals, and many of them even changed their religion, converting to Hinduism. When mosques and Islamic teachers were unable to change the situation, Maulana Ilyas Kandehlavi called on Muslims to create small groups and recover religion through "door to door" preaching. He called on them not to wait for Muslims to come to the mosque to learn Islam, but to go to them in their homes, bringing the faith, asking them to renew kalima, and inviting them to prayer in the local mosque. The main goal of the movement was to revive religious practices among Muslims in order to make them better Muslims.

Now Tablighi Jama'at became one of the widespread global Muslim movements claimed to have followers numbering between twelve million and fifteen million (Reetz 2009b). Annual congregations (*ijtimai*) in Delhi, Dahka, and Raiwind gather millions of Muslims from different countries. Now TJ as part of the Muslim mainstream has developed a more bureaucratic and hierarchical administration (Reetz 2008, 2009b), represented by a council (*mashvara*) at the local, regional, country, and global levels—a "vertical" structure (Nasridinov and Ismailbekova 2012), through which Tablighi networks in different countries are connected globally.

The Tablighi movement aims at achieving its mission based on its six principles, which lead to the "Sunnaization of Islam" (Metcalf 1996), bringing the Prophet's Sunnah—sayings and deeds—to Muslims' everyday life. The first principle is *shahada*, which every Muslim must be able to recite correctly: "There is no God but Allah and Muhammad is his Messenger." The first thing Tablighi preachers ask fellow Muslims to do is to recite or to "renew" the kalima. The second principle is *salat*, learning to pray correctly. Third is *dhikr*, remembering God—every Muslim must perform dhikr regularly and improve his religious knowledge (*ilm*). Fourth is *ikrom*, showing respect to fellow Muslims. Fifth is *niyat*, sincere intention. Tablighis must be sincere in performing their religious duties. The sixth principle is *daw'a*—*davat* in the local version—a call to Islam and to consider *daw'a* as one of the forty duties of Islam.

The preaching tour (haruj), called "davat" by Kyrgyzstani Tablighi activists, plays a major role in the implementation of these six principles, referred to as *"6 syfat"* by davatchys in Kyrgyzstan. Kyrgyzstani TJ activists conduct preaching tours both internationally and domestically, following all rules concerning length of travel, organizational structure, and expected outcomes of the tour. Leaving for tours of three, fifteen, and forty days and four months, lay Muslims are instructed to do four things to increase faith—preaching, teaching sessions, service (*khydmat*), and learning to control the ego, avoiding worldly things by less eating, less sleeping, less worldly talks, less creating of unnecessary expenses. Following the above-mentioned six principles Tablighi activists are expected to achieve self-reformation, and to strengthen their faith.

The Localization of the Transnational Tablighi Jama'at Network in Kyrgyzstan

"Our Grandfathers Never Wore T-shirts": Appearance and Clothing Style of Davatchys

"Re-Islamization" in post-Soviet Kyrgyzstan occurred in the context of nation building, where the revival of ethnic history, ethnic symbols, and ethnic language became the leading tendency of that process. This revivalist context increased the visibility of Tablighi's "alien" features. Most davatchys wear long Pakistani-style clothing, extensively use Urdu, Arabic words, the Islamic greeting style, and Koranic terminology. Furthermore, many davatchys change their Kyrgyz names to "Islamic" names—from Almaz to Abdullo, Suiun to Suleiman, Ruslan to Abdurahim, and so forth.

These cultural changes of Tablighis are seen by ethnic nationalists—who promote traditional Kyrgyz ethnic culture—as very destructive for the local culture by ultranationalists. From their perspective, davatchys as the main actors of that process are not simply changing their appearance and clothing style but introducing new ways of practicing Islam, which has a deeply destructive influence on the traditional culture of the Kyrgyz people. Involving ordinary Muslims in preaching tours and teaching them to reconstruct their ways of life according to the Prophet's Sunnahs, Tablighi's reformist activities are directed against the folk customs and traditions that the Kyrgyz people have observed for a long time. For example, it is suggested that some traditional cultural elements of funeral traditions be eliminated. The Kyrgyz funeral tradition contains a mixture of Islamic ceremonies with traditional cultural customs. One of the required elements of the Kyrgyz funeral is lamentations by women (*koshok*) and men (*okuruk*). Today even koshok is widely criticized by davatchys. Tablighis interpret koshok as an action against the power of Allah. According to their interpretation of koshsok, one is supposed to accept the will of God, and so he or she should not grieve deeply and strongly because this contradicts Islamic principles. According to ethnic nationalists Tablighi's idea of being a "good Muslim" requires the complete ignorance and destruction of Kyrgyz customs and traditions that lead to the death of Kyrgyz culture.

But another direction of the same discourse shows how religious revival and the promotion of religious rituals and symbols are seen as complimentary components of nation building. In this context, Islam as one of the markers of ethnic identity was also intensified. As a result, Islamic intellectuals and different international and local religious actors started to interpret Islamic practices as a part of ethnic symbols.

In the Muftiate's official newspaper *Islam madaniaty*, the hijab has been discussed several times in relation to ethnonational features. The hijab was compared with Kyrgyz ethnic headdress (*elechek*) for women and the religious meaning of the hijab that refers to piety and modesty was reinterpreted in relation to concepts such as independence, ethnic nationalism, and cultural tradition. This reinterpretation of the meaning of the hijab by the Muftiate stresses the "similarities" between traditional ethnic and Islamic clothing style.

Continuing this discourse, Tablighi Jama'at discuss its "imported" clothing style and appearance as the "restoration" of the cultural tradition of Kyrgyz people that was broken by the Soviets. According to one davatchy,

Our grandparents never wore T-shirts, western-style shirts, and ties, our ethnic clothing for men was long, and all our ethnic heroes [*baatyrs*], including Manas (epic hero) wore a long beard and long coat [*chapan*]. Can you find at least a picture of one *baatyr*, who wore a short dress? No. Our tribal rulers and *aksakals* (respected elders) wore a long beard that shows high moral behavior of those people. The meaning of a beard is the same in our Tablighi practice, when I wear a beard I cannot do bad things, for instance, by stealing something or going to a disco. It protects me from immoral behavior.[3]

Here the davatchy's long dress and beard are reinterpreted as a tradition. References to Manas, tribal leaders, and respected old people are used in opposition to the disco, which is associated with the western lifestyle. In response to criticism of their "alien" image, davatchys search for similarities between their sunna clothing and Kyrgyz traditional clothing to legitimize their own practices.

In Tablighi bayans, delivered for women in one of the learning sessions observed by the author, the meaning of the hijab and its similarity to traditional headdress were discussed in relation to the image of one of the key female figures in the history of Kyrgyzstan—Kurmanjan datka—a tribal leader in the nineteenth century. For example, a male speaker who came to a female taalim session to perform a monthly bayan from behind the curtain instructed that "Our Kurmanjan ene was a modest woman. She was a leader of the nation and pious women, who obeyed her husband, prayed five times, and wore elechek (ethnic headdress), covering her head in the same style as the hijab."

During that inspirational talk, Kurmanjan's name appeared several times in the same context with Khadija, Fatima, and Aisha as exemplary modest Muslim women who led pious lives. All are referred as *ene*—a Kyrgyz term referring to old and respected women. In the bayan Kurmanjan ene was seen as the Mother of the Nation who had very strong faith. And two oppositional binaries were created where on the one side lay "ethnic," "Muslim," "traditional," "heroic," and on the other side—"Western," "Russian," "Soviet," and "atheistic." It is the way "Sunnaization" is presented by davatchys in opposition to Western globalization, which has a destructive influence on the traditional lifestyle of the Kyrgyz people, where Tablighi's innovative practices are interpreted as the restoration of the tradition.

Fear of the alien appearance of davatchys with long beards is expressed in nicknames used to refer to them, including the often used "Sakalchandar," which can be translated as "one who wears a long beard," which has a negative connotation. Not many people deeply reflect on and analyze the negative consequences of the reformist ideas of davatchys as ultranationalists do, so they found something in davatchys' activities that makes them seem dangerous to society. They remain suspicious and fearful because of the davatchys' new, unusual, and unfamiliar features. Reflections of people on unfamiliar, unusual features depict the Soviet discourse on "traditional Islam," which is still alive in the society and influences the perceptions and attitudes of the Soviet generation toward Islamic global movements.

One veteran Tablighi activist, Abjapar, who was first head of the Davat

Department in the Muftiate, described how one of first jama'ats from Pakistan visited Bishkek in the 1990s:

> We met a jama'at from Pakistan in 1992, during the Friday prayer [*namaz*] in the Central Mosque, where they joined in prayer with us. After prayer they introduced themselves as preachers on haruj from Pakistan and asked the imam to help them find a place to do daw'a. Nobody understood their idea about "haruj" and "daw'a," so led them to the Muftiate to ask for a consultation with mufti Kimsanabay ajy, but he also could not understand them. Then we found a young Muslim practitioner who had graduated from a madrasa in Pakistan to help with the translation, and he was the only person who understood the meaning of haruj and explained it for us, saying that haruj is a widely practiced missionary tour in Pakistan, where he spent several years as a student in one of the madrasas and where he used to join such preaching tours. This man was from Balykchy, in the northern Issyk Kul region of Kyrgyzstan, and took them to his village to conduct davat there. Two or three young people joined them, and others stayed in Bishkek expressing suspicions about the Pakistani jama'at's visit to Kyrgyzstan and worrying about our decisions to allow foreigners to preach Islam in our country. Later we learned from that Kyrgyz man who hosted the Pakistani Tablighis in Balykchy that local people were very hostile toward them, and that is why it was impossible to conduct *gasht*.[4] Instead they stayed in the house and delivered an inspirational religious talk (bayan) for a small group of young people invited by the host.[5]

Now Abjapar laughs saying how they were afraid of those Pakistani Tablighis only because they were from another Muslim country, where Islam in their understanding was practiced differently, their appearance—long beards and long dress—made them look dangerous. He explains the great fear they had about "Pakistani Islam," which did not fit "Soviet traditional Islam." Even in witnessing their sincere behavior they could not block their own worries and suspicions. However, according to Abjapar, those young people who joined the Pakistani jama'at tour to Balykchy were impressed by the Tablighis' sincere behavior and level of religious knowledge. It was the first time they had listened to an inspirational speech about religion and had seen how a man cries asking God to send faith (*yiman*) to his Kyrgyz Muslim brothers who were drunk and entering a single mosque in Balykchy that was empty during Friday prayer time. Finding nothing dangerous in the "Pakistani" way of preaching, they did not call for a caliphate, but concentrated on the individual spiritual experience. The story shows that the young generation was more open to Tablighis and interested in the way

Islam is practiced, whereas the older generation was not much focused on the content of preaching and the level of knowledge but on the "foreign" features of the preachers.

The author heard this story from many davatchys in Issyk Kul, who told it to stress the changes that took place because of Tablighi's "positive" influence on Balykchy, which was formerly a town with a high criminal rate, a single mosque that was always was locked, and young guys addicted to alcohol. Now they describe Balykchy in a new mode with a decreased criminal rate, and with young guys who have stopped drink alcohol, are involved in *davat*, regularly attend the mosque. More than twenty mosques have been built in Balykchy, and all of them are now full for Friday prayer. Some Tablighis told this story and were proud that their town of Balykchy was the birthplace of Tablighi Jama'at, at least in the northern part of Kyrgyzstan.

The ways of retelling the same story and its context by different davatchys also depicts the complexities of the perceptions of the first Tablighi Jama'ats by local people, their fear of what they considered "alien" or " foreign" Islam, which did not fit "traditional Islam" in Soviet times, and also their doubts and questions about the consequences of changes in religious practices introduced by global movements.

Abjapar is now one of the Tablighi veterans who was eager to share with us the benefits he gained from joining the TJN. He even wrote poetic verses in which he calls people to join the movement. As an active davatchy he performed a forty-day davat to Pakistan together with his wife Aisha and regularly makes his monthly and annual davat within the country. But not all people in Kyrgyzstan share Abjapar's vision of TJ.

About twenty years have passed from the time when Pakistani missionaries first came to introduce Tablighi practices in Kyrgyzstan, where they made great efforts to overcome the suspicious and hostile attitudes of local Muslims toward early Tablighi Jama'ats. In the 1990s, davat was presented mostly by foreign jama'ats from Pakistan, but now the main actors of Tablighi networks in Kyrgyzstan are Kyrgyzstani Tablighis and they are connected to transnational TJ networks not only through markazes in Raiwind and Tablighi madrasas in Pakistan but through two other large markazes in India and Bangladesh. Emil Nasridinov and Aksana Ismailbekova (2012) report that in those countries the doors to markazes for Kyrgyzstani Tablighis were not opened at the same time. They describe how every new door depicted the phases of evolution of the TJ movement in Kyrgyzstan and its characteristics coincided with the specific features of the TJ movement in those three places.

Despite all these active developments of Tablighi Jama'at networks and their practices, perceptions and attitudes toward Tablighi missionaries are mixed and discourses around the TJ movement in Kyrgyzstan remain contested.

Introducing Tablighi Concepts: Linguistic and Sociocultural Adaptation

Linguistic tools play a significant role in introducing the transnational Tablighi network's main concepts to Kyrgyzstani Muslims. Translation, interpretation, phonetic adaptation, and the borrowing of different Arabic and Urdu terms are used by davatchys to express the meaning of faith concepts and core Tablighi practices. Metaphorical language with extensive use of Kyrgyz reference terms and rhythmical style of phrases shape Tablighi narratives close to the style of Kyrgyz oral traditions.

The meaning of the core Tablighi concept haruj, which refers to the preaching tour as a condition for the isolation of davatchy from worldly matters and is expressed by the phrase "breaking with worldly matters" (in Kyrgyz, *dunuiodon uzuluu*) and the creation of other new phrases with the word *dunuio* to intensify the same meaning. Detachment from worldly matters as expressed in Kyrgyz refers not only to physical isolation but also spiritual isolation, increasing one's spiritual reflections and immersing oneself in spirituality to achieve self-reformation. There are other phrases used by Tablighis to refer to worldly matters. "Break with worldly duties" (*dunuionun ishinen uzul*) or avoid worldly talks (*dunuionun sozun suilobo*) suggest that preachers on haruj or that female Tablighi activists involved in Taalim sessions gain a deeper spiritual experience. *Dunuio* is a worldly life in which people are very much attached to material values and lead a "westernized" lifestyle. In contrast to this, on haruj people are detached physically from worldly life and must develop the skills to become spiritually isolated from worldly matters.

All rules on haruj compel davatchys to distance themselves from worldly matters. Cell phones are not allowed; when conducting gasht, walking on the left side of the street and not looking at women are suggested. When knocking on the doors of houses, preachers should not look through the peepholes in order to avoid jealousy and greed by comparing the wealth of people living in the house. In addition to this, the members of davat should stay in the mosque during services (all days and nights of the preaching tour) and not leave unless it is necessary.

According to a Tablighi activist, who experienced three days of davat for the first time: "one's thoughts and reflections really turn toward the spiritual side, and one starts to look on his life differently. Now I see how much people's lives are attached to material values, which makes them blind to seeing the spiritual side in their everyday competition for material wealth."[6]

Tablighis avoid these worldly things not only during the preaching tour (to fully immerse themselves in the spiritual learning) but also in their everyday lives. In an interview with the author, Bermet (name has been changed), a thirty-five-year-old female informant, who did *masturat davat* six times for three days said that such avoidance helps her to keep her spirit (*ruh*) clean in everyday life. She works as an electrical engineer at the airport, where she shares an office with other female colleagues who talk a lot about fashion, furniture, cosmetics, and money. In order not to be involved in the conversation she repeats kalima and does inner dhikr silently. She believes that such worldly things lead people to bad actions (jealousy, involvement in corruption, consumerism) and completely fill one's thoughts, leaving no room for moral and spiritual values. Tablighis' personal stories revealed during the author's interviews *were* deeply reflexive and structured with clear opposing boundaries in their own lives: between material and spiritual, pious and ignorant, moral and immoral, and so on. This reflective experience became a primary condition for Tablighis in critically reconsidering their previous lifestyle and reforming it according to TJN principles, which Barbara Metcalf (1996) calls "Sunnaization."

In Bermet's case "Sunnaization" is seen as a reflective reconsideration of her own life and its reconstruction in a new way. She removed the modern sofa, table, and chairs from her flat and replaced it with Islamic decoration—placing a picture of Mecca and verses of the Koran on the wall. Besides observing the obligatory religious rituals—five times daily prayer, fasting, and so on—she finds time to attend weekly lectures delivered by the former mufti Chubak ajy, weekly taalims and bayan organized for women by Tablighis in Bishkek, to listen to recorded bayans at home on CD, and to read Fazail Amal' for her five-year-old son and twelve-year-old daughter.

Modernity is not completely ignored by many Tablighis, who continue to use some harmless modern achievements. Bermet selectively watches some television shows, including news and popular scientific programs. She understands the importance of modern education and sends her daughter to an expensive private school Dawha, where scientific subjects are taught as well as the basics of Islam. She wants her daughter to receive both types of knowledge—religious and secular—so she will not become an "educated satan" (*bilimduu shaitan*), a term used by many Tablighis to refer to Muslims who are educated but do not practice Islam. Bermet always tries to balance both sides of her daughter's life—she wears the hijab, prays, reads Fazail Amal' with her mother, and attends an Arabic-language course.

The concept of dunuio in Tablighi practices is broad—it does not reject worldly life completely, but instead teaches that a worldly life must be led appropriately. Only through experiencing the break with worldly life can one see how worldly life is constructed and how it must be reconstructed. For Tablighis' haruj life makes them detach from worldly life and then return to it, now leading it by following the Prophet's exemplary life ways. Our field data show that breaking with worldly life makes a person learn very practical worldly things, teaching, and even training davatchys through haruj activities, what to say and how to say it, how to spend money, how to treat a husband or wife, parents, and family members in this life.

Another term used to interpret the meaning of haruj for Kyrgyzstani Muslims is *meenet*, meaning hard working. According to TJ activists, life is given to build faith (*yiman*) which requires hard work in overcoming inner (ego) and external difficulties (attacks from society). One must have a strong faith to overcome these difficulties. The hard work is understood by them as global. "Meenet (hard work for rising faith) goes to every part of the world now" (*meenet but dunuiodo jurup jatat*)—say Tablighi in bayan, referring to Tablighi activities as forms of meenet. In Kyrgyzstan all the difficulties that require meenet are discussed by Tablighis in relation to their hard work against Western influence, Soviet atheistic influence, and difficulties created by nationalists against Tablighi's attempts at "purification of Islam."

Not always translating the term into the Kyrgyz language is encouraged. In some cases it is important for Tablighis to retain original Urdu or Arabic terms or names. During the davit, other than the leader (amir), group members have be in roles of different positions that change every day according to the council's (mashvara) decision, conducted every day in the morning after the first prayer. Even when a Kyrgyz equivalent is available, davatchys prefer to use foreign terms to name the role performed on preaching tour: *elon* (announcer) and *mutacalim* (speaker) during the gasht; taalim, one who leads the reading of Fazail Amal'; *dalil*—usually recruited from the locals—guide the group during the *gasht*; *Khidmat*—a service performed by the person who cooks and cleans. Retaining Arabic, Urdu words in their original form among davatchys not only shows how

Urdu became a lingua franca of the movement but also how this linguistic style became important for their belonging to the transnational network, manifesting their connections to the global Muslim network, and expressing their religious identity. Despite the republican council's suggestion and the Davat Department's attempt to Kyrgyz-size Tablighi terminology, davatchys in Kyrgyzstan extensively use Tablighi terminology in Arabic and Urdu to express their connections to the global network.

In some cases Tablighis invent metaphors from the local language to convey the meaning of Tablighi concepts and activities. In these cases they use not translation but similar-sounding metaphors in the native language. For instance, without translation, *ijhtimai* refers to Tablighi gatherings, but also to the Kyrgyz metaphor *ishtin maijy*, where *ish* means job and *mai* means buttermilk. Together they create the metaphorical meaning *outcomes of the job*. Such linguistic adaptation fits well the style of Tablighi language discussed above.

The linguistic adaptive strategies of Tablighis in Kyrgyzstan creatively reproduce the metaphorical language of the transnational TJN as the main tool for introducing Tablighi faith concepts and practices using linguistic sources of native language in combination with Arabic and Urdu words. To some extent, we can say that the rich narrative practices of TJN in Kyrgyzstan shape the "language of faith" in Kyrgyz, which has a very distinctive linguistic and performative style.

The Woman Is a Madrasa in the House: Learning a New Role for Tablighi Women

Female Tablighi activists known in Kyrgyzstan as *masturat*, interpreted as covered women, play a significant role in the localization of transnational TJ practices and the networking of its activists. Female Tablighis are recognized by their unusual appearance, wearing long dresses in dark colors and hijab. Some of them fully cover their face strictly following purdah to achieve "yakin," full devotion to faith as Tablighis explained to the author.

Kyrgyzstani Muslim women as well as other Central Asian female Muslims were traditionally involved in home-based religious cultural rituals conducting healing, mazar worship, and life-cycle rituals that remain far from preaching Islam. Habiba Fathi (1997) studied religious practices among Central Asian Muslim women, and Gillian Tett (1994) highlighted the importance of home-based ritualistic female practices in preserving Islam in Soviet Central Asia. Both authors noted the deep mixture of cultural traditional and Islamic elements in those practices. But now through the involvement of the global TJN, Muslim women in Kyrgyzstan are learning to perform new roles—preaching and teaching Islam. Scrupulous learning of Tablighi textbooks makes Tablighi women better oriented in orthodox Islam and creates a discourse on what it means to be a "good Muslim" in the Tablighi way. This causes Tablighi women to distance themselves from mazar worship, healing, and life-cycle rituals.

Female Tablighis acquire and present these new roles by attending weekly learning sessions, joining a husband or male relatives in preaching or welcoming tours, teaching the basics of Islam at home, and reading Fazail Amal' every day for children.

The weekly taalim session, an open event that lasts only an hour and focuses on reading Fazail Amal' (*Virtues of Good Deeds*),[7] is led by an experienced female Tablighi who opens and closes the taalim with a prayer (*du'a*). The author attended taalim in different neighborhoods in Bishkek, Karakol. At Bashy from six to thirty-two women gathered. In all houses or flats where taalim was conducted the author saw duva written in Arabic on a piece of paper placed on the entrance door, and some Islamic objects: a picture of Mecca, a rosary, Fazail Amal' textbooks on the shelf, CDs with bayan recordings, and so on. In towns taalim is usually conducted in the guest rooms of flats that are refurnished according to the Muslim lifestyle, with the removal of furniture—sofa, chairs, tables, and sometimes a television—associated with the Western lifestyle by davatchys. One can see mattresses (*toshoks*) placed on the floor carpets around the room where women can sit and the female Tablighi leader of the session sits in the middle, together with an appointed reader of Fazail Amal,' to whom other attendees listen, repeating ritualistic phrases. The chapters of the Fazail Amal' for every taalim are assigned by Tablighi Jama'at in the mosque, and usually cover a piece from each chapter. After reading they pray and go home.

Once during the month taalim is accompanied with bayan performed by a man from the neighborhood mosque who is an experienced Tablighi activist. In the house, the room is usually divided into two parts covered by a curtain in the corner where the man delivers bayan. The content of the bayan discusses the importance of the role of masturat, in building faith (*yimandy kuruu*) in society. This is how one preacher began his bayan in one of the sessions I attended: "Because of masturat's strong adherence to faith, it increased during the time of the Prophet. His main supporters were our Kadicha ene, Fatima ene, and Aisha ene. Many masturats suffered in the struggle for the faith, but never gave up their faith. Women are a madrasa in the house, they inspire their husbands to make davat, they teach Islam to their children and to other female Muslim colleagues. They found full happiness in the faith."

The sessions usually lasted thirty minutes and concluded with a call to masturat to keep their faith strongly, and carry this information to other Muslims—especially family members, relatives, and friends. After taalim was finished women were advised to repeat in pairs what they learned, then to do *tashkil* (invitation to a preaching tour for their husbands), make a list of *nak* (being ready to go to davat) or *niyat* (intention to go for davat) for their husbands, leave their contact information, and instruct the six-year-old daughter of the host family to give the list to the bayan speaker so that he could take the list to the mosque.

There are some requirements for hosting the taalim, which moves from one house to another every month by decision of the mosques of the town, village, or neighborhood. In the mosque the local jama'at makes a list of families who want to host taalim. If they fulfill the hosting requirements, they will be scheduled to host a taalim for the whole month. The hosting couple must be pious practicing Muslims, who observe obligatory religious rituals, and it is better if the husband is a part of the Tablighi Network. The house should be clean and contain a big room in which to conduct teaching. It is believed by Tablighis that a house or flat that hosts taalim, will be covered in light (*noor*) as a sign of blessing that includes twenty neighboring houses on all four sides. One of my informants, who was eager to host taalim invited her brother-in-law to live in her house for a month, in order to meet one of the hosting requirements according to which a man should be present in the family during taalim. Her husband died several years ago and she had three daughters, but no son.

According to Tablighi rules, women should be accompanied by their husband or male relatives to attend taalim, a requirement called *mahram*. But in Kyrgyzstan, women come alone to taalim or together with female friends. Another requirement is that after taalim women should go directly home, bringing light to their houses from taalim, keeping in their hearts all the inspiration they received from the session. On the way back home they should not be involved in worldly conversations, visit friends, or be involved in other worldly things that will disturb a person from the faith (*din*). They are not allowed to discuss even the content of the taalim. If a woman has questions she should send them to the imam of the mosque through her husband, who will bring the answer for his wife from the imam. Women have no right to ask and answer questions directly. Another central requirement for women to attend taalim is that she come with a strong sincere intention (niyat) to learn Islam. Women are advised to leave everything associated with worldly life in the house, including feelings and thoughts about worldly duties. In one of the taalims attended by the author in Uchkun, a micro district of Bishkek, the bayan speaker said that it is not good to bring small children to taalim because they might interrupt the women's learning by dividing their attention. To meet this requirement, male Tablighis have to look after children when women go to taalim to encourage their seeking of knowledge.

Aside from offering religious interpretations of its distinctive moral values, Tablighi practices respond to local needs. In Kyrgyzstan, many families are separated because of labor migration to Russia. In the context of separation of spouses, parents, and children, the Tablighi idea of a "cooperative family" (Metcalf 1996) can be seen as an alternative, where spouses and children live harmoniously, maintaining the common goal of leading a pious life through involvement in Tablighi practices of recovering religion, where a man is a spiritual leader, a woman is his supporter, and children are followers of parents. In zïyarats and bayans all family members can be seen together: children participate as mediators between men and women who are not allowed to talk face to face. Men and women are mutually dependent on each other, a Tablighi woman can make a decision for man, when writing a *nak* (readiness to join the next davat group) or *niet* (an intention to go to davat) for their husbands in tashkil, circulating the paper in the masturat group to make a list of male Tablighis with nak and niet, and leaving the husband's contacts to be invited for the next davat. Also a man's davat is nothing if his wife is not involved in TJN practices. TJ networking is significantly based on these cooperative families, in which some traditional gender roles are "reconfigured," using Metcalf's term, and challenge certain aspects of hierarchical family structures by introducing duties of the opposite gender to both sides.

Some personal stories of Tablighis show reflective and critical views of female practitioners on traditional cultural customs of the Kyrgyz people that affect the relationship between spouses as well as among all family members. The case of Bermet, one of my key informants, who found new meaning in joining TJN illustrates how she distanced herself from some cultural customs related to daughter-in-law's position in the society.

As a daughter-in-law [*kelin*] I experienced firsthand all unjust attitudes toward daughters-in-law in Kyrgyz traditional customs. I was a servant for all my in-laws, cleaning and cooking for the whole family. I had to treat my fathers- and mothers-in-law as if they were God, bowing to them every day in the morning; I had no rights in my husband's family. Islam gives me equal rights. Islam teaches, "A wife is a special gift (*amanat*) from God that places a heavy responsibility on the recipient [i.e., the husband]. He has a great responsibility for her." Woman is not a servant of people, but a servant of God. We have to bow only to God.[8]

In this example she reflects on the cultural customs that establish a hierarchy for daughters-in-law in relation to their husband's family members. As in the Indian case described by Metcalf (1996), she "finds less hierarchical familial structure and means resistant to social hierarchies" in Islam through Tablighi practices.

During the taalim observed by the author, the leader commented on the greeting style of local women who had come to listen to bayan and greeted others in the traditional way by bowing to show respect. "Bowing should be done for God only, we create a *shirk*, another God out of people, when we bow to them. We are just human beings, so we have to greet each other saying 'Assolomu alekum'" (a ritualized greeting style for Tablighi women), she explained.

In both examples traditional cultural customs are seen as unjust rules that cause inequality. However, according to Tablighis they are not rejecting but "restoring" the traditional position of Muslim women in Kyrgyzstan, recommending that a woman remains in private, in the house, rearing children according to Islam, and treating her husband as a leader in the everyday and religious spheres, inspiring, supporting, and encouraging the gaining of Islamic knowledge and performance of Tablighi duties. Masturat are allowed to perform public duties through taalim, zïyarat, and dawat, if they strictly follow the principles of gender segregation embodied in purdah by covering themselves and being accompanied by a mahram, a male relative. But these rules do not always work for many Tablighi women in Kyrgyzstan, so they combine their professional work in diverse secular settings and Tablighi duties and attend taalim without mahram; the majority wear a hijab but not nikab (full covering).

"The Name 'Tablighi Jama'at' Is Incorrect": Stressing Universal Revivalist Goals

TJ is prohibited in Russia and all of Central Asia except for Kyrgyzstan, where they remain unbanned. This does not mean, however, that the state in

Kyrgyzstan trusts them and thus provides them with full freedom. The relationship between the state and TJ is more complex and ambiguous in reality, ranging from freedom to manipulation and from cooperation to attempts to prohibit it, following neighboring countries. TJN in Kyrgyzstan is institutionalized to some extent, representing the Davat Department of the Muftiate.

According to Abdullatif Jumabaev, head of the State Commission on Religious Affairs (CRA) under the president of the Kyrgyz Republic, "TJN is now sitting on the shoulders of the Muftiate because the main function of the Muftiate is fulfilled by TJN. The Muftiate had to lead religious propagation, explaining to society the main principles of Islam and how to practice it, but they are very passive. That is why religious propagation is conducted by Tablighis, according to Tablighi Jama'at's principles"⁹

The Davat Department in the Muftiate is called the Davat and Propagation Department (*dawat jana ugut nasyiat bolumu*), and led by Eratov, who graduated from a madrasa in Raiwind, Pakistan, and is also the director of the Tablighi madrasa in Archa beshik settlement in Bishkek, students of which are involved in Tablighi practices. Eratov always emphasizes the universal functions of his department, saying that davat is not specific to TJ and began with the Prophet Muhammad. He says the aim of the department is not to build TJN but to contribute to reviving religious practices in which the state and many different groups participate. The same statements were made by Tablighi actors in interviews with the author. Davatchys hide their sectarian features and express more universal goals shared with other groups in reviving Islam in Kyrgyzstan.

The Davat Department became a mediator between the state and TJN in Kyrgyzstan. On the one hand the department head reports to the government and the CRA under the president, collects statistical data on Tablighi preaching tours within and outside the country, conducts meetings with Tablighi activists in the regions and prepares reports on those meetings, issues regulations and rules to respond to local complaints concerning the "alien" practices of Tablighi, and develops requirements for preaching tours, and so on, aimed at adapting and making TJ practices acceptable for Muslims in Kyrgyzstan. In so doing, the department head plays a key role in regulating TJN practices and assisting the state in controlling TJ activities. On the other hand the head of the Davat Department is the Tablighi practitioner actively involved in fulfilling TJ's mission, translating its main book Fazail Amal' into Kyrgyz, establishing the first Tablighi madrasa in Bishkek, and participating in Tablighi activities. He contributes to adapting Tablighi practices to the local context, issuing rules in the name of the

Muftiate in regard to Tablighi clothing style—including a suggestion to shorten Tablighi clothing and add Kyrgyz ornaments to make it not "alien" for the Kyrgyzstani people—or developing requirements for Tablighi preaching tours, making it mandatory to have an official paper from the local mosque and from police as well as permission from the family to go to davat. This was a response to people's hostile attitudes toward davatchys. But davatchys do not always accept the new requirements for doing davat.

"Davat is not selective about people [*davat adamdy tandabait*]," said one davatchy I interviewed. "If a person who was previously involved in criminal acts expresses his will to join davat, we must allow him to do it. His intention to change his lifestyle is very positive, so why would we create an obstacle to him in his motivation to learn a faith?" Usually a revisionist commission (which davatchys call "kavaib jamaat") discusses the situations of each person who plans to do davat, individually assessing not only his family and financial condition but also his intention of learning faith.

Eratov also emphasized in his interview with the author that Tablighi Jama'at is not the correct term to refer to actors involved in TJN. According to him, ordinary people invented this term, but the founder of the TJN, Maulana Muhammad Ilyas, did not like the term, and said, "I would call it 'recovering faith or raising faith'" (Kyrgyz: *Yimandy janadandyruu, kotoruu*). Eratov is eager to show the more universal features of TJN and to avoid speaking openly about its sectarian characteristics, as opposed to Jumabaev, who pointed out that the Davat Department of the Muftiate makes a call (dawa) to Islam in a very specific Tablighi way that involves Muslims in preaching tours. For Jumabaev it is not good to allow one group to dominate in the context of the re-Islamization process. "An official structure such as the Muftiate and Board of Ulema (Ulamalar Keneshi) should be free of any group's influence. But now the Muftiate is under the strong influence of the TJ. Tablighi leaders say that they are not interested in politics and official positions, but now they are entering structures such as the Muftiate and Board of Ulema and gaining high positions for their members, which contradicts their declared apolitical orientation."[10]

At the end of the interview Jumabaev emphasized that the State Commission does not work with unregistered religious organizations, saying, "TJ is not officially registered, and that is why we do not collect information about them. Without registration our state cannot prohibit it." It is not clear from this interview how other Central Asian countries did it. He mentioned the 2010 agreement among the ODKB (Collective Security Treaty Organization) member countries, in which all heads of member country Security Committees, including Kyrgyzstan's, signed the agreement in which the TJ was included on the list of terrorist organizations.

After Kazakhstan prohibited the TJ on February 29, 2013, some deputies and local activists suggested that it should also be prohibited in Kyrgyzstan. Responding to such proposals, Tablighi Jama'at activists also expressed the group's views on those issues, including the use of media sources. One energetic TJ activist wrote three articles in local newspapers, where he pointed out that instead of prohibiting this apolitical movement it would be beneficial for the society to involve Tablighi in solving problems such as ethnic conflicts and political protests, which are frequent in Kyrgyzstan. According to him, Tablighi's main idea is to call for Muslims to distance themselves from politics and to unite together, rejecting discrimination based on ethnic belonging.

The presence of Tablighi activists in official structures reflects new discourses on the meaning and role of structures that still exist such as the Muftiate and the State Commission for Religious Affairs because similar institutions were established by the Soviets to control Islam. Previous forms and functions of those structures are being challenged with entrance into them of activists of global movements, which contribute to a shift from traditional to orthodox Islam.

Religious Globalization

The TJN in Kyrgyzstan has been developed as a part of a transnational network resulting from the involvement of Kyrgyzstani Tablighis in a global religious movement, which some scholars have viewed as religion's contribution to globalization. In his book *Globalized Islam: The Search for a New Ummah*, Roy (2004, 24) pointed out that in the modern globalized world religions live beyond the cultures. The "mobility" paradigm (Sheller and Urry 2006) suggests looking at global movements together with its "mobile actors," who cross geographical, sociocultural, national, and ethnic boundaries, bringing with them new objects, sources, ideas, and practices and creating networks based on existing social and new symbolic ties. Stressing the connections between mobility, actors, and networking structures in understanding global religious movements, the "mobility" paradigm addresses not only which global practices, ideas, and structures emerge in various multiple localities, but also how local cultures are influenced by global mobilities. Dietrich Reetz (2010) claims that religious globalization has different forms, one of which emerged through the mobilities of

Muslim preachers, particularly the Tablighi Jama'at Network, and creates "alternative globalities" in opposition to Western globalization. The impact of this alternative globalization on local societies is "multifaceted . . . [and] shaped by the social and cultural experience of local society and driven by its needs, rather than by a transnational agenda" (Reetz 2013, 1).

This chapter has addressed the localization of the transnational Tablighi Jama'at Network in Kyrgyzstan that is going on not through the rejection of local traditional cultural practices, but through adaptation of its faith principles and practices to the local context. The field data presented here did not confirm the break of religion with culture, allowing "religions to live beyond the cultures," but the localization of the global TJN movement in Kyrgyzstan, mobile actors who introduce the movement's principles of global faith, concepts, and structures, creatively adapting to the local context and reinterpreting them by using local sociohistorical, cultural, and linguistic sources. Tablighi activists in Kyrgyzstan are "not passive receivers of alternative globalization" but active actors who creatively change some TJ principles in response to religious and sociocultural, political-economic challenges in the society and "far from being objects or victims of globalization, they form 'alternate globalities' in their own right who self-consciously shape their own modernity" (Reetz 2013, 14).

The localization of Tablighi Jama'at also has another direction, its "purist" ideas: its adherents' new images and practices challenge local culture and society, causing debates among different groups, in which religious actors, the state, and ordinary people are involved. These debates show how under the influence of the transnational religious movement local cultures are reconsidered in a new way, in accordance with universal Islamic values. Muslims in Kyrgyzstan, rethinking both local cultural traditions and Islamic practices under the influence of Tablighis, find ways to shift from "traditional" to orthodox Islam. In this context some groups, for instance, female Muslims, learn new roles and become involved in preaching and teaching Islam.

As the collected field data show, as a recently emerged global movement, TJ does not consist in a shift of traditional Islam (Hanafi Islam) toward fundamentalist Islam (Salafism). Instead the Tablighi Jama'at Network contributes to personalization and individualization of Islamic practice among Muslims, which causes a diversification of Islamic practices not only in the society (Akiner 2003b) but also within the family (Borbieva 2009).

CHAPTER ELEVEN

Transnational Islamic Banks and Local Markets in Central Asia

Aisalkyn Botoeva

We first established a regional financial center in Almaty, since it has a high concentration of banks. But the goal and idea was that the center would facilitate growth of Islamic finance as a niche in Kazakhstan, then in the Central Asian region, and then in NIC broadly.
> — Representative of the National Bank of Kazakhstan

How are state officials going to openly practice Islam, or actively promote us, if the state leaders are banning prayer rooms in government buildings?
> — Representative of a community of entrepreneurs, striving to establish a small-scale Islamic company in Kazakhstan

Starting in the early and mid-2000s, the Central Asian states of Kazakhstan and Kyrgyzstan have become another node in the worldwide network of Islamic financial institutions, hosting an array of such institutions that vary from large banks that serve businesses, to banks that offer retail products, and finally to microfinance companies that offer services to mostly rural populations.[1] Despite their foreign origins and their transnational scope, these institutions are framed, translated, and implemented by local actors: state regulators, religious authorities, and entrepreneurs. As the quotes above illustrate, however, these different sets of actors do not always share a singular vision of why and how Islamic financial institutions (hereafter, IFIs) should be expanding in this post-Soviet region. Contrary to some analysts' arguments that openness to IFIs is an indicator toward "Islamic activism in general" (Aliyev 2012), I argue that disaggregating the different actors within these national contexts and attending to their distinct rationales and narratives reveals a polarized dynamic. Drawing from my research on IFIs in the two countries, I aim to explore the ethical, political, and normative narratives of this triangle of actors who have been promoting IFIs in particular, as well as promoting sharia-compliant businesses in general. Such analysis gets us away from perspectives centered on the state and foreign investment (Aliyev 2012; Gresh 2007), which presume the political and economic powers to be the sole drivers in this moralized "market niche" (Pitluck 2013, 17).

Some authors equate Islamic finance with the organic food and Fair Trade movements, which are widely known examples of the struggle to make market activities more moral. As with these initiatives to make capitalism less exploitative, damaging, and hazardous, IFIs represent a moralized market. The two major moral religious precepts that are incorporated into IFIs are the avoidance of *riba* (unjustified increase, interest), and *gharar* (uncertainty, risk).[2] It is also prohibited to finance *haram*—illicit products and activities such as production and sale of alcohol, guns, tobacco, and pork and the promotion of gambling, among others. While some authors question the extent to which these precepts are actually embedded in the work of Islamic banks (Kuran 2005), heightened attention to the moral work of economic transactions offered by IFIs, as well as their explicit symbolic identity, still serve as sites for exploring the complex relations between religion, market, and state (Wolters 2013, 3). Exploring this market niche may be of further importance in light of the 2008 global financial crisis, when "the new forms of scrutiny . . . exposed finance as a social activity subject to considerable dishonesty and recklessness" (Fourcade et al. 2013, 602).

The origins of IFIs trace back to Egypt, Pakistan, Iran, and Malaysia, where they first emerged in the 1970s, and the global scope of the industry has grown rapidly since then to reach an estimated $822 billion (Imam and Kpodar 2010) to $1.3 trillion (Warde 2010) in revenue. But why has there been a rapid growth of these institutions in the Central Asian context recently? Are the states behind the wheel in the process of introducing them, or are private for-profit enterprises simply seeking new markets? Does the bottom-up revival of Islam in the region (McGlinchey 2009), through which Muslim identities are increasingly becoming a dominant part of national identities among the local population, play a significant role in this process? Or is it perhaps the financial resources available to Islamic banks from the petrodollars of the Gulf countries that make these institutions attractive to local market players? These kinds of speculations circulate among the local population, which is itself engaged in making sense of this new market phenomenon in the region. Scholars and policy analysts who have written on IFIs in the region have mostly centered their analysis on the foreign investors who made "Islamic money" available to this post-Soviet region (Gresh 2007) and state actors (Aliyev 2012) who supposedly have more open policies toward Islamic finance if they endorse Islamic activism broadly. These analyses are in line with broader theoretical camps that explain the rise of IFIs *globally* in terms of the high liquidity of capital available from the Gulf (Beck, Demirgüç-Kunt, and Merrouche 2010) and the growing global community of pious Muslims, who ostensibly strive to incorporate "Islamic guidelines for behavior in various aspects of everyday life" (Pepinsky 2013 1).[3]

What these analyses cannot explain, however, is why Kazakhstan as a state that has restrictive policies toward the practice of Islam, would nevertheless take a proactive role in establishing Islamic banks. They also fail to explain why in contexts such as that of Kyrgyzstan, where there is less state facilitation of the growth in IFIs, the networks and reach of Islamic banks and microfinance companies is nevertheless expanding. To answer these questions, I attend to the states' narratives, but also bring in the less publicized accounts of entrepreneurs and religious authorities, whose vision, strategies, and actions vis-à-vis the state and the local population are crucial in understanding this market niche in its complexity. My discussions here are based on in-depth interviews with state regulators, entrepreneurs in large and small-scale IFIs, and religious authorities in Kazakhstan and Kyrgyzstan, conducted in 2012–13. Moreover, I rely on secondary data, such as relevant newspaper articles and policy reports. Inspired by social studies of the finance and economic sociology literatures, I aim to explore this financial market niche in terms of involved actors, "who have a particular web of relations," with "contested and fallible interpretations of economic reality rather than unproblematic representations" (De Goede 2005, 23; cf. MacKenzie 2003 and Maurer 2002).

It is important to highlight what this chapter is not about. I do not aim here to bring in the voices of the broader players in conventional financial markets. Rather the chapter focuses on the narratives of proponents of sharia-compliant business owners and actors who are involved in the creation of this market niche in one way or another. Moreover, despite the differences that I must note between Kazakhstan and Kyrgyzstan, for example, varying levels of state collaboration with entrepreneurs and religious factions in the cases (see table 11.1), this chapter does not intend to present a comparative analysis of IFIs in the two settings. The multitude of IFIs

Table 11.1. The Field of Islamic Finance in Kazakhstan and Kyrgyzstan

	Kazakhstan	Kyrgyzstan
Membership in the Islamic Development Bank (IDB)	1995	1993
Legislation signed	2007	2009
Local actors that initiated promotion of Islamic Financial Institutions (IFIs)	BTA bank working group	Shamil Murtazaliev and his colleagues at EcoBank
Existing large IFIs	Al Hilal Bank, daughter of Abu Dhabi–based bank	EcoIslamic Bank, pilot project of IDB
Existing smaller-scale IFIs	— Fattah Finance, consultancy and financial broker for Islamic investments and securities — Takaful Insurance Company	— Kompanion Invest microfinance company — Kausar, microfinance company

in two countries is rather taken as constitutive of one field, and the purpose is to explore the different rationales and meanings of "Islamic finance" for three different sets of actors: the state, entrepreneurs, and religious authorities in the two countries. They all are engaged in translating what "Islamic finance" means, and offer distinct rationales. These rationales warrant our attention if we are to understand the political dynamics within developing economies, where competing visions of "fairness, moral tolerability, right and wrong courses of action" (Fourcade et al. 2013, 602) among different actors shape their strategies, actions, and perceptions of each other. After all, as economic sociologists contend, "economies are shaped by the moral dispositions and beliefs of the individuals who govern them as much as they are governed through techniques and numbers" (Fourcade et al. 2013, 603).

Foreign Investors and the State

The initial engagement of the governments of Kyrgyzstan and Kazakhstan with Islamic finance started with their membership in the Islamic Development Bank (IDB). The IDB provided $65 million and $76 million in investments to the Kyrgyzstani and Kazakhstani governments, respectively, by the year 2003 (Gresh 2007, 3–4).[4] These cash flows were primarily targeted at the construction of roads, dams, and other forms of physical infrastructure. Remarkably, both governments are also known for their systematic exclusion and eradication of Islamic groups that are not aligned with traditional Islam, broadly defined by the state and state-aligned religious authorities of each country (Jones Luong and Weinthal 2002; Khalid 2007; Naumkin 2005; Olcott 2007a). Why would they welcome investors with "Islamic money," while being so cautious about foreign Islamic groups in general? Some analysts have argued that "the policies towards this financial industry have taken their lead from the individual countries' policies towards Islamic activism in general" (Aliyev 2012, 4), concluding that the higher tolerance of activism in the religious sphere leads to more openness to Islamic finance. In contrast, drawing from my interviews with state regulators in the two countries to demonstrate, I argue that the "openness" of these states to Islamic finance is in fact driven by their vision of it as a source of viable alternative cash flows and tools for diversifying investment portfolios. Moreover, as I will demonstrate later, state policies in Kazakhstan and Kyrgyzstan that support Islamic finance have fostered strategies of prioritizing larger banks, while neglecting pious entrepreneurs who own small and medium enterprises.

According to state officials in the two settings, the emergence of IFIs followed a linear process (often traced only to the early and mid-2000s), and their gradual expansion is mostly due to their economic utility. In Kazakhstan, the state's support for Islamic finance has taken force especially after many Western banks closed channels of capital inflow as a result of the global financial crisis in 2007.[5] The following excerpt from an interview exemplifies a common narrative among state officials both in Kazakhstan and Kyrgyzstan: "Kazakhstan views Islamic finance as an alternative source of investments. At the time of the financial crises, you may remember that Western cash flows drastically shrank, and at one point became completely inaccessible to Kazakh banks, making the major 'cash pillow' absent. Our banking sector had not developed [local] deposits, because it was easier for them to attract foreign investments with lower interest rates, and then to give out loans here like hot cakes. Without the Western cash flows, the National Bank started looking for other options."[6]

In his push for Kazakhstan to become a regional Islamic financial hub, President Nursultan Nazarbayev stated that the "global economic crisis has shown that the Islamic financial and economic model is stable and viable."[7] Under the guidance of state leaders, upper-echelon political elite started to sing the chorus regarding the economic benefits of Islamic finance. This narrative is pervasive in these circles in both countries. Regulators in Kazakhstan, for example, frequently make statements along the lines that "the development of Islamic finance . . . will put [their country] in a favorable light for foreign investors, who prefer to operate in accordance with Shariah Law. Such investors are widely represented in the Middle East, Malaysia and even Europe."[8] Echoing this, Omurbek Babanov, then the deputy prime minister of Kyrgyzstan, expressed his interest in creating centers of Islamic financial services in the capital city. According to him, "the development and spread of Islamic principles of finance would yield fast and effective returns, bearing a direct impact on economic development and social welfare."[9] The instrumental rationality of IFIs is hence at the core of these state regulators' rationalization.

The high hopes of these regulators for inexhaustible investments into their markets once they declared themselves open to Islamic finance have pushed state officials to rush through and revise existing laws on banking and the securities market. In Kazakhstan, lobbying groups such as the Association for the Development of Islamic Finances (ADIF or ARIF in Russian), which included the Islamic Development Bank, Kazakh BTA bank, and state agencies such as the Ministry of Industry and Trade, made initial progress. This alliance of upper-echelon state officials and large investors has been steadily leading discussions and negotiations with large infrastructure projects and corporate clients as a priority.[10] In Kyrgyzstan, Shamil Murtazaliev, the official representative of the IDB in Kyrgyzstan, is often mentioned as the initiator of legislative changes.[11] Allegedly well connected to then president Kurmanbek Bakiev (2005–10), he facilitated the passing of a decree "On the Pilot Project of Introduction of Islamic Financing Principles in the Kyrgyz Republic" in July 2006. Based on the decree, the National Bank later adopted a statute for Islamic financing principles, with banking instruments like *mudarabah*, *ijara*, *murabaha*, *musharakah*, and *istisna'a* discussed in detail.[12] Starting in December 2006, the National Bank gained the right to hand out licenses to IFIs in the country. Moving further, "state regulators continued their talks with consultants of the IDB and investors from Malaysia, further introducing amendments in the legislation to allow micro-finance companies to offer credit in form of *mudarabah*, *musharakah*, *ijara* and others" (Wolters 2013, 13).

As a result of active state facilitation, the two largest Islamic banks in Kazakhstan and Kyrgyzstan were established. In Kazakhstan, Al Hilal was established as a daughter company of the Abu Dhabi–based bank in 2010.

The bank serves only large corporations, giving preference to corporate clients in oil and gas, rail transport and other infrastructure industries.[13] In Kyrgyzstan, EcoIslamic Bank took off as a pilot project under the aegis of the IDB in 2010, after an intergovernmental agreement was signed. Shamil Murtazaliev, who first bought the shares of a conventional Russian/Kyrgyz bank and then led the initiative to make it a pilot project of the IDB, built on the foundation of an already mature organization with core personnel, a large customer base, and its own "archetypal" form of finance and credit lending. Although already a functioning bank, according to bank managers, EcoIslamic Bank has grown considerably in size since its transition to sharia-compliant finance.[14]

The discourse of state officials, strongly anchored in their vision of Islamic finance through the lens of economic utility, has shaped their strategies of prioritizing larger banks. This is particularly true in Kazakhstan. The government even eased some of the regular requirements for the banking sector in the case of Al Hilal. For example, the bank was allowed to enter the market despite its parent bank's low (in fact absent) credit rating. It was also allowed to have a higher ratio of foreign specialists than other companies. In contrast, the initiatives of local entrepreneurs to build sharia-compliant commercial companies have not fared as well. The primary critique of these entrepreneurs is that the legislation that has been passed on Islamic banking barely touched on issues of taxation, customs, insurance, and securities. The existing legislation does not allow a full range of activities for new sharia-compliant businesses, nor are the state agencies in charge enthusiastic about passing the amendments they propose. These contentions shed light on a different side of state policies toward Islamic finance, otherwise seen as welcoming.

Legislative changes that were publicized as generally conducive to IFIs in Kazakhstan have not guaranteed favorable conditions in all cases, as evidenced by the deprivation of economic freedom to particular initiatives such as businesses striving to deliver retail products to the local population. Fattah Finance is one such company, which was established by a local devout Muslim economist as the first sharia-compliant brokerage and investment company. The company's leadership aimed to include nongovernment securities on the official list of Kazakhstan's stock exchange and to provide services to help investors analyze and make investments that were sharia-compliant. Fattah Finance's CEO Zaratkazy Nurpiisov and his colleagues, who were very optimistic about the presidential decrees on the support of Islamic finance in the country, invested considerable time, energy, and capital in researching both local and foreign markets and subsequently drafting legislation—the 2020 road map for Islamic finance development, approved by the government. They gained significant interest from potential investors in Malaysia, Brunei, and other countries with well-institutionalized IFIs. Fattah Finance's leadership signed an agreement with the state-owned Malaysian group AmanahRaya and the Development Bank of Kazakhstan (DBK) to open a second Islamic bank in the country. This bank, it was hoped, would deliver retail financial products that would finally be available to the community of devout Muslims, who have long been waiting to access sharia-compliant mortgages and loans. Despite these hopes, however, the initiative has stalled.

One of the reasons, according to Nurpiisov,[15] was the fact that Amanah-Raya had a subsidiary firm in an offshore zone in Labuan, which was blacklisted by the National Bank of Kazakhstan. According to Kazakhstani legislation, no local banks could invest in financial institutions that have any connections to this offshore zone. To resolve this technicality, the Malaysian prime minister requested that the Kazakhstani prime minister facilitate the removal of Labuan from the blacklist. The management of Fattah Finance sent official requests to the upper-echelon state officials, but once the process stalled, state officials took little further initiative to resolve the matter, attributing the lack of progress to technical problems. However, from discussions with the entrepreneurs, the reason appears to be more culturally laden than state officials seem willing to admit. According to representatives of Fattah Finance, they have already lost hope of opening the bank in the near future. The situation is a direct illustration of Ronen Palan's (2003) argument that offshore is first of all a legal space, created and enabled (or disabled) by the state, and that decisions on juridical status of a geographical space are driven by international relations. Here, local entrepreneurs estimate that the process would have taken much less time if the government had been willing to work with their Malaysian counterparts and, more important, to show support for its own devout Muslim constituents.

As the discussion above shows, the states of Kazakhstan and Kyrgyzstan viewed Islamic finance as an economic tool. Hence, I argue that it was not so much the endorsement of Islamization broadly that guided these states (Aliyev 2012), but quite the opposite—the incorporation of Islamic values into policymaking and finance was a means to expand their legitimacy with foreign investors from the Gulf, with the purpose of generating revenue. Other Central Asian states have reportedly engaged in similar practices. According to Tim Epkenhans (chapter 8, this volume), Tajik-istan's President Rahmon, despite his uneasy relationship with religious groups, has attempted to elevate Dushanbe to the "Capital of Islamic Culture" in 2010, in order for he and his administration to appeal to foreign Muslim investors and to improve their position in the Organization for Islamic Cooperation. These processes in Central Asia are very much in line with S. V. R. Nasr's (2001) observations of Pakistan and Malaysia, where he contends the state instrumentally used Islamization processes in its efforts to boost economic development and as a means to expand state power. One of the implications of this instrumental approach in my cases was the lopsided playing field, tilted by the state in favor of larger Islamic banks. Smaller-scale entrepreneurs fared worse, and therefore unsur-prisingly they criticize large state-supported banks for focusing solely on profitability, rather than the religious and ethical logics of Islamic finance. According to these entrepreneurs, large IFIs are seen as *apolitical* by the state, due to their lower interest in purporting Islamic precepts and serving the local Muslim population. While the state regulates the market and religion as separate domains, state policies toward Islam have served as another signal to smaller-scale entrepreneurs that their initiatives will not enjoy governmental support. Taking stock of recent state policies toward religion in Kazakhstan such as the ban of the Tablighi Jama'at movement in February 2013 and the 2012 ban on prayer rooms in state institutions, one of the entrepreneurs asked rhetorically, "How are state officials going to openly practice Islam, or actively promote us, if the state is banning prayer rooms in government buildings?"

Local Entrepreneurs: Applying "Islamic Finance" in Practice

The community of entrepreneurs striving to build sharia-compliant com-panies highlight the centrality of their Muslim identity in their businesses. If *instrumental rationality* was at the core of the state regulators' discourse, *value rationality*, that is, the religious identity and ethical values and prac-tices of a pious Muslim, was at the center of entrepreneurs' discussions. Founding smaller-scale brokerage and insurance companies, these entre-preneurs discovered that the playing field was not equal for all companies, and that the large Islamic banks represented the priority for the state. Consequently, there have been very few chances for smaller-scale entrepre-neurs to build linkages with the large banks, due in part to their size, but also due to the shared perception among these bottom-up enthusiasts of sharia-compliant finance that the large Islamic banks are mostly concerned with profitability, rather than with ethical business.

Attending to the less publicized narratives and experiences of these entrepreneurs is important, as they are the ones implementing Islamic finance in practice. Although the origins of IFIs in Kyrgyzstan are often tied to the initiative of the Islamic Development Bank, and in Kazakhstan to the state's active role in searching for investors and changing legislation, both state officials and entrepreneurs acknowledge that the field has been primarily driven by local enthusiasm. A representative of the National Bank of Kyrgyzstan stated that if not for Shamil Murtazaliev's own enthusiasm, EcoIslamic Bank would not have launched the pilot project in agreement with the IDB. Murtazaliev's vision of Kyrgyzstan as an Islamic financial hub in the region was instrumental in instigating new legislation supportive of Islamic finance (Aliyev 2012; Wolters 2013). Similarly, a representative of the National Bank of Kazakhstan noted in his interview that the path to introducing IFIs was initially paved by an enthusiastic group from BTA bank, which was driven by young, local professionals, some of whom were pious believers. The first large conference on Islamic finance in Kazakhstan was similarly organized and sponsored by BTA bank.

In my interviews with these entrepreneurs, they commonly started their stories with why they believed that the formation of sharia-compliant business was important. For example, Kuralai Yeldesbai, who founded the first sharia-compliant insurance company in Kazakhstan, talked about the community of pioneers in the field: "Like myself, they all initially came to Islam, started practicing it, and then gradually started learning more about Islamic finance. Being good specialists in this area . . . being educated, yes I especially like the fact that all of the people who are now enthusiasts of IF are educated . . . and being fluent in three languages, they just came to understand that it is in their hands to do good deeds not just for themselves, but for the society as well."[16]

In discussing her motivation for promoting Islamic finance, Yeldesbai explained the rationale for opening the company in terms of her own benefits as a devout believer—"I thought if I'd earned money in a non-halal sector previously, I should at least gain *sabap* [benefaction] by shifting to a halal sphere." At the same time, she connected this motivation to a second rationale that focused on benefits for the broader community of believers—"I wanted to make sharia-compliant insurance available to people who care."

In their conceptualization of Islamic finance, entrepreneurs often criticize the usurious conditions of the conventional financial market that has been too focused on "selling money for money." In Islamic financial practices, products like murabaha tackle these money-making practices and partly address the misuse of funds. Murabaha, as a kind of fiduciary sale, involves three parties: the bank, a commodity seller, and a client. The bank obtains a good from the seller and resells to the client with a profit. In these and other transactions, all information on costs should be honestly declared and rooted in real commodity trade, not just financial dealing (Wolters 2013, 5). While discussing Islamic finance as a solution may be idealistic, these views suggest a shared denunciation of the conventional financial system among a growing clique of businessmen. Zamir Pusurov, the director of Kompanion Invest in the southern Kyrgyzstani city of Osh, explains the reasons behind increasing interest in Islamic finance in terms of the general public discontent with the lack of transparency in the interest rates of conventional financial products, as well as with the generally usurious conditions of loans at conventional financial companies.[17] Hence, the themes of ethics and social justice (exemplified by principles of prohibiting the exploitation of labor and money, and equal partnership with customers) have resonated in discussions, not only with proponents of Islamic finance but also with a wider circle of people in Kyrgyzstan.

Most of the local enthusiasts of Islamic finance that I spoke with shared the sentiment that money should only be the equivalent of a commodity, and should not be torn away from tangible commodities. In an interview in September 2012, Yerlan Baidaulet, the executive director of the Islamic Development Bank in Kazakhstan and the chair of the ADIF, reiterated this point and added: "Islamic finance seeks to tie money to real commodities and services. In that sense, IF is a recipe for curing [*ozdorovlenie*, in Russian] the economy; if someone doesn't like the words 'sharia' or 'Islamic,' these are just equivalents of 'ethical.'"[18] In his discussion, the benefits of IF represented a direct critique of the existing neoliberal capitalist system: "In the last couple of centuries, there has been a powerful growth of usury, and what do we see now? What we have is constant crisis situations, social inequalities, and the narrowing of the real sector of the economy. That together with the constant growth of the financial sector, which sells money for money, reinforcing usurious approaches, quick profits, and bets. All of this tears us away from moral principles and values."[19]

As can be seen, the community of entrepreneurs conceptualizes Islamic finance as a "social project," and "something more than a credit lending institution,"[20] due to their belief in its potential to tackle existing economic problems and provide devout Muslims with the ability to incorporate religious precepts into their daily lives.

Reflecting on their experiences of implementing the principles of Islamic finance in their work, most of the respondents voiced concerns about the state's prioritization of larger IFIs, as well as with the "legitimacy" of large banks. In the past decade, local entrepreneurs in Kazakhstan and Kyrgyzstan have been involved in establishing various organizations, from microfinance to sharia-compliant insurance and brokerage companies. In Kazakhstan, however, entrepreneurs have encountered significant difficulties in turning these ostensibly Islamic companies into profitable and sustainable businesses. Their misfortunes appear to result from the uneven playing field that they shared with larger market players. The legislation on Islamic banking that was passed by the state in 2009 was created in a rushed manner, with only the banking sector in mind. This framework therefore restrains their economic activities and makes it difficult to generate profits and returns on their capital investment. Companies that were established by local entrepreneurs and aim to deliver retail products to individual customers have received little if any facilitation from the state. This is particularly well illustrated in the experience of Kuralai Yeldesbai,[21] who established Takaful, a sharia-compliant insurance company. A specialist in insurance products and a devout practitioner of Islam, Yeldesbai actively participated in drafting the roadmap and legislation for Islamic finance. The amendments that they have drafted with a close group of supporters have not, however, been passed after two years. Due to the lack of legislation on sharia-compliant insurance, her company cannot offer as wide a range of products as conventional companies can. In her understanding, the regulators have been delaying the passage of amendments partly because they are not as deeply convinced of its necessity as are local enthusiasts of sharia-compliant finance—"It's only one among a whole list of other things that they have to work on."

Technical issues related to size and profit turnaround challenge the efforts of smaller-scale entrepreneurs to tap into the resource and knowledge network of large Islamic banks. "They're just too large to be interested in us," said Yeldesbai, who had hoped to collaborate with Al Hilal when she founded her insurance company. If her suggestions of collaboration were accepted, she could have gained a large pool of customers from this one bank alone, and delivered comprehensive medical insurance coverage from within a trusted network of medical professionals. Al Hilal's management was initially interested, "but when they found out our size and portfolio, they quickly lost interest," said Yeldesbai. To be able to offer inclusive health insurance to the workers of Al Hilal, her company would need to grow and be registered as a joint-stock company.

Besides technical issues, however, the moral critique that smaller-scale entrepreneurs voiced of large IFIs indicated the low potential of collaboration in terms of knowledge and expertise sharing. Zamir Pusurov, director of Kompanion Invest, shared his experience of working for the major Islamic bank in Kyrgyzstan. At first, excited about the opportunity to gain experience at EcoIslamic Bank, he later became disillusioned by the management's way of doing business because, to his mind, they were more concerned with profitability than with honesty. In one such practice that for him served as evidence of how large IFIs bend the sharia law in their favor, is the EcoIslamic Bank's sharia board allowing loans to be granted to entrepreneurs engaged in commerce and trade that involved sales of tobacco and alcohol. The management and the sharia board would not care, as long as only 50 percent of these businesses' profits came from the sales of illicit commodities. Pusurov left EcoIslamic Bank, and was later contacted by Kompanion Invest,[22] one of the largest microfinance companies in the country, which asked him to lead their subsidiary microfinance company in the south of Kyrgyzstan according to sharia principles.

For the practicing devout Muslims who have been financially and emotionally investing in their projects, questions of religion, morality, and ethics are inseparable from their aspirations to lead sustainable, profitable, and ever-expanding commercial companies. Hence, the state's offensive on Islam is for them an open signal that their economic activities, which they would like to be compliant with sharia principles, are not going to be easily allowed. Moreover, the state's lack of support for their activities is interpreted as unwillingness to allow the strata of devout Muslims to become economically and politically active in the public domain. The technical specificities of operation among larger- and smaller-scale IFIs further catalyze the disconnection in their practices and efforts to build sharia-compliant finance. Moreover, similarly to the Tajik youth that Manja Stephan-Emmrich (chapter 12, this volume) artfully depicts, local entrepreneurs in Kazakhstan and Kyrgyzstan have been exposed to different sources of Islamic education. However, most of the "new Muslim subjectivities," as Stephan-Emmrich calls them, revolve around ideals of being an "authentic Muslim" as well as a "moral entrepreneur" who seeks economic profit through sharia-informed ethical codes. Hence, in this quest they often cast doubt on the moral legitimacy of larger IFIs. The per-

ceived lack of legitimacy is tied to the disconnection of large projects from
the demands and wishes of local devout believers and the general ulema.

Religious Authorities

The tenets of sharia are ingrained in the work of IFIs primarily through
sharia boards, which interpret and apply sharia to finance by serving as ar-
biters of what does and does not count as compliant with religious precepts.
Hence, every Islamic bank and microfinance company in Kazakhstan and
Kyrgyzstan has such a board.[23] The sharia board of Al Hilal Bank in Kazakhstan is primarily foreign, while in Kyrgyzstan IFIs work actively with
local religious authorities (including imams of mosques) and theology experts, who sit on the sharia boards of IFIs and generally serve as a support
network. Products such as musharakah and mudarabah that IFIs deliver
to their customers cannot gain popularity among customers overnight, by
order of the state, or through mere appearance in the financial market.
In order to understand the broader process of the legitimization of IFIs
in the region through the eyes of local devout believers, it is important to
address the work of imams and theologians,[24] who are arguably producing
"a value system" (Zelizer 1978, 594) that condemns the usurious practices
of the conventional financial sector and diffuses knowledge about IFIs as
more morally diligent and sustainable.

In her historical analysis of the legitimation of life insurance in the
United States, Viviana Zelizer (1978, 593) suggested that "including certain
items in the social order . . . into a market-type of exchange introduces
structural sources of strain and ambivalence into their marketing." As can
be seen from the previous sections, taking on the "Islamic" identity and
incorporating religious precepts into financial transactions did in fact produce strains and ambivalence in the relations of the state and entrepreneurs.
Drawing from my interviews with religious authorities,[25] and also a month
of ethnographic work at Kompanion Invest, I aim to shed light on the
processes in which imams lend their moral authority to IFIs as they gain
legitimacy and build bases of trust vis-à-vis their existing and potential
clientele. Studies of the bottom-up nature of Islamic revival in the country
(McGlinchey 2009) imply the growing influence of these authorities.

These religious officials equate Islamic principles of finance to the morality and honesty that they see lacking in the practices of conventional
financial practices. For them, terms such as "usury" and "aversion of uncertainties" are core precepts of the Koran. In Kyrgyzstan, in which large

segments of the population regularly borrow micro and small loans, imams report having observed general public discontent with high interest rates and with the conditions of repayment. The difficulties customers face in repaying local microfinance companies and banks are regularly publicized, leading imams to incorporate these general trends and their communities' concerns into their narratives of what differentiates "appropriate" from "inappropriate" terms of loans and credit. Imams, actively promote the "non-quantifiable element" (Maurer 2002) of Islamic finance, with the ethical principles of risk evasion and fair treatment of the borrower at the center of their vision. The imam of the central mosque in Bishkek, who is on the sharia board of EcoIslamic Bank, condemned conventional banks for their "forceful" and "confusing" methods: "If people ask me, I tell them that it's not permissible in Islam to force someone into a transaction with unclear terms, and then strip them of their property when they are unable to pay back their debt. People call me constantly, asking 'Can I take a loan here? Should I lend on these or those terms?'"[26] For the religious factions, who unsurprisingly need to address issues of misuse of loans regularly in their meetings with communities of believers, Islamic financial practices are seen as part of the solution. In their views, financing "the real needs of customers" by buying them the needed construction materials or household appliances represents a far better model than giving away cash that often gets misused by customers. In the words of the imam quote above, it is honesty (*yiman*) that is lacking among people who are used to taking loans for one purpose, but then misusing them in other ways. Honesty and integrity among both financiers and customers are thus key components in the narratives of religious authorities.

Through this process of framing Islamic finance as more morally diligent and ostensibly more sustainable, practitioners and religious authorities reject the conceptualization of money as a neutral and fungible medium of exchange (Zelizer 1998). These observations suggest that the financial products of IFIs are culturally informed as much as they are shaped by expertise and their competitiveness with other conventional products. Distinct multiple symbolizations (Parry and Bloch 1989, ch. 1) carried by IFI products and services lend them a favorable image in this context. One episode from my participant observations within Kompanion Invest, the Islamic microfinance company in the south of Kyrgyzstan illustrates this point well. One afternoon in April, when I shadowed two workers of the company, Olaberdi and Nasiba,[27] we went door to door in one of the *mahallas* around Sulaiman. The following dialogue that took place during one of the encounters with a local resident offers a vivid example of how the moral authority of imams is used:

> "Well, you also have an interest rate, isn't that an interest rate?"
> "No, it's not; we call it a *koshumcha nark* [commission fee]. Go ask your imam if you don't trust me, and see what he says about our work."

Moreover, mosques have come to serve as a physical infrastructure that is open for practicing Muslims, especially in Kyrgyzstan, and as a result have become spaces of information diffusion about Islamic precepts regarding financial deals. In the language of marketing, these religious officials (both those who are on sharia boards of local IFIs and those who are not) have been playing a crucial role in making "sales pitches" to the population of devout believers. In the words of the imam quoted above:

> The numbers of people newly entering Islam are growing. There are more people giving alms [*sadaqa*], going on hajj trips, and proselytizing [*davat*]. They are also finding out more and more that taking credit with interest rates is forbidden. We've got many people these days . . . entrepreneurs . . . the majority of them are not taking credit from conventional banks these days. They ask their communities [*jama'ats*], if they can take credit and so on. The majority of them are intentionally not using conventional banks, not because there's any kind of propaganda against banks, but because they're listening to their heart. Everyone trusts Jigitaaly *damla* [teacher], Maksat *damla* and Mahmud *damla*, and these people approve of EcoIslamic Bank whenever people ask . . . they used to be on the sharia board [of EcoIslamic Bank] if you know.

It is through such processes, depicted here only superficially, that the value system is created, which gradually promotes IFIs as reinforcing life projects and ensuring the welfare of individuals (Zorn et al. 2005). The epistemic knowledge structures offered by imams and theology experts (at least nominally and cognitively) facilitate the conceptualization of Islamic finance as constitutive of principles and practices that are antithetical to those of pervasive conventional financial institutions.

The state's more relaxed policies toward practicing Islam in Kyrgyzstan have left more space for IFIs to actively seek out and employ the expertise and authority of religious authorities as reputational guarantors, and channels of informational exchange. One of the workers at Kompanion Invest was recruited through the mosque, which he used to attend. As we discussed how he got interested in working for the company, he admitted that he had faced drinking problems and unresolved financial issues in the past. Working for a sharia-compliant company would be a way of "begging God's forgiveness," as he explained. This divide between haram (forbidden) and halal (permissible), dishonest and honest were reiterated numerous times in my conversations with workers, existing customers of Kompanion Invest, and attendees of *taalim* (Koran study) groups. In one such discussion, my respondent, a resident of Nookat in the south of Kyrgyzstan, told me about his extensive readings in a circle of practicing believers about the haram nature of conventional credit and loans.

This close collaboration with the network of imams and theology experts, however favorable to the work of IFIs, influences the formation of factions among IFIs. My interviews with imams elicited contested visions of EcoIslamic Bank as the largest IFI in terms of reach; those imams formed opposing camps that divided those who were in immediate collaboration with IFIs through membership in sharia boards and those not directly connected. One imam based his critique primarily on the lack of piety among the workers of the bank, but others questioned the reputation of the bank owner, Murtazaliev, since he was known to be involved in alcohol production in the past. Besides criticism based primarily on religious dimensions, still others suggested that EcoIslamic bank is not yet fully "Islamic," since the largest share of its profits come from cash transfers rather than Islamic financial products per se.

As authors on Islam in the region observe, many of the contributors to this volume (e.g., Borbieva, Tasar, Stephan-Emmrich, and others), Islam as a religious institution is constituted and practiced through various factions and political alliances. In my observations, EcoIslamic Bank's network of religious authorities do not overlap with that of Kompanion Invest's, and the criticism that exists between these diverse religious political cliques translates into perceptions of these IFIs as less pious and diligent, and therefore less legitimate. Hence, the religious authorities that break down into political cliques are partly the reason for a contested rather than a unified vision of what Islamic finance really is and how it should be implemented.

An Unnatural Alliance?

I have aimed in this chapter to shift the focus away from state-centered and foreign investment–centered perspectives in analyzing the emergence and expansion of Islamic financial institutions in Kazakhstan and Kyrgyzstan. Bringing in the accounts of the community of entrepreneurs and religious authorities who are engaged in the field, I have argued that Islamic finance as a moralized market niche is understood, rationalized, and promoted by these different sets of actors due to distinct value systems. The states of these countries have altered their legislation and sought international investors due to their instrumental-rational perspective of Islamic finance as an economic tool for attracting alternative, non-Western sources of finance. In their narratives, state regulators speak of IFIs as *depoliticized* and distant from any taboo discussions of religion in the public sphere. This stance in part explains why the governments favored large Islamic banks.

In contrast, the community of local entrepreneurs, striving to build smaller-scale IFIs, explain their motivation in value-rational terms, expressed in part by positioning their Muslim identity and beliefs at the center of their narratives. In collaboration with local religious authorities, they are engaged in an ongoing production of knowledge about what constitutes "proper" and sharia-compliant lending and borrowing. Their accounts contribute toward our understanding of those culturally informed political dynamics that provide broader legitimacy to IFIs in the eyes of the local population.

Due to their alleged unease with the "moral legitimacy of effortless fortunes" (Sen 1991, 38) and core rationales of committing to a financial order based on equity, mutuality, and sustainability, IFIs hold the potential for reimagining dominant Western financial systems. With these ideals in the background, preliminary research demonstrates, however, that the formation of Islamic finance in the region is far from consolidating a natural alliance of all the involved parties that some observers (Wolters 2013) hope to see. The large IFIs that have enjoyed more state support remain disengaged from smaller-scale local initiatives, and the linkages that would allow information and knowledge flows between these levels are largely absent.

CHAPTER TWELVE

Studying Islam Abroad

Pious Enterprises and Educational Aspirations
of Young Tajik Muslims

Manja Stephan-Emmrich

Between the early 1990s and 2010, a remarkable number of young Muslims in Tajikistan left their country to study Islam abroad,[1] and in the meantime many of them have returned to their homeland. Their self-representations as reawakened, pious Muslims are built on references to a "true" or "pure" Islam and attest to their imagination of "ideal" Muslim places afar that, as I will show in this chapter, in many senses serves as an antidote to their experiences of everyday life at home. With their Islamic knowledge gained abroad and their travel experiences in regions that are perceived by many Muslims in Tajikistan as sacred or educational centers of Islam, the students who return contribute to a dynamic religious field in which a wide range of religious as well as secular players, ideologies, and discourses are competing for normative power. However, the competitive character of Tajikistan's religious field is characterized not only by religious–secular tensions (Epkenhans 2010) but also by an obvious fragmentation of religious authority along social and spatial categories such as age and gender as well local and translocal points of reference (Abashin 2006; Schmitz 2015, 26–30; Stephan 2006; see also Borbieva, chapter 7, this volume).

In the atmosphere of religious awakening that was nourished by a religious liberalization in the late 1980s (Khalid 2007, 116–39; Mullojonov 2001) and the subsequent breakdown of the Soviet Union, a first generation of Tajik students went to Muslim countries such as Pakistan, Iran, Turkey, Egypt, and Saudi Arabia in order to seek Islamic knowledge (Abramson 2010, 36–43). Their educational travel abroad attests to the spiritual pursuits (*isloh*) of many Tajik Muslims in the post-Soviet moral crisis in the 1990s and documents the reconfiguration of Tajikistan's Muslims within the wider, global Muslim community (*ummah*). This reconfiguration was born of their need to emancipate themselves from the Communist and antireligious spirit of the former "colonising other" (Bissenova 2005, 261), which, by isolating Central Asian Muslims intellectually from the wider Muslim world, turned them into "ignorant Soviet Muslims."[2]

Today, about twenty years later, the academic paradigm of "post-Soviet Islamic revival" is also challenged by demographic realities—that is, a new generation of young people that did not directly experience the Soviet times. Moreover, Tajikistan's rapid integration into the global economy and the growing importance of social media (such as Facebook and mail.ru) in daily life have resulted in new spatial, virtual, and social mobilities, used especially by the young generations to transgress previous geographical, political, cultural, and social boundaries, thereby creating new or reestablishing historically existing translocal spaces (Freitag and von Oppen 2010; Glick-Schiller and Foroun 1999; Vertovec 2009). As a consequence, the religious enterprises of many Muslims in Tajikistan are more and more entangled with mobile livelihoods, global networks, and new group identities beyond national and other boundaries (Schröder and Stephan-Emmrich 2014).

Religious mobility such as the hajj pilgrimage to Mecca, the establishment of new trading networks, the growing field of international labor migration, and media-supported representations have promoted encounters with cultural diversity, divergent orthodoxies, and "other Muslims" on a large scale (Mandaville 2002; Manger 1999). The various encounters and global flows triggered the formation of new Muslim subjectivities and served as references for imagining "ideal Muslim places" afar that promise not only the realization of spiritual demands in regard to religious freedom, but also the gaining of "true" Islamic knowledge and the remaking of oneself as a pious, good Muslim. These imagined distant Muslim locales also feed notions of good morality, ideal democracy, and a Muslim modernism that links economic progress with Islamic ethics.

As the case studies in this chapter will show, the decision to pursue an Islamic education abroad is often part of an intended (international) career that links religious interest with mundane aspirations such as for economic success, moral upgrading, and social mobility. An Islamic education abroad therefore should not be read only as a purely religious matter—that is, an individual spiritual enterprise that automatically leads to pious behavior, the formation of Islamic lifestyles, a conscious Muslim self, or a religious career. Rather, I argue that religious training in foreign Muslim places is inseparably intertwined with dynamic livelihood strategies of young Tajiks (or their families) that combine spiritual needs with social mobilities, moral endeavors, and educational aspirations. Conceptually, I thus follow the anthropological approach of everyday religion: I consider the practice of Islamic education abroad as inseparable from the wider course of life that involves "different pursuits and interests, different emotions and experiences, varying periods and degrees of engagement, and complex motivations" (Schielke and Debevec 2012, 8). In an urban context such as Dushanbe, Tajikistan's capital, where I met all the students whose travel experiences I trace in this chapter, the complexity and ambiguity of everyday life is framed significantly by an unstable national economy that only provides limited future opportunities for the country's younger generation. Despite these incisive economic constraints, Dushanbe still attracts many young people from rural and peripheral areas who move to the city in the hope of finding a lucrative job, obtaining a university degree, or realizing labor migration to Moscow, Dubai, and other places in the wider world. In reality, the deficient and corrupt national universities produce masses of insufficiently trained and often disenchanted graduates who face unemployment and an uncertain future. For many of them (and their families), leaving the country in order to work or study abroad is both a socially accepted exit option and a strategy for coping with uncertainties.

At the same time, the life-worlds and future perspectives of urban Muslim youth in today's Tajikistan are still strongly influenced by a social order that, based on principles of seniority and patriarchy, determines "youth" as a short-term and transitional stage in the life course, during which young people learn to become adults in ways that are prescribed by their elders (Harris 2006; Roche 2010). As I will show later, in many Muslim families in Dushanbe, religious references play an important role in parents' efforts to cultivate the morality of their future adult sons and daughters.

Finally, this chapter illustrates how the everyday experiences of being a young and pious Muslim in urban Dushanbe is determined by an increasingly rigid secular policy advanced by the Tajik state, which promotes its own national interpretation of "Tajik" Islam, controls the Islamic education sector in the country, and stigmatizes religious otherness as politically dangerous.

The translocal trajectories that characterize the life-worlds of many young Tajiks today bear witness to their daily negotiations of various economic, social, political, and religious claims in urban Dushanbe. But what exactly motivates them to study Islam abroad? Which dreams, hopes, and aspirations mark the starting point of their educational projects abroad? And, emphasizing the time after their return, what are the realities they face back home? How do they invest their mobile experiences and educational capital in realizing their future dreams, goals, and aspirations in an urban setting that is marked by a growing competitive religious field, a social order that reproduces the power of the elders, and a secular state that is increasingly trying to regulate and control the religious practices of its Muslim citizens in public as well as in private? To address these questions, the chapter presents the case studies of Karim, Zebo, Guli, Aziz, and Samira, to give insights into the generation of Tajik students who left the country in the early or mid-2000s and have returned home only recently. Based on fieldwork that I carried out in Dushanbe and its rural surroundings between 2011 and 2013, which includes semistructured and narrative interviews with about thirty returned students, this chapter offers some snapshots on how urban pious youth negotiate their elusive future between educational aspirations, family expectations, a local imaginary of ideal Muslim places abroad, and the political claims of a rigid secular state.

A Changing Muslim Tradition

Travel with the objective of gaining knowledge about Islam has a long tradition in Tajikistan, as it does in the whole of area of the Muslim world. In a well-known hadith,[3] in which the Prophet Muhammad's appeal to Muslims "to seek knowledge even unto China" is confirmed, the obligatory dimension of Islamic education for every Muslim is underlined and spatial mobility as a core principle of Islamic learning is stressed. From the tenth century onward networks of religious learned men established themselves around centers of Islamic learning, such as Bukhara (today in Uzbekistan) and extended into areas of today's modern India, Pakistan, China, Russia, and Turkey. The Arab world (Hejaz) has always played an important role as the sacred center of Islam and was traveled by Central Asian Muslims, above all as part of the hajj, the pilgrimage to Mecca (Hurgronje 1888–89; Papas, Welsford, and Zarcone 2012). These pilgrimages, which often lasted several years, also served the acquisition of knowledge about Islam along the way (El Moudden 1990; Gellens 1990). Closely linked with the Sufi tradition of learning, these journeys in regions and places of the Middle East contributed to the origination of a "global culture" that is based on a symbolic interactive system founded on Islam, within which the Muslims of Central Asia felt themselves to be part of the ummah but were also confronted with cultural and other differences (Manger 1999, 4). In pre-Soviet times, educational journeys were overwhelmingly individual affairs, yet they were also an established aspect of many life cycles, denoted social prestige,[4] and were predominantly undertaken by men.

The interconnectivities between Muslim Central Asia and particularly the Arab region were further consolidated in the 1930s and 1950s, when Uzbek, Uyghur, and other Central Asian refugees fled the Communist regimes in China and the newly founded Soviet Union. These refugees—most of whom were (religious) intellectual elites escaping Stalinization—followed different routes (via Kashgar, British India, or Afghanistan) to Saudi Arabia, where they formed cohesive communities in Mecca and Medina that have persisted until today (Balci 2007). In the early 1990s many Saudi Arabian Central Asians returned as missionaries of Saudi Wahhabism to the newly independent states of Central Asia (Balci 2007).

As a result of Soviet secularism, the individual pursuit of Islamic studies abroad became an institutionalized and state-regulated practice that was reserved for a small group of (future) religious elite. Since historically established routes of religious travel to the Hejaz and the Middle East were diverted to new destinations within the Soviet Union (Keller 2001), a course of Islamic study outside the Tajik SSR was only possible in the two official Soviet educational centers in the neighboring republic of Uzbekistan (Tashkent and Bukhara). Under the strictest supervision of state authorities via the official muftiate for Central Asia (commonly known by its Russian acronym, SADUM), a very few educational trips to Arab countries such as Egypt, Jordan, and Yemen were approved, which served mainly the religious careers of (future) representatives of official Islam, as exemplified in the educational biographies of Islamic figures, including Hoji Akbar Turajonzoda, the former *qazy* of Tajikistan between 1988 and 1999 (Epkenhans 2011; Muminov, Gafurov, and Shigabdinov 2010). Beyond the Soviet educational system, religious training in foreign Islamic institutions was possible for the offspring of Tajik state diplomats who resided with their families in Muslim countries (Stephan 2006).

Since the 1990s, the tradition of educational journeys to Muslim places abroad has undergone a rapid metamorphosis from a predominantly state-regulated phenomenon among the religious elite to an increasingly popular religious practice that overcame not only political regulations and national boundaries but also those drawn by demographic categories such as gender, age, generation, and even social status and material wealth. Whether organized as part of national educational exchange programs, supported by international scholarships, or realized by private budgets,[5] the practice of undertaking Islamic studies abroad became widely established across Tajikistan's Muslim population as an expression of a new piety, a striving for inner reform, and a search for "true" or "authentic" knowledge about Islam.

Preferences for a particular place of study abroad are confirmed in the narratives of returned students. These preferences reflect an imagined sacred geography with particular hierarchies that, nonetheless, are not solely based on religious parameters. They are also shaped by political conditions, aspects of practicability and access, as well as by social networks of trust that cross territorial, political, and social boundaries and strongly influence the individuals' or families' choice of the place to study abroad. During the civil war in Tajikistan (1992–96), many Tajiks fled to Afghanistan and paved the way for thousands of Tajiks who followed later to study in Islamabad and other places in Pakistan. Later, Tajik labor migrants in Russia "discovered" readily accessible and low-cost options for Islamic study at Cairo's Al-Azhar University via Moscow. The obviously growing Tajik community on Cairo's outskirts tempts entire families to follow their offspring to their place of study, and Al-Azhar with its many students from Central Asia promotes the establishment of translocal marriage strategies. At the same time, Tajik pilgrims who return every year from their hajj report on how members of old established Central Asian communities in Mecca and Medina were supporting the study of Islam among their compatriots.[6] Finally, in the past few years, Islamic charities in Istanbul have started to advertise scholarships for Central Asian Muslims via the Internet, which has triggered new flows of students relocating from Tajikistan to Turkey.

To sum up, the evolving "market" of Islamic education abroad contributes to the heterogeneity and diversity of Muslim practices of religious learning in terms of form, quality, and period of study as well as preferred destinations. At the same time, it demonstrates that educational trips and the religious experiences they give rise to are no longer a privilege of a small mobile elite but have become a reality for many ordinary families irrespective of their socioeconomic origins (Goulbourne et al. 2010, 6).

State Regulations and Secular Rhetoric

The new religious mobility of Tajikistan's young Muslims seriously challenges the efforts of the political elites around President Emomali Rahmon (in office since 1992) to propagate an "authentic" and "homegrown" Tajik (ethnic) Islam. The declaration of 2009 as the "Year of Imomi A'zam Abu Hanifa" marks an obvious turning point in the official national discourse,[7] in which Islam was persistently excluded in favor of a constructed pre-Islamic Zoroastrian or Aryan civilization, and in which the cultural, intellectual, and political merits of the Persian Samanid dynasty were praised as the source of the Tajik nation and statehood (Rahmon 2001–8). By proclaiming Abu Hanifa as "son of the Tajiks," the government officially accepted Islam as a core pillar of Tajik national identity (Epkenhans, chapter 8, this volume). It also highlighted the contribution of the Tajik nation to the global history of Islam and the belonging of Tajik Muslims to the global ummah. Furthermore, in stressing principles such as "tolerance" (*tahammulpaziri*), "peace" (*oromi*), "dialogue in faith" (*guftugūhoyu mukomalai dinho*), and "cooperation" (*hamkori*), the Hanafi branch (*mazhabi hanafi*) is presented as the cultural and humanistic foundation of the Tajik nation, as well as the main source of "Taijk Islam," which embraces both orthodox principles and local traditions as well as the cultural heritage of the nation's ancestors (Rahmon 2009, 4–40). The official reading of the Hanafi branch as the foundation of a "peaceful" and "tolerant" Tajik Islam, however, is also a rhetorical response to the increasing influence of Salafi and other purist and scripturally strict interpretations of Islam in Tajikistan that, not only in the official reading but also among Islamic authorities, are depicted as "alien" and incompatible with the culturally, spiritually, and philosophically Persian and Sufi influences on Islam in Tajikistan.

The religiously liberal and open atmosphere of the 1990s came to an end with the growing influence of new and globally active Islamic players inside and outside Tajikistan. In 2001, in response to the rise of the Taliban regime in neighboring Afghanistan, President Rahmon ordered hundreds of Tajiks to return from their studies at Islamic institutions in Pakistan.[8] The government's fear of Islamic fundamentalism inside and outside the country and fear that its Muslim population would become radicalized definitely increased further around 2005, when Salafi ideologies became obviously stronger in Tajikistan's religious field (for details, see Epkenhans, chapter 8, this volume). As a result, travel regulations became stricter and a more aggressive rhetoric against the practice of religious instruction abroad was broadcast to the public. In so-called blacklists that were spread through state television and print media, popular destinations for study such as the Makki madrasa or the Jamiah Darul Uloom in Zahedon in southeastern Iran or in places in Pakistan, where religious instruction to a large degree is offered in privately funded institutions, were declared "non-legal" (*ghayriqonunī*, i.e., "beyond the law"), and educational travel to these places without state permission was officially banned.[9] At the same time, the government put more effort into promoting a "legal" and "healthy" version of Islamic education abroad within the state Islamic education sector. When in 2007 the formerly private Islamic university al-Termizi in Dushanbe was transformed into the state-controlled Abu Hanifa Islamic Institute, new exchange programs with state universities in Saudi Arabia, the United Arab Emirates (UAE), and Egypt were implemented, and Islamic education abroad became more structured, centralized, and thus easier for the government to control.[10] However, up to now the newly implemented study programs are limited and accessible overwhelmingly only for students of the Abu Hanifa Islamic Institute. The majority of Tajiks therefore organize their study trips privately and find their own ways to reach their preferred destinations abroad.

The government has also started upgrading the quality of religious teaching in order to eradicate the negative image of the Islamic educational sector in Tajikistan. In the past few years the administrative and teaching personnel of the Abu Hanifa Islamic Institute has been replaced by the first generation of graduates from Islamic universities in Saudi Arabia or Al-Azhar, and Islamic scholars from abroad are invited to teach Tajik students in Islamic subjects.

The climax of state regulatory measures so far, however, has been the presidential campaign in 2010 to recall those students who were studying abroad without state permission. Consequently, many students discontinued their studies abroad and returned home. Among the returnees, some were integrated by the government into the official Islamic education system and resumed their studies (EurasiaNet 2010). Others refused and returned with their families to their former places of studies, as in the case of Karim, a student from Al-Azhar who was forced to interrupt his studies in Islamic jurisprudence (*fiqh*) in 2010 but again left the country one year later via Moscow to Cairo. The trajectory of Karim's educational biography attests to the limits of the state's efforts to fully regulate and control the practice of religious instruction abroad. Many Tajiks who eventually succeed in pursuing study abroad rely on their relatives or classmates living in Moscow or Cairo to use their local contacts in order to circumvent visa restrictions and official bans. Nevertheless, the state's powerful rhetoric criminalizes these flows of traveling students as well as the new religious practices that they bring with them from abroad. The state rhetoric also has a powerful influence on the future careers of young returnees both in the religious and secular sector and, as we will see later, in the cases of Zebo, Aziz, and Karim.

Longing for Ideal Muslim Places Afar

Appadurai (2010, 31) refers to the creative power that imagination and fantasy occupy in the fabrication of social life in the modern world, which has made them a "social fact." For him, imagination has become "an organized field of social practice, a form of work (in the sense of both labor and culturally organized practice), and a form of negotiation between sites of agency (individual) and globally defined fields of possibility" (Appadurai 2010, 31). Dushanbe's city markets today are a hub of various global flows of goods, people, and images not only from the "West" but also from Muslim countries such as the Arab Emirates, Iran, Turkey, Afghanistan, and Pakistan. Islamic fashion and paraphernalia, Mecca wallpapers, and mobile ring tones with prayer calls or Koran recitations invite proper consumption and create new modern urban lifestyles that have made Islam more visible in Dushanbe's public than the government, with its secular political agenda, prefers. The rising Islamic commodity culture in Tajikistan's urban centers is seen in public advertisements, beauty salons, Internet cafes, and media entertainment, which fabricate the local imagery of the Muslim "other" and stimulate highly self-reflective debates about identity, belonging, and modernity (McBrien 2012). In these debates, distant Muslim places (countries, cities, holy sites) are imagined as "perfect" or ideal places. This imagery serves as an important reference point for critically assessing one's own imperfect religious life, which many of my interlocutors directly related to the narrow limitations set by the Tajik nation-state for pursuing their pious endeavors.

Consequently, the attractiveness of distant Muslim places is based on a longing for religious freedom that has been seriously curtailed by the restrictive secularization policy of the Rahmon government during recent years. This has been reflected in prohibitions, persecution, and an increased mistrust of religious movements such as the Hizb-ut-Tahrir, the Nurcu movement, members of Tablighi Jama'at, and various Salafi groups. In addition, many nonregistered mosques were closed and regulations were passed to control religious gatherings and the wearing of Islamic dress in public.[11] The transformation of the formerly private Islamic University al-Termizi into the Abu Hanifa Islamic Institute, subject to the Ministry of Education in 2007, and the ban on providing religious education (*sabaq*) on private premises or in neighborhood mosques are examples of the political leadership's attempts to implement stricter centralization and state regulation of the Islamic sector.

The inhabitants of the republic's capital city are particularly affected by the new political situation. As the seat of government, the Islamic Center, and the Islamic Institute, Dushanbe is undoubtedly crucial to the government's ambitious secularization project. Debates have thus ensued concerning the government's arbitrary understanding of democracy and the curtailing of any public discussion on religious fanaticism and its initiators. As described by the mother of a twenty-five-year-old son who has been studying Islamic jurisprudence at Cairo's Al-Azhar University since 2008:

> The Soviet era was not a good time for us, as Muslims. But nevertheless there were opportunities to pray in secret or at home or to acquire religious knowledge. But today? These days the government talks about democracy [*demokratiia*]. But in the same breath they prohibit us from sending our children to the mosque or bringing them up in a religious environment. Where is the freedom that was promised to us? What does this have to do with democracy? Ultimately, we are worse off than under the Soviets. One does not need to ask which of us are really the fanatics.

Such nostalgic sentiments are fueled by the law "On Parents' Responsibility in Bringing Up Their Children,"[12] which was passed in 2010 and perfectly illustrates how the secular political elite increasingly interferes with Muslim practices in the private sphere. Among other things, this law forbids parents to send their underage children (younger than eighteen) to the mosque or to allow them to participate in religious events and celebrations. The new political climate in the country also opposes the influence of locally and regionally popular Islamic authorities. One looks in vain for publications of popular Tajik religious scholars in bookstores around the central mosque and in the bazaars in Dushanbe, above all since the government forbade the media activities of influential preachers such as the Turajon brothers or Hojji Mirzo. Because these personalities are increasingly diverting their activities to the Internet (see Epkenhans, chapter 8, this volume) or the Tajik migrant community in Russia, it encourages the popular imaginary of better Muslim places "somewhere else" in which many Muslims look for the fulfillment of their wishes for religious freedom, a good Islamic education, and their acceptance as Muslims. One of these people is forty-eight-year-old Olima who, just a few days after our meeting, was to join her studying son and his family who had already emigrated to Cairo: "They know everything about Islam at the Al-Azhar. But here? One cannot even buy good books here. They [government officials] have forbidden everything, even *amri ma'ruf* [commanding right and forbidding wrong]. They have forbidden all good preachers here [in Dushanbe] to speak, Eshon Nurridin, Hojji Mirzo. . . . How can one learn well in such a situation? Look at Russia. Even there religious authorities may invite young people to *amri ma'ruf*. But here?"

The image of foreign Islamic educational institutions as perfect or ideal places for religious study is not only a response to the secular agenda of the Tajik state. It should also be regarded as a direct reflection of the serious shortcomings of national schools and universities.[13] Concepts of "correct education" (*ta'limu tarbiya-i durust*) associated with Islamic universities abroad such as Al-Azhar are not related only to reigning notions of "pure" and "false" contents of religious learning. The belief that these educational establishments are free of corruption, and that one's offspring are spending their time usefully in a study environment imbued with the principles of Islamic ethics is of considerable influence.

Besides highly self-reflective debates on Muslim identity and belonging, images of ideal Muslim places afar also create options for alternative concepts of being, becoming, living, and well-being. Given the uncertainties of the socioeconomic situation, unemployment, and the lack of future prospects, the local Muslim imagery as projected on distant places bolsters the hopes of many young Tajiks for material success, social mobility, and alternative concepts of living. These hopes are fueled by the increasing number of Iranian diplomats and businessmen who have opened elite restaurants on Dushanbe's main road Rudaki and send their wives to shop at the only, and rather overpriced, Iranian Supermarket in Dushanbe or in one of the newly opened city malls. But the hopes of many Muslims have also been affirmed by the returnees from Dubai, who over the past few years have been able to establish successful trading networks or have found a lucrative seasonal job there. The increasing significance of religion in Tajik society has thus led to a situation in which piety, symbolized by visible codes such as fashionable Islamic dress or beard, is also regarded as a sign of high moral standards in the urban milieu of Dushanbe. This mark of confidence is reflected, for example, in marriages or business connections in which religious capital may be transformed into social or economic capital through one's moral status as a "good bride or groom" or as trustworthy business partner (see Abramson 2010, 40; Stephan-Emmrich and Mirzoev 2016). From a religious economy perspective, an Islamic education abroad can therefore be a passport to social mobility: it enables one to refashion him- or herself as a perfect Muslim and thus increases opportunities in highly competitive realms such as the wedding market, international trade or business, and employment.

Alternative Roads to International Education, Success, and Social Status

As a striking pattern in the narrations of my interlocutors in Dushanbe, the study of Islam abroad frequently emerged as an integral part of extensive educational biographies.[14] Regarding the question of what follows after graduation from university and what future prospects graduates of state universities in Tajikistan have today, the decision to go abroad to study Islam can be identified as a strategy for educated urban youth to cope with unfulfilled promises, aspirations, and expectations that they—or their parents—first associated with a regular university program.

For many of these first-generation students, a stipend for Islamic study at the International Islamic University Islamabad (IIUI), for example, served as a welcome exit option not only to escape the civil war but also to search for alternative avenues toward a successful educational career that was interrupted at home. Young Tajik students who left the country in the early 2000s explained their decision rather with regard to unsuccessful integration into the local job market. As the case of Karim shows, pursuing an Islamic education abroad often correlates with a young person's frustration over an unfilled future. The new piety that they cultivate abroad provides a cushion for the disappointments, anxieties, and uncertainties that young university graduates experienced at home. For them, religion also offers an alternative road to pursuing a successful career—namely, to upgrade one's self-esteem outside of material and worldly concerns. Their striving for moral perfection and gaining merits for the hereafter helps them to control their own lives in uncertain times (Metcalf 1994).

Karim: A Pious Career

Karim was twenty-four years old when he went to Cairo in 2008 to study Islamic jurisprudence at the Al-Azhar University. His decision was preceded by the completion of a degree in law at the National State University in Dushanbe and several years of moving between unemployment and migration to Moscow and Dubai as a seasonal worker. His frustration and disappointment about not being able to work as a lawyer as well as numerous attempts "to do something meaningful" finally led him to religion:

> I struggled a lot to become a good lawyer. I was not driven by money or success, but I wanted to do something meaningful. But it didn't work out. A lot went wrong, and I experienced a lot of injustice [*beadolatī*]. . . . So finally, I wanted to know whether there is anything else, something better, more just, than that which I had experienced so far. . . . And I came to religion. I had no idea of Islam at that time and I was advised "if you really want to know what Islam is all about, you'll have to go to a university abroad, preferably to Egypt, to the Al-Azhar."

As in many other cases, Karim's religious awakening and his decision to study Islam abroad cannot be understood without his formative experiences as a seasonal labor migrant in Moscow, and later in Dubai. In 2008 an estimated 1.5 million Tajiks worked in Moscow, either seasonally or for longer terms (ICG 2009a). Among them, many are uneducated young men for whom migration is not only a livelihood strategy but also a "rite of passage" into adulthood (Monsutti 2007; Zmejewski 2013). In recent years, for university graduates like Karim who possess foreign-language skills (Russian, English, Arabic), Dubai has become an alternative and much more lucrative place to earn money in the tourist sector, as well as to become an "adult" person.

Studies on migration have provided adequate evidence that experiences of migration can lead to an increase in individual religiosity, encourage religious conservatism, and stimulate religious transformation at home (Brettell 2003, 75–100; van der Veer 2001, 9). Karim was influenced not only by the religious freedom that many of his fellow Tajiks experience in Moscow. It will be chiefly the negative experiences that shape Karim's life as a Tajik migrant in an urban reality that is increasingly marked by Russian nationalism and xenophobia, and that later informs his perception of Dubai as an ideal Muslim place abroad. He perceives Dubai as an absolute contrast to both Moscow and Dushanbe. Fascinated by the dynamism of Dubai, he understands its technical progress, prospering economy, and Islamic banking system as the achievements of a well-working Islamic society with strong moral values. For Karim, Dubai's hyper-image of Middle Eastern modernity embodies "the most perfect purity" (*joyi insoftarin*) and is seen as the opposite of a modern world, influenced above all by "Western" values. Karim's notion of "Western modernity" shows itself in all its sobering facets in both Dushanbe and Moscow and also includes his experience of economic deprivation, corruption, moral decline, and lack of acceptance as a Muslim and the low status occupied above all by Tajik migrants in Russian society. But it is not only in moral matters that Dubai is seen as a distant Muslim-friendly place worth emulating. The stories of success narrated by and embodied in the returning students, traders, and businesspeople make Dubai, in Tajikistan as well as in other parts of Asia, a projection surface for aspirations, illusions, and hopes for social mobility that is fed by the interplay of modernity and piety (Thangarajah 2003). The promise of acquiring religious and economic capital resulting from a stay in Dubai partly explains the growing significance that this city has acquired during the past few years as a destination for labor migration from the whole of Central Asia. Particularly for young Tajiks with a university degree such as Karim, Dubai offers a genuine alternative to Moscow in terms of earning well and engaging in a Muslim lifestyle. This again enables youth like Karim to tell the success story that is expected of migrants after their return back home. Once invited to a memorial ceremony in a Tajik family settled in the outskirts of Dushanbe, I witnessed how the host introduced a young man as a "Dubai businessman" (*dubaiskii biznesmen*) to the guests who were overwhelmingly older women, and assigned him the place of honor in the room (*bolo*), a gesture of respect that is usually reserved for elders or religious people such as Mecca pilgrims or ritual specialists.

Acquiring International Educational Capital

The positive image that Islamic education from abroad enjoys, in addition to religious and moral aspects, also embraces worldly concerns: in other words, the hope of being able to acquire international educational capital. The international prestige of universities such as Al-Azhar in Cairo or IIUI in Pakistan (which accept students from all over the world and where the courses are partly conducted in English) attracts many young people from Tajikistan who would like to acquire knowledge of foreign languages. The Tajik proverb "Zabondony—jahondony"[15] exemplifies the extent to which such high esteem is attributed to the learning of foreign languages as part of one's upbringing (*ta'limu tarbiya*) to become a thoroughly morally, culturally, and spiritually educated person embodying, within the meaning of the ancient Persian cultural tradition, *odob-u akhloq* (morality, modesty, perfected civilized and proper behavior) (Niyazi 1999, 181–82; Stephan 2010, 471).

The internationalization of education in independent Tajikistan was aimed at gaining admission to international employment markets. To do this, international standards were introduced in lycées, colleges of higher education, and universities, and private educational establishments were authorized. Consequently, the ancient proverb "Zabondony—jahondony" is also acquiring current relevance and encapsulates the high international educational aspirations of young Tajiks connected with the acquisition of foreign languages. For instance, the successful international professional careers that graduates of private Turkish high schools in Tajikistan are able to achieve in the United States, or after returning home, in private companies or international organizations are a convincing precursor of this trend. But these successful career trajectories are reserved for a very small number of young people in Tajikistan. The vast majority of young people try to acquire international skills and foreign languages in other ways. Among the students I talked with who returned to Dushanbe many were attracted by the prospect of learning internationally recognized languages such as English or Turkish. They placed their hopes in Arabic as well, which, through its religious and sacred significance as the language of Islam, would provide with them a resource to enter a secular profession such as translator, tourist guide, diplomat, and journalist, both at home and abroad.[16]

A morally charged public debate in Dushanbe about the many young male as well as increasingly female Tajik labor migrants in Russia indicates that migration to a non-Muslim foreign country for purposes of employment or study is frequently accompanied by anxieties on the part of family members at home that the son or daughter will become alienated from his/her cultural and religious traditions through contact with other (primarily Western) value systems and lifestyles. In contrast, foreign Muslim countries offer an alternative route to education for many young people striving for secular careers in an environment that is defined in a religious sense and thus is morally trustworthy. The imagined membership in the ummah creates a protected domain in which, above all, young and unmarried women can obtain international educational capital.

Samira (twenty years old), who through an announcement on the Internet obtained a scholarship for a three-year course in Islamic studies in a charitable endowment (*waqf*) in Istanbul was supported in this venture by her mother. While Samira aspired to acquire knowledge in Turkish and Arabic language, her mother hoped for a considerable moralizing effect as a result of her daughter's studying in a religious institution: "I consented immediately. Simply because she wished to study abroad in a Muslim country. That is not a problem at all. Muslims live there. They are people like us. But they have higher moral standards there. The girls live in boarding schools. They are not corrupted but learn through religion what is morally good."

Finally, there are also quite pragmatic reasons in favor of studying Islam in foreign Muslim places. First, considerably fewer resources have to be mobilized than would be required for study in a European country or the United States. This relates to lower language barriers (through Persian and Urdu in the case of Iran and Pakistan), the possibility of avoiding selection by obtaining a scholarship (through privately organized and financed trips) as well as the comparatively low financial outlay associated with study in educational centers in Iranian Zahedon or Pakistan, or at Cairo's Al-Azhar. Second, until recently, a promising opportunity to achieve residence for study purposes in Al-Azhar, for instance, was provided by the uncomplicated issue of obtaining necessary visas via transit through Moscow. Third, the social contacts that exist in foreign Muslim countries through labor migrants in Moscow and Dubai, pilgrims to Mecca, traders, and refugees from the Tajik civil war are helpful in preparing and carrying out Islamic studies in a foreign Muslim country. This interplay of language and social networks with geographical and social mobility again gives rise to translocal spaces of connectedness and mobility that embrace both the experienced realities of "here" and the imaginary "there." Moreover, these spaces create a familiar cultural or moral proximity that is reproduced through new religious affiliations and definitions of Islam and enables young people to experience alternative educational options and ideas for their future.

Following the Return Home: Navigating a Flexible Piety

The modernist reading according to which education automatically and directly guarantees development, economic success, social advancement, and a "good life," can be found in many narratives of returning Tajik students. But as the following case of Zebo and Aziz reveals, the imaginations held before a study abroad do not necessarily correspond to the reality experienced upon returning home. Students who returned from studying Islam abroad are not able in the same way or to the same extent to use the symbolic and educational capital acquired in order to fulfill their religious pursuits and secular aspirations. As we have seen, the pursuit of an Islamic education in a foreign Muslim country is closely linked to personal religious reform projects that grow out of spiritual renewal, disappointments in life, uncertainties, and the longing for an imaginary distant place full of promise. However, the new piety of the returned students has to find its way through daily routines filled with contradictions, ambiguities, and challenges, or, as Samuli Schielke and Liza Debevec (2012, 8) put it: "Everyday practice is complex in its nature, ambivalent, and at times contradictory. It is embedded in traditions, relations of power and social dynamics, but it is not determined by them."

Zebo and Aziz

In 2007, Aziz (age fourteen) and his sister Guli (age twelve) were sent by their mother Zebo to Zahedon in southeastern Iran. During their three-year stay abroad, the siblings attended elementary courses in Islamic studies, Koran reading, and Arabic language and gained advanced religious knowledge. The trip was intended by Zebo as a disciplining strategy to raise her pubescent son and daughter to become "pure" Muslims and to upgrade their moral standing in the community. However, the privately organized educational stay in Zahedon turned out to be a pious enterprise with many unintended consequences for the family when the siblings had to cancel their studies after President Rahmon launched his callback campaign in 2011. Particularly for Aziz, the premature return to Dushanbe had negative consequences for his possibilities of gaining a secular education certificate in a national secondary school in Tajikistan. When I met the family in autumn 2012, Zebo had already been struggling for more than one year with state officials to reintegrate Aziz into the secular education system. The Ministry of Education continuously rejected her numerous requests for a continuation of her son's interrupted secondary school education, first of all because of Aziz's long absence from state school and the lack of an official note on his temporary departure from school. In addition, due to their forced return Aziz was not able to submit any of the required official training certificates from Iran that would have allowed his adequate reintegration into the secular education system. For Zebo, however, the official rationales given by the state authorities are blurring the fact that the state is discriminating against her son on grounds of his religious profile and thus stigmatizing them as representatives of a "foreign" Islam incompatible with the secularized version of the "homegrown" Tajik Islam the Tajik government is trying to implement in Dushanbe's public sphere (see also Toktogulova, chapter 10, this volume). Zebo, who accompanied her children to Iran and stayed with them for a couple of months, learning Arabic and reading the Koran herself, got used to wearing a black *niqab*, a long veil that fully covers the face, neck, and breast, while her son Aziz returned with a beard. Back at home, Zebo and her son found themselves in a strictly secular environment that forced them to adjust their pious lifestyles to their educational aspirations, which, besides moral ambitions, mirror in particular the mother's wish to prepare her son for a good life in the future. This strong mundane aspiration finally induced Zebo to adapt herself to the secular realities surrounding her: before she underwent another attempt to convince the state authorities to enroll Aziz in secondary school, she instructed Aziz to shave his beard, while she replaced her black niqab with a colorful small hijab that matches the current fashion trends in Dushanbe and makes her less noticeable in the urban public.

According to Cassarino's (2004, 17) thesis on return migration, the capacities available to migrants to innovate or actively change their social (or religious) environment on their return correlate not only with the ability to mobilize various resources (technical skills, financial means, social networks). Perhaps of much greater importance are the current power hierarchies related to state policies and cultural traditions as well as processes of social (and religious) dynamics, which become even more concentrated in the complexity and ambiguity of urban life and experiences of returning students in Dushanbe. This urban complexity and ambiguity is reflected first, in the returning students' capability for investing their study experiences at home, and second, in the unexpected consequences of their study projects, which, as we have seen in Aziz's case, challenge them to balance their religious endeavors with the secular realities of everyday urban life in Dushanbe.

The presidential callback campaign had quite immediate consequences, above all for those, who, like Zebo and her children, organized their Islamic studies without the permission of the government authorities (*kumitai diny*) and returned home without an official diploma. Failure to complete study courses abroad, insufficient time to prepare for their return, and the atmosphere of mistrust that is fostered by the state's skepticism toward "foreign" interpretations of Islam were severe impediments for the returning students in reestablishing themselves in the national educational system or finding employment in the public sector (education, child care, and the health and medical sector). The religious capital that Zebo and her children had hoped to acquire from a period of study in a foreign Muslim country proved to be a social stigma for them, and prevented them from using their educational experiences to advance their secular careers.

The political constraints that returnees face in today's Dushanbe pose serious challenges, especially for those students who wish to strictly follow their new religious beliefs and turn to an Islamic lifestyle that covers all aspects of everyday life, which includes public religious expressions through body language and special dress codes. In Dushanbe's urban public, where a great variety of Islamic lifestyles and identities can be seen, the newly pious have to make recourse to religious symbols and expressions in order to demarcate their belief from that of other Muslims around them. To show their Islamic knowledge and their proximity to "sacred" places abroad, many returnees wear conspicuous Islamic clothing—as Zebo does with her black, fully covering niqab— that stands in sharp contrast to the colorful hijab and traditional dress of other Tajik women in Dushanbe. Being diacritics of great normative power in urban debates about "right" or "true" Islam, with their visibly *other* religious habits, Tajik returnee students at the same time become a particularly vulnerable group in Dushanbe's public sphere. Suspected of being "Salafi" (who are perceived in the official rhetoric as enemies of the Tajik state and nation), the newly pious are often the main targets of everyday secular politics in Dushanbe. Publicly staged luggage inspections at airports, prohibitions on entering schools, universities, and neighborhood mosques, as well as being actively monitored by the secret service fuel the politicization and criminalization of those religious expressions that are not in line with the official interpretation of Islam. Moreover, this everyday politics of state secularism also hampers the successful reintegration of the returnee students into social life, job markets, and the national educational system.

Zebo responds to this politics of distrust by cultivating a flexible piety— that is, she adapts her educational strategies and goals regarding her son, which also implicate his moral upgrading through Islamic self-fashioning, to Dushanbe's secular realities. As a single mother, Zebo is attentive in fulfilling her parental duties and preparing her son to enter university later. Practices such as adapting, adjusting, and balancing are everyday tactics of the returnee students in urban Dushanbe, which help them to navigate their own livelihood projects and future aspirations situationally—that is, by referring to a higher moral or spiritual order (set by religion) as well as to a secular order (set by the nation-state) depending on the context. As we will see later in the case of Zebo's daughter Guli, when religious instructions abroad are part of a family strategy, the symbolic capital gained there preserves the moral reputation of the family, even if individual members partially give up their religious endeavors afterward.

Negotiating Young Women's (Im)Mobility

Local power politics are found not just in Tajikistan's political sphere. They also appear in the context of the individual's position in the generational order and have a particular effect on culturally determined concepts of gender and youth (Harris 2004, 2006; Roche 2010). The educational biographies of Guli and Samira, presented below, offer a specific gender perspective on the differing consequences of religious instruction abroad on the spatial and social mobility of young, unmarried women.

Guli and Samira grew up in an urban social environment in which female modesty and notions of attractive marriage partners are often debated in religious terms and with regard to global images of the ideal Muslim woman (McBrien 2012). Consequently, young Muslim women in Dushanbe have to negotiate their aspirations for education within the social norms and moral expectations of family members, relatives, and neighbors. The following contrasting examples illustrate how, following the return home, the conversion of study experiences abroad into various forms of capital is determined by individual as well as collective interests and leads to differing opportunities for mobility on the part of young, unmarried women.

Guli: Immobility within Mobility

When young Tajik Muslim women travel to foreign Muslim countries for the purpose of study, an older, usually female, member of the family or another unmarriageable kin (*mahram*) has to accompany them. This is a mandatory precondition for unmarried women to become mobile across regional and social boundaries at all. Moreover, abroad this practice also reproduces cultural gender concepts developed at home and reinforces their effectiveness.

In 2007, Guli was sent to Zahedon in southeastern Iran by her mother together with her older brother Aziz and the family of her mother's sister in order to attend courses in reading the Koran and in Arabic. Guli was thirteen years old at the time. During her three years of education there, her freedom of movement was restricted to visits to the religious courses in town, and to the rooms occupied by her aunt and her family in the flat of the Baluchi family who hosted them. Since Guli also attended the religious courses together with her aunt, she barely had any opportunity to gather personal experiences in the foreign country, except for those that had been prepared by her family beforehand. Moreover, on her return to Dushanbe, Guli was restricted even more firmly than before to the area of the home. Her mother has not reregistered her for school and she is only allowed to leave the flat in her mother's company. Apart from her cousins with whom she studied in Zahedon, Guli is no longer allowed to meet people of her own age.

Guli's example shows how mobility for purposes of education, during which considerable geographical distances are covered, can ultimately lead to increased immobility for young, unmarried women both abroad and once they are back home. As in Guli's case, many parents in Dushanbe combine a period of study in a foreign Muslim country with the goal of guiding their daughters from puberty to maturity (*baloghat*). As a novel way for parents to express their piety toward that of other Muslims around them, this practice of social upbringing at the same time shows the close relationship between conveying religious knowledge and forming good (traditional) morality (*odob*), as expressed in the term *ta'limu tarbiya* (Stephan 2010, 471). However, the spatial shift of moral education from the intimate space of "home" (the household, kin group, neighborhood) to foreign places abroad underlines the power of the local image of ideal Muslim places afar for shaping Muslim subjectivities in Dushanbe. Besides, the government's rigid restrictions on Muslim religious life foster local aspirations for a trusted or distant place close to home and encourage many parents to send their children away. Facilitating a good moral upbringing for their daughters in a foreign Muslim country enables parents to successfully present them on the marriage market (Schröder and Stephan-Emmrich 2014, 8–11).

Guli's educational biography is strongly influenced by the fact that following her parents' divorce she and her brother grew up without a father, and her mother had barely any social contacts in Dushanbe that could support her in bringing up her children. The lack of support, the social stigma of living without a husband, and the everyday urban routine that, particularly for young adolescents, provides a narrow range of opportunities, unsettled the mother and promoted anxieties about endangering the daughter's good reputation (*obrū*), preventing her from enjoying a better life later on. A period of studying in an Islamic country removes any possible doubts about Guli's good reputation and that of her family. In a social environment in which the hijab has in the past few years established itself as a symbol of urban living and has largely lost its earlier significance as an expression of particular religious piety, a period of Islamic education abroad symbolizes capital that enables Guli (and her mother) to enhance her female morality vis-à-vis the other young women wearing the hijab in Dushanbe. Guli's stay in Zahedon and the parental intentions linked to it have produced a life pattern for Guli in which education—religious in this case—serves less as preparation for a subsequent professional career than for her future role as an honorable wife and daughter-in-law. This promotes the concept of youth as a transitional phase that allocates young people in Tajikistan the role of "learners," who at an early stage and under the guidance of their elders are prepared for their future role as adults. Religion in this context is subject to the dominating influence of adults and, in contrast to the following case of Samira, is not available to Guli as a resource in developing an alternative identity during adolescence (Stephan 2013).

However, the strong moral symbolism inherent in Guli's religious instructions abroad also disrupted the educational goals of Guli's mother Zebo. Because she had herself obtained a degree from Tajik National University, Zebo's notion of a good life for her daughter entailed plans for an academic career. But after divorce, Zebo fell into a vulnerable position that forced her to accept her sister's husband as guardian of her and her children's reputation. When the sister's husband, who experienced a spiritual awakening in the early 2000s, decided to send his family to Zahedon in order to increase his religious credibility, Zebo was persuaded by her sister to send her daughter and son with them. Zebo agreed, hoping that both religious instruction abroad and a university career at home would increase her children's chances to live a good life in future. Eventually, and due to her relatives' pressure, Zebo adjusted her educational aspirations for her daughter and invested all of her maternal endeavors in maintaining Guli's moral reputation and finding a good husband for her.

Samira: Self-Empowerment through Religion

An Islamic education abroad is not so much a free ticket to a religious or an educational career as an alternative road to social mobility. As we have seen, the refashioning of Muslim selves in Tajikistan produces a wide range of translocal parental education strategies regarding adolescent daughters, which embrace sacred geographies and evoke strong moral connotations. But the highly moralized local debates on religious instruction abroad do not automatically lead to increased female immobility. At the same time, they can empower in particular young urban Muslim women to use religion as a culturally and socially accepted resource in order to pursue individual future aspirations and academic careers and to develop their own identities and lifestyles beyond the prevailing gender order. Let us again look at Samira, who in 2010 returned from her Islamic studies in Istanbul.

I got to know Samira in the autumn of 2011 in the offices of the Islamic Renaissance Party of Tajikistan (IRPT) in Dushanbe where the female members of the party regularly meet. At that time, Samira was doing an internship as part of her recently begun studies in journalism at a public institution of higher education in Dushanbe. Before that she had finished a program in Islamic studies at a Turkish Sufi endowment from 2007 to 2010. During her internship, Samira was able to make new social contacts that provided her with professional experience and helped her to get a little closer to achieving her plans for the future. These networks also opened up ways to use religion as a resource in order to develop her own female Muslim identity, which in many ways deviates from the traditional gender order commonly envisioned for young women with its norms and limited mobility (see the case of Guli presented earlier). Through her close contacts with Islamic activists in the party, Samira acquired access to an emancipatory feminist circle that combined Islam and modernity and challenged current secular interpretations of religion. She explained her understanding of modern activist Muslim women: "Because we wear a headscarf and pray, many believe that we are uneducated and are only waiting to be married and to stay at home. But that is not true. We have decided to wear a headscarf by our own free will. And we are educated and modern women too! We know our rights as women better than those [women] who have nothing at all to do with religion."

Of primary importance in the discussions of the IRPT were both the religious and educational capital that Samira acquired abroad during the time she studied in Istanbul. It enabled her not only to obtain a status of trust mentioned above but also to create an opening for dialogue on an equal footing with women, despite sometimes extreme differences in age. Ultimately, Samira's Islamic education abroad promoted her mobility back home and enabled here to accumulate social capital in order to continue to pursue both her professional and religious goals. Together with a female friend, whom she had gotten to know during her work in IRPT, Samira developed the idea of establishing a taxi company in Dushanbe that would be completely devoted to enhancing female mobility in the city. This example clearly shows how new hopes can arise from study experiences abroad. Moreover, it illustrates how symbolic capital can, at least potentially, be transformed into economic capital. This in turn promises young, educated women like Samira social mobility that enables them to combine a religious background, professional aspirations, and emancipation from social norms and predominant gender expectations.

This positive moral image is associated not just with foreign universities. Regarding higher education for women, a matter on which the whole family decides, domestic Islamic educational establishments also provide a protected space in which young women can realize their educational aspirations without endangering their moral standing. My surveys among female students at the Abu Hanifa Islamic Institute in Dushanbe reveal that in many cases parents only agree to their daughters' wish to study on the condition that they study at an Islamic educational institution. Such decisions are frequently the result of a process of negotiation within the family in which parents try to harmonize their own and their daughters' educational aspirations with the social expectations of an urban environment that is strongly characterized by patriarchal principles and a gender order that limits young women's mobility outside the private sphere.

Against this background, the experience of self-empowerment through religion is often supported by a religious family background. Unlike Guli and her family, who started their religious enterprises just recently, Samira grew up in a religious environment. Her older sister, who studies at the Abu Hanifa Islamic Institute in Dushanbe and serves as a role model for Samira, had already paved the way for Samira to convince her parents to allow her to pursue her educational goals abroad.

Religious Mobility and Self-Empowerment

Dale Eickelman and James Piscatori in *Muslim Travellers* (1990) point out that religiously motivated travel is primarily a social activity that is led by personal motives, socioeconomic conditions, and political interests and, therefore, is filled with meanings that go beyond a single religious dimension. As this chapter has illustrated, an Islamic education abroad can serve either as an alternative pathway to international educational capital in order to pursue future aspirations linked with economic success and upward social mobility, or as a cultural strategy to realize educational goals or the collective moral upgrading of a family. In addition, an Islamic education abroad promotes freedom to experience self-empowerment, moral superiority, and forms of youthfulness. Therefore, to focus solely on religious motivations obscures the fact that religious training abroad can produce important social, religious, and economic capital that is deliberately converted once students return home.

Tracing the juncture of religion, education, youth, and livelihood, this chapter counterbalances the ongoing academic and political debates on Islamic revivalism in Tajikistan. These debates have so far been dominated by issues of political and social security, and they often foster what John Heathershaw and David Montgomery (2014) identify as "the myth of post-Soviet Muslim radicalization in Central Asia." The wide range of possible motivations and consequences of studying Islam abroad instead shows that the young Tajiks involved can in no way be regarded as a homogeneous group of Muslims who have become religious "radicals" during their time outside of their home country and who experience problems with reintegrating on their return. For many of them, their experiences while abroad serve as more of a cushion than a potential catalyst for disappointment and frustration. Furthermore, their new piety embraces daily efforts to refashion themselves as moral subjects rather than motivating them for political activism.

However, with its recent introduction of stricter regulations, the Tajik state implemented a powerful tool to illegalize the educational careers of young Muslims and to define new hierarchies in the imagined sacred landscape of Islamic education abroad. While national study programs in Saudi Arabia, Egypt, and the UAE train the future Islamic elite and enable professional religious careers in the state sector, the privately organized and often insufficiently prepared educational trips to Iran, Pakistan, and Egypt lead young Tajik Muslims into an uncertain future once they return home (Schmitz 2015, 18–19). Due to the nonlegal status of their education, they are not able to use their translocal experiences as a resource to pursue a professional religious or secular career in Dushanbe. Consequently, many of them return to their former places of study. Thus, in many ways the experiences of Karim, Zebo, Aziz, and Guli are illustrations of how Tajik students of Islam, who started their educational endeavors in the early or mid-2000s and then returned home without official diplomas, respond to the unexpected consequences of their religious endeavors.

In addition to the effects of strict secular policies, an obviously fragmented sacred landscape of Islamic education shapes the return experiences of young Tajik students of Islam in Dushanbe. The growing market of educational opportunities abroad has paved the way for the emergence of new interpretations of Islam that seriously challenge local Islamic traditions. Among returnees in Dushanbe, the strong influence of Salafi ideologies is hotly debated and feeds into a greater awareness of belonging to an imagined "Persian Islam" and the dissociation from an "alien" Arab Islam that is associated with stricter religious practice, intolerance of spiritual and philosophical readings of Islam, and conspicuous Islamic appearance. The resulting translocal or transnational fields of Muslim discourse and practice that young Tajiks engage with bear witness to the "pluralization of Islam" since independence (Khalid 2007, 123; see also Jones, Introduction, this volume). At the same time, these new border-crossing religious fields obviously interrogate those anthropological and other studies that still fall into the trap of "methodological nationalism" (Wimmer and Glick-Schiller 2002) or "regionalism" and deal with Islam in Tajikistan mostly within the conceptual container of the post-Soviet nation-state or Central Asia as a homogeneous region.

The students' aspirations and future wishes associated with a faraway Muslim country do not always concur with the reality experienced after return. Or to put it in more concrete terms, religious mobility does not always facilitate (female) students' agency. Morality (i.e., symbolic capital) as well as various knowledge and language skills (i.e., educational capital) acquired as a result of studying abroad are used in the urban context at home in very different ways. For some there are opportunities to develop a modern Muslim identity or even to achieve professional successes (Samira). For others, the religious capital associated with a period of studying in foreign Muslim countries leads to a stronger attachment to collective and often gendered (family) strategies, the aim of which is less a professional career than a successful marriage (e.g., Guli).

One pattern however links all the biographies of the returning students presented here. Their travel reports are stories of a spiritual awakening (*isloh*) in which the true or pure Islam experienced while abroad is presented as a solution or an alternative. The strong moral dimension linked to this religious experience offers a scope for self-empowerment, in which disappointed secular careers, socioeconomic uncertainties, and a lack of recognition and acceptance are cushioned, and alternative routes to social recognition are revealed. This gives rise to a new piety that reveals strong links abroad and simultaneously requires demarcating the "other" in the home country as "wrong," "impure," or "ignorant" in order to be able to differentiate oneself (Armbrust 2006). This turns a period of studying in a distant Muslim country into a subjective success story that can be told to those who stayed behind at home.

The new religious mobility of Tajik Muslims is embedded in local imaginations about better or ideal Muslim places far away that in many respects may be considered "as antidotes to the finitude of social experience" (Appadurai 2010, 53). Studying Islam abroad is on the one hand strongly borne out by these local projections. On the other hand, the returning students, with their translocal experiences, affiliations, and livelihoods, are themselves carriers of these images and fantasies. What Appadurai noted about the role of the mass media in creating global flows applies equally in the case of returning students. Their travel reports and their embodied religious experience (Islamic dress, pious lifestyle, divergent religious practices) are "semiotic diacritics of great power" (Appadurai 2010, 53). They bear new images of Islamic lifestyle and piety, notions of modernity, democracy, and Islamic economy. At the same time, they document a new translocal space in which a constant interaction takes place between here, as it is actually experienced, and an imaginary there. Since many programs of study abroad are offered especially for nonlocals, that is, "foreign" Muslims, and many students, like Guli, have only limited contact with the local population, the Muslim "other" abroad can only be perceived though a filter (Abaza 1994). Preexisting images and projections therefore often remain intact abroad, are brought back home, and confirmed in travel reports or described in an exaggerated form to the disadvantage of other experiences that do not fit. Thus, the interaction between here and there is neither equivalent nor balanced. The predominance of the imagined there is rather reproduced both at home and abroad. This strong attraction of Muslim foreign countries has developed from a need for identity that Sean McLoughlin (2010, 223–24) describes as "an Islamic homing desire," which is not the same thing as a desire for a homeland. This need is far from new. It represents an old Muslim tradition associated with travel to imagined Muslim sacred or learning centers, which in modern Tajikistan, however, takes shape in a rigid national state secularism and in the lack of future prospects for young people.

CONCLUSION

Central Asia as Part of the Islamic Core

Pauline Jones

Central Asia has long been treated as peripheral to world history—a victim to the shift in the "world historical centre of gravity . . . outward, seaward, and westward" since the fifteenth century (Frank 1992, 44). Perhaps less well recognized is that it has also long been relegated to the periphery of the Islamic world. Geography tells a large part of the story here too. Central Asia's location between the "barbarian nomads on its north and Chinese civilization at its east" and its cultural connection to both meant that Central Asia was and would always remain on the outer frontier of Islamic civilization (Bregel 1980, 1).[1] The Russian Empire's gradual yet steady conquest of the region in the nineteenth century,[2] with its alternating policies of toleration and suppression toward Islam, introduced new (albeit tractable) barriers to Central Asia's full incorporation into the Islamic world (for details, see, e.g., Carrère d'Encausse 1994; Crews 2003). Under Soviet rule (1917–91), these barriers took on both an ideological and administrative form that made them seemingly insurmountable. Following the Bolshevik Revolution, Central Asia endured not only the brutal atheistic campaign to eliminate religion (Keller 2001) but also the structural reorganization of the Russian Empire into administrative units based on officially recognized nationalities (Sabol 1995). The region's Muslim identity was thus challenged on two fronts, creating the potential for a further distancing from the Islamic world in geographical as well as religious terms. Indeed, the predominant view has long been that the imposition of Russian and especially Soviet rule over Central Asia severed its connection to the rest of the Islamic world (DeWeese 2002).

As the chapters in this edited volume suggest, however, the states and societies that compose Central Asia have much in common with their counterparts in other parts of the Islamic world, including both the so-called Arab Muslim core and predominantly Muslim countries in other regions (such as Southeast Asia and Africa) that have similarly been relegated to a peripheral status (see, e.g., Mehmet 2002; Von der Mehden 1993; Ware 2014). They have experienced many of the same historical and political trends: colonialism, revivalism, Islamism,[3] and nationalism. They also face a similar struggle between political and religious leaders who feel compelled to endorse a singular state or "official" interpretation of Islam and a society that encompasses multiple forms of Islamic belief and practice—often described as syncretism outside the Arab world.

Historical and Political Trends

Albeit later than most other parts of the Islamic world, Central Asia also fell victim to imperialist ambitions that led to the European[4] conquest and subjugation of Muslim lands from the seventeenth through the nineteenth centuries.[5] As it was for other predominantly Muslim regions, moreover, Central Asia's experience under colonial rule was formative. Russian and later Soviet colonialism imposed unpopular social and political changes that evoked impassioned and collective responses. Just as they did under European colonial rule, Islamic religious leaders served both as a means to enhance the Russian Empire's social and political control and to mobilize armed resistance against Russian occupation (Motadel 2014). Sufi sheikhs, for example, led anticolonial struggles and also accommodated colonial rule in India and Iraq under the British, in Algeria and Senegal under the French, and in the Caucasus and Central Asia under the Russians (see, e.g., Abun-Nasr 2013, 200–234; Buehler 1998, 168–89; Zelkina 2000, 169–202). Similar to European colonialism in other parts of the Islamic world, Russian rule in Central Asia also inspired advocates of modernizing reforms (*Jadids*) to emerge and gain support, or "revivalist movements," which often served as the catalyst for Muslim resistance to colonial rule (see, e.g., Voll 1999). Although by no means inevitable, Jadidism in Central Asia was a direct response to Russian conquest,[6] which forced Central

Asian intellectuals to decide how best to preserve Central Asian culture given the challenges of the modern world—in short, "to reconcile Islam with a modernity they very much admired" (Khalid 1998, 2).

It was not the Russian but the Soviet Empire, however, that laid the foundations for Central Asia to undergo two of the other seminal trends that most other predominantly Muslim regions experienced during the twentieth century—nationalism and Islamism.[7] Much like their European counterparts in Africa, Asia, and the Middle East, the Soviets enacted policies and demarcated borders that reified certain ethnic groups and ultimately constructed national identities. The "self-defined 'professional ethnographers'" charged with assigning ethnic categories to the various peoples of the Soviet Union, moreover, drew inspiration from the dominant role they believed ethnographic information played in the European colonial project (Hirsch 2005, 52–55).[8] Armed with both scholarly expertise and the "local knowledge" that local elites supplied often as a means to promote the interests of their own communities (Hirsch 2005, 10), Soviet ethnographers identified the ethnic groups that eventually served as the basis for the delimitation of national boundaries throughout the Soviet Union (Hirsch 2005, 145–86). In Central Asia these efforts resulted in five major ethnic groups receiving the status of "titular nationalities"—that is, territorial units established in their name, which granted them some degree of political and cultural autonomy—and the designation of these units as a Soviet Socialist Republic (SSR): Turkmen (Turkmen SSR), Kyrgyz (Kyrgyz SSR), Uzbeks (Uzbek SSR), Tajiks (Tajik SSR), and Kazakhs (Kazakh SRR).[9] Much like other parts of the Islamic world in the aftermath of empire, these territorial units served as a potent vehicle for demanding and receiving independence following the collapse of the Soviet Union in the form of nation-states: Turkmen SSR became Turkmenistan, the Kyrgyz SSR became Kyrgyzstan, and so on.

Also similar to the postcolonial experience of many other Muslim polities, Islamism emerged as one of many social and political forces seeking to influence how these nation-states were constructed and governed but was ultimately subordinated to secular nationalism. Consequently, Central Asian states and societies experienced a similar "disjuncture between what the [former] have viewed as the proper course of development and the values that [the latter] holds near and dear" (Nasr 1999, 561). In other parts of the Islamic world, this disjuncture fostered the emergence of Islamist movements that challenged state authority by articulating an alternative vision of development in accordance with societal values (Nasr 1999, 561). It also laid the foundations for the religious revivalism that has swept across Muslim societies since the 1970s and bolstered support for these movements (see, e.g., Esposito 1991). Although they have not yet experienced either of these phenomena to the same degree, Central Asian states and societies are certainly not immune. Indeed, they share many of the factors that helped to fuel both Islamist movements and religious revivalism elsewhere: corruption, economic decline, and repression (see, e.g., Jones Luong 2003).

Singular versus Multiple Interpretations of Islam

One of the primary reasons that Central Asia has been considered peripheral to the Islamic world is the prevalence of traditional forms of Islamic belief and practice, which have long coexisted with scriptural forms. Although hardly unique to Central Asia,[10] the pluralism that characterizes Central Asian Muslims (see, e.g., Jones Luong, Introduction, this volume) has led to the common misperception that Central Asian Islam is somehow not real or is inauthentic (DeWeese 1994). Observers from both outside and within the region thus viewed Central Asia's "Islamic revival" following the Soviet collapse with a particular set of assumptions that ironically placed Central Asia more firmly in the orbit of the Islamic world. First, because the reference point for what "true Islam" entails was the Arab core, the presumption was not only that the religious revival was about making Central Asians good Muslims but also that making them good Muslims meant greater compliance with scriptural forms of belief and practice. Second, because scriptural forms of Islamic belief and practice were conflated with fundamentalism, the presumption was that the revival would be unidimensional—that is, traditional beliefs and practice would give way to scriptural forms. And finally, because fundamentalism was viewed as inherently political, the presumption was that Central Asia's religious revival would be unidirectional—that is, Central Asian Muslims would become radicalized. In sum, the revival could only take one form— conservative and political.

The characterization of the revival as such also led observers to presume both that outside influence—specifically, radical Islamist groups—would dominate the revival and that Central Asians would be particularly susceptible to this influence. This affected not only the foreign policies that states within and outside the Islamic world adopted toward the region but also the domestic policies that Central Asian governments adopted toward Islam. Although in the first few years after independence, state and religious leaders alike celebrated their Islamic heritage and criticized Soviet policies that curtailed religious freedom (Khalid 2007, 132–33), they soon began—although to varying degrees—to reinstitutionalize the Soviet practice of sponsoring a singular "official" interpretation of Islam. As in other parts of the Islamic world, this impulse to regulate the dominant religion stems primarily from the fear that Islam will serve as an alternative ideology that diminishes loyalty to the regime, and hence, a potent source of political mobilization against the regime. Also similar to the experience of many of their counterparts in predominantly Muslim countries, the very regulations created to control the potential for religion to mobilize opposition have themselves had the perverse effect of fostering popular resistance in a variety of forms that challenge the stability of Central Asian governments (for details, see Gamza and Jones Luong 2014).

Future Research

Although perhaps peripheral in terms of geography, Central Asia shares much in common with the Islamic core. Not only have the states and societies that compose the region experienced many of the same historical and political trends, but they also face a similar struggle between political and religious leaders' desire for a singular state or "official" interpretation of Islam on the one hand and a society that encompasses multiple forms of Islamic belief and practice on the other. Comparisons that highlight these similarities as well as take into account the differences across the Islamic world are a fruitful avenue for future research.

NOTES

Introduction

1. The examples are numerous. I include here only a representative sample: Haghayeghi 1994; Hunter 2001; Lipovsky 1996; Olcott 1994; and Rashid 2002.

2. These states were among the fifteen that emerged after the collapse of the Soviet Union in 1991.

3. Rasanayagam (2006a) is an important exception.

4. For an overview, see Petros 2004; Tazmini 2001; and Yilmaz 2007.

Chapter One. The Social Significance of Islam in Post-Soviet Central Asia

1. The official name of the Muftiyat is Religious Council of Muslims of Kyrgyzstan (Kyrgyzstan Musul'mandar din bashkarmasy).

2. M. Ibraev, personal communication, May 14, 2013.

3. As of June 2012, 1 U.S. dollar = 46 som.

4. *Shahada* or faith in one God and the Prophet Muhammad is used as a measurement of religious belief.

Chapter Two. Beyond Piety

1. The analysts' focus on Muslims in the Fergana Valley is not unique (see, e.g., Bringa 2002, 33).

2. John Heathershaw and Nick Megoran (2011) provide a thorough critique of the tendency for journalists and academics to promote representations of Islamic identities that "endanger" Central Asia.

3. About 80 percent of Uzbekistan's 29 million population are self-identifying Muslims.

4. The names of the individuals, except the two heroines, are pseudonyms.

5. I use these women's real names per their request. In the following paragraphs, however, I refer to Hayethon as Ruhshonoz.

6. Contrary to the Uzbek state's reports about tremendously improved health-care quality, some sources suggest that Uzbekistan's health-care system was in no better shape in 2011 than it was in the 1990s. In this context, traditional healers had to cater to an increasing number of patients (see, e.g., http://www.eurasianet.org/node/64509, accessed November 21, 2011).

7. I have translated this pamphlet from Russian into English.

8. Ruhshonoz was among those who believe that Kaaba, a large cube-like building located inside the mosque known as *al-Masjid al-Haram* (the Sacred Mosque) in Mecca, symmetrically reflects a house in heaven called *al-Baytu l-Ma'mur* (the house or the place of worship of angels).

9. For example http://news.uzreport.uz/news_1_e_86319.html, accessed May 1, 2015.

10. See more at http://www.fergananews.com/article.php?id=3836, accessed May 10, 2015.

11. For a historical overview of "the unregistered," see Tasar, chapter 6, this volume.

12. Bennetts (2010) does not indicate over how many years these tele-healings had this number of viewers.

13. See http://www.scientificremoteviewing.com/main-menu/dzhuna-the-healer/, accessed February 1, 2011.

14. She is often referred to as a healer and scientist. Eugenia Davitashvili or Djuna is Georgian. She is president of the International Academy of Alternative Sciences "Djuna." She holds the Order of Friendship of Peoples. Djuna is a member of the Political Consultative Council of the president of the Russian Federation and head of the Regent Council of the Russian Noble society, New Russia Elite. She is also a colonel-general in the Medical Military Service and a holder of the Highest International Medical Reward Order of Albert Schweitzer.

15. Belyaev's concept of "heterodox religious worldviews" implies that there are "orthodox" religious worldviews, which is a theological and not an anthropological claim.

16. Rasanayagam (2010, 212) argues, "ideas from what might be termed 'New Age' healing such as bioenergy, as well imagery from the biomedical tradition . . . is not unique to healing in Uzbekistan."

Chapter Three. Radical Islam from Below

Research for this article was supported by the Czech Science Foundation under project no. P408/10/P596.

1. I use "radical" as a description in relation to Islamic ideology. "Islamic fundamentalism," or "radical Islam," is discussed in the scholarly literature in relation to the term "Islamism": as a subset (Fuller 2003), or differentiation (Roy 1994). Some prefer the term "Islamic activism" or "Islamic revivalism" (e.g., Esposito 1992, ICG 2005b).

2. Sharia law is a body of moral and religious law derived from religious prophecy. A caliphate is a form of Islamic government led by a caliph, or the chief Muslim civil and religious ruler.

3. The Ferghana Valley (22,000 square miles) is a densely populated zone in the heart of Central Asia, divided among Uzbekistan, Kyrgyzstan, and Tajikistan. It is also one of the religious and agricultural centers of the region.

4. Research on the HBT's practice in Uzbek Ferghana Valley has been largely impossible for political reasons.

5. Through accommodation of these changes or in opposition to them. For more see Dudoignon and Noack 2014.

6. For more see also Marcus 1995.

7. In addition, my field research drew on details provided in archival sources in the State Archive of the Russian Federation (GARF) in Moscow, Harvard University's records from the Russian State Archive of Contemporary History (RGANI) in Widener Library, and the State Archive of Uzbekistan (GAU) between 2002 and 2008.

8. Broader ethnographic research on the rhetoric of radical Islamic groups was hampered by the fact that in the ruling context of the Central Asian countries many informants were not willing to discuss the research question out of the fear of persecution by the government or of being associated with these movements.

9. In Tajikistan, they referred to them as *jawan mullas* (cf. Dudoignon and Noack 2014, 19).

10. For a more detailed description of the official party policy during this period, see Tasar, chapter 6, this volume.

11. Author interviews, Ferghana Valley, Uzbekistan, September 2007 and May 2008.

12. Today official documentation is accessible in the Soviet archives, including the collection of RGANI and GARF (fonds 6991).

13. For instance, older people from the Asht region in Tajikistan visited the mosque in the Uzbek city of Qoqand. Within society it was conceptualized that in this way the elders were able to follow the example of the Prophet Muhammad and represent their families and communities before God. Author interviews, Ferghana Valley, Uzbekistan, May–June 2008 and Dushanbe, Tajikistan, June 2011.

14. Regular reports of these activities, authored by members of the Soviet apparatus, are available in the archives.

15. Author interview, Yozyovon, Ferghana Valley, Uzbekistan, September 2007. For more on the approach of the local authorities toward Islam in the Ferghana Valley during this period, see Exnerova 2006.

16. For instance, the son of the famous ishon in Mindon, (Abdullah) Abdul Majid (1911–88), was appointed to the position even though he was not religiously educated. Author interview, Mindon, Ferghana Valley, Uzbekistan, May 2008. On the link between the structures of kolkhoz and Islamic congregations, see Dudoignon and Noack 2014; Roy 1997; and Sukhareva and Bikzhanova 1955.

17. The Mir Arab secondary school in Bukhara resumed operations in 1948, and in 1969 the Tashkent Islamic Institute, named after Imam al-Bukhari, a school

of higher learning, was founded and began to operate in 1971. Enrollment at both schools was kept low (fifty people were accepted at Mir Arab and thirty students at Tashkent Islamic Institute every two years). Students from all over the Soviet Union were eligible to study there, including Chechens, Ingush, Kazakhs, and Tajiks (author interview, Uyghur, Uzbekistan, May 2008). Later, during the Soviet era, enrollment at the madrasa was raised to two hundred and at the institute to one hundred (Utorbaev 1990, 2). After graduating, Mir Arab students were sometimes sent to universities in foreign countries, such as Egypt, Libya, and Saudi Arabia.

18. Imam *khatib* (person who delivers the sermon, usually the imam) of the Khanaqa mosque in Marghelan Sobir-qori, for example, studied in Bukhara but he claimed that all the required knowledge was available in Marghelan (author interview, Marghelan, Uzbekistan, May 2008).

19. For instance, the father of Mohammadjon, born in 1958 in the Toshloq region, found it beneficial to dedicate his seventh and final child to Islam. To this end, and for many years, he supported his son's education with different religious authorities (author interview, Kurghonche, Uzbekistan, September 2007).

20. People could thus spend time within this system, studying for up to twenty years, without being seriously harassed by the Soviet authorities (author interviews, Ferghana Valley, Uzbekistan, May 2008).

21. He studied with Mohammad Ali Qori over a period of five to six years, three times per week (author interview, Marghelan, Uzbekistan, May 2008).

22. Author interview, Marghelan, Uzbekistan, May 2008. See also Babadzhanov, Muminov, and von Kügelgen 2007, 25.

23. Author interview, Qoqand, Uzbekistan, September 2007.

24. Author interview, Yozyovon, Uzbekistan, May 2008.

25. Author interview, Chohi, Balkh Province, Afghanistan, November 2008.

26. Rahmatulla Alloma and Abduvali Qori, for instance, would come to Tashkent five or six times a year to meet Arabic students and order religious literature, at least five or six copies of each, as well as to participate in religious lessons (Olcott 2007, 14). However, contact was restricted by the Soviet authorities, especially after the Soviet invasion of Afghanistan (author interviews, Mazar-e-Sharif and Kabul, Afghanistan, November 2008, April 2011).

27. The official who reported this case (the *upolnomochennyi*, meaning "pleni-potentiary," for the Ferghana oblast in 1980) used this figure to complain that of these 850 people only 11 had discovered the "right" place, that is, in Tashkent University's East Faculty. Another 32 studied at Bukhara and Tashkent Islamic institutes. The other 800 were used by illegal religious figures to teach the younger generation the Arabic language and train them in the recitation of the Koran. They were then supposed to go on to study at religious institutes. (State Archive of the Russian Federation, 1980. Author interviews, Marghelan, Ferghana Valley, Uzbekistan, May 2008.)

28. Within his family, he passed all his knowledge to his oldest son Mukhtoriddin, who was born before the revolution in 1916 and who never attended a Soviet school. In contrast, his younger brothers matriculated through the Soviet education system and later worked within government structures (author interview, Vuadyl, Uzbekistan, May 2008).

29. There was a migration of ulema to the kolkhozes during the 1930s and 1940s, as is evident in biographies printed locally in the Ferghana Valley during the post-Soviet period (Babadzhanov 2014, 204).

30. Author interview, Yozyovon, Uzbekistan, May 2008.

31. For more on the fatwas of SADUM, see Babadzhanov 2001b. The majority of local scholars based their work on Hanafi *madhaab* (schools of Islamic jurisprudence) and arguments.

32. For details, see Jones, Introduction, this volume.

33. Author interviews in the Ferghana Valley, Uzbekistan, September 2007 and May–June 2008.

34. Information about the Mujaddidiya's discourse during the period under discussion is limited and informants were not willing to discuss it out of the fear of persecution or of being associated with these movements by the Uzbek government. The analysis relies on the primary data published in other scholarly works. The ethnographic research on Islam in the Ferghana Valley reveals details about their practice toward other religious actors at that time.

35. According to Mohammad Sodiq, the Mujaddidiya was inspired in this respect by contact with students from Arabic countries in Tashkent who performed prayers differently, including pronouncing the name of Allah aloud, raising hands, citing the sunnah of the Prophet. The students claimed that local Muslims did not fulfill the sunnah of the Prophet, but followed what Abu Hanifa said, and in their informal lessons they focused on explaining what sunnah was and why it was necessary to follow it (Yusuf 2007, 203–4).

36. Cited in his sermons on the same subject in the 1990s (Frank and Mamatov 2006, 78).

37. "Wahhabis" is a term that the opponents of the Mujaddidiya among other religious actors and elders, and later the Central Asian governments, used to denote the group because of its opposition to the locally used Hanafi madhhab. At that time, however, few people realized there was a difference, and a mixup occurred (author interview, Yozyovon, Uzbekistan September 2007). Ahmadjon-aka also eventually joined the Mujaddidiya. The Soviet regime, however, imprisoned both proponents of the Mujaddidiya and other scholars following the local Hanafi madhhab (author interview, Toshloq, Uzbekistan, September 2007).

38. People paid mullahs three to ten rubles, or one kilogram of meat, for the rituals at that time (author interview, Olti Oriq, Uzbekistan, September 2007).

39. Sverkhontura's son recalls an event when the scholar threw a teapot at Rahmatulla at one of their discussions during which Rahmatulla was trying to win Sverkhontura over to his side (author interview, Yozyovon, Uzbekistan, May 2008).

40. While the Mujaddidiya leaders started to say that it was necessary to revive local Islam, questioned the political status of Islam and discussed the situation in Iran or the Israeli–Palestinian conflict, the older Islamic scholars were afraid because of the "illiteracy" of the people who associated Islam with the rituals. Babadzhanov, Muminov, and von Kügelgen 2007, 100. See also al-Hindustani 1988, 118.

41. In addition, Yaacov Ro'i (2000, 346) finds in his analysis of the Soviet archival

sources from 1983 that the mullahs reportedly asked people to boycott registered mosques, to refuse the services of the governmental clergy, and not to buy meat, sweetmeats, and other "unclean" products in government stores.

42. Author interview, Yozyovon, Uzbekistan, May 2008; translation of ayat by T. J. Irving.

43. Perestroika (literally, restructuring) refers to the reforms implemented by the Soviet leader Mikhail Gorbachev in the 1980s.

44. Abduvali Qori's relative, however, claimed that the scholar had been under the continuous surveillance of secret organs of the state since the late 1970s (Human Rights Watch 1996).

45. For some it was as if this were a "game with Islam," practically encouraging the Islamization of young people (Babadzhanov 2014, 220).

46. The community's religious authorities and the descendants of local religious scholars denounced these "Wahhabists" but this only served to further polarize the conflict (author interviews, Ferghana Valley, September 2007 and June 2008).

47. Author interview, Eskiarab, Uzbekistan, September 2007.

48. Author interview, Uyghur, Uzbekistan, May 2008.

49. However, he sought to ensure that the Islamic revival and the imams in the local mosques remained under his control (Babadzhanov, Muminov, and von Kügelgen 2007, 137).

50. For detailed information about the power dynamics in Qoqand at that time, see Hilgers 2009. There were instances of the beating of imams in other towns of Ferghana (Babadzhanov, Muminov, and von Kügelgen 2007, 140–41).

51. They later called themselves the "Shari'a Militia" (Babadzhanov 2014, 241).

52. According to some, Adolat even carried out kidnappings of children from families of those imams who were not willing to support the Mujaddidiya (Babadzhanov, Muminov, and von Kügelgen 2007, 141). At the same time, this group came up with the idea of pressing for an Islamic state as a mean of purifying Islam. Similar actions were, however, used by other Islamic actors at that time, especially in the cities of Andijan and Namangan. Among others, Dowud-khon Ortikov, the radical supporter of the Sufi Qadiri order, restored the mosque of Aziz Hoja Ishan to his control in 1990 by putting pressure on neighbors and people living in the area that had originally been *vaqf* of the madrasa. This was done in the name of creating the Islamic republic of Uzbekistan. He was also an active supporter of the creation of a so-called Islamic region, complete with its own army (Olcott 2007, 25–26).

53. Author interview, Namangan, Uzbekistan, June 2008.

54. Abduvali Qori played a decisive role in persuading Tahir Yuldashev to leave the building of the Namangan oblast administration. See the interview with his relative, Kamalov (Firdavsii 2006). Yuldashev was one of its leaders who later became leader of the IMU. At that time, he was a twenty-four-year-old dropout from Bukhara Technological Institute.

55. Author interview, Eskiarab, Uzbekistan, September 2007.

56. Author interview with native from Asht, Khojent, Tajikistan, April 2011.

57. Author interview, Ferghana, Uzbekistan, May 2008.

58. Probably because he helped Islam Karimov persuade Yuldashev to leave the Namangan state administration building without a fight and thus managed the calls for an Islamic state in the Ferghana Valley without violence.

59. For which he was harassed by the authorities. Soon after the arrest and disappearance of Abduvali Qori in 1995, the firm was closed and the money was passed to the government (Mirsaitov and Saipov 2006).

60. He never even ate meals outside his house for fear of being poisoned (Human Rights Watch 2006).

61. Author interview with civil society worker, Jalalabad, Kyrgyzstan, June 2009. Similarly, in neighboring regions of Tajikistan some people were denied drivers licenses and passports since their facial appearance (bearded men in particular) did not comply with official "standards" (author interview with lawyer, Khojent, Tajikistan, June 2011). In Kyrgyzstan in 2007 the government first sought to deny girls the right to have a photograph of themselves wearing the hijab in their passports, but it was later forced to accept these photographs (ICG 2009, 21).

62. Author interviews with expert on Islam and lawyer, Jalalabad, Osh, Kyrgyzstan, June 2011.

63. Author interview with civil society worker, Jalalabad, Kyrgyzstan, June 2009.

64. Author interview with former human rights activist, Jalalabad, Kyrgyzstan, June 2011.

65. However, there were attempts to blame religious organizations for the interethnic violence, which many in southern Kyrgyzstan perceived negatively. The religious authorities reportedly helped to calm the situation, and it is believed that Islam has stood against national divisions (author interviews in Osh, Jalalabad, Kyrgyzstan, June 2011).

66. In 2012, after being criticized by politicians that "far from doing its best to counter extremism, the *muftiate* itself had become infected with extremist ideas," the institution embarked on a complex internal reorganization in order to improve its effectiveness in the fight against extremism and to achieve its goal of acting as the country's spiritual guide (Sultanov 2012).

67. Author interview with businessman and HBT sympathizer, Jalalabad, Kyrgyzstan, June 2011.

68. Author interview with civil society worker, Bishkek, Kyrgyzstan, July 2011. Some did this apparently after receiving bribes from a religious entity.

69. According to research carried out by the ICG, not a single graduate of the theological faculty at Osh University has managed to find work in one of the city's mosques. The local imams supported this image in order to retain their own position of authority: "Better the elderly imam from your own community than a young graduate from elsewhere." Many young people, however, do not want to work in a village mosque, where salaries are low and the only congregants are elderly village men (ICG 2003b, 28).

70. According to Kudratullo Mekhmankulov, teacher of Arabic, the Batyrov Friendship of Peoples University in Jalalabad (ICG 2003b, 29).

71. In Jalalabad, some girls stopped attending the state-run school because

of harassment on the part of teachers and the management (or even classmates). According to one civil servant, she encountered only one case where a girl was forced to wear a hijab; this was when the parents had cut her hair in order to compel her to wear a scarf. Other girls stated that they believed in what their Prophet and the Sunnah said, that when a girl starts to differentiate between the right and the left hand, she should wear a scarf (author interview, Jalalabad, Kyrgyzstan, June 2009). Girls have also often been taken out of state schools in order to improve their potential for securing a good marriage.

72. Author interview with civil servant, Bishkek, Kyrgyzstan, June 2011.

73. Author interview with lawyer, Osh, Kyrgyzstan, June 2011.

74. State officials portrayed them as holding fanatical beliefs. "What can you expect from that kind of study if their only textbook is the Koran? They will be fanatics" (author interview, Bishkek, Kyrgyzstan, June 2011).

75. And have not been sought for their knowledge by others outside of their community (author interviews, Jalalabad, Kyrgyzstan, June 2011).

76. Author interview with the muftiate official, Jalalabad, Kyrgyzstan, June 2011.

77. Corruption, along with a lack of religious experts in their ranks, have been the main reasons for the low levels of authority of the muftiate. Author interviews with lawyer, HBT sympathizer, Osh, Jalalabad, Kyrgyzstan, June 2011.

78. Unlike in the past, younger scholars have been more highly recognized as being real authorities than the carriers of local knowledge among older generations.

79. Author interview, Osh, Kyrgyzstan, June 2011.

80. For some he was the only real authority in the South when compared to others (author interviews, Osh, Jalalabad, Kyrgyzstan, June 2011).

81. Most recently, due to allegations of the misappropriation of funds for hajj (RFE/RL 2011b). He has been known to criticize the muftiate for its encouragement of "distorted practices" since it allows morally suspect clergy to collect fees in return for the administration of life-cycle rites, with the muftiate, in turn, extracting its own cut. Members of the family identified themselves as proponents of Salafi Islam (McGlinchey 2009, 19).

82. "In order to go on a 40-day pilgrimage, men must acquire three signatures for the Muftiate—one from their families, one from their local imam, and one from their local police precinct. They also must prove that they have sufficient funds to support their family while away. . . . These missions can last just a few days. But some go on for 40 days, or even four months, although such long sojourns are now strictly regulated in Kyrgyzstan" (Schenkkan 2011).

83. Author interview with HBT sympathizer, Jalalabad, Kyrgyzstan, June 2011.

84. Author interview with expert on Islam, Jalalabad, June 2011.

85. The mayor said this when calling into question the data of the deputy head of Kyrgyzstan's National Security Committee, Kolbay Musaev. According to him, Musaev says that there are about twelve thousand to fifteen thousand HBT supporters. "I am sure that in fact their numbers are much higher, especially in the southern provinces" (Kutueva 2011).

86. Author interview with expert on Islam, Jalalabad, Kyrgyzstan, June 2011.

Similarly in 2001, a member in Kara-Suu and his fellow members wrote on the bulletin boards in the elections booth, "We will vote only for a caliphate," and other members in Aravan wrote, "At the elections, we vote against everybody." During the referendum other members wrote, "We want a caliphate" (ICG 2003a, 21).

87. HBT "Muborak iidi Ramazon tabrigi" Congratulations on blessed Ramadan, December 5, 2002 (ICG 2003a, 27).

88. To the contrary, if the police have not beaten them, "it means we have not earned anything: if the police oppose us, the reaction of people is much stronger" (ICG 2003a, 38).

89. See also Khamidov, chapter 9, this volume.

90. Author interview with government official, Bishkek, Kyrgyzstan, June 2011.

91. Author interview with civil society worker, Bishkek, Kyrgyzstan, June 2011.

92. Author interview with HBT sympathizer, Jalalabad, Kyrgyzstan, June 2011.

93. But the local mullahs are being criticized for knowing very little about this organization and its ideas. They find it hard to comment on it in their sermons (author interviews, Bishkek, Jalalabad, June 2011).

94. When asked if members of other parties meant that there would also be non-Muslims, he answered that this was of no concern (author interview with expert on Islam, Jalalabad, Kyrgyzstan, June 2011).

95. Author interview with government official, Bishkek, Kyrgyzstan, June 2011.

96. In comparison with Uzbekistan and Tajikistan to some extent, in Kyrgyzstan they did not torture them; they were imprisoned for a maximum of four to five years, sometimes even given a suspended sentence, and sometimes sent to a colony. Only in a few cases did they resort to the use of force; generally, they pursue a more or less soft policy toward religious activists (author interview with former civil society worker, Jalalabad, Kyrgyzstan, June 2011).

97. Although local Islamic scholars do not aim to become members of the HBT.

98. Author interview with HBT sympathizer, Jalalabad, Kyrgyzstan, June 2011.

Chapter Five. Subversives and Saints

This research on Sufism in Central Asia was conducted under the auspices of an Edward A. Hewett Fellowship from the National Council for Eurasian and East European Research (NCEEER), an IREX Fellowship, an American Councils Fellowship, a State Department Critical Language Scholarship, and a Columbia University Travel Grant. I wish to thank these organizations for their generous support.

1. Groups commonly cited by Central Asian governments as "extremist" or "Wahhabi" include: Hizb-ut-Tahrir; the Islamic Movement of Uzbekistan; al-Qaeda; the Taliban; and Pakistan's Lashkar-e Taiba.

2. See http://www.azan.kz, accessed January 9, 2014.

3. See Tim Epkenhan (chapter 8, this volume) for more details on how popular religious authorities in Tajikistan avoid getting publicly involved with the High Council of ulamo—and even disregard their decrees.

4. *Partokratiia* refers to the nomenklatura-based ex-apparatchik ruling elites in the former Soviet Union.

5. In 1991, Yeltsin appointed Akhmet Arsanov, the grandson of Deni Arsanov (a famous Chechen Naqshbandi sheikh in the twentieth century), as the Russian presidential representative in Chechnya.

6. Born Said Atsayev.

7. For fatwas from Chechnya, see http://dumm.ru/catalog/80/sort/name/page_0, accessed January 9, 2014.

8. Today, at various Islam-related competitions held in Chechnya, contestants are rewarded for knowing about the lives of Sufi saints (*awliya*), and at religious foundations named after Sufi saints (e.g., Shaykh Abd al-Rahman al-Sughuri in Makhachkala) in Dagestan students are encouraged to learn about the spiritual history and achievements of Sufis in the region.

9. Numerous other religious figures have been killed recently in Dagestan, including the imam of the central mosque in the city of Buinaksk. In addition, Sirajudin Israfilov, the imam of a Sufi mosque in the town of Derbent, was shot dead in his home. Chirkeisky had an estimated 10,000 to 50,000 religious pupils, yet over 100,000 people attended his funeral in the town of Chirkeisk. A previous assassination attempt on his life had failed in 2007.

10. See the newspaper *Islom Nuri* (1990), and the journals *Sovet Sharqi Musulmonlari, Movarounnahr Musulmonlari,* and *O'zbekiston Musulmonlari.*

11. For a summary of official points of view, see Aminov (1997, 531–37, section "Dini").

12. Anniversaries of Timur, Bobur, Ulug'bek have also been commemorated.

13. *Milliy Tiklanish,* October 21, 1997, 7. *Khoji Abdulghafur Razzoq Bukhoriy. Tariqatga Yo'llanma. Naqshbandija ta'limoti asosida* (Tashkent, 2003), 18–21. With a foreword by Najmiddin Komilov.

14. Sadriddin Salim Bukhari's *Dilda Yar* (1993), a popular book on the history, doctrine, zikr, and *adab* of the Naqshbandi Sufi order, emphasizes Bahauddin's support for honest laborers and the poor.

15. For instance, for Ramadan the nationally broadcast *Radio Oriat Dono*—FM 106.5 MHz—prepares several religious enlightenment (*dini-ma'rifi*) programs, including "Ramazon Fonusi" (Lighthouse of Ramadan) and "Ko'ngil Hilvati" (Paradise of the soul), in tandem with Sufi tales and Sufi philosophical essays, such as "Ihyo-ul-ulum ad-din" by Ghazzali (Olcott 2007b).

16. Born in 1939, Khaja Ahmadjon Makhdum Khanafi-Naqshbandi Mujaddidi is a well-known Sufi sheikh in Uzbekistan's Surxondaryo oblast. He received his first religious education from his father, Shoh-Murod Mukhdum, and then studied with a number of prominent Sufis, including Muhammadjan Hindustani. Mujaddidi runs a *hujra* to teach the principles of sharia and Sufism.

17. Born in 1916, Ghulom-ota Normat still resides in his native town of Kuyi Girvan, near Namangan. After the war, he joined the Namangan *halqa* and accepted a small group of students to whom he transmitted basic Sufi practices, including vocal zikr. He received his religious education in Sufi practices from his father Narmat-Muhammad.

18. Dowud-khon is from the Qadiriya brotherhood. Born in 1929, he lives in Namangan. He believes that zikr and ritual dance gave him special physical and

spiritual strength. In his hujra, which opened in 1983, Dowud-khon lectures on the proper reading of the Koran (*qira'at, tajwid*), on mystical poetry, and on Sufi rituals (*dhikr, jahr*).

19. For more on Muslim women "clerics" and religious authorities in Central Asia, see Fathi 1997, 2010; Harris 2004; Kandiyoti and Azimova 2004; Sultanova 2011.

20. See Peshkova (chapter 3, this volume) for an in-depth discussion of female healers in Uzbekistan.

21. In addition to these community gatherings, otinlar in Bukhara lead religious ceremonies for important holidays like Navruz and the birthday feast (*mavlud*) of the Prophet Muhammad. The Soviet attempt to politicize these local traditions illustrates how the overlapping rituals of Sufism and local practices in Central Asia forced the Soviets to occasionally change how these practices were framed. For instance, the Soviets banned Navruz as a "Muslim" holiday in the 1930s, but then they reinstated it as a "pre-Islamic" festival of "Zoroastrian" origin.

22. From the word "dastarkhan," meaning tablecloth.

23. Shrines were renovated during the Soviet period to showcase the region's cultural heritage, but not to encourage pilgrims to make use of these sacred sites.

24. The burial sites of Islamic saints, local rulers, learned scholars, warriors, or pre-Islamic figures have always been popular sites of pilgrimage in Uzbekistan. Some of the most popular pilgrimage sites in Uzbekistan are connected to the memory of the family of the Prophet Muhammad. For instance, the complex of Shah-i Zinda features the grave of the Prophet Muhammad's cousin Qusam ibn Abbas, who was killed near Samarkand in the late seventh century. Though Imam Ali, the Prophet Muhammad's cousin and son-in-law, never visited Central Asia, a number of shrines in Central Asia are associated with him, such as Shahimardan in Uzbekistan. Shrines dedicated to Imam Ali can also be found in Turkmenistan and throughout the Ferghana Valley. Thus, the memory of the Prophet and him is memorialized by the governmental embrace and promotion of these sacred spaces. Other popular shrines in Uzbekistan include those associated with prophets (such as Prophet Daniel), and famed theologians (Imam Muhammad ibn Ismail al-Bukhari).

25. Though Uwais-bobo (or Uwais al-Qarani) was a contemporary of the Prophet Muhammad, he never met him—yet he claimed to have received the teachings of the Prophet Muhammad through an inward transmission. Other tombs dedicated to this seventh-century prototypical Sufi saint are found in Damascus, Raqqa, and near Zabid in Yemen.

26. However, Sadriddin Salim Bukhoriy does mention one story about a Sufi sheikh who called upon the help of Bahauddin Naqshband against the Bolsheviks. Bukhoriy claims the deceased saint answered that the bad situation of Uzbek Muslims under the Bolsheviks was due to their lack of faith: neither jihad nor any other action save for the restraint and total belief of the believers would be acceptable to combat the Bolsheviks' repression.

27. In Uzbek, the term used for "saint" is *vali* or *pir* (Louw 2006). The term *pir* is usually used for the founder of a Sufi order (Bosworth 1995).

28. Fatkhullo Sharifzade (Fatkhulla Sharipov) was born in Kizyl, Tajikistan in

1942 and died on January 21, 1996. In 1989, he quit his position as a manager of the water service to serve as the mufti of the main mosque in Hissar.

29. Similarly, in my research in Kazakhstan and Kyrgyzstan, the only books on Sufism for sale at the mosques and nearby shops were books written by the local muftiate.

30. Through interviewing Sufi sheikhs, khatibs, ulema, professors, and Islamic scholars in Tajikistan, I acquired a rich understanding of the ways in which Sufism is supported at the national and local levels.

31. Haji Isma'il Pirmuhammad-zadeh, an imam in the Hissar region of Tajikistan, is the leader of the Naqshbandi–Mujaddidiya brotherhood. He had few students during Soviet rule, but now runs a large hujra at his mosque.

32. For this research, I visited all the major shrines in Turkmenistan to record the rituals practiced at these shrines, interview those visiting the shrines about their pilgrimages, and study how shrine pilgrimage and the beliefs underlying it play a prime role in religious expression in Turkmenistan and create a unique and communal religious identity that is intimately tied by the authorities at the state level to the national project.

33. In 1987, there were only four functioning mosques in the Turkmen SSR; by 1992, there were already eighty-three.

34. President Niyazov deported as many as three hundred foreign Islamic teachers in 2000. In June 2001, the government closed the madrasa in the town of Dashoguz, leaving only one institution in the country available to provide Islamic education— the theological faculty at the Turkmen State University in Ashgabat, which has been merged with the history department. When I tried to enter the university, I was denied access.

Chapter Six. Unregistered

1. KRBMA 2597/2s/131/39 (March 13, 1988). KRMBA refers to the archival records of the Council for the Affairs of Religious Cults (CARC) and the CRA.

2. The Central Asian muftiate's formal title was the Spiritual Assembly of the Muslims of Central Asia and Kazakhstan (Russian, *Sredneaziatskoe dukhovnoe upravlenie musul'man*; Uzbek, O'rta Osiyo va Qozog'iston Musulmonlari Idorasi).

3. On Soviet citizens' recourse to the shadow economy for obtaining basic supplies and goods, see Feldbrugge 1984; Hessler 2004, 251–96; and Moskoff 1990, 94–112.

4. Unregistered Orthodox practices in the USSR have received little scholarly attention. For a recent discussion of Soviet policies against Orthodox shrine pilgrimage, see Panchenko 2012.

5. The 1929 Law on Religious Associations specified the procedure for establishing a house of worship but had nothing to say about informal congregations or itinerant religious figures. That this omission was not addressed during Stalin's 1943–44 religious reforms is due to the likelihood that such a prohibition would have encumbered the wartime state's attempts to fuel patriotic sentiment using religion. Its enforcement, moreover, would have entailed widespread police action at a time when memories of the Great Terror remained fresh.

6. Decrees of the Communist Party's Central Committee served as a tacitly acknowledged body of "law" that could override legislation formally codified by the Soviet government (Solomon 1996).

7. KRBMA 2597/2s/3/15 (October 17, 1945).

8. KRBMA 2597/1s/1/128 (September 30, 1946).

9. KRBMA 2597s/1s/4/251 (March 13, 1947).

10. During the 1940s the number of registered mosques numbered in the single digits in each of the Central Asian republics (Ro'i 2000, 183–98).

11. CARC's first chairman, Ivan Vasil'evich Polianskii (d. 1956), was an NKVD colonel (Bociurkiw 1996, 69).

12. KRBMA 2597/1s/11/42 (March 31, 1949). In one particularly egregious example, CARC forwarded the names of 495 unregistered figures across Kyrgyzstan to the republican Ministry of Finance, with no results. KRBMA 2597/1s/10/20 (April 15, 1949).

13. These included Article 19 of the Order of the USSR Supreme Soviet dated April 30, 1943 ("On Income Taxes from the Population"), a "Clarification" from the People's Commissariat of Finance dated April 17, 1944, a law of the Council of Ministers dated December 3, 1946 ("On the Procedure for Taxing Religious Cult Functionaries") and Circular Letter No. 870 of the Ministry of Finance dated December 13, 1946, of the same name (Chumachenko 2002, 79–81).

14. KRBMA 2597/1s/10/187 (January 13, 1950).

15. KRBMA 2597/1s/12/64 (December 16, 1949). This very likely stemmed from the fact that the laws' authors principally had in mind functionaries of the Russian Orthodox Church, which, due to its historically hierarchical structure, dealt with a miniscule number of unregistered priests.

16. KRBMA 2597/1s/4/392 (January 22, 1948).

17. Postanovlenie TsK KPSS ot 10 noiabria 1954 g. "Ob oshibkakh v provedenii nauchno-ateisticheskoi propagandy sredi naseleniia" (Zalesskii and Kupchenia 1983, 62–63).

18. KRBMA 2597/1s/28/12 (April 22, 1953).

19. KRBMA 2597/1s/28/12 l. 3 (May 6, 1953).

20. KRBMA 2597/1s/25/297 (January 13, 1953). Akhtiamov did express astonishment, though, underlining this sentence in the report and noting in the margin: "A mosque has been functioning since 1924 and the district government does not know about it?!"

21. KRBMA 2597/1s/28/149 (July 6, 1953).

22. KRBMA 2597/1s/29/57–8 (October 5, 1953). As was often the case in Central Asia, his authority stemmed from kinship. Tagaev's father, Togay Satylganov, was considered a "great mullah" until he and his family were exiled from Przheval'sk to Ukraine in 1930 or 1931 as kulaks. Tagaev studied religion with his father in exile, and when the latter died toward the end of the war in Ukraine, he returned to Kyrgyzstan.

23. KRBMA 2597/1s/29/65 (October 5, 1953).

24. BM JT 1516/1/59/5 (December 1957).

25. KRBMA 2597/1s/45/119 (December 13, 1955). In the words of the deputy in Osh, "the women who do not have children but want to [get pregnant] gather in one building

where Akrom to'ra eshon engages in various bodily movements [as if] copulating with them, and pushes some so far to the point of exasperation that they express a supposed desire for sexual relations. One must note that the husbands intentionally send their wives to Akram to'ra eshon for this kind of 'healing' even though they know about all this."

26. BM JT 1516/1/49/2 (October 9, 1956).

27. BM JT 1516/1/44/20 (April 2, 1955). As he noted, "among them only ten or eleven people possess some ability to read and can manage a tiny bit with some of the principal dogmas of Ismailism. The rest are almost completely illiterate."

28. KRBMA 2597/1s/70/74 (November 25, 1958).

29. KRBMA 2597/1s/61/124 (January 22, 1958).

30. These practices, of course, may or may not have been the defining feature of an individual's religiosity or a barometer of religion's importance in his or her identity and life.

31. BMJT 1516/1/85/98 (May 26, 1960).

32. On Khrushchev's idealism, see LaPierre 2012.

33. During the antireligious campaign, SADUM lost the autonomy it had enjoyed in the 1950s, with severe restrictions placed on its fundraising channels. Even in the realm of registered religion, however, the muftiate fared much better than the Russian Orthodox Church. As the Metropolitan Nikolai (1892–1961) told CAROC chairman Karpov shortly before resigning from his bishopric, "the current line aims to destroy the church, and religion generally, in even more systematic and thorough fashion than in the 1920s" (Danilushkin 1997, 495).

34. O'zRMDA r-2456/1/515/23 (early 1971).

35. On the history of this vitally significant shrine, see Ogudin 2003.

36. KRBMA 2597/1s/79/21–2 (June 30, 1959).

37. Little reliable information exists concerning this community. The documentation lists twenty sheikhs at the shrine, five of them "chief sheikhs," and features biographical information on some of them. If the representatives are to be believed, a number of them had participated in the *qurboshi* resistance and some even had criminal records for violent behavior. Nishan Madaliev, for example, spent eight years in prison in the 1930s for "beating someone almost to death" in the course of a scuffle. Another sheikh, identified only by the surname Abbos, "is himself a narcotics user and all the *anasha* smokers and narcotics addicts congregate at his place." It goes without saying that this information merits a healthy dose of skepticism, given the anticlerical spirit of the day and the representatives' long-standing loathing and frustration with the unregistered at the Throne of Solomon. KRBMA 2597/1s/83/89 (April 15, 1959).

38. This decree marked the commencement of Khrushchev's antireligious campaign in Central Asia. RGANI 5/33/125/1–109 (1959).

39. KRBMA 2597/1s/83 181 (April 10, 1959).

40. KRBMA 2597/1s/95/10 (February 15, 1962).

41. KRBMA 2597/1s/99/30 (May 22, 1963).

42. KRBMA 2597/1s/101/3 (February 25, 1964).

43. KRBMA 2597/1s/104/20 (June 10, 1964).

44. KRBMA 2597/1s/99/4 (March 18, 1963).

45. KRBMA 2597/1s/83/66 (March 25, 1959).

46. KRBMA 2597/1s/87/29 (June 2, 1961).

47. KRBMA 2597/1s/98/34 (February 1963).

48. KRBMA 2597/2s/49/30 (February 23, 1961). A local bureaucrat lamented that urban authorities ignored his repeated requests to replace the sheikh "with an honest person."

49. Although the sheikhs remained in place, the number of pilgrims descending upon the Throne of Solomon on 'Eid ul-Adha decreased by 80–90 percent after the campaign's inauguration and never fully recovered to levels of the 1950s. This radical change resulted from measures taken by Uzbekistan's KGB to block trucks, buses, and other vehicles carrying pilgrims to the Throne of Solomon and other major shrines in the days preceding 'Eid ul-Adha during the campaign years. Thus, although the campaign failed to unseat any sheikhs from the shrine, it did have a dramatic effect on the character of Central Asian shrine pilgrimage, which, ethnographic accounts and oral histories suggest, became more centered on weekly visits to local community shrines rather than annual pilgrimages to high-profile sites throughout the 1960s–1980s.

50. KRBMA 2597/1s/79/40–41 (June 25, 1959).

51. For more on the fascinating story of this shrine-cum-state health resort, and its virtual takeover by an extended family of dynastic sheikhs in the 1950s, see Tasar (forthcoming).

52. Such punitive taxes could range in amount from the highly dramatic figure of 134,000 rubles assessed upon five unfortunate unregistered figures in 1960 in Tajikistan to the more typical figure of 61 to 85 rubles, which roughly corresponded to the average monthly salary at the time. BMJT 1516/1/85/55 (June 11, 1960); 1516/2/36/30 (May 4, 1964); 1516/2/47/38 (July 7, 1965).

53. The sources have little to say about their membership. It appears likely that their composition depended on personal relationships and local dynamics.

54. In 1985 alone, Kyrgyzstan's commissions "heard and analyzed around 1,000 of the clergy's sermons." By 1986 they had compiled a list of 648 unregistered figures in the republic, compared to 368 in 1984 and 250 in 1972. In the same year, one report noted that 66 provincial and district commissions functioned alongside 406 "assistance groups" at the village and collective farm level, which met "every quarter or every month" to "hear reports about the work of rural and village assistance groups, analyze sermons, and transmit the results of visits to prayer houses and information about violations [of the law] uncovered therein." KRBMA 2597/2s/128/5 (February 12, 1986); 2597/2s/130/32 (January 30, 1987); 2597/2s/120/154 (February 20, 1984); 2597/2s/93/105 (February 22, 1972); 2597/2s/130/56 (January 30, 1987).

55. GARF r-6991/6/1345/39–41 (April 5, 1978).

56. O'zR MDA r-2456/1/674/52 (January 13, 1983).

57. KRBMA 2597/2s/120/102 (February 18, 1983).

58. GARF r-6991/6/1798/6 (February 18, 1980).

59. KRBMA 2597/2s/89/39 (February 16, 1967).

60. KRBMA 2597/2s/92/75 (October 21, 1971).

61. GARF r-6991/6/1345/41 (April 5, 1978).

62. GARF r-6991/6/1348/38 (August 14, 1978).

63. O'zRMDA r-2456/1/674/53 (January 13, 1983) and 60 (January 17, 1983).

64. GARF r-6991/6/1798/6 (February 18, 1980). The total tax came to 6,100 rubles or roughly 200 rubles per individual, a considerable amount encompassing several months' salary for the average citizen.

65. The CRA instructed republican representatives to explore the idea at some point in the mid-1970s. As the representative in Kyrgyzstan reported, "as regards the experiment of attaching certain unregistered *moldo*s to registered mosques, so far we have only made the first few steps. In one of the districts in Osh province, we attached two such functionaries to a mosque. . . . We will position these attached functionaries as assistants to the primary imams, to avoid any violations of legislation concerning religious cults." KRBMA 2597/2s/102/159 (December 2, 1976). Other documentation explicitly stated that "attachment" occurred "at the recommendation of the Council." KRBMA 2597/2s/109/22 (February 15, 1979).

66. Apparently local officials had much leverage in selecting these figures. Undoubtedly everything depended on interpersonal relations and connections, offering an echo of the ad hoc relationships that defined Church–state relations in the mid-1930s. As one reported noted, "the most loyal part of the unregistered clergy" underwent "attachment" "with the agreement of local organs of power." KRBMA 2597/2s/125/38 (February 18, 1985).

67. KRBMA 2597/2s/102/159 (December 2, 1976).

68. KRBMA 2597/2s/125/38 (February 18, 1985).

69. KRBMA 2597/2s/130/33 (January 30, 1987). Of the 20,300 rubles in charity received by the one registered mosque in Talas province in 1982, for example, 16,700 rubles came from its 57 "attached" mullas. In 1986 the corresponding figures for the same mosque were 18,000 out of 21,500 rubles, while the registered mosque in the mountain settlement of At-Bashy, Naryn province, received 7,009 of its 9,434 rubles in receipts that year from unregistered mullas.

70. KRBMA 2597/2s/130/111 (December 24, 1987).

71. Here I do not mean to suggest that the closure of illegal mosques did not take place. It did. Throughout the 1970s the authorities shuttered an average of 5–10 such prayer houses in Kyrgyzstan a year. The number of unregistered mosques known to the CRA in the republic dropped from 138 in 1979 to 75 in 1980 to 36 in 1981. However, without additional information it is impossible to assess the precise impact of these actions. Closure had taken place before. In the last years of the 1940s, for example, zealous local government officials routinely closed down mosques but imposed no monitoring mechanism, meaning that in the space of as little as a few days believers could reassemble in the structure once more—often for many years with no retaliation.

72. KRBMA 2597/2s/121/3–4 (April 19, 1983). The "Islamic Factor" is a concept coined by Soviet political scientists to refer to the political instability Islam could supposedly generate among Muslims, worldwide and in the Soviet Union (e.g., Polonskaia 1986, 13–14).

73. KRBMA 2597/2s/105/33 (August 7, 1981). The emphasis on the unregistered connection of this Muslim activation emerged in a CRA decree lambasting the representative in Qurghon Tappa: "Among the unregistered clergy there is a not inconsiderable number of charlatans and swindlers [*avantiuristov*], who transmit every variety of provocative rumor bearing an antisocial character. It should not be forgotten that the unregistered clergy is betting on imperialism and the foreign Islamic reaction in its aspiration to fan the flames of religio-nationalistic sentiment among Soviet Muslims." KRBMA 2597/2s/105/26 (July 24, 1981). Again, none of this rhetoric translated into any apparent policy action on the ground.

74. KRBMA 2597/2s/121/8–9 (April 27, 1983). "Proponents of these [Shiite] formations are almost considered blasphemes from the Muslim faith by the Muslim believers of our republic."

75. KRBMA 2597/2s/121/3 (April 19, 1983).

Chapter Seven. The Ascendance of Orthodoxy

1. From a storied well in the Kaaba in Mecca.

2. These categories are purely heuristic. They do not encompass all aspects of Central Asian Islamic spirituality. Although Vernon James Schubel (2010, 459) identifies a similar set of three categories, Adeeb Khalid suggests that pre-Soviet occupational guilds were another important site of spiritual education and practice (1998, 28; see also Sultanova 2011, 66–68). These traditions interact and inform each other in ways I address below, which is to say that this scheme should not be taken as a revival of the orientalist distinction between scholarly/urban/literate Islam and folk/rural/illiterate Islam.

3. This was true primarily in settled areas. Among nomadic groups, access to education was intermittent and depended on periodic visits from traveling clerics from the settled regions (Khalid 1998, 26–27). There is less documentation of female education, but girls and young women also acquired some education, probably in the homes of female religious authorities called *otin-oyis* (Fathi 2006; Khalid 1998, 27).

4. The "scope" of religion is "the range of social contexts within which religious considerations are regarded as having more or less direct relevance" (Geertz 1968, 112).

5. Although I do not address the colonial period specifically, these processes had already begun under the tsarist regime (see, e.g., Abdurakhimova 2002).

6. *Sredneaziatskoe dukhovnoe upravlenie musul'man.*

7. An extensive network of unregistered congregations, study circles, and Sufi orders continued to operate. These were led by clerics who either did not want or were unable to register with SADUM (Ro'i 2000, 345). See Tasar (chapter 6, this volume) for a carefully researched discussion of the persistence of unregistered religious activity during the Soviet era.

8. Even practices that had only tenuous links to Islam, once they were associated with a "Muslim" ethnic group, were newly constructed as Muslim. This was true, for example, of Nooruz, a holiday in March that celebrates the coming of spring. During the Soviet era, it came to be known as "Muslim New Year," since it was most popular in Muslim regions of the USSR, even though it is more likely to have originated in Zoroastrianism (Khalid 2007, 99).

9. Anyone with professional ambitions, much less ambitions within the Communist Party, was wise not to betray religious convictions publicly.

10. This is not to suggest that Islam was not long an important component in local identities. See M. Nazif Shahrani (1984) on Central Asia and Abdessamad Dialmy (2007) for a broader discussion of Islam and identity.

11. A certain amount of disagreement persisted, particularly between SADUM and individual congregations. See Ro'i's exhaustive discussion (2000, 121–34).

12. "Kyrgyzstani" refers to the Kyrgyz Republic. "Kyrgyz" refers to the ethnic group.

13. At independence, Kyrgyzstan had thirty-nine mosques. As of 2009, there were over seventeen hundred mosques, six religious colleges, and one university (USDS 2011, 1). It is common knowledge in Kyrgyzstan that Middle Eastern, especially Arab sources, have funded a significant quantity of the growing number of mosques and madrasas and provide scholarships for students to study Islam in Kyrgyzstan and abroad (e.g., Abramson 2010; Bissenova 2005).

14. SCRA's refusal to register a group of Ahmadiyya Muslims, whose interpretation of Islam contrasts sharply with that of the Muftiate (but is not political or extremist) can be understood as a sign of the state's willingness to uphold the Muftiate's authority (Bayram and Kinahan 2014, 6).

15. See Julie McBrien (2006), who examines state fears of extremist Islam.

16. A book on Islam for children includes a picture of a young boy kissing the Kyrgyz flag. Underneath the picture are words taken from a Hadith: "Faith means loving one's homeland" (Seidalieva 2012, 7).

17. Most Central Asians still use Persian-derived words for God, (e.g., *Kudai* in Kyrgyz). The most devout Muslims prefer the Arabic "Allah," but even they often use both. For simplicity's sake, I use "God," noting usage in direct quotations.

18. Nearly all the books I cite here include the following statement on the copyright page: "This book has been printed with the permission of the Spiritual Directorate of Kyrgyzstan Muslims," together with a number and a date.

19. Koran interpretations are given in Kyrgyz in the pamphlet. I have provided the relevant passages from a recognized English version. This is taken from Arberry (1955, 339).

20. The speaker is referring to sections of the Koran, not the entire Koran.

21. This is not to say that official Islam does not value community. Many of the Muftiate's texts and sermons include advice about solving problems in the family or neighborhood, but the advice usually identifies changes in individual behaviors that can ideally improve social relations.

22. In a survey of Muslims in four Central Asian republics, Ro'i and Wainer (2009, 307) found that 22 percent of respondents prayed five times a day and 12 percent prayed once or twice a day.

23. Unfortunately, the article is no longer accessible. I last accessed it June 6, 2013.

24. Here I draw on Geertz's account of Islam in Morocco, where faithful varied from viewing the Koran as a "fetish radiating barakah" to venerating it as "a body of precepts to be memorized, comprehended, and observed" (Geertz 1968: 73).

Interestingly, official Islam in Kyrgyzstan includes observances that depend on belief in the holiness of the physical manifestation of scripture. For example, the faithful are directed not to handle a Koran without first performing ritual ablutions (*daarat*) (e.g., Ibraev 2013, 8).

25. It is also possible that the shared rejection of shirk indexes a shared Islamic heritage, but this seems less likely in light of other ethnographic evidence. Rasanayagam's study in Uzbekistan, for example, reveals discursive shifts among traditional healers who only since independence have begun to construct their power and authority in ways that align with scripturalist discourses against shirk and bidayat (2006b).

Chapter Eight. Islam, Religious Elites, and the State in Post–Civil War Tajikistan

1. About 90 percent of Tajikistan's population (in 2015, eight million) are Sunni Muslims of the Hanafi law school. Some 3 percent are Ismaili Muslims of the Nizari *tariqa* (path) who recognize the Agha Khan as their forty-ninth hereditary imam. Tajikistan's Ismaili community regulates its religious affairs reclusively and there is virtually no interaction between Sunni and Ismaili religious specialists; therefore, this chapter deals with only Sunni Muslims and their leaders.

2. For a few years now, private media in print and online, such as the Tajik weeklies *Millat* (www.millat.tj), *Nigoh*, *Ozodigon* (www.ozodagon.com), *Tojikiston* (www. tojnews.org), *Faraj* (www.faraj.tj), and the private media group Asia Plus (www. islamnews.tj) have established special rubrics and report frequently about Islamic affairs and religious authorities.

3. Although survey data on religious perception in Tajikistan should be handled with care (see, e.g., Ro'i and Wainer 2009), both the available data and qualitative research confirm a significant increase of religious activities among the population.

4. Similar developments can be observed in Kazakhstan and Uzbekistan, where Nazarbayev and Karimov have identified a "good" traditional (local) and a "bad" nontraditional (foreign) Islam (Karimov 1998; Nazarbaev 2003).

5. The Arabic plural term *ulema* (Tajik: *ulamo*) means generally "scholars" but is used almost exclusively for the Islamic sciences. Islamic religious specialists are frequently described as "clergy" or "clergymen," a term insinuating a formal hierarchy, which does not exist in an Islamic context. Thus, I prefer to apply the original Arabic/ Tajik terms.

6. Transparency International ranks Tajikistan among the most corrupt regimes (154th out of 178), Freedom House considers the country as "not free." Some 1 million Tajiks, predominantly men, are on seasonal and permanent labor migration in Russia and face increasing xenophobic violence and appalling living conditions. Since 2008 the population in the Rasht/Gharm Valley (east of Dushanbe) has experienced continuous violence between local armed groups and government security forces. There were violent clashes in Kulob (2008), Khujand (2010), and in Gorno-Badakhshan Autonomous Region's capital Khorugh (2012 and 2014).

7. While the majority of scholars associate the perestroika and glasnost years in the

1980s with the Islamic revival in Central Asia, Stéphane Dudoignon (2011) identifies earlier periods of Islamic revival in Soviet Tajikistan, initially with the establishment of "official" religious institutions between 1943 and 1948, followed by the general amnesty 1953 after Stalin's demise. The "mutation" is associated with political Islamic activists in Central Asia challenging not only the political system but also the authority of the established religious specialists, who initiated the "revival" in the 1950s and 1960s.

8. An imam khatib (or *sarkhatib*) as "leader of a prayer" organizes the important congregational Friday prayer in a Friday mosque.

9. Friday mosques (*masjidi jome*) as well as the regular five-times-daily-prayer mosques (*masjidi panj vaqta*) and their religious personnel have to be registered with the authorities and according to the DRA in 2010, there were 314 registered Friday mosques and some 3,000 regular five-times-prayer mosques in Tajikistan.

10. In 2004, I was able to observe a negotiation between local communities and authorities regarding a mosque in southern Tajikistan. Since the suggested imam khatib would have created tensions with the authorities and ultimately have been rejected by the regional representative of the DRA, local government representatives suggested recommending a less well-known person, who was eventually appointed. However, the initially suggested imam khatib worked "unofficially" in the mosque. The reluctance to enforce the appointment or dismissal of an imam khatib by the High Council of Ulema and the DRA might be related to Turajonzoda's term in office as *qozi-kalon*. Turajonzoda had successfully negotiated the statutes for the *qoziyot* with the then Council of Ministers in June 1991 (before independence) and increased the independence of his office. These statutes gave him far-reaching competences to hire and fire imam khatibs.

11. http://islamnews.tj/tajikistan/564-v-tadzhikistane-nachalas-proverka-deyatelnosti-imam-hatibov-sobornyh-mechetey.html, accessed February 20, 2013.

12. This paper is based on long-term fieldwork in Tajikistan since 2002. Since then, I have surveyed seventeen religious specialists in southern (i.e., Khatlon and the districts under Republican administration) and eight in northern (Sughd) Tajikistan.

13. Interestingly, some academics loyal to the government and representatives of urban civil society have cultivated a discourse on the alleged "tolerant" and moderating impact of Sufism on religious communities in recent years, which, however, resonates more with international academics and diplomats (Olcott 2007) than with the perceptions and practices of local religious communities (see O'Dell, chapter 5, this volume).

14. This is apparently changing gradually. Although foreign religious education is still a highly contested issue (Abramson 2010), with an increasing number of religious specialists graduating from Islamic universities, the acceptance and importance of formal degrees might increase.

15. Conversely, a refusal to register with the DRA generates religious capital as well, although with a different audience in mind.

16. Qumsangiri passed away on November 22, 2012, during the drafting of this chapter.

17. Nuriddinjon was appointed imam khatib of Xalifa Abdulkarim Friday mosque.

However, he resigned in January 2011 (with ten other imam khatibs in the Dushanbe area) and his younger brother Mahmud asumed the position until the mosque's demotion to a five-times-daily-prayer mosque in May 2012 (Nozimova and Epkenhans 2013).

18. The Qadiriyya (which originally emerged in Bagdad in the twelfth century) and Naqshbandi (which originated in Bukhara in the fourteenth century) are Sunni Sufi orders and represent a "normative" interpretation of the Islamic tradition. Formalized structures, for instance "convents" (*xonagoh*, *zawiya*, or *tekke*), have not been reestablished in post-Soviet Central Asia and the teaching circles (*halqa* or *mahfil*, sometimes "cells"—*hujra*) work informally.

19. The funeral of *domullo* Pir Muhammad "Sangi Kulula" close to Sari Xosor in the remote Baljuvan district (east of the Norak reservoir and north of Danghara) in 1968 was attended by several thousand mourners and turned—according to local lore—into a popular demonstration of the people's repudiation of Soviet atheist propaganda (Dudoignon 2011, 75; Nasriddinov 1995, 296).

20. Especially the concept of *xalvat dar anjoman* is central to the Naqshbandi tradition (Algar 1976) demanding from a follower a strict devotion to God without neglecting his political role in society.

21. Information based on observations and conversations with Pir Ismoil Muhammadzoda during March and September/October 2010 in Dushanbe and Hisor. Pir Ismoil conducts various rites of passage, such as *nikoh* (marriage), *xatnazur* (circumcision), and *janozat* (funeral) services, for members of the dominating elite. However, he also "performs" at more mundane events, such as the opening of a restaurant or another business.

22. Information is based on interviews with *dehqon* farmers in Vahdat and Fayzobod in July 2003, March 2004, and August 2008. Futurists' deals (i.e., companies that supply farmers with seeds and other inputs for a fixed price below market rates) have ruined many of Tajikistan's cotton-farming communities (see ICG 2005a).

23. In March 2009, the state news agency Khovar and the government mouthpiece *Jumhuriyat* (March 20, 2009) published an article in which a Tajik journalist in Moscow presented the alleged KGB file of Turajonzoda under the alias "Abdukarimov" (after his grandfather). According to this "file," Turajonzoda was recruited by the KGB in 1971 (during his undergraduate studies at Miri Arab) and reported frequently to Tashkent and Moscow. Considering the strong anti-Uzbek sentiment in Tajikistan, the innuendo that Turajonzoda is an Uzbek spy has a serious connotation (http://www.jumhuriyat.tj/index.php?art_id=1925, accessed May 3, 2013).

24. S. Rašidzoda, "Masjid joi ibodat ast, na joi siyosat," *Faraj* 8 (325), February 20, 2013, 1, 10.

25. I am grateful to Johan Rasanayagam for a lively discussion on Bourdieu that needs to be continued.

26. Between 2008 and 2012, I collected 142 recordings (*nasihat*, *xutba*, and *posuxi pursišho*) of six different religious specialists, often with the label *amr ba ma'ruf.* The audio and video DVDs of popular imams—such as Hoji Mirzo, who attracts a younger audience—are distributed promptly nationwide and sold inexpensively (sometimes for less than one somoni, around twenty cents in United States dollars).

27. The IRPT also maintains Facebook (https://www.facebook.com/www
.nahzat.tj) and Twitter (https://twitter.com/nahzat_tj) accounts as well as a YouTube
channel (http://www.youtube.com/user/nahzattj). The IRPT homepage operates a
"flag counter" that identifies the Web site's visitors. In September 2012, 30 percent (or
9,600) were from Tajikistan, 22 percent from Russia, 9 percent from the United States,
followed by Germany, Egypt, and Iran (each with some 4.5 percent). The Turajon Web
page does not have a "flag counter," but in the question-and-answer section (see below)
a significant percentage of questions come from Tajiks in Russia.

28. The design of the Web site www.turajon.com was relatively stable, but in
October 2012 the architecture of the site was changed completely. The *suol va javob*
section from Nuriddinjon could be found at http://www.turajon.com/lib/savolu_
javob/nuriddin.htm (accessed October 10, 2012) and only selections of the *suol va javob*
section were copied into the new one at http://www.turajon.org/faq.php, accessed
October 12, 2012. Since 2013, the Web site has operated stably under the URL www.
turajon.org (Nozimova and Epkenhans 2013).

29. The separation of the ritual (*ibodot*) from the law (*mu'omalot*) is a modern
construct and often fails to "appreciate both the *legal* ramifications of *'ibādāt* rituals
and the *moral* ramifications of those 'strictly legal' provisions of *mu'ālamāt*" (Hallaq
2010, 144).

30. Hanafi scholars are not in agreement regarding women's mosque attendance.
See Epkenhans 2010, 334; http://www.rferl.org/content/article/1055440.html, accessed
October 10, 2012.

31. For instance, *Safinai Umed* publishes a series of articles on female personalities
in early Islamic history with a strong idealization of their specific female qualities.
"Bonuvoni sahoba: Asmo," *Safinai Umed* 1 (2012), 36–38.

32. See Nuriddinjon *Nasihat ba javonon* DVD 1 (2009). Hoji Mirzo, who supports
a nongovernmental organization project against domestic violence in Kulob, made a
similar statement (DVD *Dar bobi modar*, 2009).

33. Holiqov was replaced in February 2015 as chairman of the DRA by Sulaymon
Davlatov, the former rector of the Islamic University.

34. A copy of the official (and obviously confidential) letter circulated on several
Tajik Web sites such as that of the IRPT (http://www.nahzat.tj/1/item/6344-maktubi-
kumitai-dina-protokolro-zamina-mesozad, accessed May 13, 2013).

35. The last official campaign to promote Zoroastrianism took place in the
early 2000s with the publication of a university history textbook by the Ministry
of Education (Ne'matov 2003) and an essay by (then) adviser of President Rahmon
Ibrohim Usmonov (2001).

36. *Vovchik* is an abbreviation of *vahhabovchik* for "Wahhabi," a term used for the
"opposition" in the civil war. Followers of the government were dubbed *yurchik*, from
the Russian given name Yuri.

37. In an interview shortly before his assassination, Sangak Safarov claimed descent
from a sayyid family (i.e., the family of the Prophet Muhammad) and maintained that
his grandfather was ešoni Sulton, an eminent local religious authority in the Darvoz,
Tavildara, and Qarategin region. Ešoni Sulton competed with a prominent Basmachi

leader, Faizal Maksum, and was eventually executed by him 1922. Safarov framed his motivation to fight against the Garmis/Qaroteginis in terms of revenge for his grandfather. In addition, he portrayed his uncle, Mullo Abdulhaq, as a mixture of an Islamic saint and Iranian mythological hero or an image modeled after Ferdousi's *Shahname* (Medvedev 1994, 188–90).

38. The construction of the Friday mosque for a congregation of approximately 50,000 is a joint venture with Qatar, which contributes two-thirds of the budget. http://www.ozodi.org/content/article/24351221.html, accessed May 3, 2013.

39. See *Jumhuriyat*, July 9, 2009, "Imomi A'zam va ahloqi umumiinsoni." The article was reproduced on the *Khovar* homepage, http://khovar.tj/archive/7549-imomi-azam-va-ahloi178i-umumiinsoni250.html, accessed May 3, 2013.

40. Rahmon's interpretation of Abu Hanifa coincided in time with the repercussions of the 2008 financial and economic crisis on Tajikistan. While the economy and—most important—the remittances from labor migrants in Russia did not contract in 2008, the crisis hit Tajikistan seriously in 2009–10.

41. Rudaki was a ninth-century poet (born in Panjikent) and Kaykavus b. Iskander was the eleventh-century author of a Persian mirror for princes, known as *Qabus-nama* or *Nasihat-nama*.

42. The celebrations culminated in an international symposium, "The Heritage of Imam Azam Abu Hanifa and Its Significance in the Dialogue of Civilizations," under the auspices of Rahmon in October 2009 with some five hundred invited participants (among them the late sheikh al-Azhar, Tantawi).

43. Interview with a government official in Dushanbe, March 2010.

44. Interview with a government official in Dushanbe, March 2010. The textbook was composed by an authors' collective recruited from the Oriental Studies Department, Ministry of Culture, Ministry of Education and the DRA.

45. The law regulates ceremonies and festivities related to *zodruz* (birthday, only to be celebrated within the family, §3.8), *xatnazur* (circumcision, to be celebrated with a maximum of 60 guests and only one meal, §3.9), *tuyi* (wedding, two celebrations are allowed with a maximum of 350 guests, §3.10), *janoza* (funeral, maximum 80 guests can be invited for the *ta'om*—funeral feast, §3.11).

46. The chairman of the DRA (four since 2002) is traditionally a (former) MVD/KGB official with a university degree in Oriental studies.

47. *Sredneaziatskoe dukhovnoe upravlenie musul'man.*

48. Abdulqodirzoda, a Kulobi, was until 2010 a relatively unknown official in the DRA. He is a graduate of the International Islamic University in Islamabad and has taught at the Islamic University al-Tirmizi in Dushanbe.

49. The university's dean and teaching staff were replaced and the teaching program was changed to BA and MA programs (interview with a former lecturer at the university in Dushanbe, December 2010).

50. http://www.ozodi.org/content/article/2245826.html, accessed October, 5, 2012. Interestingly, the IRPT did not reject the directive on principle, but suggested issuing the list monthly (instead of biannually or annually) in order to respond to recent developments.

51. On the tenth of the Islamic months Muharram (*aśura*), Shiites commemorate the martyrdom of al-Husayn, the third imam and son of Ali ibn Abi Talib (the cousin and brother-in-law of the Prophet Muhammad) in 680 CE.

52. H. Qosimi, "Zaruratu islohot dar šuroi ulamoi islomi," *Najot* 24 (June 13, 2012), 5–6. The Arabic term *fitna* has a connotation of secession, upheaval, and chaos within the (Muslim) community. Historically, fitna refers to the civil war within the Islamic caliphate after the assassination of Uthman in 656 AD.

53. http://www.ozodi.org/content/article/24598382.html, accessed May 3, 2013.

54. The High Council of Ulema and the Islamic University operate a department for legal advice (*fatvo*) and a Web site (http://muftiyat.tj/), which reportedly enjoys increasing popularity.

Chapter Nine. When Religion Resorts to Violence

1. The number of mosques and seminaries quadrupled and their attendance increased immensely since 1991. According to statistics of the Kyrgyz State Agency for Religious Affairs, in 1991 there were only 39 mosques in Kyrgyzstan. By 2005, their number had reached 2,500. The number of unregistered mosques and associations is several times higher than official figures, according to estimates by independent scholars.

2. The IMU was established in the late 1990s by a group of Uzbekistani émigré Muslim militants who escaped Uzbekistan in the early 1990s. The group fought alongside the United Tajik Opposition during the civil war in Tajikistan from 1993 to 1997. The IMU's stated goal is to overthrow the regime of the Uzbek president Islam Karimov.

3. Author's interviews with Kyrgyzstani scholars, Bishkek and Osh, August–September 2009.

4. Various restrictions on operations of foreign religious organizations that the government has imposed since 2006 made it difficult for foreign sponsors to fund the Nookat riots. Author's interview with local officials, Nookat, July 2009.

5. Author's interview with an HBT member, Kara-Suu, August 2009.

6. As one Kyrgyz observer with links to HBT claimed: "[Kyrgyz] officials claim that they are Muslims, but their policies show that they are infidels and agents of the West and Israel. They crack down on Muslims at the request of the Jews, and they allow the Americans to freely operate a military base. . . . Of course, Muslims must oppose these policies." Author's interview with a member of HBT, Kara-Suu, September 2009.

7. In a recent case, Mikhail Kalishevskii, a Moscow-based scholar of Central Asia, claimed that the wave of unrest in several Muslim countries in September 2012 set off by an American-made video that provided a negative depiction of the Prophet Muhammad was "the clash of civilizations, a confrontation between Islam and Christianity; therefore, the West's response must be firm." "Tsena svobody, ili plokhoe kino, vzorvavshee mir," *Ferghana.ru*, September 25, 2012, http://www.fergananews.com/article.php?id=7498.

8. Observant Muslims in southern Kyrgyzstan are aware that large Muslim

populations reside in Western countries and influence politics in their host countries through grassroots activism, elections, and mass media. Author's interviews with residents in Nookat, Kara-Suu, Aravan, and Uzgen, July–August 2009.

9. Manas Isakov, a former leader of Nookat's Muslim initiative group, which was accused of organizing the riot, is an ethnic Kyrgyz.

10. Author's interview with an imam khatib of the Aravan central mosque, July 2009.

11. Author's interview with imams in Osh and Aravan, June–July 2009.

12. Author's interview with Uzbek and Kyrgyz historians of Islam in Central Asia, Bishkek, and Tashkent, 1999.

13. Author's interview with Kyrgyz journalists, January 2005.

14. Author's interviews with local officials in Aravan, Kara-Suu, Nookat, and Uzgen, July–October 2009.

15. Author's interviews with local officials in Aravan, Kara-Suu, Nookat, and Uzgen, July–October 2009.

16. Author's interviews with local officials in Uzgen, Aravan, Nookat, and Kara-Suu, June–November 2009.

17. Author's interview with a local official, Kara-Suu, August 2009.

18. Interview with Ashurali, head of one of the Kara-Suu kvartal'nyi komitet, Kara-Suu, August 2009.

19. Interview with Abdulajjan Hamidov, an Aravan resident, October 2009.

20. Author's interviews with Abdulwohid Isabaev, Aravan, June 2009.

21. Author's interview with an Aravan local official, August 2009.

22. Author's interview with Abdygany Aliev, former head of the Nookat administration, July 2009.

23. "Anti-Terrorism Crackdown Fuels Discontent in Southern Kyrgyzstan," *EurasiaNet*, August 7, 2006, http://www.eurasianet.org/departments/insight/articles/eav080806.shtml.

24. "Anti-Terrorism Crackdown Fuels Discontent."

25. "V Kirgizii zametno aktivizirovalas' rabota Hizb-ut-Tahrir," *Kazakhstan Segodnia*, July 31, 2008.

26. Orozo-Ayt is a celebration to mark the end of the holy month of Ramadan. It is also known as the feast of "Eid-al-Fitr."

27. Author's discussions with local officials, journalists, and political analysts in Osh and Bishkek, July–August 2009.

28. Author's interview with Abdygany Aliev, the former akim of the Nookat raion, August 2009, and with Adaham Isakov, leader of the initiative group released from prison in May 2010, August 2012.

29. Author's interviews with local officials and residents, Nookat, August 2009.

30. Author's interviews with local officials and residents, Nookat, August 2009.

31. "Otchet po 'nookatskim sobytiiam' komissii pri Ombudsmene Kyrgyzskoi Respubliki," March 2, 2009.

32. Author's interview with Adaham Isakov, leader of the Nookat initiative group, August 2012.

33. Author's interview with Adaham Isakov, August 2012.

34. Author's interview with Nookat residents, July–August 2009.

35. Author's interview with Osh-based journalists, July–August 2009.

36. Author's interview with Abdygany Aliev, former akim of the Nookat raion, and several Nookat residents, August 2009.

37. Author's interview with Zahidzhan Abidzhanov, deputy head of the Nookat raion administration, August 2009.

38. Dmitrii Kabak and Dinara Saiakova, "Ekspertnoe zakliuchenie (Amicus curiae) po voprosu o sobliudenii prava na svobodu veroispovedaniia," May 13, 2009, http://prava.kloop.kg/?p=876.

39. Author's interview with Abdygany Aliev, former akim of the Nookat raion, August 2009.

40. Interview with Abdygany Aliev, August 2009.

41. Author's interview with Akram, a Nookat-based businessman, Nookat, July 2009.

42. Author's interview with a group of Nookat residents, August 2009.

43. Interview with Nookat residents, August 2009.

44. Author's interview with a Nookat-based businessman, Nookat, July 2009.

45. Author's interviews with Abdygany Aliev, Zahidzhan Abidzhanov, and two local officials in Nookat who requested anonymity, August 2009.

46. Author's interviews with eyewitnesses of the Nookat events, August 2009.

47. Author's interview with eyewitnesses of the Nookat events and Soip-qori, August 2009.

48. Interview with eyewitnesses of the Nookat events and Soip-qori, August 2009.

49. Interview with eyewitnesses of the Nookat events and Soip-qori, August 2009.

50. Author's interview with officials in Kara-Suu, July 2009.

51. Author's interview with Akhmat Rakhimov, the mayor of Kara-Suu, July 2009.

52. Interview with Akhmat Rakhimov, July 2009.

53. Author's interview with a group of Kara-Suu-based residents and clerics, July 2009.

54. Author's interview with Misha, an assistant to the Kara-Suu mayor, August 2009.

55. Interview with Misha, August 2009.

56. Interview with Misha, August 2009.

57. Interview with Misha, August 2009.

58. Author's interview with Kara-Suu residents.

59. Author's interview with Rakhimov Akhmad, the mayor of Kara-Suu, July 2009.

60. Author's interview with Akhmedov Sobir, chairman of the Kara-Suu kvartal'nye komitety council, July 2009.

61. Interview with Akhmedov Sobir, July 2009. Author's interview with Aiub, an HBT activist in Kara-Suu, August 2009.

62. "V Oshe rastet chislo storonnikov partii 'Hizb-ut-Tahrir,'" RFE/RL Russian Service, October 19, 2011, http://rus.azattyk.org/content/kyrgyzstan_islam_osh/24363972 .html. "Kadyr Malikov: esli v Ferganskoi doline budet aprobirovana teoriia 'uprav-

liaemogo khaosa,' to sushchestvuet ugroza dlia iuga Kyrgyzstana," *Information Agency 24.kg*, January 25, 2011.

Chapter Ten. The Localization of the Transnational Tablighi Jama'at Network in Kyrgyzstan

1. *Ziyarat* (Ar.) refers to pilgrimage to holy sites, but in TJ practice in Kyrgyzstan the term refers to visiting davatchys.

2. Author's field notes, Karakol, June 2012.

3. Author's interview, Osh, August 2012.

4. Tablighi practice that refers to the visit of davatchys to the neighborhood knocking on each door and inviting Muslims to the mosque to join in prayer.

5. Author's interview, Bishkek, September 2012.

6. Author's interview, Bishkek, September 2012.

7. *Fada'il-I A'mal* covers the virtues of salat, dhikr, charity, hajj, ritual salutation to the Prophet, and the Koran. For more information, see Reetz (2008, 2009b). In Kyrgyzstan, both Kyrgyz and Russian translations are used in taalim sessions.

8. Author's interview with Tablighi women, Bishkek, May 2012.

9. Author's interview with Jumabaev, Bishkek, September 2012.

10. Author's interview with Jumabaev, Bishkek, September 2012.

Chapter Eleven. Transnational Islamic Banks and Local Markets in Central Asia

The author gratefully acknowledges all the respondents who shared their insights and time. Thanks also to all the participants of the mini-conference on Islamic Finance, who provided feedback on the earlier version of this chapter presented as a paper at the Society for the Advancement of Socio-Economics conference in July 2013. The Central Asian Studies Institute of the American University of Central Asia hosted the author as a visiting fellow during fieldwork, and Hazeltine fellowship of Brown University provided financial support. Finally, gratitude is extended to Pauline Jones for inviting me to contribute to this edited volume as well as for her ongoing encouragement and support.

1. In this chapter, I include all these types of financial companies in IFIs as well as brokerage and insurance companies that identify themselves as sharia-compliant.

2. *Riba* is a prohibition on charging interest due to the view of interest as exploitative (Mills 1999), in contrast to profit earned by active labor. *Gharar* is the prohibition of ambiguous and uncertain contracts. Hence, transactions should avoid "all contracts that contain uncertain counter values in exchange (e.g., the sale of fruit before it has ripened)" (Mills 1999, 5).

3. I call these two perspectives undersocialized economic and oversocialized cultural for their exaggerated emphasis on economic incentives and cultural identity, respectively.

4. Kyrgyzstan became an IDB member in 1993 and Kazakhstan became an IDB member in 1995. Kazakhstan also hosts the IDB's regional office in Almaty (Gresh 2007, 3–4).

5. Author's interview with Aidyn Tairov, financial director/chief accountant at Al Hilal Bank. Almaty, Kazakhstan, November 26, 2012.

6. Author's interview with Timur Omarov, head of the Islamic Finance development, Department of Regional Financial Development Center in Almaty and Islamic Finance, National Bank of Republic of Kazakhstan. Almaty, Kazakhstan, June 13, 2013.

7. From the speech of Nursultan Nazarbayev at the Organization of Islamic Cooperation in 2011, http://www.arabnews.com/node/382230/.

8. Aibek Bekzhanov, a specialist in Islamic financing from the Almaty Regional Finance Center, http://centralasiaonline.com/en_GB/articles/caii/features/main/2012/05/11/feature-01/.

9. "Bishkek nameren stat' islamskii fintsentrom," http://www.islamnews.ru/news-61641.html.

10. This has been done primarily through the implementation of a forty-one-point government roadmap for Islamic finance that envisages amending taxation rules and introducing other legislative changes favorable to Islamic banks. The roadmap consists of eight chapters, and lists the tasks that various state and public organizations are charged with fulfilling by 2020. Hence, it is a comprehensive guideline that seeks to facilitate "the expansion of Islamic finance infrastructure, the establishment of more Islamic finance services including new banks, more educational and scientific work, a closer cooperation with foreign partners and the development of state organs" (Wolters 2013, 9).

11. Author's interview with Arzykan Osmonova, head of the department, National Bank of Kyrgyz Republic. Bishkek, Kyrgyzstan, April 2, 2013.

12. *Mudarabah* is a profit-and-loss–sharing agreement, where the bank provides financial capital, and the lender, here defined as the partner, implements a business. *Murabaha* is a type of fiduciary sale, where the bank purchases commodities for the customer and adds a commission fee. *Musharakah* operates as a joint venture in which the involved partners (the bank and the customer) agree in advance on profit sharing and estimated losses are divided proportionally to the shares of each partner (Warde 2010).

13. For details, see its Web site: http://www.alhilalbank.kz/en/ibank/.

14. Currently, the bank's network includes 120 branch offices throughout the country, and over 100,000 customers who use a variety of services, such as Islamic deposits, banking cards, and halal cash transfers. Author's interview with Askat Chonorov, director of complex servicing department, EcoIslamic bank. Bishkek, Kyrgyzstan, October 31, 2012.

15. From Nurpiisov's interview to Interfax-Kazakhstan, February 2012, http://www.interfax.kz/?lang=eng&int_id=13&category=exclusive&news_id=65/.

16. Author's interview with Kuralai Yeldesbai, founder of Takaful Insurance Company. Almaty, Kazakhstan, June 14, 2013.

17. Author's interview with Zamir Pusurov, director of Kompanion Invest. Osh, Kyrgyzstan, March 7, 2013.

18. This interview was published on September 29, 2012, on the Web site www.muslimwomen.com.kz/, which is no longer accessible.

19. Author's interview with Yerlan Baidaulet, executive director of the Islamic Development Bank in Kazakhstan and chair of the ADIF, June 12, 2013.

20. Interview with Baidaulet, June 12, 2013.

21. Interview with Yeldesbai, June 14, 2013.

22. Author's interview with Erkeaiym Baialieva, chief development officer at the Kompanion Development Agency. Bishkek, Kyrgyzstan, February 20, 2013.

23. This excludes brokerage and insurance companies mentioned in the previous section.

24. Future fieldwork will include the accounts of religious authorities in Kazakhstan.

25. Interviews were conducted with those who serve on sharia boards of the local bank and microfinance company, as well as the broader community of imams.

26. Interview with Toktomushev Maksatbek *damla*, imam at the Central Mosque in Bishkek. Bishkek, Kyrgyzstan, February 9, 2013.

27. Names have been changed to maintain confidentiality.

Chapter Twelve. Studying Islam Abroad

1. The majority of Muslims in Tajikistan (over 90 percent) are Sunnis, adhering to the Hanafi branch. There are also Ismaili communities living mainly in the eastern part of the country, the Pamir region.

2. The self-image of Tajikistan's Muslims as "ignorant" (in Arabic *jahil*, in Tajik *besavod*, *nodono*) harks back to a discourse that was an integral part of the official atheist propaganda in Soviet times but gained new meaning in the course of the post-Soviet preaching of Islam (*da'wa*) (Bobrovnikov 2011).

3. In Arabic *'Utlub il 'ilma wa law fis-sin.*

4. Educational journeys were frequently the privilege of prosperous families that could afford to dispense with a family member's provision of subsistence over a longer period or were restricted to students in Islamic educational establishments (madrasa), diplomats, or traders (see Eickelman 1985; Eickelman and Piscatori 1990).

5. Since most Tajiks do not finance their studies with scholarships but privately, one can only speculate on exact figures. According to official data, 1,400 Tajik students were studying Islam in another Muslim country in 2010. However, the actual figure must be assumed to be considerably higher, since 4,000 Tajiks are estimated to be studying in educational establishments (madrasas, universities) in Pakistan alone (Lemon 2010).

6. The annual number of hajj pilgrims from Tajikistan varies according to the national quotas set by the Saudi Arabian government. While in 2010, 5,500 Tajik made the hajj pilgrimage to Mecca, the number increased to 6,000 in the following years. In 2013, however, the Saudi Arabian government reduced the number of Tajik pilgrims to 4,800.

7. Abu Hanifa (699–767) is the founder of the Hanafi school of law. On the seventeenth anniversary of Tajikistan's independence, President Rahmon announced that 2009 would be the Year of Imam-i Azam Abu Hanifa in Tajikistan.

8. More than seven hundred students were brought back to Tajikistan per flight.

Author's interview with Yusufi, a former journalist working for Radio Free Liberty in 2001. Dushanbe, July 16, 2013. See also Abramson (2010, 40–41.)

9. Author's interview with Yusufi, July 16, 2013. See also Abramson (2010, 40).

10. Students are equipped with a monthly scholarship and free accommodation and food, and their curriculum includes secular subjects such as math, geography, and foreign languages.

11. Stronger regulations were introduced by the "Law on Traditions, Festivities, and Ceremonies" in 2007 and by the "Law on Freedom of Conscience and Religious Associations" in 2009 (Qonuni Jumhurii Tojikiston dar borai ozodi vijdon va ittihodiyahoi dini [Dushanbe: Irfon]). See also Epkenhans, chapter 8, this volume.

12. "Qonunhoi Jumhurii Tojikiston dar borai ma'suliyati padaru modar dar borai ta'limu tarbiyai farzand."

13. Many national educational establishments in Dushanbe currently lack qualified teachers and there is inadequate teaching material, which, if it exists at all, is out-of-date. The teachers' poor pay compels them to take on secondary employment. The consequences are that lessons frequently do not take place, that many teachers are badly motivated in exercising their profession, and that a pervasive culture of corruption reinforces social distinctions and the relevance of ethnic and regional affiliations. Many schoolchildren are left on their own due to the lack of care and responsibility, and they spend their mornings on the street. These educational realities are in sharp contrast to the expectations that the government dictates in its agenda for schools and universities. This also includes compensation for the moral education of children and young people that is currently largely handled by the private Islamic educational sector and is to be transferred as part of a national program to educate citizens.

14. The majority of returning students I met in Dushanbe came from families with an academic background but were not necessarily brought up in a family environment close to religion. Depending on their age, many had completed a secular higher education or just completed their studies at a secular university.

15. "Possessing knowledge of [foreign] languages means understanding the world."

16. These findings agree with my observations in the Abu Hanifa Islamic Institute in Dushanbe: Among the male and female students, many stated that the purpose of their Islamic education is not to pursue a religious career but rather an international education career in a Muslim country such as Turkey, Saudi Arabia, or the United Arab Emirates.

Conclusion

1. The region's slow and contested conversion to Islam, which lasted from the eighth until the eighteenth century, also contributed to this peripheral status (for details, see, e.g., Foltz 1999).

2. This occurred over nearly a century and under three tsars: Alexander I (1801–25), Nicholas I (1825–55), and Alexander II (1855–81).

3. Islamism is synonymous with "Islamic activism" or "the active assertion and promotion of beliefs, prescriptions, laws, or policies that are held to be Islamic in character" (ICG 2005b, 1; see also Hirschkind 1997).

4. Although some would question the notion that Russia is a part of Europe, that Russia was acting as a European colonizer in Central Asia during this period was taken for granted (Khalid 1998, 51).

5. Importantly, European conquest and subjugation did not begin with Napoleonic conquests in 1798, as is the commonly held view, but rather, with Dutch colonization of the East Indies, which began in the seventeenth century (Lapidus 1999, 471–73).

6. Jadidism was primarily concerned with modernizing elementary education, which it viewed as the key to reversing the cultural decay among Muslims in the Russian Empire. The term *Jadidism* originated with the Crimean Tatar reformer Ismail Bey Gaprinskii, who introduced "the new (i.e., phonetic) method (*usul-i-jadid*) of teaching the Arabic alphabet" (Khalid 1998, 89).

7. The Basmachi rebellion, which began in 1916 and continued until the early 1930s is often mischaracterized as a national liberation movement. In fact, it was a fragmented and local response to Russian colonial policies that produced severe economic hardship (see, e.g., Khalid 1998, 285–86).

8. The Soviets also drew heavily on the European ideal of the nation-state in developing their own conceptualization of the nation.

9. The Kyrgyz were initially called Kara-Kyrgyz. The Kazakhs were initially called Kirgiz. The process of national delimitation began in 1924 and was not completed until 1936. The delimitation actually created a hierarchy among ethnic groups, with only some receiving the highest designation of SSR. The Karakalpaks, for example, were identified as a major ethnic group in the 1920s and given their own autonomous oblast in 1925 but never became an Autonomous Soviet Socialist Republic (ASSR) or SSR. For details, see Jones Luong 2002, 51–101.

10. In other parts of the Islamic world, these traditional beliefs and practices might be described as "folk piety" or "popular Islam" (see, e.g., Gaffney 1992). For a description of the diversity of beliefs and practices among South Asian and African Muslims, see, for example, Reetz 2009a.

REFERENCES

Abashin, Sergei. 2006. "The Logic of Islamic Practice: Religious Conflict in Central Asia." *Central Asian Survey* 25, no. 3, 267–86.

Abaza, Mona. 1994. *Islamic Education, Perceptions, Exchanges: Indonesian Students in Cairo*. Paris: Association Archipel.

Abdurakhimova, Nadira A. 2002. "The Colonial System of Power in Turkestan." *International Journal of Middle East Studies* 34, no. 2, 239–62.

Abdylda uulu, Düishön ajy, and Özübek ajy Chotonov. 2002. *Musulman baldary üchün adep-ahlak kitebi*. Bishkek: Tehnologiya.

Abdyldaev, D. 2003. "Biz Markumdu Kanda Uzatabyz" [How we honor the dead]. *Islam Madaniyaty* 32, no. 48 (September): 2.

Abramson, David. 2010. "Foreign Religious Education and the Central Asian Islamic Revival: Impact and Prospects for Stability." *Silk Road Paper*. Central Asia-Caucasus Institute, Paul H. Nitze School of Advanced International Studies.

Abramson, David, and Elyor E. Karimov. 2007. "Sacred Sites, Profane Ideologies: Religious Pilgrimage and the Uzbek State." In Sahadeo and Zanca, *Everyday Life in Central Asia*, 319–38.

Abun-Nasr, Jamil M. 2013. *Muslim Communities of Grace: The Sufi Brotherhoods in Islamic Life*. New York: Columbia University Press.

Ackerman, Susan E. 2005. "Falun Dafa and the New Age Movement in Malaysia: Signs of Health, Symbols of Salvation." *Social Compass* 52, no. 4, 495–511.

Adams, Laura L. 2010. *The Spectacular State: Culture and National Identity in Uzbekistan*. Durham, NC: Duke University Press.

Ahmed, Akbar S. 1992. *Postmodernism and Islam: Predicament and Promise*. London: Routledge.

Ahmed, Leila. 1992. *Women and Gender in Islam: Historical Roots of a Modern Debate*. New Haven, CT: Yale University Press.

Ahmed, Leila. 2011. *A Quiet Revolution: The Veil's Resurgence, From the Middle East to America*. New Haven, CT: Yale University Press.

Ahmedov, B. A. Mirzo. 1994. *Ulughbek: Badi—Tuzitalgan va Tuldirilgan Ikkinchi Nashri*. Ezuvchi.

Aitmatov, Chingiz. 1988. *The Day Lasts More than a Thousand Years*. Bloomington: Indiana University Press.

Aitpaeva, Gülnara. 2009a. "The Dispute on Pilgrimage to Sacred Sites among Kyrgyz Muslims." In *Sacred Sites of Ysyk-Köl: Spiritual Power, Pilgrimage, and Art*, edited by Gülnara Aitpaeva and Aida Egemberdieva, 224–36. Bishkek: Aigine Cultural Research Center.

Aitpaeva, Gülnara. 2009b. "Sacred Sites in Kyrgyzstan: Spiritual Mission, Health and Pilgrimage." In *Nature, Space and the Sacred: Transdisciplinary Perspectives*, edited by S. Bergmann, P. M. Scott, M. Jansdotter Samuelsson, and H. Bedford-Strohm, 249–63. Burlington, VT: Ashgate.

Aitpaeva, Gülnara, Gülmira Aldakeeva, and Aida Egemberdieva. 2010. "Katardagy Islam ököldörü je azyrky Kyrgyzstandagy moldolor fenomeni (Talas oblastynyn misalynda)." In Aitpaeva and Agemberdieva, *Jalal-Abaddagy yiyk jerler jana el daanyshmandygy*, 413–36

Aitpaeva, Gülnara, and Aida Egemberdieva. 2010. *Jalal-Abaddagy yiyk jerler jana el daanyshmandygy*. Bishkek: Aigine Cultural Research Center.

Aitpaeva, Gülnara, Aida Egemberdieva, and Mukaram Toktogulova. 2007. *Mazar Worship in Kyrgyzstan: Rituals and Practitioners in Talas*. Bishkek: Aigine Research Center.

Akbarzadeh, Shahram 1996. "Why Did Nationalism Fail in Tajikistan?" *Europe-Asia Studies*, 48 (7): 1105–29.

Akhmedova, Umida, and Oleg Karpov. 2008. *Bremya devstvannosti* [The burden of virginity]. Accessed October 13, 2012. https://www.youtube.com/watch?v=gSb_5rD6nYs&feature=gv.

Akiner, Shireen. 2003a. "The Search for a Rational Balance between Religiosity and Secularity in the Post-Soviet Muslim States." In *Islam and the Secular State*, edited by W. Schneider-Deters, 235–48. Tashkent: International Fund of Imam al-Bukhari and Friedrich Ebert Foundation.

Akiner, Shireen. 2003b. "Polarization of Islam in Post-Soviet Central Asia." *Religion, State and Society* 31, no. 2, 97–122.

Algar, Hamid. 1976. "The Naqshbandi Order: A Preliminary Survey of Its History and Significance." *Studia Islamica* 44, 123–52.

Algar, Hamid. 1995. "Naqshbandiyah," *Oxford Encyclopedia of the Modern Islamic World*. Vol. 3. Oxford: Oxford University Press.

al-Hindustani, Muhammad Ibn Rustam. 1988. "Otvety vnosyshim nedopustimye novshestva v religiiu." In Babadzhanov, Muminov, and von Kügelgen, *Disputes on Muslim Authority in Central Asia*, 117–25.

Aliyev, Fuad. 2012. "The Politics of Islamic Finance in Central Asia and South Caucasus." *Voices from Central Asia* 2 (July). Washington, DC: Central Asia Program, George Washington University. http://centralasiaprogram.org/blog/2012/07/08/the-politics-of-islamic-finance-in-central-asia-and-south-caucasus/.

Allsworth, Edward. 1989. "Religious and National Signals in Secular Central Asian Drama." In *Muslim Communities Reemerge: Historical Perspectives on Nationality, Politics, and Opposition in the Former Soviet Union and Yugoslavia*, edited by Andreas Kappeler, Gerhard Simon, Georg Brunner, and Edward Allworth, 80–110. Durham, NC: Duke University Press.

Al-Suwaidi, Jamal. 1995. "Arab and Western Conceptions of Democracy." In *Democracy, War, and Peace in the Middle East*, edited by David Garnham and Mark Tessler, 82–115. Bloomington: Indiana University Press.

Aminov, Murod, et al. 1997. *O'zebkiston Respblikasi Entsiklopediya*. Tashkent: Bosh Tahririyati.

Andreev, M. S. 1927. "Sredne-aziatskaja versija Zolushki (Sandril'ony)." *Sv. Paraskeva Pjiatnitsa*. "Div-I Safid." In *Po Tadzhikistanu*, Vyp. 1, Tashkent, 60–76.

Andrew, Christopher. 2006. *The World Was Going Our Way: The KGB and the Battle for the Third World: Newly Revealed Secrets from the Mitrokhin Archive*. New York: Basic Books.

An-Nabhani, Taqiuddin. 1998. *The Islamic State*. London: Al-Khilafah Publications.

Ansari, Ali. 2012. *The Politics of Nationalism in Modern Iran*. Cambridge: Cambridge University Press.

Antze, Paul, and Michael Lambek. 1997. *Tense Past: Cultural Essays in Trauma and Memory*. New York: Routledge.

Appadurai, Arjun. 1996. *Consumption, Duration, and History in Modernity at Large*. Minneapolis: University of Minnesota Press.

Appadurai, Arjun. 2010. *Modernity at Large: Cultural Dimensions of Globalization*. Minneapolis: University of Minnesota Press.

Arberry, Arthur John. 1955. *The Koran Interpreted*. New York: Macmillan.

Armbrust, Walter. 2006. "Audiovisual Media and History of the Middle East." In *History and Historiographies of the Modern Middle East*, edited by Amy Singer and Israel Gershoni, 288–312. Seattle: University of Washington Press.

Asad, Talal. 1986. The Idea of an Anthropology of Islam. In *Occasional Papers Series*. Washington DC: Center for Contemporary Arab Studies, Georgetown.

Asad, Talal. 1993. *Genealogies of Religion: Discipline and Reasons of Power in Christianity and Islam*. Baltimore: Johns Hopkins University Press.

Asad, Talal. 1999. "Religion, Nation-State, Secularism." In *Nation and Religion: Perspectives on Europe and Asia*, edited by P. van der Veer and H. Lehmann, 178–97. Princeton, NJ: Princeton University Press.

Asad, Talal. 2003. *Formations of the Secular: Christianity, Islam, and Modernity*. Stanford, CA: Stanford University Press.

Ashymov, Daniar. 2003. "The Religious Faith of the Kyrgyz." *Religion, State and Society* 31, no. 2, 133–38.

Atayeva, Nadejda, 2014. "Uzbekistan: 'Traitors to the Motherland' Are Named." Accessed August 6, 2015. http://nadejda-atayeva-en.blogspot.com/2014/12/uzbekistan-traitors-to-motherland-are .html.

Azamatov, Danil D. 1998. "The Muftis of the Orenburg Spiritual Assembly in the 18th and 19th Centuries: The Struggle for Power in Russia's Muslim Institution." In *Muslim Culture in Russia and Central Asia from the 18th to the Early 20th Centuries, Vol. 2: Inter-Regional and Inter-Ethnic Relations*, edited by Anke von Kugelgen, Michael Kemper, and Allen J. Frank, 355–38. Berlin: Klaus Schwarz Verlag.

Babadzhanov, Bakhtiyar. 1999. "The Fergana Valley: Source or Victim of Islamic Fundamentalism?" In *Political Islam and Conflicts in Russia and Central Asia*, edited by Lena Jonson and Murad Esenov, 112–23. Stockholm: CA&CC Press.

Babadzhanov, Bakhtiyar. 2000. "Sredneaziatskoe dukhovnoe upravlenie musul'man: predistoriia i posledstviia raspada" [Spiritual Administration of the Muslims of Central Asia]. In *Mnogomernye granitsy Tsentral'noi Azii* [The multidimensional borders of Central Asia], edited by A. Malashenko and M. B. Olcott, 55–69. Moscow: Carnegie Center.

Babadzhanov, Bakhtiyar. 2001a. "Khudzhra." In *Islam na territorii byvshei Rossiiskoi imperii: Entsiklopedischeskii slovar' no. 3* [Islam on the territory of the former Russian Empire: encyclopedic dictionary no. 3], edited by S. M. Prozorov, 116–17. Moscow: Vostochnaia literatura RAN.

Babadzhanov, Bakhtiyar. 2001b. "O fetvakh SADUM protiv 'neislamskikh obychaev'" [The fatwas of SADUM against "non-Islmic customs"]. In *Islam na postsovetskom prostranstve: vzgliad iznutri* [Islam in the post-Soviet space: a view from within], edited by A. Malashenko and M. B. Olcott, 55–69. Moscow: Carnegie Center.

Babadzhanov, Bakhtiyar. 2001c. "Mudzhaddidiia." In *Islam na territorii byvshei Rossiiskoi imperii: Entsiklopedischeskii slovar no. 3* [Islam on the territory of the former Russian Empire: encyclopedic dictionary no. 3], edited by S. M. Prozorov, 68–69. Moscow: Vostochnaia literatura RAN.

Babadzhanov, Bakhtiyar. 2001d. "Mohammadjan Hindustani and the Beginning of the 'Great Schism' among Muslims of Uzbekistan." In *Politics and Islam in Russian and Central Asia*, edited by Stephan Doudoignon and Hisao Komatzu, 195–220. London: Routledge.

Babadzhanov, Bakhtiyar. 2003. "Babakhanovy." In *Islam na territorii byvshei Rossiiskoi imperii. Entsiklopedischeskii slovar no. 4* [Islam on the territory of the former Russian Empire: encyclopedic dictionary no. 4], edited by S. M. Prozorov, 12–14. Moscow: Vostochnaia literatura RAN.

Babadzhanov, Bakhtiyar. 2004. "From Colonization to Bolshevization: Some Political and Legislative Aspects of Molding a 'Soviet Islam' in Central Asia." In *Central Asian Law: An Historical Overview*, edited by Wallace Johnson and Irina F. Popova, 153–72. Lawrence: University of Kansas Press.

Babadzhanov, Bakhtiyar. 2014. "The Economic and Religious History of a Kolkhoz Village: Khojawot from Soviet Modernisation to the Aftermath of the Islamic Revival." In *Allah's Kolkhozes. Migration, De-Stalinisation, Privatisation and the New Muslim Congregations in the Soviet Realm*, edited by Stéphane A. Dudoignon and Christian Noack, 202–64. Berlin: Klaus Schwarz Verlag.

Babadzhanov, Bakhtiyar, and Muzaffar Kamilov. 2001. "Muhammadjan Hindustani (1892–1989) and the Beginning of the 'Great Schism' among the Muslims of Uzbekistan." In *Islam in Politics in Russia and Central Asia (Early Eighteenth to Late Twentieth Centuries)*, edited by Stéphane A. Dudoignon and Hisao Komatsu, 195–219. London: Kegan Paul.

Babadzhanov, Bakhtiyar, and Muzaffar Kamilov. 2001a. "Khindustani." In *Islam na territorii byvshei Rossiiskoi imperii: Entsiklopedischeskii slovar no. 3* [Islam on the territory of the former Russian Empire: encyclopedic dictionary no. 3], edited by S. M. Prozorov, 116–17. Moscow: Vostochnaia literatura RAN.

Babadzhanov, Bakhtiyar, Muminov, A. K., and von Kügelgen, A. 2007. *Disputes on Muslim Authority in Central Asia (20th Century)*. Almaty: Daik Press.

Bacon, Elizabeth. 1980. *Central Asians under Russian Rule: A Study in Culture Change*. Ithaca, NY: Cornell University Press.

Balci, Bayram. 2003. *Missionaires de l'Islam en Asie Centrale: Les Ecoles Turques de Fethulla Gulen* [Missionaries of Islam in Central Asia: The Turkish Schools of Fethulla Gulen]. Paris: Institut Français d'Etudes Anatoliennes, Maisonneuve et Larose.

Balci, Bayram. 2007. "Central Asian Refugees in Saudi Arabia: Religious Evolution and Contributing to the Reislamization of Their Motherland." *Refugee Survey Quarterly* 26, no. 2, 12–21.

Balci, Bayram. 2010. "The Jama'at al Tabligh in Central Asia: A Mediator in the Recreation of Islamic Relations with the Indian Subcontinent." In *China and India in Central Asia: A New "Great Game"?*, edited by Marlène Laruelle, Sébastien Peyrouse, Jean-François Huchet, and Bayram Balci, 235–48. New York: Palgrave.

Baldick, Julian. 1993. *Imaginary Muslims: The Uwaysi Sufis of Central Asia*. New York: New York University Press.

Baran, Emily. 2014. *Dissent on the Margins: How Soviet Jehovah's Witnesses Defied Communism and Lived to Preach about It*. New York: Oxford University Press.

Baran, Zeyno. 2004. "Understanding Sufism and Its Potential Role in U.S. Policy." *Nixon Center Conference Report*, March, 1–25.

Basilov, Vladimir. 1987 "Popular Islam in Central Asia and Kazakhstan." *Journal of the Institute of Muslim Minority Affairs* 8, no. 1 (January): 7–17.

Bat, Yeor, Miriam Kochan, and David Littman. 2002. *Islam and Dhimmitude: Where Civilizations Collide*. Madison, NJ: Fairleigh Dickinson University Press.

Bayram, Mushfig. 2011. "Uzbekistan: New Haj Pilgrimage, Same Old Restrictions." Forum 18, November 7. Accessed May 14, 2013. http://www.forum18.org/Archive.php?article_id=1634.

Bayram, Mushfig, and John Kinahan. 2014. "Kyrgyzstan: Religious Freedom Survey." *Forum 18 News Service*. http://www.forum18.org/archive.php?article_id=2013.

BBC Monitoring. 2012. Tashkent Channel One. "Uzbek Leader Urges Muslim Clergy to Inform People of Events in Arab World." August 31. Tashkent.

Beck, Thorsten, Asli Demirgüç-Kunt, and Ouarda Merrouche. 2010. "Islamic vs. Conventional Banking Business Model, Efficiency and Stability." Policy Research Working Paper 5446. Washington, DC: World Bank Development Research Group.

Bellér-Hann, Ildikó. 2001. "Rivalry and Solidarity among Uyghur Healers in Kazakhstan." *Inner Asia* 3, 73–98.

Belousova, Ekaterina. 2002. "The Preservation of National Childbirth Traditions in the Russian Homebirth Community." *SEFA Journal* 7, no. 2, 50–77.

Belyaev, Demyan. 2010. "'Heterodox' Religiosity in Russia after the Fall of Communism: Does It Challenge 'Traditional' Religion?" *Religion, State and Society* 38, no. 2, 135–51.

Bennetts, Mark. 2010. "Afternoon Tea with a Soviet Psychic." In *Sputink International*. Accessed March 16, 2015. http://sputniknews.com/analysis/20101011/160907529.html.

Bennigsen, Alexandre, and S. Enders Wimbush. 1985. *Mystics and Commissars: Sufism in the Soviet Union*. London: C. Hurst.

Bissenova, Alima. 2005. "Central Asian Encounters in the Middle East: Nationalism, Islam and Postcoloniality in Al-Azhar." *Religion, State and Society* 33, no. 3, 253–63.

Blain, J., and R. J. Wallis. 2002. "Sites, Sacredness, and Stories: Interactions of Archaeology and Contemporary Paganism." *Folklore* 114, no. 3, 307–21.

Blakkisrud, Helge, and Shahnoza Nozimova. 2010. "History Writing and Nation Building in Post-Independence Tajikistan." *Nationalities Papers*, 32, no. 2, 173–89.

Bobrovnikov, Vladimir. 2011. "The Contribution of Oriental Scholarship to the Soviet Anti-Islamic Discourse: From the Militant Godless to the Knowledge Society." In *Heritage of Soviet Oriental Studies*, edited by Michael Kemper and Stephan Conermann, 66–85. New York: Routledge.

Bociurkiw, Bohdan. 1996. *The Ukrainian Greek Catholic Church and the Soviet State*. Edmonton: Canadian Institute of Ukrainian Studies Press.

Borbieva, Noor O'Neill. 2009. "Islam and the International Sector: Negotiations of Faith in the Kyrgyz Republic." Working Paper no. 364. The Helen Kellogg Institute for International Studies. http://kellogg.nd.edu/publications/workingpapers/WPS/364.pdf.

Borbieva, Noor O'Neill. 2012a. "Foreign Faiths and National Renewal: Christian Conversion among Kyrgyz Youth." *Culture and Religion* 13, no. 1, 41–63.

Borbieva, Noor O'Neill. 2012b. "Empowering Muslim women: Independent Religious Fellowships in the Kyrgyz Republic." *Slavic Review* 71, no. 2, 288–307.

Botobekov, Uran. 2001. "Spreading the Ideas of the Hizb at-Takhrir al-Islami in South Kyrgyzstan." In *Islam in the Post-Soviet Space: A View from Within*, edited by Aleksei Malashenko and Martha Brill Olcott, 129–52. Moscow: Carnegie Institute.

Bourdieu, Pierre. 1971. "Genèse et structure du champ religieux." *Revue française de sociologie* 12, no. 3, 295–334.

Bourdieu, Pierre. 2011. *Religion*. Frankfurt: Suhrkamp.

Bowen, John R. 1993. *Muslims through Discourse: Religion and Ritual in Gayo Society*. Princeton, NJ: Princeton University Press.

Bregel, Yuri. 1980. "The Role of Central Asia in the History of the Muslim East." Institute of Asian and African Affairs, Hebrew University of Jerusalem, Occasional Paper no. 20, 1–19. New York: Afghanistan Council.

Brenner, Louis. 2001. *Controlling Knowledge: Religion, Power and Schooling in a West African Muslim Society*. Bloomington: Indiana University Press.

Brenner, Suzanne. 1996. "Reconstructing Self and Society: Javanese Muslim Women and 'the Veil.'" *American Ethnologist* 23, no. 4, 673–97.

Brettell, Caroline. 2003. *Anthropology and Migration: Essays on Transnationalism, Ethnicity, and Identity*. Walnut Creek, CA: AltaMira Press.

Bringa, Tone. 2002. "Islam and the Quest for Identity in Post-Communist Bosnia-Herzegovina." In *Islam and Bosnia: Conflict Resolution and Foreign Policy in Multi-Ethnic States*, edited by M. Shatzmiller, 24–34. Montreal: School of Policy Studies Queen's University.

Brown, Bess. 1992. "Central Asia's Diplomatic Debut." *RFE/RL Research Report* 9, no. 6.3, 20–25.

Buehler, Arthur F. 1998. *Sufi Heirs of the Prophet: The Indian Naqshbandiyya and the Rise of the Mediating Sufi Shaykh*. Columbia: University of South Carolina Press.

Bukhari, Sadriddin Salim. 1993. *Dilda Yar: Hazarat Bahauddin Naqshband*. Tashkent: Ghafur Ghulam Nomidagi Adabiyat va Sanat.

Carmichel, David, et al. 1994. *Sacred Sites, Sacred Places*. London: Routledge.

Carrère d'Encausse, Hélène. 1994. "'Systematic Conquest' and 'Organizing and Colonizing the Conquered Territories.'" In *Central Asia, 130 Years of Russian Dominance: A Historical Overview*, 3rd ed., edited by Edward Allworth, 131–71. Durham, NC: Duke University Press.

Cassarino, Jean-Pierre. 2004. "Theorizing Return Migration: A Revisited Conceptual Approach to Return Migrants." EUI Working Paper RSCAS 2004/2. European University Institute: Badia Fiesolana.

Central Intelligence Agency (CIA). 2013. *The World Factbook*. https://www.cia.gov/library/publications/the-world-factbook/geos/kg.html.

Chalko, Thomas. 2001. "Is Chance or Choice the Essence of Nature?" *Natural University Journal of Discovery* 2 (March): 3–13.

Chaudet, Didier. 2008. "Islamist Terrorism in Greater Central Asia: The 'Al-Qaedaization' of Uzbek Jihadism." *Russie.Nei.Visions* 35, 1–29.

Chilanzar District Criminal Court, Tashkent City. 2009. "Verdict: *Tashkent City Criminal Prosecutor vs. Maksim V. Popov*." June 9.

Chotonov, Özübek aji. 2006. *Yiman tarbiyasy baldar üchün*. Bishkek: Dilazyk.

Chumachenko, Tat'iana. 2002. *Church and State in Soviet Russia: Russian Orthodoxy from World War II to the Khrushchev Years*. Armonk, NY: M. E. Sharpe.

Chvir, L. A. 2006. *Obriady i verovaniia uigurov v XIX–XX vv.: ocherki narodnogo islama v Turkestane* [Rituals and beliefs of Uyghurs in the nineteenth–twentieth centuries: Essays on folk Islam in Turkestan]. Moscow: Vostochnaia literatura RAN.

Cleek, Ashley. 2012. "Uzbekistan Goes After Islam with Clothing Ban and Cameras." March 16. Accessed May 10, 2013. *Eurasianet*. www.eurasiasnet.org/node/65142.

Collins, Kathleen. 2007. "Ideas, Networks, and Islamist Movements: Evidence from Central Asia and the Caucasus." *World Politics* 60, no. 1, 64–96.

Committee on Religious Affairs of the Republic of Uzbekistan. 2012. "Peace And Tranquility: A Priceless Gift." Accessed May 13, 2013. http://religions.uz/rus/news/mir_i_spokoystvie_besenniy_dar.mgr.

Cook, Michael. 2000. *Commanding Right and Forbidding Wrong in Islamic Thought*. Cambridge: Cambridge University Press.

Crews, Robert. 2003. "Empire and the Confessional State: Islam and Religious Politics in Nineteenth-Century Russia." *American Historical Review* 108, 50–83.

CXW. 2006. "Kamalov Killed—Links with Extremists Alleged by Law Enforcement Agencies." August 8. Cited from *Vechernii Bishkek*, August 7, 2006. Accessed September 9, 2013. http://www.neweurasia.net/politics-and-society/kamalov-killed-links-with-extremists-alleged-by-law-enforcement-agencies/.

Danilushkin, M. B. 1997. *Istoriia Russkoi Pravoslavnoi Tserkvi: tom I, 1917–1970* [History of the Russian Orthodox Church: vol. 1: 1917–1970]. Saint Petersburg: Voskresenie.

Davis, Eric. 1987. "The Concept of Revival and the Study of Islam and Politics." In *The Islamic Impulse*, edited by Barbara Freyer Stowasser, 37–58. London: Croom Helm.

Deeb, Lara. 2006. *An Enchanted Modern: Gender and Public Piety in Shi'i Lebanon*. Princeton, NJ: Princeton University Press.

De Goede, Marieke. 2005. *Virtue, Fortune and Faith*. Minneapolis: University of Minnesota Press.

DeWeese, Devon. 1994. *Islamization and Native Religion in the Golden Horde: Baba Tukles and Conversion to Islam in Historical and Epic Tradition.* University Park: Pennsylvania State University Press.

DeWeese, Devon. 2002. "Islam and the Legacy of Sovietology: A Review Essay on Yaacov Ro'i's Islam in the Soviet Union." *Journal of Islamic Studies* 13, no. 3, 298–330.

Dialmy, Abdessamad. 2007. "Belonging and Institution in Islam." *Social Compass* 54, no. 1, 63–75.

Dudoignon, Stéphane. 1998. *Communal Solidarity and Social Conflicts in Late 20th Century Central Asia: The Case of the Tajik Civil War.* Tokyo: University of Tokyo Press.

Dudoignon, Stéphane. 2011. "From Revival to Mutation: The Religious Personnel of Islam in Tajikistan, from De-Stalinization to Independence." *Central Asian Survey* 30, no. 1, 53–80.

Dudoignon, Stéphane, and Christian Noack. 2014. *Allah's Kolkhozes: Migration, De-Stalinisation, Privatisation and the New Muslim Congregations in the Soviet Realm.* Berlin: Klaus Schwarz Verlag.

Eickelman, Dale. 1985. *Knowledge and Power in Morocco: The Education of a Twentieth-Century Notable.* Princeton Studies on the Near East. Princeton, NJ: Princeton University Press.

Eickelman, Dale. 1992. "Mass Higher Education and the Religious Imagination in Contemporary Arab Societies." *American Ethnologist* 19, no. 4, 643–55.

Eickelman, Dale. 2003. "Communication and Control in the Middle East: Publication and Its Discontents." In *New Media in the Muslim World: The Emerging Public Sphere*, edited by Dale Eickelman and Jon W. Anderson, 33–42. Bloomington: Indiana University Press.

Eickelman, Dale, and James Piscatori, eds. 1990. *Muslim Travellers: Pilgrimage, Migration, and the Religious Imagination.* London: Routledge.

Eickelman, Dale, and James Piscatori. 1996. *Muslim Politics.* Princeton, NJ: Princeton University Press.

Eisenstadt, S. N. 2000. "The Reconstruction of Religious Arenas in the Framework of 'Multiple Modernities.'" *Millennium: Journal of International Studies* 29, no. 3, 591–611.

Eisenstadt, S. N. 2003. *Comparative Civilizations and Multiple Modernities.* Leiden: Brill.

El Moudden, Abderrahmane. 1990. "The Ambivalence of *rihla*: Community Integration and Self-Definition in Moroccan Travel Accounts, 1300–1800." In Eickelman and Piscatori, *Muslim Travellers*, 60–84.

el-Zein, Abdul Hamid. 1977. "Beyond Ideology and Theology: The Search for the Anthropology of Islam." *Annual Review of Anthropology* 6, 227–54.

Epkenhans, Tim. 2010. "Muslims without Learning, Clergy without Faith: Institutions of Islamic Learning in the Republic of Tajikistan." In *Islamic Education in the Soviet Union and Its Successor States*, edited by Michael Kemper, Raoul Motika, and Stefan Reichmuth, 313–48. London: Routledge.

Epkenhans, Tim. 2011. "Defining Normative Islam: Some Remarks on Contemporary Islamic Thought in Tajikistan." *Central Asian Survey* 30, no. 1, 81–96.

Ernst, Carl. 2011. *Sufism: An Introduction to the Mystical Tradition of Islam.* Boston: Shambhala.

Esposito, John. 1991. "Trailblazers of the Islamic Resurgence." In *The Contemporary Islamic Revival: A Critical Survey and Bibliography*, edited by Yvonne Yazbeck Haddad, John Obert Voll, and John L. Esposito, 37–56. Westport, CT: Greenwood Press.

Esposito, John. 1992. *The Islamic Threat: Myth or Reality?* New York: Oxford University Press.

EurasiaNet. 2010. *Tajikistan: Dushanbe Forcing Students Abroad to Return Home.* November 29. http://www.eurasianet.org.

Exnerova, Vera. 2006. "Caught between the Muslim Community and the State: The Role of the Local Uzbek Authorities in Ferghana Valley, 1950s–1980s." *Journal of Muslim Minority Affairs* 26, no. 1, 101–12.

Expert Working Group. July 4, 2012. "Uzbekistan: While Islamic Weddings Become Popular It Irritates the Government." July 4. Accessed May 10, 2013. http://en.hrsu.org/archives/1577.

Falkowski, G. E. 1989. "Letter from Moscow: Complementary Medicine under Glasnost." *British Medical Journal* 299, 1608–9.

Fathi, Habiba. 1997. "Otins: The Unknown Women Clerics of Central Asian Islam." *Central Asian Survey* 16, no. 1, 27–43.

Fathi, Habiba. 2006. "Gender, Islam, and Social Change in Uzbekistan." *Central Asian Survey* 25, no. 3, 303–17.

Fathi, Habiba. 2010. "Female Mullahs, Healers and Leaders of Central Asian Islam: Gendering the Old and New Religious Roles in Post-Communist Societies." In *Ethnicity, Authority and Power in Central Asia: New Games Great and Small*, edited by Robert L. Canfield and Gabriele Rasuly-Paleczek, 174–95. New York: Routledge.

Feldbrugge, F. J. M. 1984. "Government and Shadow Economy in the Soviet Union." *Soviet Studies* 36, no. 4, 528–43.

Fergananews.com. 2009. "O'zbekistonda 'Nur' Diniy Oqimiga Mansublikda Ayblangan Sudlanuvchilarga Hukm O'qildi" [In Uzbekistan verdict is read for defendants accused of membership in the 'Nur' religious movement]. February 17. Accessed May 13, 2013. http://uzbek.fergananews.com/article.php?id=1350.

Fergananews.com. 2009. "Uzbekistan: Women in Bukhara Are Prohibited from Attending Mosques." August 17. Accessed May 13, 2013. www.fergananews.com/news.php?id=1324.

Ferghananews.com. April 29, 2010. "Uzbekistan: nachalsia zakrytyi sud nad zhurnalistom Khairullo Khamidovym: ego i eshche 14 chelovek obviniaiut v sozdanii nezakonnykh religioznykh organizatsii" [Uzbekistan: closed trial begins for journalist Hayrullo Hamidov. He and 14 other people accused of forming an illegal religious organization]. April 29. Accessed May 4, 2010. http://www.ferghana.ru/news.php? id=14633&mode=snews.

Fergananews.com. 2012. "Popularity of 'Muslim' Weddings Concern Country's Leadership." April 7. Accessed July 20, 2012. www.fergananews.com/news.php?id=18987.

Fergananews.com. 2012. "Uzbekistan: student Islamskogo Instituta stal zhertvoi religioznykh korruptsionerov" [Uzbekistan: Islamic Institute student becomes victim of corrupt religious officials]. February 15. Accessed May 13, 2013. www.fergananews.com/article.php?id=7278.

Firdavsii. 2006. "Imam Mukhammadrafik Kamalov: v Tsentralnoi Azii vedetsa nepravilnaia politika otdeleniia gosudarstva ot religii" [Imam Mukhammadrafik Kamalov: Central Asia conducts an incorrect policy of separation of church and state]. May 5. Fergana. ru. Accessed September 9, 2013. http://www.fergananews.com/articles/4388.

Fish, M. Steven. 2011. *Are Muslims Distinctive? A Look at the Evidence.* Oxford: Oxford University Press.

Foltz, Richard. 1999. *Religions of the Silk Road: Overland Trade and Cultural Exchange from Antiquity to the Fifteenth Century.* New York: St. Martin's Press.

Fourcade, Marion, Philippe Steiner, Wolfgang Streeck, and Cornelia Woll. 2013. "Moral Categories in the Financial Crisis." *Socio-Economic Review* 11, no 3, 601–27.

Frank, Allen J., and Jahangir Mamatov. 2006. *Uzbek Islamic Debates. Texts, Translations, and Commentary.* Springfield, VA: Dunwoody Press.

Frank, Andre Gunder. 1992. "The Centrality of Central Asia." *Studies in History* 8, no. 1, 43–97.

Freitag, Ulrike, and Achim von Oppen. 2010. "'Translocality': An Approach to Connection and Transfer in Area Studies." In *Translocality: The Study of Globalizing Processes from a Southern Perspective*, edited by Ulrike Freitag and Achim von Oppen, 1–12. Boston: Brill.

Froese, Paul. 2008. *The Plot to Kill God: Findings from the Soviet Experiment in Secularization.* Berkeley: University of California Press.

Fuller, Graham E. 2003. *The Future of Political Islam*. New York: Palgrave Macmillan.

Gaffney, Patrick D. 1992. "Popular Islam." *ANNALS of the American Academy of Political and Social Science* 524, no. 1 (November): 38–51.

Gammer, Moshe. 2005. "Between Mecca and Moscow: Islam, Politics and Political Islam in Chechnya and Daghestan." *Middle Eastern Studies* 41, no. 6 (November), 833–48.

Gamza, Dustin, and Pauline Jones Luong. 2014. "Religious Regulation and Political Mobilization in Central Asia." Paper presented at the Annual Meeting of the American Political Science Association, Washington, DC, August 28–31.

Ganev, Venelin I. 1995. "Post-Communism as an Episode of State Building: A Reversed Tillyan Perspective." *Communist and Post-Communist Studies* 38, no. 4 (December): 425–45.

Garagozov, Rauf. 2005. "Collective Memory and Memory Politics in the Central Caucasian Countries." *Central Asia and the Caucasus* 6, no. 30, 51–60. http://www.ca-c.org/online/2005/journal_eng/cac-06/06. gareng.shtml.

Geertz, Clifford. 1968. *Islam Observed: Religious Development in Morocco and Indonesia*. Chicago: University of Chicago Press.

Gellens, Sam I. 1990. "The Search for Knowledge in Medieval Muslim Societies: A Comparative Approach." In Eickelman and Piscatori, *Muslim Travellers*, 50–65.

Gellner, Ernest. 1981. *Muslim Society*. Cambridge: Cambridge University Press.

Gellner, Ernest. 1993. "Marxism and Islam: Failure and Success." In *Power-Sharing Islam?* edited by Azzam Tamimi, 33–42. London: Liberty for Muslim World Publications.

Ghafurov, Bobodzhan. 1998. *Tojikon* [The Tajiks]. Dushanbe: Irfon.

Glick-Schiller, Nina, and Georges E. Fouron. 1999. "Terrains of Blood and Nation: Haitian Transnational Social Fields." *Ethnic and Racial Studies* 22, no. 2, 340–66.

Goldman, Marshall I. 1983. *U.S.S.R. in Crisis: The Failure of an Economic System*. New York: Norton.

González, Alessandra L. 2011. "Measuring Religiosity in a Majority Muslim Context: Gender, Religious Salience, and Religious Experience among Kuwaiti College Students—A Research Note." *Journal for the Scientific Study of Religion* 50, no. 2, 339–50.

Goulbourne, Harry, Tracy Reynolds, John Solomos, and Elisabetta Zontini, eds. 2010. *Transnational Families: Ethnicities, Identities and Social Capital*. London: Routledge.

Grant, Bruce. 2011. "Shrines and Sovereigns: Life, Death, and Religion in Rural Azerbaijan." *Comparative Studies in Society and History* 53, no. 3, 654–81.

Gresh, Geoffrey F. 2007. "The Rise of Islamic Banking and Finance in Central Asia." *Fletcher School Online Journal for Issues Related to Southwest Asia and Islamic Civilization* (Fall): 1–12.

Gross, Jo-Ann. 1992. *Muslims in Central Asia: Expressions of Identity and Change*. Durham, NC: Duke University Press.

Gross, Jo-Ann. 1995. "Naqshbandi." *The Encyclopedia of the Modern Middle East*. New York: Macmillan.

Gross, Jo-Ann. 1999. "The Polemic of 'Official' and 'Unofficial' Islam." In *Islamic Mysticism Contested: Thirteen Centuries of Controversies and Polemics*, edited by Frederick de Jong and Bernd Radtke, 520–40. Boston: Brill.

Gross, Jo-Ann. 2013. "Foundational Legends, Shrines, and Isma'ili Identity in Tajik Badakhshan." In *Muslims and Others in Sacred Space,*" edited by Margaret Jean Cormack, 164–92. Oxford: Oxford University Press.

Gupta, Akhil. 1995. "Blurred Boundaries: The Discourse of Corruption, the Culture of Politics, and the Imagined State." *American Ethnologist* 22, no. 2, 375–402.

Hafez, Sherine. 2011. *An Islam of Her Own: Reconsidering Religion and Secularism in Women's Islamic Movements*. New York: New York University Press.

Haghayeghi, Mehrdad. 1994. "Islamic Revival in the Central Asian Republics." *Central Asian Survey* 13, no. 2, 249–66.

Haghayeghi, Mehrdad. 1996. *Islam and Politics in Central Asia*. Hampshire: Macmillan.

Hall, Stuart. 1997. "The Work of Representation." In *Representation: Cultural Representations and Signifying Practices*, edited by Stuart Hall, 13–74. London: Sage.

Hallaq, Wael B. 2009. *Shari'a: Theory, Practice, Transformations*. Cambridge: Cambridge University Press.

Hallaq, Wael B. 2010. "Islamic Law: History and Transformation." In *Islamic Cultures and Societies to the End of the Eighteenth Century*, edited by Robert Irwin, 142–83. Cambridge: Cambridge University Press.

Hamidov, Hayrullo. 2007. "Odamlar Orasida" (unavailable).

Hamidov, Hayrullo. Feburary 15, 2011. "Mahbuslarga Sog'inch Xati" [A letter for those who long for prisoners]. Excerpted from the article: "Hayrullo Hamidov Will Not Be Released on Amnesty: An Interview with Dilnoza Hamidova." *Ozodlik* [Radio Free Europe/Radio Liberty]. Accessed May 15, 2013. http://www.ozodlik.org/content/article/2310027.html.

Hamidov, Hayrullo. 2015. "Ishid Fitnasi." Accessed August 6, 2015. https://www.youtube.com/watch?v=V6D3dg3iqOo.

Harris, Colette. 2004. *Control and Subversion: Gender Relations in Tajikistan, Anthropology, Culture, and Society*. Sterling, VA: Pluto Press.

Harris, Colette. 2006. *Muslim Youth: Tensions and Traditions in Tajikistan*. Boulder, CO: Westview Press.

Heathershaw, John. 2009. "Tajikistan's Virtual Politics of Peace." *Europe-Asia Studies* 61, no. 7, 1315–36.

Heathershaw, John, and Nick Megoran. 2011. "Contesting Danger: A New Agenda for Policy and Scholarship on Central Asia." *International Affairs* 87, no. 3, 589–612.

Heathershaw, John, and David Montgomery. 2014. "The Myth of Post-Soviet Muslim Radicalization in the Central Asian Republics." London, Chatham House Research Paper.

Heathershaw, John, and Sophie Roche. 2011. "Islam and Political Violence in Tajikistan. An Ethnographic Perspective on the Causes and Consequences of the 2010 Armed Conflict in the Kamarob Gorge." *Ethnopolitics Papers* 8, 1–21.

Hegarty, Stephen. 1995. "The Rehabilitation of Temur: Reconstructing National History in Contemporary Uzbekistan." *Central Asia Monitor* 1, 28–35.

Hegland, Mary E. 2010. "Tajik Male Labour Migration and Women Left Behind: Can They Resist Gender and Generational Hierarchies?" *Anthropology of the Middle East* 5, no. 2, 16–35.

Henkel, Heiko. 2007. "The Location of Islam: Inhabiting Istanbul in a Muslim Way." *American Ethnologist* 34, no. 1, 57–70.

Hessler, Julie. 2004. *A Social History of Soviet Trade: Trace Policy, Retail Practices, and Consumption, 1917–1933*. Princeton, NJ: Princeton University Press.

Hilgers, Irene. 2009. *Why Do Uzbeks Have To Be Muslims? Exploring Religiosity in the Ferghana Valley*. Berlin: LIT Verlag.

Hirsch, Francine. 2005. *Empire of Nations: Ethnographic Knowledge and the Making of the Soviet Union*. Ithaca, NY: Cornell University Press.

Hirschkind, C. 1997. "What Is Political Islam?" *Middle East Report*. October/December, 12–14.

Hizb-ut-Tahrir. http://www.hizbuttahrir.org.

Horvatich, Patricia. 1994. "Ways of Knowing Islam." *American Ethnologist* 21, no. 4, 811–26.

Human Rights Watch. 1996. "Persistent Human Rights Violations and Prospects for Improvement." Report 8, no. 5 (May). Accessed September 9, 2013. http://www.hrw.org/reports/1996/UZBEK.htm.

Human Rights Watch. 1998. "'Islamic Extremism' Masks Human Rights Crackdown in Uzbekistan." *Weekly Newsletter,* May 25. https://www.hrw.org/news/1998/05/25/islamic -extremism-masks-human-rights-crackdown-uzbekistan.

Humphrey, Caroline, and Nicolas Thomas, eds. 1994. *Shamanism, History and the State.* Malden, MA: Blackwell.

Humphrey, Caroline, and A. Tulokhonov, eds. 2001. *Kul'tura i priroda vo vnutrennei Azii* [Culture and environment in inner Asia]. Novosibirsk: Nauka.

Hunter, Shireen. 2001. "Religion, Politics, and Security in Central Asia." *SAIS Review* 21, no. 2, 65–90.

Hunter, Shireen, Jeffrey L. Thomas, and Alexander Melikishvili. 2004. *Islam in Russia: The Politics of Identity and Security.* Armonk, NY: M. E. Sharpe.

Huntington, Samuel. 1993. "Clash of Civilizations?" *Foreign Affairs* 72, no. 3 (Summer): 22–49.

Hurgronje, Christiaan S. 1888–89. *Mekka* (dt.) 2 Bände. + Bilderatlas. Haag: Nijhoff.

Ianovskaia, Maria. April 27, 2010. "Sem' let tiurmy za bor'bu so SPIDom: kak 'seli' Maksima Popova" [Seven years in prison for the fight against AIDS: how they "got" Maksim Popov]. *Fergananews.ru,* April 27. Accessed October 12, 2012. http://fergananews.mirror.tengu.ch/ articled7e5.html?id=6557.

Ibraev, Mambetasan. 2013. *Yiman jana Islam sharttary* [Requirements of faith and Islam]. Bishkek: Dilazyk.

Ibrohimov, Abduqahhor, et al. 1996. *Vatan Tuyg'usi.* Tashkent: O'zbekistan.

Ilkhamov, Alisher. 2006. "The Phenomenology of 'Akromiya': Separating Facts from Fiction." *China and Eurasia Forum Quarterly* 4, 39–48.

Imam, Patrick, and Kangni Kpodar. 2010. "Islamic Banking: How Was It Diffused?" International Monetary Fund Working Paper 10/195.

Insoll, Timothy. 1999. *The Archaeology of Islam.* Sussex: Wiley-Blackwell.

Institute for War and Peace Reporting. 2012. "Islamic Clothing Vanishes from Tashkent Markets." March 14. Accessed May 13, 2013. http://iwpr.net/report-news/islamic-clothing -vanishes-tashkent-markets.

International Crisis Group (ICG). 2003a. "Radical Islam in Central Asia: Responding to Hizb-ut-Tahrir." Asia Report, no. 58. Accessed August 29, 2013. http://www.crisisgroup.org/en/ regions/asia/central-asia/058-radical-islam-in-central-asia-responding-to-hizb-ut-tahrir .aspx.

International Crisis Group (ICG). 2003b. "Central Asia: Islam and the State." Asia Report no. 59, Osh/Brussels. http://www.crisisgroup.org/en/regions/asia/central-asia/059-central-asia -islam-and-the-state.aspx.

International Crisis Group (ICG). 2005a. "The Curse of Cotton: Central Asia's Destructive Monoculture." Asia Report no. 93, Osh/Brussels.

International Crisis Group (ICG). 2005b. "Understanding Islamism." Middle East/North Africa Report no. 37, Cairo, Egypt, Brussels, Belgium. Accessed September 14, 2013. http:// www.crisisgroup.org/~/media/Files/Middle%20East%20North%20Africa/North%20 Africa/Understanding%20Islamism.

International Crisis Group (ICG). 2009a. "Tajikistan: On the Road to Failure." Asia Report no. 162, Dushanbe/Brussels.

International Crisis Group (ICG). 2009b. "Women and Radicalisation in Kyrgyzstan." Asia Report no. 176, Osh/Brussels. Accessed September 9, 2013. http://www.crisisgroup.org/~/media/Files/asia/ central-asia/kyrgyzstan/176_women_and_radicalisation_in_kyrgyzstan.

Islamic Educational, Scientific, and Cultural Organization (ISESCO). January 1, 2007. "Medals Offered to Officials in Tashkent Capital of Islamic Culture." Accessed May 13, 2013.

http://www.isesco.org.ma/index.php?option=com_k2&view=item&id=6702:ISESCO%20 Medals%20offered%20to%20officials%20in%20Tashkent%20Capital%20of%20Islamic%20 Culture&Itemid=74&lang=en.

Islom.uz. 2013. "Mir i spokoistvie—bestsennyi dar" [Peace and tranquility is a priceless thing]. Accessed May 13, 2013. www.islam.uz/home/news/uzbekistan/1445-l--r.html.

Jalilov, Chubak ajy. 2014. *Baktyluuluktun formulasy*. Bishkek: Dilazyk.

Jones Luong, Pauline. 2002. *Institutional Change and Political Continuity in Post-Soviet Central Asia: Power, Perceptions, and Pacts*. Cambridge: Cambridge University Press.

Jones Luong, Pauline. 2003. "The Middle Easternization of Central Asia." *Current History* 102, no. 666 (October): 333–40.

Jones Luong, Pauline. 2014. *Measuring Religiosity in Central Asia: The Pluralism of Piety and Its Political Implications*. Manuscript, University of Michigan.

Jones Luong, Pauline, and Erika Weinthal. 2002. "New Friends New Fears in Central Asia." *Foreign Affairs* 81, no. 2 (March–April): 61–70.

Jonikhonov, Maqsud. 2011. "Uzbek Pundit Fears 'Immoral' Internet Pages May Pose Threat to Youth." Tashkent Khalq Sozi, January 28. Foreign Broadcasting Information Service (FBIS) translation from Uzbek.

Jumhurii Tojikiston. 1998. *Qonuni Jumhurii Tojikiston dar borai din va taškilothoi dini* [Law of the Republic of Tajikistan on religion and religious associations]. Dushanbe: Irfon.

Jumhurii Tojikiston. 2007. *Sanadhoi me'yorii huquqi oid ba tanzimi an'ana va jašnu marosimho* [Law on regulating traditions, festivities, and ceremonies]. Dushanbe: Nashriyoti Sharqi ozod.

Jumhurii Tojikiston. 2009. *Qonuni Jumhurii Tojikiston dar borai ozodii vijdon va ittihodiyahoi dini* [Law of the Republic of Tajikistan on the freedom of conscience and religious associations]. Dushanbe: Irfon.

Jumhurii Tojikiston. 2011. *Qonuni Jumhurii Tojikiston dar boraoi ma'suliyati padaru modar dar ta'limu tabiyai farzand* [Law of the Republic of Tajikistan on the responsibility of the father and mother in the education and upbringing of a child]. Dushanbe: Irfon.

Kamalov, Ekin. 2012. "Southern Kyrgyzstan Fears Influence of Hizb ut-Tahrir." *Central Asia Online*, November 30. Accessed September 9, 2013. http://centralasiaonline.com/en_GB/ articles/caii/features/main/2012/11/30/feature-01?mobile=true.

Kamilov, Najmiddin. 1995. *Najmiddin Kubra, Abdullah Qadiri Nomidagi Khalq Merosi*. Tashkent: Uzbekistan.

Kamp, Marianne R. 2001. "Three Lives of Saodat: Communist, Uzbek, Survivor." *Oral History Review* 28, no. 2, 21–58.

Kamp, Marianne R. 2006. *The New Woman in Uzbekistan: Islam, Modernity, and Unveiling under Communism*. Seattle: University of Washington Press.

Kamrava, Mehran. 2006. *The New Voices of Islam: Rethinking Politics and Modernity: A Reader*. Berkeley: University of California Press.

Kandiyoti, Deniz. 2007. The Politics of Gender and the Soviet Paradox: Neither Colonized, nor Modern? *Central Asian Survey* 26, no. 4, 601–23.

Kandiyoti, Deniz, and Nadira Azimova. 2004. "The Communal and the Sacred: Women's Worlds of Ritual in Uzbekistan." *Journal of the Royal Anthropological Institute* 10, no. 2, 327–49.

Karagiannis, Emmanuel. 2009. *Political Islam in Central Asia: The Challenge of Hizb ut-Tahrir*. London: Routledge.

Karim, B. 1997. *Faryodi solho: Hujjat, dalel, tabsira, khulosa* [Recalling the years: Documents, proofs, collections, conclusions]. Moscow: Transdornauka.

Karimov, Islom. 1998. *Uzbekistan on the Threshold of the Twenty-First Century: Challenges to Stability and Progress*. New York: St. Martin's Press.

Keller, Shoshana. 2001. *To Moscow, Not Mecca: The Soviet Campaign Against Islam in Central Asia, 1917–1941*. Westport, CT: Praeger.

Keller, Shoshana. 2007. "Going to School in Uzbekistan." In Sahadeo and Zanca, *Everyday Life in Central Asia*, 248–65.

Kemper, Michael, and Stephan Conermann. 2011. *The Heritage of Soviet Oriental Studies*. New York: Routledge.

Kendzior, Sarah. 2012. "Digital Freedom of Expression in Uzbekistan." New America Foundation. Accessed October 12, 2012. http://newamerica.net/sites/newamerica.net/files/policydocs/KendziorFINAL7172012.

Kenjaev, Safarali. 1993. *Tabadduloti Tojikiston* [The transformation of Tajikistan]. Vol. 1. Dushanbe: Fondi Kenjaev.

Khalid, Adeeb. 1998. *The Politics of Muslim Cultural Reform: Jadidism in Central Asia*. Berkeley: University of California Press.

Khalid, Adeeb. 2003. "A Secular Islam: Nation, State, and Religion in Uzbekistan." *International Journal of Middle Eastern Studies*, no. 35, 573–98.

Khalid, Adeeb. 2007. *Islam after Communism: Religion and Politics in Central Asia*. Berkeley: University of California Press.

Khalid Masud, Muhammad. 2000. *Travellers in Faith: Studies of the Tablighi Jama'at as a Transnational Islamic Movement for Faith Renewal*. Boston: Brill.

Khazanov, A. M. 1994. "Underdevelopment and Ethnic Relations in Central Asia." In *Central Asia in Historical Perspective*, edited by Beatrice F. Manz, 144–63. Boulder, CO: Westview Press.

Khushkadamova, Khalima. 2010. "Women's Self-Immolation as a Social Phenomenon." *Sociological Research* 49, no. 1, 75–91.

Kislyakov, Nikolaj. 1966–76. *Tadžiki karategina i darvaza*. 3 vols. Dushanbe: Doniš.

Klimovič, Lyucian. 1965. *Islam*. Mosow: Nauka.

Knorr Cetina, Karin, and Alex Preda, eds. 2005. *The Sociology of Financial Markets*. Oxford: Oxford University Press.

Knysh, Alexander. 2002. "Sufism as an Explanatory Paradigm: The Motivations of Sufi Resistance Movements in Western and Russian Scholarship." *Die Welt des Islams* 42, no. 2, 139–73.

Knysh, Alexander. 2007. "Contextualizing the Salafi-Sufi Conflict (from the Northern Caucasus to Hadramawt)." *Middle Eastern Studies* 43, no. 4 (July): 503–30.

Kolig, Erich. 2012. *Conservative Islam: A Cultural Anthropology*. Lanham, MD: Lexington Books.

Kotkin, Stephen. 1995. *Magnetic Mountain: Stalinism as a Civilization*. Berkeley: University of California Press.

Kramer, Annette. 2001. "Crisis and Memory in Central Asian Islam: The Uzbek Example of the 'Otin' and 'Xalfa' in a Changing Environment." In *Crisis and Memory in Islamic Societies: Proceedings of the Third Summer Academy of the Working Group Modernity and Islam Held at the Orient Institute of the German Oriental Society in Beirut*, edited by Angelika Neuwirth and Andreas Pflitsch. Beiruter Texte Und Studien, Bd. 77. Beruit: Ergon Verlag Wurzburg in Kommission, 366–67.

Krauss, Steven Eric, Azimi Hamzah, and Fazila Idris. 2007. "Adaption of a Muslim Religiosity Scale for Faith Communities in Malaysia." *Review of Religious Research* 49, no. 2, 147–64.

Krivosheev, P. S. , U. A. Rustamov, and N. I. Hasanov, eds. 1987. "Zakon, religiia, tserkov" [Law, religion, and church]. Tashkent.

Kubik, Jan. 2009. "Ethnography of Politics: Foundations, Applications, Prospects." In *Political Ethnography. What Immersion Contributes to the Study of Power*, edited by Edward Schatz, 25–52. Chicago: University of Chicago Press.

Kuchumkulova, Elmira. 2007. "Kyrgyz Nomadic Customs and the Impact of Re-Islamization after Independence." PhD dissertation, University of Washington.

Kumkova, K. 2012. "Silly Dictator Story #7: 1000 Weddings in Uzbekistan (Whether You Like It or Not)." *Eurasianet.org*, July 12. Accessed July 19, 2012. http://www.eurasianet.org/65656.

Kuran, Timur. 2005. "The Absence of the Corporation in Islamic Law: Origins and Persistence." *American Journal of Comparative Law*, no. 53, 785–834.

Kutueva, Aizada. 2011. "The Doubts about the Data of Kyrgyzstan's State National Security Committee on the Number of Supporters of the Extremist Organization Hizb ut-Tahrir." September 12, 24 news agency. Accessed September 9, 2013. http://eng.24.kg/community/2011/09/12/20253.html.

Ladbury, Sarah, and Seema Khan. 2008. *Increased Religiosity among Women in Muslim Majority Countries*. Birmingham: University of Birmingham Press.

Lamoreaux, Naomi. 1994. *Insider Lending: Banking, Personal Connections, and Economic Development in Industrial New England*. Cambridge: Cambridge University Press.

Lapidus, Ira. 1996. "State and Religion in Islamic Societies." *Past and Present* 151, 3–27.

Lapidus, Ira. 1999. *The Cambridge Illustrated History of the Islamic World*. Cambridge: Cambridge University Press.

LaPierre, Brian. 2012. *Hooligans in Khrushchev's Russia: Defining, Policing, and Producing Deviance during the Thaw*. Madison: University of Wisconsin Press.

Laruelle, Marlene. 2007. "The Return of the Aryan Myth: Tajikistan in Search of a Secularized National Ideology." *Nationalities Papers* 35, no. 1, 51–70.

Lemon, Edward. 2010. "Tajikistan: Dushanbe Forcing Students Abroad to Return Home." November 29. http://www.eurasianet.org/node/62460.

Liebelt, Claudia. 2008. "Touristinnen, nicht Arbeiterinnen! 'Philippinische Pflegekräfte in Israel auf Pilgerfahrt' im Heiligen Land." In *Migration und Religiöse Dynamik: Ethnologische Religionsforschung im Transnationalen Kontext*, edited by Andrea Lauser and Cordula Weiss-köppel, 173–95. Bielefeld: Transcript Verlag.

Lipovsky, Igor. 1996. "The Awakening of Central Asian Islam." *Middle Eastern Studies* 32, no. 3, 1–21.

Louw, Maria E. 2007. *Everyday Islam in Post-Soviet Central Asia*. London: Routledge.

Lubin, Nancy, and Barnett R. Rubin. 1999. *Calming the Ferghana Valley: Development and Dialogue in the Heart of Central Asia*. New York: Century Foundation Press.

Lynch, D. 2001. "The Tajik Civil War and Peace Process." *Civil Wars* 4, no. 4, 49–72.

MacKenzie, Donald. 2003. "Opening the Black Boxes of Global Finance." Paper presented at the workshop "Approaches to Global Finance." University of Warwick, February.

Mahmood, Saba. 2005. *Politics of Piety: The Islamic Revival and the Feminist Subject*. Princeton, NJ: Princeton University Press.

Makhmudov, A. 2010. "Travlia Umidy Akhmedovoi vyplesnulas' na stranitsy gazet" [The case of Umida Akhmedova splashed across the newspapers]. Fergana.ru, February 22. Accessed October 13, 2012. http://www.fergananews.com/article.php?id=6480.

Makris, G. P. 2007. *Islam in the Middle East: A Living Tradition*. Malden: Blackwell.

Malashenko, Andrey. 1999. "Islam and Politics in Central Asian States." In *Political Islam and Conflicts in Russia and Central Asia*, edited by Lena Jonson and Murad Esenov, 9–18. Stockholm: CA&CC Press.

Mandaville, Peter G. 2002. "Reimagining the *Ummah*? Information Technologies and the Changing Boundaries of Political Islam." In *Islam Encountering Globalization*, edited by Ali Mohammadi, 61–90. New York: Routledge.

Mandaville, Peter G. 2005. "Sufis and Salafis: The Political Discourse of Transnational Islam."

In *Remaking Muslim Politics: Pluralism, Contestation, and Democratization*, edited by Robert Hefner, 302–25. Princeton, NJ: Princeton University Press.

Manger, Leif O. 1999. "Muslim Diversity: Local Islam in Global Contexts." In *Muslim Diversity: Local Islam in Global Contexts*, edited by Leif O. Manger, 1–36. Richmond, UK: Curzon Press.

Mansurov, Shamuhiddin, ed. 1990. *Ghaiblar Khailidan Yangan Chiragh.* Tashkent: Uzbekistan.

Marcus, George E. 1995. "Ethnography in/of the World System: The Emergence of Multi-Sited Ethnography." *Annual Review of Anthropology* 24, 95–117.

Markazi islomshinosi (dar nazdi Prezidenti Jumhurii Tojikiston) [The Center for Islamic Studies (under the President of the Republic of Tajikistan)]. 1998. *Ethnography through Thick and Thin.* Princeton, NJ: Princeton University Press.

Markazi islomšinosi (dar nazdi Prezidenti Jumhurii Tojikiston), ed. 2009. *Šarhi musnadi Abuhanifa (r) bo qalami Mullo Aliqorii Hanafi (rh)* [Exposition to the sources of Abuhanifa (r) by Mullo Aliqorii Hanafa (rh)]. Dushanbe: ER-graf.

Marranci, Gabriele. 2008. *The Anthropology of Islam.* Oxford: Berg.

Matsuzato, Kimitaka, and Magomed-Rasul Ibragimov. 2005. "Islamic Politics at the Sub-Regional Level in Dagestan: Tariqa Brotherhoods, Ethnicities, Localism and the Spiritual Board." *Europe-Asia Studies* 57, no. 5 (July): 753–79.

Maurer, Bill. 2002. "Repressed Futures: Financial Derivatives' Theological Unconscious." *Economy and Society* 31, no. 1, 15–36.

Maxala.org. 2012. "Imamy Uzbekistana obsudili 'arabskuiu vesnu'" [Imams of Uzbekistan discussed the "Arab Spring"]. November 19. Accessed November 30, 2012. maxala.org/politika /0296-imamy-uzbekistana-obsudili-arabskuyu-vesnu.html#.UZE-jaKmiAg.

Mayer, Ann Elizabeth. 2006. *Islam and Human Rights: Tradition and Politics.* Boulder, CO: Westview Press.

McAndrew, Siobhan, and David Voas. 2011. "Measuring Religiosity Using Surveys." *Survey Question Bank: Topic Overview* 4, 1–15.

McBrien, Julie. 2006. "Listening to the Wedding Speaker: Discussing Religion and Culture in Southern Kyrgyzstan." *Central Asian Survey* 25, no. 3, 314–57.

McBrien, Julie. 2009. "Mukadas's Struggle: Veils and Modernity in Kyrgyzstan." *Journal of the Royal Anthropological Institute* 15, s.1, S127–S144.

McBrien, Julie. 2012. "Watching *Clone*: Brazilian Soap Operas and Muslimness in Kyrgyzstan." *Material Religion* 8, no. 3, 374–96.

McBrien, Julie, and Mathijs Pelkmans. 2008. "Turning Marx on His Head: Missionaries, 'Extremists' and Archaic Secularists in Post-Soviet Kyrgyzstan." *Critique of Anthropology* 28, no. 1, 87–103.

McGlinchey, Eric. 2004. "Constructing Militant Opposition: Authoritarian Rule and Political Islam in Central Asia." Paper prepared for the Yale Lecture Series on Central Asia. April 6.

McGlinchey, Eric. 2007. "Divided Faith: Trapped Between State and Islam in Uzbekistan." In Sahadeo and Zanca, *Everyday Life in Central Asia*, 305–18.

McGlinchey, Eric. 2009. "Islamic Revivalism and State Failure in Kyrgyzstan." *Problems of Post-Communism* 56, no. 3, 16–28.

McGlinchey, Eric. 2011. *Chaos, Violence, Dynasty: Politics and Islam in Central Asia.* Pittsburgh: University of Pittsburgh Press.

McLoughlin, Sean. 2010. "Muslim Travellers: Homing Desire, the *Umma* and British-Pakistanis." In *Diasporas: Concepts, Intersections, Identities*, edited by Kim Knott and Sean McLoughlin, 223–29. London: Zed Books.

Medvedev, Vladimir. 1994. "O saga Bobo Sangak: Voine" [The saga of Bob Sangak: war]. *Dru-zhba Narodov* 6, 187–204.

Mehmet, Ozay. 2002. *Islamic Identity and Development: Studies of the Islamic Periphery*. New York: Routledge.

Meijer, Roel. 2009. *Global Salafism: Islam's New Religious Movement*. London: Hurst.

Metcalf, Barbara. 1994. "'Remaking Ourselves': Islamic Self-fashioning in a Global Movement of Spiritual Renewal." In *Accounting for Fundamentalisms*, edited by Martin E. Marty and R. Scott Appleby, 706–25. Chicago: University of Chicago Press.

Metcalf, Barbara. 1996. *Making Muslim Space in North America and Europe*. Berkeley: University of California Press.

Mirsaitov, I., and A. Saipov. 2006. "Byvshie soratniki Takhira Iuldasheva rasskazyvaiut o tom, chto takoe 'Islamskoe dvizhenie Uzbekistana' segodnia" [Former supporters of Tahir Yulda-shev discuss what the "Islamic Movement" is today]. *Fergana.ru*. April 16. Accessed September 13, 2013. http://www.fergananews.com/articles/4348.

Moaddel, Mansoor. 2005. *Islamic Modernism, Nationalism, and Fundamentalism. Episode and Discourse*. Chicago: University of Chicago Press.

Moaddel, Mansoor, ed. 2007. *Values and Perceptions of the Islamic and Middle Eastern Publics*. New York: Palgrave Macmillan.

Monsutti, Alessandro. 2007. "Migration as a Rite of Passage: Young Afghans Building Mascu-linity and Adulthood in Iran." *Iranian Studies* 40, no. 2, 167–85.

Montgomery, David. 2007. "*Namaz*, Wishing Trees, and Vodka: The Diversity of Everyday Re-ligious Life in Central Asia." In Sahadeo and Zanca, *Everyday Life in Central Asia*, 355–70.

Moskoff, William. 1990. *The Bread of Affliction: the Food Supply in the USSR during World War II*. New York: Cambridge University Press.

Motadel, David. 2014. *Islam and the European Empires*. Oxford: Oxford University Press.

Muftiyat. 2013. *Islamic Institutions in Kyrgyzstan*. Accessed April 12, 2013. http://muftiyat.kg/ category/mod.

Mullojonov, Parviz. 2001. "The Islamic Clergy in Tajikistan since the End of the Soviet Period." In *Islam in Politics in Russia and Central Asia*, edited by Stéphane A. Dudoignon and Hisao Komatsu, 221–50. London: Kegan Paul.

Muminov, Ashirbek, Uygun Gafurov, and Rinat Shigabdinov. 2010. "Islamic Education in Soviet and Post-Soviet Uzbekistan." In *Islamic Education in the Soviet Union and Its Successor States*, edited by Michael Kemper, Raoul Motika, and Stefan Reichmuth, 107–67. London: Routledge.

Mustafina, R. M. 1992. *Predstavleniia, kul'ty, obriady u Kazakhov* [Superstitions, cults, and ritu-als of the Kazakhs]. Alma-Ata: Kazakhstan.

Myrzabekov, Ashad. 2004. "Allaga shirk keltirüü" [Worshipping idols other than God]. *Islam Madaniyaty* 36, no. 52, 3.

Najibullah, Farangis. 2003. "Central Asia: A Visit to Ferghana Valley—Exploring the Roots of Religious Extremism." *Ferghana News*. Accessed May 11, 2015. http://enews.ferghana.ru/ article.php?id=220.

Narmatov, Abdyshükür. 2011. *Juma Kutbasy* [Friday sermon] (video).

Nasr, S. V. R. 1999. "European Colonialism and the Emergence of Modern Muslim States." In *The Oxford History of Islam*, edited by John L. Esposito, 549–600. New York: Oxford University Press.

Nasridinov, Emil, and Aksana Ismailbekova. 2012. "Transnational Social Networks and Tra-jectories of Religious Practices and Discourses of Kyrgyz Dawatchis." *Transnational Social Review—A Social Work Journal*, no. 3, 177–95.

Nasriddinov, Hikmatullo. 1995. *Tarkish*. Dushanbe: Afsona.

Naumescu, Vlad. 2007. *Modes of Religiosity in Eastern Christianity: Religious Processes and Social Change in Ukraine*. Berlin: LIT, Global Book Marketing.

Naumkin, Vitalii Viacheslavovich. 2005. *Radical Islam in Central Asia: Between Pen and Rifle*. Lanham, MD: Rowman and Littlefield.

Nazarbaev [Nazarbayev], Nursultan. 2003. *Kriticheskoe desiatiletie* [The critical decade]. Almaty: Atamura.

Nazarov, Bakhtiyar A., and Denis Sinor, eds. 1993. *Essays on Uzbek History, Culture, and Language*. Bloomington: Indiana University, Research Institute for Inner Asian Studies.

Ne'matov, N. 2003. *Ta'rixi xalqi Tojik* [The history of the Tajik people]. Dushanbe: Sarparast.

Niyazi, Aziz. 1999. "Islam and Tajikistan's Human and Ecological Crisis." In *Civil Society in Central Asia*, edited by M. Holt Ruffin and Daniel C. Waugh, 180–97. Seattle: University of Washington Press.

Niyazov, Saparmurat. 2005. *Rukhnama: Reflections on the Spiritual Values of the Turkmen*. Ashabat, Turkmenistan: Ashabat Press.

Niyazova, Makhinur. 2012. "The Leader of Hizb ut-Tahrir Local Unit, So-called 'Emir' of the Region, Detained in Jalal-Abad City (Kyrgyzstan)." August 27. Accessed September 9, 2013. http://www.khilafah.com/index.php/news-watch/central-asia/14556-the -leader-of-hizb-ut-tahrir-local-unit-so-called-qemirq-of-the-region-detained-in-jalal -abad-city-kyrgyzstan.

Norris, Pippa, and Ronald F. Ingelhart. 2011. *Sacred and Secular: Religion and Politics Worldwide*. 2nd ed. Cambridge: Cambridge University Press.

Northrop, Douglas. 2001. "Subaltern Dialogues: Subversion and Resistance in Soviet Uzbek Family Law." *Slavic Review* 60, no. 1, 115–39.

Northrop, Douglas Taylor. 2004. *Veiled Empire: Gender and Power in Stalinist Central Asia*. Ithaca, NY: Cornell University Press.

Nourzhanov, K. 2005. "Saviours or Robber Barons? Warlord Politics in Tajikistan." *Central Asian Survey* 24, no. 2, 109–30.

Nozimova, Shahnoza, and Tim Epkenhans. 2013. "Negotiating Islam in Emerging Public Spheres in Contemporary Tajikistan." *Asiatische Studien Études Asiatiques* 67, no. 3, 965–90.

Nuriddinov, Š., and Imomov, A. 2009. *Tajribai rasmigardonii masjidho dar šahri Dušanbe* [The practice of registering mosques in the city of Dushanbe]. Dushanbe: Devaštič.

O'Dell, Emily J. 2013. "Waging War on the Dead: The Necropolitics of Sufi Shrine Destruction in Mali." *Archaeologies: Journal of the World Archaeological Congress*, December, 506–25.

Office of Muslim Affairs. 2012. "Tezis 47: Yurt Tinchligi—Oliy Saodat!" [Sermon no. 47: peace in the homeland is supreme happiness!]. November 9.

Ogudin, V. L. 2003. "Tron Solomona: istoriia formirovaniia kul'ta" [The throne of Solomon: history of the formation of a cult]. In *Podvizhniki Islama: kul't sviatykh i sufizm v Srednei Azii i na Kavkaze* [Followers of Islam: the cult of saints and Sufism in Central Asia and the Caucasus], edited by S. N. Abashin and V. O. Bobrovnikov, 63–75. Moscow: Vostochnaia literatura RAN.

Olcott, Martha Brill. 1987. *The Kazakhs*. Stanford, CA: Hoover Institution Press.

Olcott, Martha Brill. 1994. "Central Asia's Islamic Awakening." *Current History* 93 (April): 150–54.

Olcott, Martha Brill. 2007a. "Roots of Radical Islam in Central Asia." Carnegie Papers 77. Washington, DC, Carnegie Endowment for International Peace.

Olcott, Martha Brill. 2007b. "Sufism in Central Asia: A Force for Moderation or a Cause of Politicization?" Washington, DC, Carnegie Papers.

Olcott, Martha Brill. 2012. *In the Whirlwind of Jihad*. Washington, DC: Carnegie Endowment for International Peace.

Omelicheva, Mariya Y. 2007. "Ethnic Dimension of Religious Extremism and Terrorism in Central Asia." Paper presented at the Annual Meeting of the International Studies Association, Chicago, February 28–March 3.

Orozbekova, Cholpon. 2005. "Vybory v Kyrgyzstane proshli pod znakom traibalizma" [Elections in Kyrgyzstan were marked by tribalism]. Institute for War and Peace Reporting, February 21.

Orozbekova, Cholpon. 2009. "Kyrgyz Presidential Election Failed to Meet Key OSCE Commitments, Despite Some Positive Elements." OSCE/ODIHR press release, July 24.

OSCE/ODIHR. 2008. "Comments on the Draft Law of the Republic of Tajikistan 'The Law of the Republic of Tajikistan about Freedom of Conscience and Religious Unions.'" REL-TAJ/100/2008. www.legislationonline.org.

O'zbekiston Telekanli [Uzbekistan State Television]. 2014. "Xiyonat" [Betrayal]. December 17. Accessed August 6, 2015. https://www.youtube.com/watch?v=IntQoRMiOio&list=UUx6 CIX5LtVh59T67e_lnn2Q.

Ozodlik Radiosi (RFE/RL Uzbek Language Service). "Hayrullo Hamidov: Ozod Etilganimdan Xursandman!" [I am glad to have been set free!] February 11. Accessed August 6, 2015. http://www.ozodlik.mobi/a/26842496.html?utm_medium=twitter&utm_source=twitterfeed.

Palan, Ronen. 2003. *The Offshore World: Sovereign Markets, Virtual Places and Nomad Millionaires*. Ithaca, NY: Cornell University Press.

Panchenko, Alexander. 2012. "'Popular Orthodoxy' and Identity in Soviet and Post-Soviet Russia: Ideology, Consumption, and Competition." In *Soviet and Post-Soviet Identities*, edited by Mark Bassin and Catriona Kelly, 321–40. New York: Cambridge University Press.

Papas, Alexandre, Thomas Welsford, and Thierry Zarcone, eds. 2012. *Central Asian Pilgrims. Hajj Routes and Pious Visits between Central Asia and the Hijaz*. Berlin: Klaus Schwarz Verlag.

Parry, Jonathan, and Maurice Bloch. 1989. *Money and the Morality of Exchange*. Cambridge: Cambridge University Press.

Paul, Jürgen. 1991. *Die politische und soziale Bedeutung der Naqšbandiyya in Mittelasien im 15. Jahrhundert*. Berlin: De Gruyter.

Pedersen, Morten A. 2012. "Proposing the Motion: Morten Axel Pedersen." *Critique of Anthropology* 32, no. 1, 59–65.

Pepinsky, Thomas. 2013. "Development, Social Change, and Islamic Finance in Contemporary Indonesia." *World Development* 41 (January): 157–67.

Peshkova, Svetlana. 2006. "Otinchalar in the Ferghana Valley: Islam, Gender, and Power." Manuscript. Department of Anthropology, Syracuse University.

Peshkova, Svetlana. 2009. Bringing the Mosque Home and Talking Politics: Women, Space, and Islam in the Ferghana Valley. *Contemporary Islam: Dynamics of Muslim Life* 3, no. 3, d251–73.

Peshkova, Svetlana. 2014. *Women, Islam, and Identity: Public Life in Private Spaces in Uzbekistan*. Syracuse: Syracuse University Press.

Petros, Tiffany. 2004. "Islam in Central Asia: The Emergence and Growth of Radicalism in the Post-Communist Era." In *The Tracks of Tamerlane: Central Asia's Path to the 21st Century*, edited by Dan Burghart and Theresa Sabonis-Helf, 139–55. Washington, DC: National Defense University, Center for Technology and National Security Policy.

Peuch, Jean C. 2004. "Turkey: Fethullahci Schools—A Greenhouse for Central Asian Elites?" RFE/RL. Accessed July 9, 2010. http://www.rferl.org/content/article/1053209.html.

Pew Research Center. 2013. *The World's Muslims: Unity and Diversity*. http://www.pewforum.org/2012/08/09/the-worlds-muslims-unity-and-diversity.

Pew Research Center. 2014. *Russians Return to Religion, but Not to Church.* http://www.pewforum .org/2014/02/10/russians-return-to-religion-but-not-to-church.

Peyrouse, Sebastien. 2007. "Christians as the Main Religious Minority in Central Asia." In Sahadeo and Canca, *Everyday Life in Central Asia,* 371–83.

Pitluck, Aaron. 2013. "Islamic Banking and Finance: Alternative or Façade?" In *The Oxford Handbook of the Sociology of Finance,* edited by Karin Knorr Cetina and Alex Preda, 431–49. Oxford: Oxford University Press.

Polat, Abdumannob. 2000. "The Islamic Revival in Uzbekistan: A Threat to Stability?" In *Islam and Central Asia: An Enduring Legacy or an Evolving Threat?* edited by R. Z. Sagdeev and S. Eisenhower, 39–57. Washington, DC: Center for Political and Strategic Studies.

Poliakov, Sergei, ed. 1992. *Everyday Islam: Religion and Tradition in Rural Central Asia.* Armonk, NY: M. E. Sharpe.

Polonskaia, L. R. 1986. "Vvedenie" [Introduction]. In *Islam v sovremennoi politike stran Vostoka* [Islam in the contemporary politics of the countries of the East], edited by L. R. Polonskaia, 1–10. Moscow: Nauka.

Ponomarev, Vitalii. 2009. "Kyrgyzstan: narusheniia prav cheloveka v sviazi s delom o 'Nookatskih sobytiiah'" [Kyrgyzstan: violations of human rights in connection with the "Nookat events"]. Report of the Moscow-based human rights center Memorial, January 27.

Privratsky, Bruce G. 2001. *Muslim Turkistan: Kazak Religion and Collective Memory.* Surrey: Curzon Press.

Prozorov, S.M. 2001. *Islam na territorii byvshei Rossiiskoi imperii: Entsiklopedicheskii slovar'. No. 3* [Islam on the territory of the former Russian Empire: Encyclopedic dictionary no. 3]. Moscow: Vostochnaia literatura RAN.

Rabinow, Paul. 2003. *Anthropos Today: Reflections on Modern Equipment.* Princeton, NJ: Princeton University Press.

Radio Free Europe Radio Liberty (RFE/RL). 2011a. "Ethnic Uzbek Imam Freed from Detention in Kyrgyzstan." February 3. Accessed September 9, 2013. http://www.rferl.org/content/ uzbekistan_imam_kygyzstan/2296884.html.

Radio Free Europe Radio Liberty (RFE/RL). 2011b. "Chief Kyrgyz Mufti Faces Accusations." September 2. Accessed May 18, 2015. http://www.rferl.org/content/kyrgyzstan_mufti_hajj _accusations/24316078.html.

Radio Free Europe Radio Liberty (RFE/RL). 2012a. "Tashkent Mayor Seeks to Tone Down Extravagant Weddings." September 24. Accessed September 24, 2012. http://www.rferl .org/23718526.html.

Radio Free Europe Radio Liberty (RFE/RL). 2012b. "Kyrgyz Grand Mufti Resigns Amid Controversy." July 17. Accessed May 14, 2015. http://www.rferl.org/content/kyrgyz-grand -mufti-chubak-hajji-jalilov/24647660.html.

Radtke, B. 2002. "Wali." In *The Encyclopedia of Islam.* New edition, edited by P. J. Bearman, T. Bianquis, C. E. Bosworth, E. van Donzel, and W. P. Heinrichs. Vol. 11, 109–12. Leiden: Brill.

Radnitz, Scott. 2005. "Networks, Localism and Mobilization in Aksy, Kyrgyzstan." *Central Asian Survey* 24, no. 4, 405–24.

Rahimov, Nabi. 2002. *Duhovnij Polet Nafisahon Khadji.* Tashkent: M.A.N.T. Uzbekistana.

Rahimzoda, H., and Axmadov, S. 2000. *Ta'rixi din* [The history of religion]. Dushanbe: NPZ.

Rahmon[ov], Emomali. 2001. *Istiqloliyat ne'mati bebahost* [Independence is a priceless blessing]. Dushanbe: Šarqi ozod.

Rahmon[ov], Emomali. 2001–8. *The Tajiks in the Mirror of History: From the Aryans to the Samanids.* 3 vols. London: River Editions.

Rahmon[ov], Emomali. 2002. *Istiqloliyati Tojikiston va ehyoi Millat* [The independence of Tajikistan and the resurrection of the nation]. Vol. 2. Dushanbe: Irfon.

Rahmon[ov], Emomali. 2006. *Dar borai din* [On relgion]. Dushanbe: Šarqi ozod.

Rahmon[ov], Emomali. 2009. *Imomi A'zam va guftugūi tammadunho: Imomi A'zam va huvijati millī.* [The Great Imam and dialogue of civilizations: The Great Imam and national identity]. Dushanbe: Adib.

Rahnamo, Abdullo. 2008. *Hizbi dini va davlati dunyavi* [The religious party and the secular government]. Dushanbe: Irfon.

Rahnamo, Abdullo. 2009. *Ulamoi Islomi dar Tojikiston* [The Islamic ulema in Tajikistan]. Dushanbe: Irfon.

Rahnamo, Abdullo. 2011. *Islom va amniyati milli dar Tojikiston* [Islam and national security in Tajikistan]. Dushanbe: Irfon.

Rapport, Nigel. 2010. *Human Nature as Capacity: Transcending Discourse and Classification.* New York: Berghahn Books.

Rasanayagam, Johan. 2006a. "Post Soviet Islam: An Anthropological Perspective." Introduction to Special Issue. *Central Asian Survey* 25, no. 3, 219–33.

Rasanayagam, Johan. 2006b. "Healing with Spirits and the Formation of Muslim Selfhood in Post-Soviet Uzbekistan." *Journal of the Royal Anthropological Institute* 12, no. 2, 377–93.

Rasanayagam, Johan. 2010. *Islam in Post-Soviet Uzbekistan: The Morality of Experience.* Cambridge: Cambridge University Press.

Rashid, Ahmed. 1994. *The Resurgence of Central Asia: Islam or Nationalism?* Oxford: Oxford University Press.

Rashid, Ahmed. 2002. *Jihad: The Rise of Militant Islam in Central Asia.* New Haven, CT: Yale University Press.

Raximzoda, H., and Axmadov, S. 2000. *Ta'rixi din* [The history of religion]. Dushanbe: NPZ.

Reetz, Dietrich. 2008. "The 'Faith Bureaucracy' of the Tablighi Jama'at: An Insight into Their System of Self-Organisation." In *Colonialism, Modernity, and Religious Identities: Religious Reform Movements in South Asia*, edited by Gwilym Beckerlegge, 98–124. Oxford: Oxford University Press.

Reetz, Dietrich. 2009a. "Conflicts in Islam on the Asian and African 'Periphery': Doctrines, Cultures, and Politics." In *Religions and the Modern World*, edited by Giovanni Filoramo and Roberto Tottoli, 478–513. Turin: Einaudi.

Reetz, Dietrich. 2009b. "Tablighi Jama'at." In *The Oxford Encyclopedia of the Islamic World Volume 5*, edited by John L. Esposito, 293–99. New York: Oxford University Press.

Reetz, Dietrich. 2010. "'Alternate Globalities?' On the Cultures and Formats of Transnational Muslim Networks from South Asia." In *Translocality: The Study of Globalizing Processes from a Southern Perspective*, edited by Ulrike Freitag and Achim von Oppen, 293–334. Leiden: Brill.

Reetz, Dietrich. 2013. "Travelling Islam: Madrasa Graduates from India and Pakistan in the Malay Archipelago." ZMO Working Paper.

Reliefweb. 2007. "Religious Discontent Evident in the Ferghana Valley." January 17. Accessed May 18, 2015. http://www.reliefweb.int/rw/rwb.nsf/db900sid/KHII-6XK3C6?OpenDocument.

Reynolds, Michael. 2005. "Myths and Mysticism: A Longitudinal Perspective on Islam and Conflict in the North Caucasus." *Middle Eastern Studies* 41, no. 1 (January): 31–54.

Roberts, Sean R. 2007. "Everyday Negotiations of Islam in Central Asia: Practicing Religion in the Uyghur Neighborhood of *Zarya Vostoka* in Almaty, Kazakhstan." In Sahadeo and Zanca, *Everyday Life in Central Asia*, 339–54.

Roche, Sophie. 2010. "Domesticating Youth: The Youth Bulge in Post-Civil War Tajikistan." Dissertation, Martin Luther University Halle-Wittenberg.

Ro'i, Yaacov. 1995. "The Secularization of Islam and the USSR's Muslim areas." In *Muslim Eurasia: Conflicting Legacies*, edited by Yaacov Ro'i, 5–20. London: Frank Cass.

Ro'i, Yaacov. 1997. *La Nouvelle Asie Centralle ou la fabrication des nations*. Paris: Seuil.

Ro'i, Yaacov. 2000. *Islam in the Soviet Union: From the Second World War to Gorbachev*. New York: Columbia University Press.

Ro'i, Yaacov, and Alon Wainer. 2009. "Muslim Identity and Islamic Practice in Post-Soviet Central Asia." *Central Asian Survey* 28, no. 3, 303–22.

Roy, Olivier. 1994. *The Failure of Political Islam*. Cambridge, MA: Harvard University Press.

Roy, Olivier. 2000. *The New Central Asia: The Creation of Nations*. New York: New York University Press.

Roy, Olivier. 2004. *Globalized Islam: The Search for a New Ummah*. New York: Columbia University Press.

Ryskulov, Nimatulla, and Rahat Möküyeva. 2012. *Men emne üchün hijab kiyishim kerek?!!!* [Why must I wear hijab?!!!]. Bishkek: Proselytism and Propaganda Division, Spiritual Directorate of Kyrgyzstan Muslims.

Sabol, Steven. 1995. "The Creation of Soviet Central Asia: The 1924 National Delimitation." *Central Asian Survey* 14, no. 2, 225–41.

Sadriddin. 2009. "Navbat 'Nurchilarga' keldi" [Uzbek: it's the Nurchilars' turn now]. Ozodlik Radiosi [RFE/RL], February 13. Accessed August 5. 2010.http://www.ozodlik.org/content/Article/1492796.html.

Safronov, R. 2000. "Islam in Turkmenistan: The Niyazov Calculation." In *Islam and Central: An Enduring Legacy or an Evolving Threat?* edited by R. Sagdeev and S. Eisenhower, 73–92. Washington, DC: Center for Political and Strategic Studies.

Sahadeo, Jeff, and Russell Zanca, eds. 2007. *Everyday Life in Central Asia: Past and Present*. Bloomington: Indiana University Press.

Saidazimova, Gulnoza. 2005. "Kyrgysztan: Hizb ut-Tahrir Rallies in South, Urges Election Boycott." February 9. RFE/RL. Accessed September 9, 2013. http://www.rferl.org/content/article/1057368.html.

Saidazimova, Gulnoza. 2007. "Banned Islamic Group Hizb ut-Tahrir Continues to Gain Members." August 13. Eurasianet.org. Accessed September 13, 2013. http://www.eurasianet.org/departments/insight/articles/pp081407.shtml.

Šarifzoda, A., and Qozimi, Z. 2011. *Emomali Rahmon va soli Imomi A'zam* [Emomali Rahmon and the year of Imomi A'zam]. Dushanbe: Irfon.

Saroyan, Mark. 1994. "Authority and Community in Soviet Islam." In *Accounting for Fundamentalisms: The Dynamic Character of Movements*, edited by M. Marty and R. Appleby, 513–30. The Fundamentalism Project, 4. Chicago: University of Chicago Press.

Saroyan, Mark. 1996. "Beyond the Nation-State: Culture and Ethnic Politics in Soviet Transcaucasia." *Transcaucasia, Nationalism, and Social Change: Essays in the History of Armenia, Azerbaijan, and Georgia*, edited by Ronald Grigor Suny, 401–26. Ann Arbor: University of Michigan Press.

Saroyan, Mark. 1997. *Minorities, Mullahs, and Modernity: Reshaping Community in the Late Soviet Union*, edited by Edward W. Walker. Berkeley: University of California Press.

Sarygulov, Dastan. 2001. *Tengirdin jolunan adashkan adam* [The human being who has strayed from the way of Tengir]. Bishkek: Suröt-Basma-Salonu.

Schenkkan, Nate. 2011. "Kyrgyzstan: Islamic Revivalist Movement Quietly Flourishing." October 25. Accessed September 9, 2013. http://www.eurasianet.org/node/64378.

Schielke, Samuli, and Liza Debevec. 2012. "Introduction." In *Ordinary Lives and Grand Schemes: An Anthropology of Everyday Religion*, edited by Samuli Schielke and Liza Debevec, 1–16. New York: Berghahn Books.

Schmitz, Andrea. 2015. *Islam in Tadschikistan: Akteure, Diskurse, Konflikte* [Islam in Tajikistan: actors, discourses, conflicts]. Berlin: Stiftung Wissenschaft und Politik.

Schröder, Philipp, and Manja Stephan-Emmrich. 2014. "The Institutionalization of Mobility: Well-being and Social Hierarchies in Central Asian Translocal Livelihoods." *Mobilities.* DOI:10.1080/17450101.2014.984939.

Schubel, Vernon James. 1999. "Post-Soviet Hagiography and the Reconstruction of the Naqshbandī Tradition in Contemporary Uzbekistan." In *Naqshbandis in Western and Central Asia: Change and Continuity*, edited by Elisabeth Özdalga, 73–87. Istanbul: Swedish Research Institute.

Schubel, Vernon James. 2010. "Islamdyn ar türdüülüktü: Borborduk Aziyada chynygy Islamdy izdöö." In *Žalal-Abaddagy yjyk žerler žana él daany yjyk ük* [Sacred sites in Jalal-Abad and traditional wisdom], edited by Gülnara Aitpaeva, 455–70. Bishkek: Aigine Cultural Research Center.

Schwab, Wendell. 2015. "Islam, Fun, and Social Capital in Kazakhstan." *Central Asian Affairs* 2, 51–70.

Seidalieva, S. 2012. *Biz yimanduu baldarbyz* [We are honest children]. Bishkek: Dilazyk.

Seifert, A. 2008. "'Natsionalizatsiia' Islama, transformatsiia i vlast': nadlezhashchee upravlenie u svetskih gosudarstv s musul'manskimi bol'shinstvami naseleniia" [The "nationalization" of Islam, transformation and power: appropriate governance in secular states with a Muslim majority]. *Materialy mezhdunarodnogo "kruglogo stola"* [Proceedings of an international roundtable]. Bishkek: Kyrgyzstan.

Shahrani, M. Nazif. 1984. "'From Tribe to *umma*': Comments on the Dynamics of Identity in Muslim Soviet Central Asia." *Central Asian Survey* 3, no. 3, 27–38.

Shahrani, M. Nazif. 1991. "Local Knowledge of Islam and Social Discourse in Afghanistan and Turkistan in the Modern Period." In *Turko-Persia in Historical Perspective*, edited by Robert L. Canfield, 161–99. Cambridge: Cambridge University Press.

Shahrani, M. Nazif. 1993. "Central Asia and the Challenge of the Soviet Legacy." *Central Asian Survey* 12, no. 2, 123–35.

Shahrani, M. Nazif. 1994. "Islam and the Political Culture of 'Scientific Atheism' in Post-Soviet Central Asia: Future Predicament." *Islamic Studies* 33, nos. 2/3, 139–59.

Sharipov, Schkovorodyuk, et al. 2009. "Zakluchenie . . . na osnovanii postanovlenie sledovatelia po osobo vazhnym delam Otdel po rassledovaniiu prestuplenii prokuratury goroda Tashkenta O. Kh. Musaeva" [Expert finding commissioned by O. Kh. Musaev, investigator for especially important cases, Tashkent City Criminal Investigation Division, Tashkent City Prosecutor's Office]. August 5. Accessed October 12, 2012. http://news.fergananews.com/archive/2010/zakl.html.

Sheller, Mimi, and John Urry. 2006. "The New Mobilities Paradigm." *Environment and Planning* 38, no. 2, 207–26.

Sievers, Eric W. 2003. *The Post-Soviet Decline of Central Asia: Sustainable Development and Comprehensive Capital*. London: Routledge.

Solomon, Peter H. 1996. *Soviet Criminal Justice under Stalin*. New York: Cambridge University Press.

Soucek, Svat. 2000. *A History of Inner Asia*. Cambridge: Cambridge University Press.

Starrett, Gregory. 2010. "Islam and the Politics of Enchantment." *Journal of the Royal Anthropological Institute* 15 (May): S222–S240.

State Archive of the Russian Federation. 1980. "Informatsiia o prokhozhdenii religioznogo prazdnika 'Kurban-uzyit' v 1980 godu na territorii Ferganskoi oblasti." [Information about the observance of the religious holiday "Kurban-uzyit" in the year 1980 on the territory of Ferghana oblast]. Fond 6991, Opis 3.

Stephan, Manja. 2006. "'You Come to Us Like a Black Cloud': Universal versus Local Islam in Tajikistan." In *The Post Socialist Religious Question: Faith and Power in Central Asia and East-Central Europe*, edited by Chris Hann, 147–67. New Brunswick, NJ: Transaction.

Stephan, Manja. 2010. "Education, Youth and Islam: The Growing Popularity of Private Religious Lessons in Dushanbe, Tajikistan." *Central Asian Survey* 29, no. 4, 469–83.

Stephan, Manja. 2013. "Duschanbe—Moskau—Kairo: Transnationale religiöse Erziehungspraktiken tadschikischer Familien in der Migration" [Dushanbe–Moscow–Cairo: Transnational religious education practices of Tajik families in migration]. In *Neue Zeiten, neue Räume: Kindheit und Familie im Kontext von (Trans-)Migration und sozialem Wandel* [New spaces, new times: childhood and family in the context of (trans-) migration and social change], edited by Christine Hunner-Kreisel and Manja Stephan, 125–40. Bielefeld: VS-Verlag.

Stephan-Emmrich, Manja, and Abdullah Mirzoev. 2016. "The Manufacturing of Islamic Lifestyles in Tajikistan through the Prism of Dushanbe's Bazaars." *Central Asian Survey* 35, no. 2, 157–77.

Suchman, Mark. 1995. "Managing Legitimacy: Strategic and Institutional Approaches." *Academy of Management Review* 20, no. 3, 571–610.

Sukhareva, Olga. 1960. *Islam v Uzbekistane* [Islam in Uzekistan]. Tashkent: Fan.

Sukhareva, O. A., and M. A. Bikzhanova. 1955. *Proshloe i nastoiashchee seleniia Aikyran* [The past and present of the village of Aikyran]. Tashkent: Izdatel'stvo AN Uzbekskoi SSR.

Sultanov, Asker. 2012. "Kyrgyz Mufti's Office Reformed to Better Fight Terrorism." Central Asia Online, November 8. Accessed September 9, 2013. http://centralasiaonline.com/en_GB/articles/caii/features/main/2012/11/08/feature-01.

Sultanova, Razia. 2000. "Qadiriyya Dhikr in Ferghana Valley." *Journal of the History of Sufism*, 534–35. Simurg: Society for the Study of Oriental Culture, Istanbul.

Sultanova, Razia. 2011. *From Shamanism to Sufism: Women, Islam and Culture in Central Asia*. London: I. B. Tauris.

Tabyshalieva, Anara. 2000. "The Kyrgyz and the Spiritual Dimensions of Daily Life." In *Islam and Central Asia: An Enduring Legacy or an Evolving Threat?* edited by Roald Sagdeev and Susan Eisenhower, 27–38. Washington, DC: Center for Political and Strategic Studies.

Tabyshalieva, Anara. 2003. "Political Islam in Kyrgyzstan." *OSCE Yearbook 2002*. Baden-Baden: Institute for Peace and Security Policy at the University of Hamburg.

Tarschys, Daniel. 1993. "The Success of a Failure: Gorbachev's Alcohol Policy, 1985–1988." *Europe-Asia Studies* 45, no. 1, 7–25.

Tasar, Eren. Forthcoming. "Sufism on the Soviet Stage: Holy People and Places in Central Asia's Sociopolitical Landscape after World War II." In *Sufism in Central Asia*, edited by Devin DeWeese and Jo-Ann Gross.

Tashkent Channel One. 2009. "Uzbek Prominent Cleric Urges People to Show Patience, Satisfaction." November 6. FBIS translation from Uzbek.

Tashkent Channel One. 2011. "Meeting in Uzbek Capital Discusses Fighting 'Alien Ideologies.'" Feburary 14. FBIS translation from Uzbek.

Tashkent Channel One. 2012. "Uzbek TV Urges Vigilance against Media 'Plots' of 'Big Powers.'" September 21. FBIS translation from Uzbek.

Tashkent Channel Two. 2011. "Uzbek TV Show Describes Rock, Rap as 'Satanic.'" February 6. FBIS translation from Uzbek.

Tashkent Mulkdor. 2004. "Uzbekistan: Tashkent's Chief Imam Instructs on Observing Ramadan." October 8. FBIS translation from Uzbek.

Tashkent Turkiston. 2011. "Uzbek Paper Says 'Evil Goal' Behind St. Valentine's Day." February 12. FBIS translation from Uzbek.

Tazmini, Ghoncheh. 2001. "The Islamic Revival in Central Asia: A Potent Force or a Misconception?" *Central Asian Survey* 20, no. 1, 63–83.

Tett, Gillian. 1994. "'Guardians of the Faith?': Gender and Religion in an (ex)Soviet Tajik Village." In *Muslim Women's Choices: Religious Belief and Social Reality*, edited by Camillia Fawzi El-Solh and Judy Mabro, 128–51. Providence, RI: Berg.

Thangarajah, C. Yuvy. 2003. "Veiled Constructions: Conflict, Migration and Modernity in Eastern Sri Lanka." *Contributions to Indian Sociology* 37, nos. 1–2, 141–62.

Tokhtakhodjaeva, Marfua. 2008. *The Re-Islamization of Society and the Position of Women in Post-Soviet Uzbekistan*. Inner Asia Series. Folkestone, UK: Global Oriental.

Toychiyev, Nasriddin-Damulla. 2007. "The Call of the Suffering Heart: In the Shadow of the Joyful Opening of Qoqan's Friday Mosque. The Abominable Surreptitious Actions of the Hypocrites [acting] under a Religious Guise." In Babadzhanov, Muminov, and von Kügelgen, *Disputes on Muslim Authority in Central Asia*, 126–40.

Tucker, James. 2002. "New Age Religion and the Cult of the Self." *Society*, 39, no. 2, 46–51.

Tucker, Noah. 2013. "Domestic Shapers of Eurasia's Islamic Future: Sheikhs, Scholars, Society and the State." Presentation at the Islam in Eurasia Policy Conference, Kennan Institute, Washington, DC, June 6–7.

Turajonzoda, Akbar. 1995. "Religion: The Pillar of Society." In *Central Asia: Conflict, Resolution, and Change*, edited by Roald Sagdeev and Susan Eisenhower, 265–71. Washington, DC: Eisenhower Institute.

Turajonzoda, Akbar. 2006. *Shariat va jomea* [Religious law and society]. Dushanbe: Nodir.

Turajonzoda, Akbar. 2007. *Joygohi masjid dar Islom* [The place of the mosque in Islam]. Dushanbe: Nodir.

Turajonzoda, Akbar. 2011. *Joygohi zan der Islom* [The place of women in Islam]. Dushanbe: Šujoiyon.

Turner, Bryan S. 1994. *Orientalism, Postmodernism and Globalism*. London: Routledge.

Tyson, David. 1997. "Shrine Pilgrimage in Turkmenistan as a Means to Understand Islam among the Turkmen." *Central Asia Monitor* 1, 15–32.

United Nations Population Division. 2011. *World Population Prospects: The 2010 Revision*. Accessed May 13, 2013. http://esa.un.org/wpp/population-pyramids/population-pyramids.htm.

United States Department of State (USDS). 2011. *Annual Report on International Religious Freedom: Uzbekistan*. Accessed May 13, 2013. http://www.state.gov/j/drl/rls/irf/religiousfreedom/index.htm??dlid=192941.

United States Department of State (USDS). 2013. *International Religious Freedom Report*. Bureau of Democracy, Human Rights and Labor. http://www.state.gov/documents/organization/222545.pdf.

Uralov, Dengiz. 2012. "Tashkent Calling." *Transitions Online*, December 3. Accessed May 13, 2013. http://www.tol.org/client/article/23495-tashkent-calling.html/?print.

Usman, Arif. 1993. *Bahauddin Naqshband va uning Ta'limati Haqida* [About Bahouddin Naqshband and his teachings]. Tashkent: Universitet.

Usmanov, M. A., ed. 1989. *Islam: Sprovochnik* [Islam: A guide]. Tashkent: Uzbek Soviet Encyclopediasi Bosh Redaksia.

Usmon, I. 2001. *Tojikon: Surudi ta'rixi xalq va zamin* [The Tajiks: a hymn on the history of the people and the territory]. Dushanbe: Payvand.

Utorbaev, G. 1990. "Podgotovka musul'manskikh bogosluzhitelei" [Preparation of Muslims to serve God]. *Komsomolets Uzbekistana*, October 12.

Uzdaily. 2012. "Khokim Tashkent utverdil pravila provedeniia svadeb i torzhestv" [Tashkent hokim approved rules on the conduct of weddings and celebrations]. September 10. Accessed May 14, 2013. http://lifestyle.uzdaily.uz/articles-id-12681.htm.

Uzmetronom. October 6, 2012. "Zampolity, Politruki . . ." [Commissars, political commissars . . .]. Accessed October 19, 2012. http://www.uzmetronom.com/2012/10/06/zampolity_politruki .html.

Uznews.net. April 30, 2010. "Klassik uzbekskogo kino Malik Kayumov Predan Zemle." http://www.uznews.net/news_print.php?nid=13542&lng=ru. Accessed May 3, 2010.

Uznews.net. September 27, 2012. "Googoosha's Music Video Is a Gift for Chroniclers of Karimov's Dictatorship." Accessed May 13, 2013. www.uznews.net/news_single.php?lng=en&cid=30&nid=20906.

Uznews.net. 2013. "Gulnara Karimova Uses Foul Language on Twitter." May 3. Accessed May 13, 2013. www.uznews.net/news_single.php?lng=en&sub=&cid=30&nid=22625.

van der Veer, Peter. 2001. "Transnational Religion." Paper presented at the Conference on Transnational Migration: Comparative Perspectives. Princeton University, June 30–July 1.

Varisco, Daniel Martin. 2005. *Islam Obscured: the Rhetoric of Anthropological Representation.* New York: Palgrave Macmillan.

Vazirligi, T. H. 1993. *Qari-Niyazi.* Tashkent: Uzbekistan Pedagogika Fanlar Ilmi-Tadqiqat Institutik.

Vertovec, Steven. 2009. *Transnationalism.* London: Routledge.

Voll, John O. 1994. "Central Asia as Part of the Modern Islamic World." In *Central Asia in Historical Perspective,* edited by Beatrice Manz, 62–81. Boulder, CO: Westview Press.

Voll, John Obert. 1999. "Foundations for Renewal and Reform: Islamic Movements in the Eighteenth and Nineteenth Centuries." In *The Oxford History of Islam,* edited by John L. Esposito, 509–47. New York: Oxford University Press.

Volosovich, Aleksei. 2010. "Expertnoe zakluchenie: tvorchestvo Umidy Akhmedovoi oskorbilo traditsii naradov Uzbekistana" [Expert finding: the work of Umida Ahmedova insulted the traditions of the peoples of Uzbekistan]. *Ferghananews.ru,* January 18. Accessed May 14, 2013. http://www.fergananews.com/article.php?id=6434.

Volosovich, Aleksei. 2010. "Protsess: kak sudili Umidu Akhmedovu" [The trial: how Umida Akhmedova was prosecuted]. *Ferghananews.ru,* February 15. Accessed October 12, 2012. http://www.fergananews.com/article.php?id=6472.

Von der Mehden, Fred R. 1993. *Two Worlds of Islam: Interaction between Southeast Asia and the Middle East.* Gainesville: University Press of Florida.

Warde, Ibrahim. 2010. *Islamic Finance in the Global Economy.* 2nd ed. Edinburgh: Edinburgh University Press.

Ware, Rudolph T., III. 2014. *The Walking Qur'an: Islamic Education, Embodied Knowledge, and History in West Africa.* Chapel Hill: University of North Carolina Press.

White, Stephen. 1996. *Russia Goes Dry: Alcohol, State and Society.* New York: Cambridge University Press.

Wilson, Andrew. 2005. *Virtual Politics: Faking Democracy in the Post-Soviet World.* New Haven, CT: Yale University Press.

Wimmer, Andreas, and Nina Glick-Schiller. 2002. "Methodological Nationalism and Beyond: Nation-state Building, Migration and the Social Sciences." *Global Networks* 2, no. 4, 301–34.

Wolters, Alexander. 2013. "Islamic Finance in the States of Central Asia: Strategies, Institutions, First Experiences." *Forschungspapiere Research Papers,* no. 2013/01, 1–28.

Xojaev, Sobir. 2002. *Ta'rixi xalqi Tojik: Kitobi darsi baroi sinfi 7* [History of the Tajik people: textbook for the seventh grade]. Dushanbe: Sarparast.

Ya'qubov, Yusufshoh. 2001. *Ta'rixi xalqi Tojik: Kitobi darsi baroi sinfi 6* [History of the Tajik people: textbook for the sixth grade]. Dushanbe: Sarparast.

Yemelianova, Galina. 2010. *Radical Islam in the Former Soviet Union*. New York: Routledge.

Yilmaz, Kiril. 2007. "The Rise of Radical Political Islam in Post-Soviet States: Fiction or Reality?" In *Understanding and Responding to the Terrorism Phenomenon: A Multi-dimensional Perspective*, edited by O. Nikbay and S. Hancerli, 103–15. Amsterdam: IOS Press.

Yoldosev, Harzulla. 1993. "Hazrat Haqida Ibratli Rivayatlar." *Bukhara Hakikati*, September 9.

Yountchi, Lisa. 2011. "The Politics of Scholarship and the Scholarship of Politics: Imperial, Soviet, and Post-Soviet Scholars Studying Tajikistan." In *The Heritage of Soviet Oriental Studies*, edited by M. Kemper and S. Conermann, 217–40. New York: Routledge.

Youtube. 2010. Pokhorony Malika Kayumova [The burial of Malik Kayumov]. May 1. Accessed May 14, 2013. http://www.youtube.com/watch?v=_SQfh_TqBfg.

Yurchak, Alexei. 2006. *Everything Was Forever, Until It Was No More: The Last Soviet Generation*. Princeton, NJ: Princeton University Press.

Yusuf, Shaikh Muhammad-Sodiq. 2007. "O raznoglasiiakh" [On disagreements]. In Babadzhanov, Muminov, and von Kügelgen, *Disputes on Muslim Authority in Central Asia*, 197–249.

Zakonuz.narod.ru. 1998. "Ukaz Presidenta Respubliki Uzbekistan, 28 oktiabr, No. UP-2100" [Decree of the president of the Republic of Uzbekistan, October 28, 1998, No. UP-2100]. Accessed May 13, 2013. http://zakonuz.narod.ru/newpage314.htm.

Zalesskii, A. M., and T. G. Kupchenia, eds. 1983. *O religii i tserkvi: sbornik vyskazyvanii klassikov marksizma-leninizma, dokumentov KPSS i Sovetskogo Pravitel'stva* [Religion and Church: a collection of the classics of Marxism-Leninism, the CPSU, and the Soviet government]. Minsk: Belarus.

Zarcone, Thierry. 1995. "Sufi Movements: Search for Identity and Islamic Resurgence." In *Central Asia: Emerging New Order*, edited by K. Warikoo, 63–79. New Delhi: Har Anand Publications.

Zelizer, Viviana. 1978. "Human Values and the Market: The Case of Life Insurance and Death in 19th-Century America." *American Journal of Sociology* 84, no. 3, 591–610.

Zelizer, Viviana. 1998. "How People Talk about Money." *American Behavioral Scientist* 41, 1373–83.

Zelkina, Anna. 2000. *In Quest of God and Freedom: The Sufi Response to the Russian Advance in the North Caucasus*. New York: New York University Press.

Zmejewski, Weronika. 2013. "'Nach Moskau gehen:' Männliche Arbeitsmigration zwischen Tadschikistan und Russland" ["Go to Moscow": male labor migration between Tajikistan and Russia]. Master's thesis, Humboldt University of Berlin.

Zorn, Dirk, Frank Dobbin, Julian Dierkes, and Man-Shan Kwok. 2004. "Managing Investors: How Financial Markets Reshaped the American Firm." In *The Sociology of Financial Markets*, edited by Karin Knorr Cetina and Alexandru Preda, 269–89. London: Oxford University Press.

INDEX

séances, 34, 38–39, 40, 41

secularism, 29–30, 98, 189, 207, 269–71, 273, 278; rejection of, xiv; religion and, 6–7, 10, 81; self-proclaimed, 54; state, 200, 201, 203–4, 267, 281, 289

security, 200; challenges, 174; maintaining, 126; national, 68; political, 287; social, 287; state, 82, 83, 85, 125

security forces, 81, 84, 86–87, 138, 174, 202, 210, 220

self-empowerment, 284–86; religious mobility and, 286–89

self-evaluation, introverted acts of, 53–54

self-identification, 3, 4, 5, 11, 30–31, 32, 117

self-reformation, 228, 233

self-relatedness, 37, 39, 40

seminaries: increase in, 206; registration of, 210–11; unregistered, 205

Senior Citizens Day, 211, 216

Seryayev, Charygeldi, 117–18

Shah-i Zinda, 108, 305n24

shahada, 100, 227, 295n4

Shamanism, 7, 106, 117, 125

shamans, 106, 129, 135, 168

Shanazarov, Ergeshaly, 211, 214

sharia, 65, 67, 154, 255, 304n16, 321n1; adopting, 74; concept of, 175; understanding of, 165

sharia boards, 258, 260, 261, 323n25

sharia law, 55, 72, 250, 297n2; IFIs and, 257, 258

sheikhs, 99, 137, 138–39, 178, 306n30, 308n37, 309n49, 309n51; Naqshbandi, 112, 115; Qadiri, 115, 116; Sufi, 109, 110–11, 126; unregistered, 139

Shia Islam, 114, 116, 146, 181

shirk, 41, 168–69, 240, 313n25

shrines, 120, 306n32, 309n49; meals at, 121; renovation of, 350n23; as state health resorts, 309n51; Sufi, 109, 115, 121–22, 123, 124, 156

SNB, 211, 212, 213, 214, 215, 216; public festivities and, 217; Uzbek Security Service and, 210

social consequences, 93–95

social control, 79, 84–87

social dynamics, 196, 279

social environment, 14, 283

social interaction, 81–82, 166, 175

social issues, 79, 82–83, 92, 93, 271

social mobility, 7, 264, 273, 274, 276, 278, 279, 282, 286; education and, 284; spiritual needs and, 265

social networks, 278, 280

social norms, 282, 286

social order, 74, 109, 181, 182, 197, 258; Islamic concepts of, 173; religiously legitimized, 178; Tajik, 265

social problems, 89, 91, 185

social relations, 42, 312n21

social space, 175, 176, 178

social status, xvi, 268, 274

social welfare, 157, 159

socialism, 73, 159

Socialist legality, 142; rule of law and, 128

sociocultural adaptation, 233–36

socioeconomic variables, 22, 268, 273, 286

Sodiq, Muhammad, 64, 299n35

Somonid Dynasty, 187, 188

sorcerers, 48, 49, 129, 135

Soviet Socialist Republic (SSR), 50, 292

Soviet Union, disintegration of, 3–4, 5, 8, 50, 99, 295n1

Spiritual Administration, 58, 84, 225

spiritual awakening, 35–36, 43, 284, 288

spiritual beings, relations with, 39–40

Spiritual Directorate of Kyrgyzstan Muslims, 161, 312n18

spiritual leaders, 40, 60, 107

spiritual network, expending, 43–46

spiritual order, 47, 281

spirituality, 30, 33, 36, 38, 50, 42, 52, 117, 123, 158, 159, 211, 234, 264, 279; Islamic, 156, 157, 172, 311n2

Stalin, Joseph, 82, 93, 112, 136, 314n7; registration requirements of, xv; religious reforms and, 128, 131, 132, 147, 306n5; repression by, 137; Sufi literature and, 105

state: foreign investors and, 248–53; religion and, 20, 21–22, 201, 205, 206–10, 219, 246; resistance to, 100; Sufism and, 126; TJ and, 227, 241

State Agency for Religious Affairs, 207, 210

State Commission for Religious Affairs (SCRA), 161, 242, 243, 312n14

Stephan-Emmrich, Manja, xvi, 257, 261

Made in the USA
Middletown, DE
03 January 2021

30700048R00214